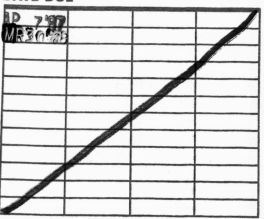

Parties and Elections in the United States

JOHN A. CRITTENDEN
Indiana State University

PRENTICE-HALL, INC.   Englewood Cliffs, New Jersey 07632

Library of Congress Cataloging in Publication Data

CRITTENDEN, JOHN A.
   Parties and elections in the United States.

   Includes bibliographical references and index.
   1. Political parties—United States—History.
2. Presidents—United States—Election—History.
3. United States–Politics and Government.
I. Title.
JK2261.C836   324'.0973   81-5123
ISBN 0-13-650903-7   AACR2

*Editorial/production supervision and interior
design by Linda Schuman
Cover design by Wanda Lubelska
Manufacturing buyer: Edmund W. Leone*

PRENTICE-HALL INTERNATIONAL, INC., *London*
PRENTICE-HALL OF AUSTRALIA PTY. LIMITED, *Sydney*
PRENTICE-HALL OF CANADA, LTD., *Toronto*
PRENTICE-HALL OF INDIA PRIVATE LIMITED, *New Delhi*
PRENTICE-HALL OF JAPAN, INC., *Tokyo*
PRENTICE-HALL OF SOUTHEAST ASIA PTE. LTD., *Singapore*
WHITEHALL BOOKS LIMITED, *Wellington, New Zealand*

For
Alan and *Drake*

Contents

9
Campaigns   220

10
Elections   247

11
Partisanship in Government   276

Illustrations

Illustrations

Tables

Preface

This book presents a wide-angle view of American electoral politics. Unlike many works of its kind, it contains historical and comparative material, as well as discussions of social forces, organized influence, and political ethics. In the late 1970s, when most of the text was written, the dominant mood in the United States was one of dissatisfaction and uncertainty. Electoral democracy seemed at times to be faltering, even though it had been central to our civilization in the past. Now, as the book's finishing touches have been completed, the election of 1980 is less than six months behind us. Although there are portents of change, the signs (as usual) are mixed. The parties still appear to be weak, and the nation's major difficulties remain well beyond the reach of easy solutions.

To a degree, the following pages reflect the centrist view that elections should be regarded as sovereign activity and that this probably requires a strong system of competing parties. However, this notion is loosely applied; it is not raised to the level of thoroughly reasoned argument. The book discusses scholarly disagreements on many matters, and much of the other information it provides bears no close relationship to particular viewpoints. My main hope is that readers of varying persuasions will find this to be a balanced work that helps them clarify their own thoughts about the place of elections in our political life.

In preparing the manuscript, I have become indebted to associations extending over many years, more immediate assistance, and the larger community of scholars. Indeed, such contributions are so extensive that I could not possibly identify all of them. However, it should be said that the scholars who most personally affected my views on parties and elections were the late E. E. Schattschneider and Sigmund Neumann. Each was a major student of politics, and each cared deeply about the contribution politics could make to human well-being. I hope that this book reflects those values and that it meets scholarly standards they would respect.

I owe my wife Susan a very special word of thanks. She has sharpened her interests since the early days in Virginia politics, and her outlooks have affected my thinking more than she realizes. She has given me constant encouragement in the pursuit of this project, while making me acutely aware of grass-roots problems through her investigative reporting.

I also want to express my gratitude to our mutual friend, Carl Elliott. Carl's careful appraisal of the initial outline and conceptual statement added immeasurably to whatever merit this book possesses. He has freely given me the benefit of his extensive knowledge of the political process and congressional operations. The personal support and active interest of Glenn and Eleanor Perry and Jamie and Bob Griffin is also greatly appreciated.

A number of scholars provided critical comments on some or all of the manuscript at its various stages and by doing so helped me to improve the quality of the final product. These scholars include Hugh Bone, University of Washington; Rita M. Cooley, New York University; Robert Craig, University of New Hampshire; John C. Donovan, Bowdoin College; Richard A. Joslyn, Temple University; David W. Moore, University of New Hampshire; and Richard Murray, University of Houston. None of these persons, of course, bears any responsibility for the content of the book. I only wish I could have taken better advantage of their excellent advice. Jeff Fishel provided early encouragement which I hope he has no cause to regret.

Various associates at Indiana State University have been helpful in discussing particular matters, and secretaries and librarians (among others) have been most forbearing. Tracey Pierce in particular should be singled out for her extraordinary service in typing and manuscript preparation. Rose Marie Baer, Laurie Marshall, and Brent Meyer helped out on a number of chores, and I obtained valuable information from Charles King, Eugene Dyche, Bob Puckett, John Corrigan, Bill Matthews, Woody Creason, Jim McDowell, Reuel Ash, Dean Myers, Bill Maxam, and Bill Harader. Dean Effie Hunt and the chairman of the Political Science Department, Arthur Dowell, were at all times helpful and supportive. Emily Alward, Purdue reference librarian, gave assistance well beyond the call of duty.

I should also like to thank John Busch, Stan Wakefield, and Linda Schuman, among others at Prentice-Hall. Pat Cahalan provided a vigorous and expert job of copyediting for which I am most grateful.

Last but not least, I want to express my appreciation to all those persons in Vigo County and the state of Indiana who contributed to my political education in the world of practical politics. My assurance on a number of points owes much to associations with these people and to experience as a Terre Haute precinct committeeman.

With all this help, it becomes almost embarrassing to assure the reader that all errors in this book—whether of fact, interpretation, or judgment—are mine and mine alone.

1

Political Parties in a World Context

Since politics is as old as the human race, it has often touched ordinary lives in recognizable ways. Thus, machines of a sort were present in ancient Rome as early as 67 B.C., and there may have been a shadowy element of choice in the designation of ancient English kings.[1] Machiavelli's accounts of medieval Florence depict a tumultuous succession of factional struggles. Even so, few people in premodern times could choose their place in society, and most people had little contact with the government.

MODERNIZATION

But beginning in Europe, a number of interconnected changes gradually produced a different kind of society. As the technology of printing improved (it was already developed by Machiavelli's time), religious and political doctrines were more intensively propagated. Expanded use of money stimulated individual risk taking. People moved about more frequently, cities grew in size, and maritime centers expanded their contacts with the wider world. As European governments increased their authority, there came to be larger numbers of taxpayers, litigants, soldiers, victims, political beneficiaries, and (gradually) nationalists. All of this was well under way by 1800. In the next 180 years, society changed even more rapidly as new developments in transport, production, warfare, communication, and medicine touched the lives of more and more people. Social scientists often apply the

[1]James C. Scott, *Comparative Political Corruption* (Englewood Cliffs, N.J.: Prentice-Hall, Inc., 1972), p. 93; Roy F. Nichols, *The Invention of Political Parties* (New York: Macmillan, Inc., 1967), pp. 2–3.

term *modernization* to such changes and others to which they were linked.[2]

Modernization led to greater political interest and activity by non-privileged persons. The belief that government should take the needs of ordinary people into account became more difficult to ignore, leading eventually to the systems of mass voting that emerged in the nineteenth century. And with mass voting came modern parties to channel votes and organize electoral politics.

Mass Participation

Political participation refers to many kinds of activities, and people take part to varying degrees. Their efforts to affect the actions of government may be legal or illegal, successful or unsuccessful. People may work through groups, they may engage in symbolic acts (such as mass demonstrations and hunger strikes), and they may riot or rebel. Although political participation is rarely construed to include such involuntary acts as paying taxes or going to jail, some analysts include various mental states and personal behavior, such as consuming political information and expressing opinions.[3] In most societies most people confine themselves to the "easier" forms of participation—applauding a candidate, but *not* running for office; voting, but *not* working actively in campaigns; supporting a guerrilla uprising, but *not* joining it.

These less demanding activities, however, are crucial to mass influence. People must become politically aware before they can organize and assert political demands. If opinions circulate widely, rulers cannot afford to ignore them. Voting may give ordinary people a real share in political power. Keep in mind, however, that even "easy" forms of participation never involve everybody. Even in the most modern societies, a fair number of people are politically inert at any given time.

In trying to understand how parties came about, we can assume that as societies modernized, traditional ruling groups usually resisted the intrusion of new power seekers and that leadership conflicts became more broadly based. Modernization also encouraged voluntary associations to form as people discovered new threats and opportunities amidst social change. Such tendencies produced interest groups and political movements as well as political parties.[4]

Political parties. The term *political party* is extremely difficult to define because it can refer to so many different kinds of entities. Indeed, there is

[2]For a rigorous account, see Joseph LaPalombara and Myron Weiner, "The Origin and Development of Political Parties," in *Political Parties and Political Development*, ed. LaPalombara and Weiner (Princeton, N.J.: Princeton University Press, 1966), pp. 3–42. For a major treatment of history in its broadest terms, see William H. McNeil, *A World History*, 2nd ed. (New York: Oxford University Press, 1971).

[3]Myron Weiner, "Political Participation: Crisis of the Political Process," in *Crises and Sequences in Political Development*, ed. Leonard Binder et al. (Princeton, N.J.: Princeton University Press, 1971), pp. 161–164.

[4]Ibid., p. 186; Gabriel Almond and G. Bingham Powell, Jr., *Comparative Politics* (Boston: Little, Brown & Company, 1966), pp. 74–80.

no definition on which political scientists are agreed. For the purposes of this book, a political party is any continuing organization, identified by an official label, that presents candidates for public office at mass elections. Each of the key elements in this definition can be interpreted loosely or restrictively, depending on the purpose at hand.[5]

The baseline of modern political parties is that they function as vehicles of mass political participation. Even where elections are only support rituals, parties are still relevant. Rulers who will not permit their power to be contested may have to maintain one party if others are to be excluded. In this situation, a party naturally lends itself to other forms of mass organizing as well.

In societies where genuine electoral contests take place, parties offer important advantages to key groups. *Office seekers* want electoral organizations that will improve their chances of winning. *Voters* support parties in order to make their vote more meaningful. *Traditional elites* may hope that parties will tame the revolutionary potential of mass voting. In fact, in modern history no nation that has held elections for any extended time has lacked parties.

MAJOR DIFFERENCES

Because parties vary so, political scientists have devised special concepts to deal with the many different types.[6] Among the more general and important distinctions are the following:

1. Strength or weakness of the parties
2. Democratic or authoritarian nature of the party system
3. Number of parties that play significant roles.

These matters are interrelated, and analysis of them should reflect that fact. Some political systems have no significant parties, illustrating a relationship between points 1 and 3. Democratic party systems provide important choices between parties, which usually implies more than one party, and this suggests a connection between 2 and 3. More speculatively, if democratic political systems cannot accommodate very strong parties, or if they cannot do without parties entirely, there is a relationship between the first two points. To shed further light on these variations, we now consider each in turn.

[5]This definition contains some elements proposed by Joseph LaPalombara, *Politics Within Nations* (Englewood Cliffs, N.J.: Prentice-Hall, Inc., 1974), p. 509; and Giovanni Sartori, *Parties and Party Systems* (New York: Cambridge University Press, 1976), I, 63. For a different approach, thoughtfully developed and well off the beaten track, see Kay Lawson, *The Comparative Study of Political Parties* (New York: St. Martin's Press, 1976), pp. 3–4.

[6]The work of Maurice Duverger is especially notable: *Political Parties* (London: Methuen & Co., Ltd., 1955). See the introduction to this book for one of the major statements on party origins.

Strong Parties versus Weak Parties

Estimates of party strength involve a good deal of guesswork. A party can obtain strength from "institutionalization"—that is, long experience with its own organizational practices may make it flexible and adaptable. Such a party is also less likely to simply reflect the particular groups that happen to support it at a given time.[7] Party regimes that have successfully resisted coups are probably hardy.

Other indications of strength come from looking at the leaders of a country. Do parties control access to leadership positions, or are the parties dependent on the leaders? Does the leadership retain its position through independent mass appeals, or does party organization restrain the leaders somewhat? Widespread support may be the best indicator of party strength. A strong party represents many groups in a society, and a strong party *system* exists when a large proportion of the population supports the existing parties.

Political parties are not universal, and nations where they do not exist are "systems without parties"—obviously the weakest instances of all. Mass participation has not always resulted in strong parties. In Latin America and the Middle East, for example, personality and military power have often made parties inconsequential. Mass elections were unknown in any country before the late eighteenth century, and most earlier political systems therefore lacked parties, even though they occasionally had cliques or factions that resembled parties to a degree. Today, there may be a few traditional societies that have not yet held elections, but the trend toward modernization suggests that all nations have at least one party in their future. In some nations parties are now so weak that they are little more than paper organizations. Many of these nations are probably, for practical purposes, systems without parties.

Democratic versus Authoritarian Parties

Some years ago, the late Sigmund Neumann argued that dictatorship versus democracy was the fundamental cleavage of our time. He thought that a genuine party implied the existence of competing parties, and he considered a totalitarian one-party system to be a contradiction in terms.[8]

Today, scholars tend to view parties as aspects of mass politics that appear in all political systems, democratic or not. Perhaps this more inclusive notion reflects a more tolerant view of one-party regimes—and a more skeptical stance towards democratic parties. However, the gulf between democratic and authoritarian parties is still very wide. The most common definition (such as the one presented above) assumes that parties are electoral organizations. Technically, this includes both dictatorial and democratic parties, but the definition is more appropriate for democracies where elections are the focus of the *most important* party activity; in authoritarian

[7]Samuel P. Huntington, *Political Order in Changing Societies* (New Haven, Conn.: Yale University Press, 1968), pp. 12–24, 408–412.

[8]Sigmund Neumann, ed., *Modern Political Parties* (Chicago: University of Chicago Press, 1956), pp. 1, 396, 403.

societies, electoral activity is of less concern than the direct exercise of political power.

All of the nations in Table 1–1 have competitive party systems, and this feature may be a democratic requirement. In democratic nations concepts of freedom and equality have required that the people be regarded as sovereign, and contested elections have become the primary method of insuring that government will be accountable to the people. Since parties are almost certain to emerge whenever elections are held, and since parties dominate election outcomes, it is easy to understand the close relation between democracy and competing parties.

Yet one cannot be certain that this aspect of the democratic process is more significant than others in a final sense. Scholars today tend to attach less significance to the role of parties in maintaining democracy than they did a generation or so ago. Leon Epstein, for example, believes that parties have become targets of general dissatisfaction. He notes that English practices, often emulated in the past, have appeared uncreative in the 1950s and 1960s. In both Europe and the United States, today's parties derive from past eras, and one wonders if they will adapt to new problems.[9]

Table 1–1
Practicing Democracies in 1979 Ranked by Population

1. India	610	14. Sweden	8
2. United States	215	15 Austria	8
3. Japan	113	16. Switzerland	6
4. West Germany	61	17. Finland	5
5. United Kingdom	56	18. Denmark	5
6. Italy	56	19. Norway	4
7. France	53	20. Israel	4
8. Spain	36	21. New Zealand	3
9. Canada	23	22. Ireland	3
10. Netherlands	14	23. Jamaica	2
11. Australia	14	24. Costa Rica	2
12. Venezuela	12	25. Trinidad and	
13. Belgium	10	Tobago	1
		TOTAL	1,324
		(About 33% of world population)	

Source: Population in millions as of 1976 as per Arthur S. Banks, *Political Handbook of the World* (New York: McGraw Hill Book Company, 1979), pp. 612–614. This table is based on Robert Dahl's list of "fully inclusive polyarchies" in his *Democracy in the United States*, 3rd ed. (Chicago: Rand McNally College Publishing Company, 1976), p. 47. Nations under 1 million population are excluded. There are at least two of these (Iceland and Luxembourg) and there may be others. I have excluded Sri Lanka, Colombia, Greece, and Lebanon, which Dahl regarded as special cases of one sort or another. As of 1979, these countries plus Portugal, Mexico, Greece, Turkey, and Malaysia might be regarded as important borderline cases. I include Spain because of events that began in 1976. None of the twenty-five nations in this table conforms completely to democratic ideals.

[9]Leon Epstein, "Political Parties," in *Handbook of Political Science,* ed. Fred I. Greenstein and Nelson W. Polsby (Reading, Mass.: Addison-Wesley Publishing Company, 1975), IV, 266–270.

Nevertheless, many political scientists still think party performance is essential to effective democracy. They see competitive parties as the best means of giving ordinary people real responsibility for their own government; they believe that parties are necessary to simplify complex issues, recruit leaders, sustain willingness to compromise, provide essential continuity over time, and organize both government and popular opinion around the questions that matter most to most people.

General comments on democracy. Some people are not interested in the requirements of democratic politics. They may believe that democracy is an archaic residue of eighteenth-century political thought, or that it is a victim of bureaucracy (or elite rule), or that mass publics do not behave in ways consistent with democratic principles. For many, democracy suffers from terminal illness.

However, one can make a good case, despite current pessimism, that democracy has strengthened its position in the world over the last twenty, fifty, or hundred years. Electorates are larger, freedom less circumscribed, opportunities for poor people more extensive, blatant racial and religious repression much less common. Large areas of Africa, the Middle East, and Asia have achieved political independence from European colonial powers.

Taken as a group, nondemocratic nations appear less securely established and less united. For example, war between any of the nations listed in Table 1-1 is almost unimaginable, but the Soviet-Chinese border is the scene of massive troop concentrations. With few exceptions, internal problems of the democracies pale in comparison to difficulties faced by most other countries.

True, there are not very many democratic nations. About two-thirds of the world's population, and about four-fifths of the world's nations, are not democratically governed. Keep in mind, however, that nondemocratic regimes can be very dissimilar. Often there is little resemblance in their ideological thrust, extent of mass participation, or basis of ruling power. The twenty largest nondemocratic nations, for example, have remarkably little in common.[10]

Events in Spain show that democratic elections can still excite the imagination. Generalissimo Franco said in 1938, "We do not believe in government through the voting booth. The Spanish national will was never freely expressed through the ballot box. *Spain has no foolish dreams.*" Not long after Franco's death, however, Spaniards took part in their first free election in forty-one years. A wide variety of parties contested, and the turnout was extremely high. One activist exclaimed, "It is so normal that it makes you think we have been living in a democracy for the past 40 years."[11]

[10]The twenty largest nondemocratic nations are as follows (in order of decreasing population): China, USSR, Indonesia, Brazil, Bangladesh, Pakistan, Nigeria, Vietnam, Philippines, Thailand, Egypt, Poland, South Korea, Iran, Burma, Ethiopia, Argentina, South Africa, Zaire, and Yugoslavia. I exclude Mexico, Turkey, and Colombia from this list because they are designated as borderline cases in Table 1-1.

[11]"Voters Say 'Si' to Democracy," *Time,* June 27, 1977, pp. 18–22.

Authoritarian systems. Authoritarian rule in the contemporary period does not necessarily mean that a party is the only vehicle of power, or even the most important one. For example, in Franco Spain (1939–1976) the Falangist party enjoyed a formal monopoly, but landowners, industrialists, and church organizations exerted some autonomous influence. In the early 1970s Spain may even have been a "no-party" system.

Instances where a party takes on a totalitarian or hegemonic role usually reflect Leninist organizational doctrines. The Bolsheviks have always perceived themselves as a self-conscious minority waging eternal war against a more powerful traditional order. To win this struggle, Lenin designed a party that combined centralized control with astute use of small group dynamics and mass psychology. Such a vehicle did not have to remain the exclusive property of communism; the basic ideas could be picked up by any social element seeking power in a divided society.[12]

A number of regimes have tried to use authoritarian parties to produce rapid social change. Such a party (often termed "party of mobilization") tries to organize, indoctrinate, and motivate the mass population. The Communist parties in China and the Soviet Union are the most notable examples, and they directly affect about 28 percent of the world's population. However, mobilizational parties in smaller countries have often been less successful. Rapid development is a difficult task—especially when the sense of national identity is weak, the resource base inadequate, or traditional outlooks too strong. A political party may be the best available instrument for social change but the risk of failure is great. Factors other than a single strong party have probably contributed to successes in China and the Soviet Union.[13]

In the mid 1960s observers of African politics frequently thought that one-party systems were the wave of the future. Of course, not all of the new regimes were of the mobilizational type. However, those in Ghana, Mali, and Guinea definitely were. In 1966 police and army elements successfully overturned Nkrumah's repressive apparatus in Ghana. In 1968 the Keita regime in Mali quickly succumbed to a military uprising after a "people's militia" had arrested some army officers. Although the regime of Sekou Touré in Guinea still survives, it has become dependent on outside help and no longer seems to enjoy conspicuous mass appeal.[14]

Since they often have skills that are in short supply, military forces provide an alternative to the party of mobilization. You might suppose that military regimes would also be less vulnerable to overthrow. However, in the African experience to date, military coups have been followed by countercoups, and regimes based on military personnel have been no more

---

[12]Samuel P. Huntington, "Social and Institutional Dynamics of One-Party Systems," in *Authoritarian Politics in Modern Society,* ed. Samuel P. Huntington and Clement H. Moore (New York: Basic Books, 1970), p. 13. See also *Political Order in Changing Societies,* pp. 336–343.

[13]Both of these societies are very large in area and population. China enjoyed a cultural identity that was nurtured in one of the world's oldest and most distinguished civilizations. Russia was beginning to experience impressive economic growth before the Bolshevik revolution.

[14]*Africa South of the Sahara 1976–1977* (London: Europa Publications Limited, 1976), pp. 17–18, 360, 534. (Contributions by Ruth First, Dennis Austin, and Donal B. Cruise O'Brien.)

successful than their civilian counterparts in achieving self-sustained economic growth.[15]

Scholars are divided on the future of the authoritarian party. Juan Linz argues that we have seen its "overthrow, transformation or decay." He feels that authoritarian governments will continue to be numerous but that bureaucracy and some dominant organized interests will provide the main underpinning. Such regimes may not be very successful in particular instances, he suggests, but they are easier to establish than either totalitarian or democratic regimes. Among nations that have never experienced political liberalism in any form, Linz feels that the alternative to a particular authoritarian regime could simply be change to a different, equally authoritarian one.[16]

Samuel Huntington, on the other hand, believes that in the long run, complex modern society makes authoritarian government dependent on the hegemonic party. He speculates that, once established, one-party regimes can go through a number of phases. In the end the crucial issue is whether the party can retain a monopoly of legitimacy. If the party is too intent on restricting genuine participation and competition it can become unwieldy and ineffective.[17]

NUMBER OF PARTIES

It is convenient, even inevitable, that people should classify nations in terms of the number of parties. Thus, we often speak of the United States as a two-party system, the Soviet Union as a one-party system, Italy as a multiparty system, and so forth. Of course, one cannot be too literal; only parties of some importance are taken into account, and the criteria for exclusion may vary. Systematic description on this basis may be helpful even if the number of parties tells us little about relationship of parties to other institutions, types of leadership, ideological differences among parties, and other important matters.

Without becoming too elaborate, one can work with some such scheme as the one that follows. Classsification cannot be mechanical, and some nations have experienced such rapid change or are so new that they defy classification. For example, Mauritania achieved independence in 1960 and soon adopted a one-party system, in spite of the fact that three illegal groups operated in exile or underground. Although a bloodless coup produced a military regime in 1978, the rulers apparently intend to create new mass-based institutions in the future.

[15]Ruth First, "Political and Social Problems of Development," in *Africa South of the Sahara*, pp. 18–22.

[16]Juan Linz, "Totalitarian and Authoritarian Regimes," in Greenstein and Polsby, eds., *Handbook of Political Science*, III, 353–357.

[17]Huntington and Moore, *Authoritarian Politics*, pp. 4, 24–44.

Types of Political Systems[18]

Party Systems
 Noncompetitive
  1. One-party authoritarian
 Competitive
  2. Competitive one-party
  3. Two-party
  4. Multiparty
Systems without Parties
 Preparty
 Parties repressed
 Parties "on paper"

Although I have already discussed systems without parties, it may be worth repeating that "no-party" systems *can* exist in a literal sense. Nations that have not yet held elections on a regular basis, regardless of the historical period, are preparty: They have not yet reached the stage where there are any party tasks to perform. Rulers can also prevent parties from functioning. Even if a repressed party remains active underground, those in power can prevent it from offering candidates for public office. Finally, parties can be so weak that there is little point in considering them.

In such a context, the view that some Americans express—that we should leave our elections to the individual voter, with parties playing no significant role—seems strange indeed. Conditions in societies without parties are generally unappealing, and no persisting system of democratic elections without parties has ever existed in any nation. If such an arrangement could be devised, it would probably be too confusing to provide meaningful leadership alternatives. Even so, antiparty sentiment is quite strong in the United States.

Those who maintain parties act out of self-interest, yet there is little reason to believe that politics without parties in a country such as the United States would be more "pure" or more responsive. Most likely, "no-party" politics would not be democratic at all, although it might resemble the American situation of the 1770s and 1780s. According to one study, the lack of parties in those years thwarted ordinary people with its "looseness, semi-invisibility, disorder, personal ties, and confusion of faction." Those with access to inside information had a distinct advantage in "working" the system.[19]

Of course, lack of a precedent should not decide the issue. Alternative channels of political action might make it possible for the nation that invented modern parties to get along without their playing any significant role. But would things be better or worse? Some critics believe that weak-

---

[18]The most rigorous discussion of classification schemes based on number of parties is to be found in Sartori, *Parties and Party Systems,* esp. pp. 39–51, 119–131, 185–192, 217–255.
 [19]William N. Chambers, *Political Parties in a New Nation* (New York: Oxford University Press, 1963), p. 27.

nesses inherent in partyless politics already characterize America's present political situation.

Competitive one-party systems. Competitive one-party systems differ from the authoritarian systems discussed earlier. Free elections are held, but the voters consistently award decisive power to a single party. *The major party's success results from a series of authentic contests with other parties that have one-sided outcomes.* India and Japan offer the leading examples.

An important, if uncertain, boundary separates the authoritarian from the competitive one-party system. To determine where the one leaves off and the other begins, one must examine the particular case. Mexico, for example, is difficult to evaluate. The dominant PRI (Party of Revolutionary Institutions) is a vehicle of national unity that began in 1929 as an effort to consolidate the gains of the 1910 Mexican Revolution. There are four "official" opposition parties, but their representation in the legislature is miniscule. Real power is in the hands of the president, and some say that where necessary to win, the PRI resorts to election fraud or repression.[20] Nevertheless, the PRI appears to be genuinely popular, and scholars have admired its contribution to national stability.

The two kinds of one-party systems resemble each other in some respects, and the one-party device may be convenient to societies on the move and short of political leadership. However, when we consider such basic principles of political democracy as widespread participation, political competition, and political freedom, the differences are enormous.

In general, one-party politics is consistent with democracy only if other parties may organize and contest elections. Internal battles are inevitable in most parties, and there is little evidence that they assure the rank and file a real choice of party leaders. Nor do independent candidacies usually offer an entrenched party a serious challenge. Therefore, whenever a party persists without organized opposition, one must suspect that competition is being suppressed. Democratic one-party systems retain their democratic credentials by contesting against other parties (however weak) and not by claiming that they are internally competitive. The point applies generally to the United States, but primary elections (to be discussed later in this chapter) complicate the issue somewhat. One-party dominance in some American states is another complication.

Two-party systems. In a two-party system minor parties exist, but they are not strong enough to prevent one of two major parties from obtaining a majority and governing alone. Furthermore, the two parties alternate in holding power. Many have praised the two-party system for its unambiguous assignment of governing responsibility and its provision of a clear-cut alternative to the governing party.

However, the number of two-party systems is small, and it is difficult to decide what nations qualify. Scholars usually cite the United States, Great Britain, Canada, New Zealand, and Australia as the main examples, but

[20]Sartori, *Parties and Party Systems*, p. 234.

there are difficulties even with these.[21] In the United States alternation between Democrats and Republicans occurs only over long time periods, and the constitutional structure permits deadlock as well as party control. New Zealand and Australia also seem to be slow in alternating party control. In Canada, minor parties have often prevented either the Liberals or Conservatives from getting a majority of parliamentary seats. Australia has a third party—the Country party—in close and permanent alliance with the Liberals.

Even Great Britain is becoming less clearly a two-party nation. Neither of the two elections in 1974 gave either major party as much as 40 percent of the vote. The Liberal party, Ulster Unionists, Scottish Nationalists, and Welsh Nationalists retained small numbers of seats, and such groups may become more important in the future. Even though the election of 1979 restored the older pattern, the country may be heading toward an era of coalition governments.

It would seem that the two-party system is a special case with tendencies towards either a one-party or a multiparty system. Nevertheless, two parties are dominant in each of the five nations discussed above. In England, for example, the Conservative and Labour parties have usually won better than 90 percent of the vote in general elections and an even higher percentage of seats in the House of Commons. In the United States, minor-party or independent candidates won less than 1 percent of all congressional contests between 1932 and 1968.

There are a number of similarities among these five two-party systems. In general, winning elections takes precedence over ideological purity; a major party in a two-party system takes its votes where it can find them. Also, the ideological distance between parties is usually not very great. America's Democratic and Republican parties tend to be especially loose coalitions, and this may permit them to contain the important political forces to a greater degree than major parties in the other four nations.

The type of electoral system traditionally used in England tends to reinforce the two-party system in these nations. Simple pluralities received in single-member districts generally determine who wins elections. Victory goes to those who are "first past the post," and it is "winner take all" in each district. Minor parties receive no elective posts unless they obtain pluralities in particular districts, and scattered support in a number of districts is of no value.

Multiparty systems. There are different kinds of multiparty systems, but we shall not bother with refinements. The usual complaint against these systems has been that they produce unstable government. Nevertheless, a number of multiparty systems are highly stable: West Germany, Belgium, Ireland, Sweden, and Norway are examples. One analyst suggests that in such cases the parties cluster into two coalitions. Centrist issue positions dominate, but neither coalition occupies the center as such. He argues that the real instability of a multiparty system comes about when a centrist

[21]Ibid., p. 187.

coalition confronts a deeply divided opposition. In such a situation, no single element of the opposition has the strength to rule by itself. Differences in party outlooks make it impossible for major elements in opposition to compromise with each other, and in trying to outbid each other they set a tone of political extremism. Relationships among the parties, not the number of parties, is what produces the instability.[22]

It is difficult to argue that two-party systems are superior to multiparty systems in an absolute sense. A nation's parties grow out of its unique experiences. According to Sartori, the more stable multiparty systems tend towards a lack of ideological differences among relevant parties and an absence of strong "antisystem" parties. There is also a tendency for alternative coalitions to resemble the mechanics of two-party competition.[23]

Multiparty systems usually go hand in hand with electoral systems that have elements of proportional representation, and this may reflect a multiparty preference. Continental European nations began with simple plurality procedures, and when more than two parties appeared, there was support for procedures that would represent these parties more equitably.[24] Perhaps the retention of plurality elections in England and the United States resulted from a different preference.

A general note. Some of the preceding distinctions may be slightly overstated. Even American parties may play "mobilizational" roles to a degree, and even hegemonic parties may have coalitional elements that strike bargains. Major factions in the Democratic and Republican parties may even give American electoral politics some of the characteristics of a multiparty system.

Before moving on to the next chapter, it would be well to supply more background to the emergence of democratic politics in the West. A few general variables explain many of the differences between the United States and other Western nations. Matters of timing, or the order in which important events occurred, have had considerable impact. Similarities among the various systems help us to perceive distinctive features of American politics more clearly.

THE UNITED STATES AND EUROPE

Democracy as we know it was not an inevitable outcome of modernization, and it only emerged after some unusual turns of history. Three of these were especially important. First, Parliament began to compete effectively with the monarch in seventeenth-century England. The competition stabilized after a long period of struggles came to an end in 1688, and the system gradually evolved towards parliamentary supremacy. Shared power was a novelty in European practice, and surprisingly enough, it produced stronger rather

[22]Ibid., pp. 131–145.
[23]Ibid., pp. 178–179.
[24]Leon Epstein, *Political Parties in Western Democracies* (New York: Frederick A. Praeger, Publishers, 1967), pp. 37–40.

than weaker government. European settlement of North America was a second development. Established European practices often had little relevance here, and the new continent often spawned utopian hopes. The French Revolution was a third major episode. Until 1789, France's absolute monarchy had been the dominant model for European government. Afterwards, the English system became the standard for imitation.

In the wake of these events, politics in the West moved towards a competitive party form as the suffrage expanded. In Europe this required a long struggle to transform the inherited patchwork of voting rights that had linked small numbers of privileged individuals with particular corporate bodies in medieval times. Reform required that voting rights be extended to new sectors of the population and that a notion of individual (rather than organic) representation be developed. It was also necessary to standardize voting procedures and to eliminate various practices that made voters unequal.[25]

Early Differences

Forerunners of modern democratic parties emerged in seventeenth-century England. For a long time the Whigs and Tories functioned as informal *legislative* organizations; they did not develop organizations outside Parliament until the 1830s, and they did not have to compete before a mass electorate until the 1870s. The English system permitted rising middle-class elements to participate in politics, and each party strongly identified with existing institutions. This helped to establish the moderate tone of English politics on a lasting basis.

The first parties with genuine *mass support* appeared in the United States in the 1790s (or in the 1830s in the opinion of some scholars). This nation had fewer obstacles to mass participation than the European nations. Federalists and Jeffersonians were less exclusive than their English counterparts, and the suffrage was broader.

One might wonder why parties did not appear earlier in the United States. Voting on a wide scale always brings parties to the fore, yet politics in the colonies and early states was individualistic or factional, rather than partisan.

The answer lies in the lack of common nationhood until late in the eighteenth century. Much of the voting took place in small community settings of a few hundred persons. There were few natural social gatherings, roads were poor, postal service uncertain. Voters had only limited influence. In such circumstances, parties might have been convenient, but they were not indispensable.[26] With constitutional ratification the scale of government expanded enormously. Voters could now have very significant influence, and electoral organizations that could function over wide areas became more necessary.

At first, distrust of parties was common in both Europe and America. Those who created parties seemed to be unaware of doing so and, like

[25]The sequences were extremely complex. See Stein Rokkan et al., *Citizens Elections Parties* (New York: David McKay Company, Inc., 1970), pp. 147–168.
[26]Chambers, *Political Parties in a New Nation*, pp. 23–25.

Jefferson, disparaged them. Proponents of democracy argued that the people *should* rule; they did not understand that electoral organizations might be a necessary means to that end. In the usual eighteenth-century view, parties (or *factions* as they were often called) served special interests and fostered discord. Perhaps this skeptical view of parties was natural. Broadening political participation made factions more noticeable, and democracy was controversial.[27] Moreover, earlier religious controversies had shown that doctrinal divisions could be dangerous. Since human beings like to rationalize, it was never difficult to impute partisanship to the *other* side of a controversy while ignoring one's own partiality.

Paradoxically, modern parties took shape a good deal later in England than in the United States, yet they were quickly accepted there. Walter Bagehot's *The English Constitution* (written in 1867) proves the point. Some scholars have argued that parties should enjoy a similar eminence in the United States, but the American public has never supported this view. Americans created the first modern parties, but they continue to distrust them.

When viewed in comparative perspective, the persistence of antiparty outlooks in the United States is unusual and not easily accounted for. Perhaps we saw political democracy as such a natural state of affairs that we failed to appreciate the practical devices needed to achieve it. In the United States, voting seemed to give citizens influence almost automatically, and the suffrage seemed to come almost as a "free gift." It followed that Americans rarely had to struggle for the right to organize in the electoral arena or to argue forcefully for the advantages of party over other forms of political organization.

By 1787 this country retained no significant remnants of monarchy, feudalism, or an established church, and this meant that most barriers to representation in Europe had little effect here. The electoral vote system might have insulated the presidency from the mass electorate, but the natural workings of party competition soon nullified that possibility. In the 1830s Americans began to use elections as a method of filling many state and local administrative positions. Aside from persisting racial barriers, electoral democracy spread rapidly in the United States and met with little resistance. European nations were more resistant to political democracy and lagged behind the United States in extending voting rights. Opposition to traditional power also required more continuous struggles before it could be influential.[28]

Effects of governmental structure. In all Western nations, government took definite form before parties came into being. Parties did not create new governmental structures to suit themselves; they had to adapt to existing

---

[27]Austin Ranney and Willmoore Kendall, *Democracy and the American Party System* (New York: Harcourt Brace Jovanovich, 1956), chap. 6.

[28]Information on developments in Europe is to be found in Rokkan et al., *Citizens Elections Parties*, pp. 33, 79–85, 148–166.

ones. An especially crucial issue was the nature of the executive. In Europe, parties could control the executive only through the legislature. In the United States, however, an electoral coalition could win the presidency without winning a majority of congressional seats. As a result, an important stimulus for party unity in European legislatures was lacking in the United States.

Parties also adapted to differences in regional organization. In the United States, Canada, Australia, and Switzerland, the government was *federal:* Special regional units shared constitutional authority with the central government. In each of these nations, parties organized first at the local or regional level; today they are still federations of regional units rather than unified national bodies. *The United States represents the extreme case.* The earliest mass parties began here before many of the centralizing forces of modern life had begun to take effect. It is not surprising, therefore, that American parties today are the most decentralized of any in the world.[29]

Spoils, Membership, and Socialism

America's parties were well established a half century before the country began to set up a merit system for governmental employees. This permitted American politicians to look on administrative positions as "jobs" they could use to reward workers and supporters. Even a modest start toward merit did not get underway at the national level until 1883. Many states and localities began much later.

In Europe extensive party organizations did not develop until the latter part of the nineteenth century, *after* effective civil service reforms were in place. Open competition and tenure protection were routine for most English civil service positions by 1870, although vigorous competition for parliamentary seats was still in its infancy. By the time mass politics arrived, the European parties could not rely on government jobs as the major spur to party effort, and this is one reason why they developed mass dues-paying memberships. American parties, on the other hand, persisted as skeletal organizations run by professional politicians.

Once they had learned to rely on spoils, American politicians were reluctant to change. Merit principles took hold only gradually, and in at least a few places "jobs" still remain the life blood of politics. One could even argue that American parties have *never* devised an adequate substitute for patronage.[30] A declining number of available jobs helps to account for the weaker condition of American parties in recent years, but failure to place reliable party support on a different basis probably results from antiparty outlooks. Most Americans would agree with Artemus Ward when he said "I am not a politician and my other habits are good."[31]

---

[29]Epstein, *Western Democracies,* pp. 31–36.
[30]Ibid., pp. 23, 105.
[31]William Safire, *Safire's Political Dictionary* (New York: Random House, Inc., 1978), p. 550. Safire describes some different types of American politician: "a *professional politician* is usually a technician without ideology; a POL is one of *the boys in the backroom:* a GOPHER is the lowest political functionary . . . and an OLD PRO knows enough ropes to hang himself."

Socialist working-class parties, an important element in European politics, were always a negligible force here. Among the possible reasons is the fact that the early industrial revolution (1780–1848) was not nearly as disruptive here as in Western Europe. By the time Europe's parties had formed, much of the population lived in large urban centers. Europe also had many more industrial workers when mass parties emerged, and many of these had already joined trade unions and listened to voices of social protest. All of this is very different from the rural and small-town origins of American electoral politics.

Special American Practices

In this country, partisan politics took a distinctive turn when the states placed political parties on a statutory footing, beginning in the 1880s, and when the parties began to use the direct primary as the principal method of nomination, about 1900.

Statutory enactments. In Europe, political parties have remained essentially private associations. They enjoy no special public status in the law, and they are subject only to minimal regulations. In the United States, however, detailed state laws define parties in official terms and prescribe rights of participants. Statutes may also dictate the precise organizational structures and details of party procedure, although these usually coexist with rules issued by official party bodies.

For example, Indiana's statutes contain more than three hundred pages of material dealing with parties and elections. These specify the party committees and how they shall be composed, officers of committees and how they shall be chosen, time and place of organizing party committees, composition of state and county election boards, and many other matters. Nearly all of this material dealing with elections is of at least potential concern to the parties, even when it does not describe parties as such. Examples would be provisions concerning voter registration, poll watchers, and compensation of precinct election officers.

Placing details of party organization in the statutes does not necessarily mean that parties are "regulated" in the usual sense. Legislators, after all, are usually representatives of the major parties, and legal enactments have often reflected partisan custom and convenience. Putting parties on a statutory footing could legitimize party activity, and it could buttress the position of major parties vis à vis lesser electoral organizations.

The direct primary. The direct primary is basically a preliminary election that determines the party's nominees. Stated differently, the primary designates candidates who will run with a party label in the general election.[32]

---

[32]Some primary contests may be final: convention delegates, precinct committee people and the like. In some cases, nonpartisan officeholders are also designated in the primary. State presidential primaries may or may not determine national convention delegates or commit delegates to specific contestants. Frequently, the most important aspect of the presidential primary is what it reveals about the relative popularity of the contestants. The actual nominations for president are made in the national conventions.

Detailed state laws regulate primaries just as they do general elections. Government funds pay the costs of administering the one, just as the other. Features of the primaries vary greatly from state to state, but direct primaries determine nominations for nearly all important offices in this country. *The practice is unique.* Some parties in other nations canvass their membership before selecting candidates, but *only* the United States has a comprehensive system of primary elections. Elsewhere, it is expected that leaders of freely formed party associations will designate their candidates. Americans have distrusted and feared control by political leaders.

Why did American politics move in these unusual directions? The introduction of secret voting provides an important clue. When the United States began to adopt the Australian (secret) ballot in 1888, the practice was to have the ballot carry party labels. This departure from Australian practice may have been necessitated by the much larger number of elective offices in the United States. Without party labels on the ballot, the voters would certainly have had difficulty sorting out party nominees for minor offices. The government printed the ballots, and it was therefore necessary to draft legal standards by which a party could qualify for a place on the ballot. From this entering wedge, the law moved rapidly by natural stages to comprehensive treatment of parties in the statutes.[33]

Changes with Similar Effects

Finally, we should note certain developments that affected the Western democracies in a like manner, although to a variable degree. One of the most important of these was secret voting, adopted in most nations between 1872 and 1918. Ballot secrecy has made the consequences of personal pressures unobservable in most cases. When the vote is secret, neither party organizations, nor peers, nor superiors can be certain that they control a particular person's vote. The secret ballot also enables more people to *abstain* from politics by not voting at all. Even those who do vote can isolate themselves from the political process and develop the view that a person's political preferences are nobody else's business. Secrecy thus permitted a certain individualism in voting. The voter no longer had to be a footsoldier in a group or party cause; he could pick and choose, dissemble and resist. With the registration of preferences no longer an inherently public process, only a minority of political activists would be publicly and continuously involved in elections.[34]

Patterns of mass communications also changed in Europe and the United States in similar ways, but the United States was often in the forefront. Political tracts began to circulate in Europe after the invention of printing in the fifteenth century. By the late 1,600s, newspapers were transmitting political information to small circles of readers in England. Indeed, newspapers may not have reached a large public in any country until the 1870s or so.

[33]Howard R. Penniman, *Sait's American Parties and Elections,* 5th ed. (New York: Appleton-Century-Crofts, Inc., 1952), p. 192.
[34]Rokkan et al., *Citizens Elections Parties,* pp. 35–36, 153–154.

The strong partisanship of early newspapers was directly related to their limited circulation. Huge increases in the circulation of individual papers first occurred in the United States in the 1880s and 1890s, perhaps because of this country's higher levels of literacy. *As circulation expanded, the papers tended to become less partisan.* Owners did not want to lose subscribers who adhered to other political views. A somewhat similar shift occurred a bit later in most of Western Europe. These changes in mass communication meant that parties were no longer the only channels to the mass electorate. Parties and candidates in all nations had to adapt to the new media situation and, in a sense, compete with it. Along with secret voting, changing media were becoming important agents of a more individualized electoral politics.

Television (politically important only since 1952) commands an even larger audience than the mass circulation dailies. In all of these countries, the audience is even less differentiated politically. As a result, TV newscasters try to avoid even the appearance of partisanship. Television permits efficient communication between candidates and voters with no apparent need of party intermediaries. Its ability to individualize politics and to weaken party organization is therefore even more pronounced than that of the newspapers.[35]

These tendencies have been especially pronounced in the United States, for several possible reasons. The American people have been more affluent, and a strikingly high proportion of them have continuously moved about over an enormous geographical area. As a result, communication techniques that do not depend on face-to-face contacts have been both more necessary and easier to develop. These same factors help account for the more advanced state of professional public relations and advertising in the United States. Skills honed in the commercial arena have been adopted by candidates who wished to use the media for effective political campaigns. In recent years, American-style public relations and television campaigns have been increasingly influential in Europe as well.

CONCLUSION

Partisan activity is a response to organizational needs in mass politics. Mass participation is still spreading, and nothing is certain about how the opportunities it presents will be worked out. Partisan politics can be fateful activity because it may either frustrate or enhance the surge of ordinary people towards a meaningful role in political decision making. In the democracies, authentic party competition can be expressed through a single party under certain conditions, as well as through two-party or multiparty systems. American electoral politics differs from practices in other democratic nations, but one can easily understand many of the variations. A number of factors have been moving the democratic nations towards a more individualistic politics, and this seems to imply a weaker role for parties.

[35]Epstein, *Western Democracies,* pp. 233–238.

However, taken as a whole, our analysis suggests that the situation in nations with very weak or nonexistent parties is distinctly unenviable. While a lack of parties does not necessarily specify the root of all major misfortunes, it really is possible that parties are instruments of human welfare, and that like some other institutions, their proper functioning contributes to the general good.

In the world today, mass participation has become so important that governments must somehow conform to the idea of equality even if they do not consult their subjects. As Leonard Binder puts it, "Under modern conditions a legitimate government is elected by the people, or is trustee for the people, or works in the interest of the people, or is a reflection of certain qualities of the people, or reflects what the people will become in the future."[36] One can, of course, wonder how many rulers are genuinely concerned about "the people." But even with full allowance for misuse of the term *democracy,* egalitarianism remains a powerful and continuing force in world politics.

Unfortunately, genuine democracy is far from universal. One can even say that it is nonexistent when measured against a pure ideal. Democracy requires political freedom to organize and compete, as well as reliable methods of imposing peoples' wishes on government. Even with mass participation and universal suffrage, people may lack needed political skills. Important groups may not support democratic values, and serious inequalities may persist.

In recent years we have heard that Americans are disillusioned with electoral politics. If this is true, perhaps Americans yearn for some substitute method of coping with their central concerns. However, in the pessimistic mood of the 1970s, we also heard that Americans are disillusioned with many other things, including achievement, technology, and child rearing.[37] The 1980s may witness a search for a new set of principles or a return to the older certitudes that were so vigorously attacked in the 1970s. Dissatisfaction with our worldly success and concern about declines in productivity and education are likely to persist. We can be certain that one way or another our electoral politics will affect the way we deal with such concerns as we face the uncertainties of the years ahead.

[36]Binder, "Crises of Political Development," in Binder et al., *Crises and Sequences,* pp. 56–57.

[37]There is a possible misunderstanding about disillusionment which we will get to later in the book.

2

American Political History

Many Americans find history uncongenial. Our society has changed almost constantly since its founding, and attention has usually been focused on the present or the future. Today, when the future appears uncertain, taking stock of our past may help us understand where we are going. History offers an important avenue to self-understanding. The materials of the past may encourage us to view the human situation in a dispassionate way, and they may help us to understand the nature of greatness. Nevertheless, the individual who approaches history in a spirit of celebration would do well to recall the advice in Ecclesiastes — "Do not ask why the old days were better than these; for that is a foolish question."

Scholars tend to agree that party politics in the United States has gone through five major phases, sometimes separated by transition periods. In each phase, two parties dominated. Even when the names of these parties did not change (as with the third, fourth, and fifth systems), the constellation of political forces differed.

The following scheme may help you to fix the main sequences in your mind. It takes the Civil War and the Great Depression as milestones that give us four major periods:

Periods and Phases of U.S. Political History[a]

1. The Early Republic, 1789–1860
    Early Creation of Parties
    First Party System: 1800–1816
        Transition
    Second Party System: 1832–1852
        Transition

2. Civil War and Its Aftermath, 1860–1868
3. The Republican Era, 1868–1932
    Third Party System: 1868–1896
    Fourth Party System: 1896–1932
4. The New Deal Era, 1932–?
    Fifth Party System: 1932–?
    Transition?

ᵃDates are approximate.

This arrangement places us in the fourth period but does not decide whether the fifth party system is still operating. Quite possibly, parties are again in a transition phase.[1]

AMERICA'S FIRST PARTIES

Partisan politics was quite intense in the early years of the Republic, and America's first two-party system was not very stable. Activists did not accept party formations as either desirable or natural, and each party's tolerance of the other was low. Uncertainty, fear of subversion, and emotionalism were hallmarks of the period.

The nation's first two political parties, the Federalist and Jeffersonian-Republican parties, had evolved from old fights over ratification of the Constitution, but they were not simply a reincarnation of them. At least twelve of forty-three members of the Constitutional Convention who had supported ratification were Jeffersonian Republicans by 1791.[2] The party's two main leaders, Jefferson and Madison, had favored ratification, and by 1800 support for the Constitution was practically universal. Issues of economic development, foreign policy, and constitutional interpretation had elements of continuity with the past, but in their specific form they were new.

The presidency was already the matrix of American party politics. The uncertainties of the electoral vote system had yielded to a recognition of the simple fact that to win the presidency one needed a *national* political coalition. Hamilton's fiscal program had shown how the executive could shape key decisions in the new nation, and the president's special prerogatives in foreign affairs had become matters of practical urgency to American politics after war between Britain and France placed new pressures on the country.

[1]This chapter is heavily indebted to Richard B. Morris, *Encyclopedia of American History* (New York: Harper & Row, Publishers, Inc., 1976) for chronological details. Other consistently important sources are Wilfred E. Binkley, *American Political Parties* (New York: Alfred A. Knopf, Inc., 1962); John A. Garraty, *A Short History of the American Nation* (New York: Harper & Row Publishers, Inc., 1974); and Samuel Eliot Morrison, Henry Steele Commager, and William E. Leuchtenburg, *The Growth of the American Republic*, 6th ed. (New York: Oxford University Press, 1969). The main source for voting statistics is *Congressional Quarterly's Guide to U.S. Elections* (Washington, D.C.: Congressional Quarterly Inc., 1976).

[2]William N. Chambers, *Political Parties in a New Nation* (New York: Oxford University Press, 1963), p. 104.

The Federalist party faded almost as soon as the first system of competitive parties was fully established. Hamilton's programs did not broaden the party's appeals, and since the French had aided the colonies in their war of independence, the English affinities and social manners of the Federalists were usually a political liability. The party developed serious factional divisions, and it watched helplessly while population almost doubled between 1790 and 1810. The decade ending 1820 brought another seven states and a third more people into the Republic. The Federalists were not able to keep up.

It is not easy for modern Americans to get a proper feeling for those early years. Aristocratic outlooks born in feudal Europe affected the meaning of words in common usage as late as 1815. *Politics,* for example, was "the science of government." *Industry* meant *diligence,* and *radical* meant *primitive.* There was, moreover, a rich vocabulary of disparagement: *vulgar,* for example, referred to the common people and meant *plebeian, mean, low.* The poor were *vile,* and a foreign peasant was a *boor.* Over the years, we have cleaned up the language and made it fit for use in a democratic society. We forget these and other things, including:

> How the past smelled, how it reeked of horse manure.
>
> How much dirty drudgery and hard physical labor there was about doing or making anything. How much hard work was done by women and children.
>
> How slowly the news got around and how little of it there was.
>
> How dark the streets were at night, and how dark it was indoors. How dim candlelight was.[3]

Transition

As the Federalist party withered, ambitious politicians swelled the Jeffersonian-Republican ranks. Antiparty feeling was still strong, and many hoped that the period after 1817 would be an "era of good feeling." Although the apparent intention was a system without parties, the congressional caucus of the Jeffersonian-Republican party made the presidential nominations, and the men so designated were associated with a party label. The caucus always gave the incumbent president a second term. Furthermore, when it was time for a new selection it always preferred the individual who had been secretary of state under the previous president. The secretary of state, in turn, had usually served as a leader in Congress. Thus, after Thomas Jefferson served for two terms, his secretary of state, James Madison, followed him to the presidency. Madison also served two terms, and Secretary of State James Monroe succeeded him. Lacking an organized opposition, the party lost all definition on issues. There were no well-defined divisions, despite the weaknesses of the Madison and Monroe presidencies. In 1820, the caucus was so poorly attended that it made no formal

---

[3]E. E. Schattschneider, *Two Hundred Million Americans in Search of a Government* (New York: Holt, Rinehart & Winston, 1969), pp. 50–51, 87–88, 102–103. Copyright © 1969 by Holt, Rinehart & Winston, Inc. Reprinted by permission of Holt, Rinehart & Winston.

nominations, and Monroe's candidacy for a second term went unopposed. A confusing train of events followed after the election of 1820. Presidential ambitions quickly pitted John C. Calhoun (secretary of war) against William H. Crawford (secretary of the treasury). Secretary of State John Quincy Adams stayed aloof from the unseemly struggles. Crawford's followers in the Senate blocked Calhoun at every opportunity and even refused to approve military nominations that he recommended. Retaliatory moves led to charges against Crawford before a congressional investigating committee in 1823.

Meanwhile, nominating activity for the 1824 election began early. Calhoun announced his candidacy in 1821. In the following year the Tennessee and Kentucky legislatures nominated Andrew Jackson and Henry Clay, respectively. The next year, 1823, brought the nomination of John Quincy Adams by a Boston meeting and William Crawford's nomination by a rump group of the congressional caucus. However, in September 1823 Crawford suffered a paralytic stroke and ceased active campaigning. Calhoun then withdrew in exchange for the vice presidential position on both the Jackson and Adams tickets. Jackson began to attack "King Caucus" and pressed for the right of the people to choose the president.

The 1824 election produced the following results:

	Electoral Votes
Jackson	99
Adams	84
Crawford	41
Clay	37
TOTAL	261

Jackson received a plurality of electoral votes, but he lacked a majority, and the contest had to be resolved in the House. For the first time, observers paid considerable attention to the popular vote. Here, too, Jackson was in the lead but again he lacked a clear majority. However, only eighteen of the twenty-four states had chosen their electors by popular vote, and in only four states were voters able to choose among all four candidates.

A letter in a newspaper printed before the balloting clouded the maneuvering that now took place in the House: According to the letter, Clay would support Adams in exchange for appointment as secretary of state. Clay was speaker of the House, and since he did not finish among the top three, he could not be chosen president. However, he was very conscious of his power and, after temporizing for weeks, finally threw his support to Adams, thus making him the next president.

Many thought that Adams's subsequent appointment of Clay as secretary of state confirmed the prediction in the letter. The incident tainted Clay's career and embittered Jackson. He had been deprived of what he considered his rightful prize, and the man responsible was in position for the party's next nomination. He wrote to a friend that "the Judas of the West has closed the contract and will receive the thirty pieces of silver."

COMPROMISE AND DEVELOPMENT
IN THE SECOND PARTY SYSTEM

In the winter of 1824–1825, not surprisingly, the most prominent leaders of the Jeffersonian-Republican party divided into two groups, the National Republicans (Adams and Clay) and the Democratic Republicans (Jackson). These groups evolved into the political parties of the second system.

Between 1824 and 1828, the presidential vote expanded more than threefold, and population growth could account for only a small part of the increase. In 1828 four more states (in fact all but two of the twenty-four) selected their electors by popular vote, and the popular vote was beginning to receive more attention. More important, the choice between Adams and Jackson provided a more focused competition. Although the Jackson men defeated them resoundingly in 1828 and 1832, competition from the National Republicans was stronger than that usually provided by the Federalists under the first party system.

The population—12.9 million in 1830—was increasing by a third every ten years. Politics was becoming more "popular"—that is, more people were participating in it—and leaders were expected to fit the common mold. Politics also began to be more fun. Leaders could enjoy the stratagems of politics, and voters could participate in mass parades and political rallies. The more substantial figures, such as Stephen A. Douglas, John C. Calhoun, Henry Clay, Martin Van Buren, and Daniel Webster, raised political practice to a fine art.

By 1832 the Jackson men had acquired recognized leaders and party organization in every state. In September 1831 the Anti-Masonic party held the country's first national nominating convention—introducing the method that would be used to nominate all persons elected president henceforth.[4] The Jackson men followed suit in May with their national convention, an assemblage of local machines that had little to do except ratify Jackson's choice of Martin Van Buren as running mate. The presidency, now free of the congressional caucus, could develop its own powers in a truly independent fashion.

The Jackson men were soon to become the "Democratic" party, a formation its twentieth-century descendant clearly resembles. The Democrats appealed to the mass of commoners, generated controversial issues from a strong presidency, developed patronage on a new scale, and brought a professional politician (Martin Van Buren) into national prominence for the first time. On the issues, the Democrats were antimonopoly, anticorporation, and antibank.

Jacksonian democracy contributed a new style to American electoral politics. Officeholders emphasized that they were representatives, appealing

[4]In a sense, the Federalists were first with a national nominating convention in 1808. However, they held it without public notice and closed its sessions to the public. This prevented it from serving as a party rally—one of the notable features of the post-1832 conventions. Paul T. David, Ralph M. Goldman, and Richard C. Bain, *The Politics of National Party Conventions* (Washington, D.C.: The Brookings Institution, 1960), p. 14.

vigorously to voters in their "campaigns." For the first time, a president had a "kitchen cabinet" to advise him. Politicians justified their enthusiastic practice of the spoils system (always an element of American politics) as a way of getting citizens to participate in self-government. As Jacksonian practices matured, large numbers of short-term elective offices became the norm. The result was the long, or "bedsheet," ballot and even more continuous partisan campaigning.

In 1834 there was a gathering of opposition forces that referred to themselves as the Whigs. In a sense, these people stood for a transparently simple principle: The outs might win, if they could only pool their forces against the ins. Elements joined in Whiggery buried their other differences in sincere or cynical detestation of "executive usurpation."

The group included National Republicans, who favored energetic policies of internal improvements; "states' righters" of varying shades; Democrats who were disgruntled with Jackson or Van Buren (the latter was especially repugnant to many southerners) and various other elements. The Whigs included northern manufacturers and southern planters, as well as people of culture who did not like the anti-intellectualism they discerned in Andrew Jackson.

The Democrats, of course, claimed that the Whigs were just a resurrection of the Federalists. But this was not really the case. Daniel Webster had been a Federalist, but most Whigs had been Republicans. Moreover, many former Federalists (including James Buchanan and Roger Taney) supported Jackson. Jackson, after all, had fought in the Revolutionary War and had feuded with Thomas Jefferson. The Whig outlook was commercial and cosmopolitan but not aristocratic. Unlike the Federalists, Whig leaders enjoyed partisan politics and were often very good at it.[5]

In 1836 the Whigs were unable to agree on a single candidate. However, they adopted the strategy of having state legislatures nominate individuals with strong local followings: Daniel Webster from Massachusetts, Hugh White from Tennessee, and William Henry Harrison from Ohio. (Technically, the Anti-Masonic party nominated Harrison, but this group had been largely absorbed by the National Republicans, and Harrison was a Whig.) The Whigs hoped that multiple candidacies would prevent anyone from getting a majority of the electoral vote. Whig electors could then unite to support one candidate or throw the election into the House. The strategy did not succeed, but the competition against the Democrats was indeed formidable.

The second party system assumed its characteristic form in 1840, the year the Whigs improved on techniques invented by the Jacksonians. The Whigs passed over controversial statesmen such as Clay and Webster and picked a military hero (War of 1812) whose views were largely unknown. They presented General Harrison (of a distinguished family, with a comfortable personal income) as a plain man of the people who lived in a log cabin and drank hard cider. His opponent, Van Buren, they averred, was luxuriat-

[5]Glyndon G. VanDeusen, "The Whig Party," in *History of U.S. Political Parties,* ed. Arthur M. Schlesinger, Jr. (New York: Chelsea House Publishers, 1973), I, 333–363.

ing in a palatial White House, dining on foreign delicacies and expensive wines. The Whigs did not adopt a platform, and they avoided taking stands on issues in the campaign. The party used placards, campaign hats, floats, and transportable log cabins as it sang its way through the campaign to the tune of "Tippecanoe and Tyler Too." The chanting refrain of that song was especially effective: "Van, Van, is a used up man."

Again there was an extraordinary increase in voter participation: from 1.5 million in 1836 to 2.4 million in 1840. The emphasis on personalities, the liveliness of the campaigns, and the closeness of the competition plausibly account for this upsurge, since the same states had popular voting both times. The pattern of close two-party competition maintained itself until the late 1840s or early 1850s, when it began to disintegrate under the stress of sectional conflict.

By the 1840s, the country was increasingly preoccupied with western expansion. Territorial advance, which had been relatively slow for two hundred years, now accelerated rapidly. Americans realized that the whole continent would soon be theirs, and the westward surge of settlement suddenly became an irresistible force. Indeed, by 1848, in only three years, the Republic had acquired vast territories from Mexico and Great Britain that set its basic modern shape.

It is paradoxical that 1844 was the only year that the Whigs ever nominated a candidate (Henry Clay) who had been an outstanding party leader with known positions. Whig nominees in other years were all nonpolitical military heroes. Polk, a dark-horse nominee, had beaten Clay in an extremely close election. In resisting pressures for the annexation of Texas, Clay had misjudged the national mood.

Polk's expansionist successes strained the Democratic party. Northern elements felt that he was too pro-Southern in his policies and in 1846 tried unsuccessfully to exclude slavery by legislation from any territory acquired from Mexico. By this time, the commitment to slavery in the South had reached a point of no return. Territorial expansion stimulated sectional rivalries that threatened to upset the balance between slave and free states. The fact that most of the new territory offered no practical prospects for the extension of slavery did not reassure anyone. The nation moved inexorably towards a sectional showdown.

Under the surface, however, less dramatic events were laying the groundwork for a different future. By the 1850s automatic machinery was turning out screws and files. American clocks, pistols, rifles, and locks were recognized as outstanding. A national economy was intruding on small local markets—making them increasingly interdependent. Innovations in textiles and sewing led to a thriving ready-made clothing industry by the 1850s, and steam power was expanding economic activity on many fronts.

More dramatic changes occurred as urban populations grew, sometimes swamping the capacity of the primitive municipal services of the time. Frontier violence and Indian "removal" had their counterpart among the urban poor. In fact ethnic and religious conflicts produced sustained rioting in Baltimore, Philadelphia, New York, and Boston between 1830 and 1860—perhaps the most massive urban violence America ever experienced.[6]

In 1848 the Democrats nominated a conservative general, Lewis Cass, and tried to keep the slavery issue out of the platform, but antislavery elements seceded from the party, and the Southern planters, oppositionists since the nullification controversy of 1832, began to return. The Southern commitment to slavery was becoming monolithic. Far from being viewed as a necessary evil, an elaborate propaganda extolled slavery as the ideal social system. Southerners who spoke out against slavery would be assaulted or driven away.

In the North, abolitionist sentiment subjected the second two-party system to heavy strain. William Lloyd Garrison, for example, had almost been killed by a Boston mob in 1835. Now he was arguing that the North should withdraw from a compact that sheltered slavery, and in 1854 he burned a copy of the Constitution while proclaiming before a public gathering "So perish all compromises with tyranny!" The slavery issue, long compromised or suppressed in American politics, could no longer be contained.

The Whig party succumbed to mounting pressures. In 1852 (its last real presidential effort) its highest vote was the 51.4 percent it received in Kentucky. In eight other states it received less than 40 percent of the vote. These included five Southern states plus Maine, New Hampshire, and Wisconsin, where the minor Free Soil party received some support. As before, the Whigs' presidential strategy had been to count on the issueless appeal of a popular military hero, in this case Winfield Scott. This had worked reasonably well when the dominant mood of the country was to suppress the slavery controversy, but it was utterly inadequate now. A growing antislavery sentiment in the Northern wing of the party repelled the Southern Whigs, and most of them defected to the Democrats.

Transition

The growing clash between North and South proceeded by stages that cannot be detailed here. By 1856 rival settlers in Kansas were already in a state of civil war. The Whigs were finished, and a new major party, the Republican, held its first convention and nominated John C. Fremont. The party had begun in 1854 as a leaderless movement united in opposition to the Kansas-Nebraska Act. Free-Soilers, Independent Democrats, and Conscience Whigs made up its basic elements; they were joined by temperance enthusiasts and Know-Nothings after 1856. The Republicans called for admission of Kansas as a free state and upheld congressional authority to control slavery in the territories. They also favored rapid development of the West and a railroad to the Pacific.

The balloting in 1856 revealed an ominous sectional cleavage. Although Republicans received no votes whatever in twelve Southern states,

---

[6]Richard Maxwell Brown, "Historical Patterns of Violence in America," in *Violence in America,* ed. Hugh Davis Graham and Ted Robert Gurr (New York: Bantam Books, Inc., 1969), pp. 53–54.

they obtained 39 percent of the total electoral vote. With the midterm elections of 1858, Republicans obtained control of the House of Representatives as tensions continued to mount. John Brown's effort to start a slave insurrection in Virginia, his capture by Robert E. Lee, and his subsequent hanging polarized emotions North and South.

Seven weeks after Lincoln's decisive victory in 1860, Southern troops began seizing United States forts and arsenals; by February, seven states had seceded. The seceding states framed a constitution and set up a provisional government with Jefferson Davis as provisional president. Lincoln took office about three weeks later. On April 12 South Carolina's shore batteries opened fire on Fort Sumter and forced its commanding officer to surrender.

THE CIVIL WAR PERIOD

It was this young nation's worst debacle. Deaths from all causes in the two armies totalled about 620,000—more Americans than were killed in battle (not a precisely comparable concept) in both world wars combined. The 1860 population was, of course, only about a third the size of the 1914 population and less than a quarter the size of the 1940 population. It was the only American war in which the civilian population (in the South) had a direct encounter with modern military violence.

The brutalizing effect of the war on American society lasted for decades. The Civil War drew the bulk of federal troops off the western lands by 1862, and five years of bloody Indian encounters followed. The methods of the struggle left a legacy of vigilantism, outlawry, and night riding. Lynch-mob violence became much more common after 1865. Family feuds in the Appalachian Mountains had their origins in the raids of rival guerrilla bands, as did similar quarrels in Texas and the Southwest. The war also reinforced the materialism of American society, since the importance of business and manufacturing to the Union victory had been clear to everyone. Corruption and insensitivity suffused the following years as Americans abandoned themselves wholeheartedly to a race for personal gain.

The scope of the disaster still resists our full comprehension. Negro slavery was at least two thousand years old by 1860, but none of the major ethical traditions of Western civilization had totally repudiated it.[7] Despite the obvious evil of slavery in North America, it had taken two centuries for a strong abolitionist sentiment to develop. The problem was especially difficult in this country because of rigid attitudes towards interracial marriage and excessive devotion to short-run material profit.

The party system had tenaciously resisted the resort to violence. Although sectional compromises and attempted compromises were hardly noble, they did demonstrate flexibility and realism. But there were also significant political weaknesses. The feebleness of the Whigs by 1856 robbed the two-party system of its moderating potential and rewarded ex-

[7]David Brion Davis, *The Problem of Slavery in Western Culture* (Ithaca, N.Y.: Cornell University Press, 1966).

tremism in both sections. Also, the South, by refusing to accommodate itself to Lincoln's victory in 1860, clearly went beyond what was in the best political interest of its dominant groups. However, the basic failure lay in the country's inability to sustain a gradual reform of slavery that could wean the South from dependence on it.

Both the Union and the Confederacy continued to hold elections during the war. A fascinating study suggests that the Confederate effort to function without political parties may have contributed to its defeat. States' rights pressures continuously hindered the war effort in the South, and a party system might have been able to offset them to some degree. In the North the Republican party linked state and national governments in a relatively cohesive prosecution of the war effort. Even the Democratic opposition may have contributed to the North's organizational superiority. By way of contrast, opposition to Jefferson Davis took the form of an "undifferentiated bickering resistance" that was extremely difficult to cope with.[8]

A Look Ahead

The sixty-four years that separate the beginning of the Grant administration from the Franklin Roosevelt administration witnessed an incredible transformation of American life. Politically, it was a period of continuous Republican dominance. The only Democratic presidents between 1868 and 1932 were Grover Cleveland and Woodrow Wilson. However, the election of 1896 divides this period into two quite distinct phases. The social and economic context of American politics in these years also needs to be differentiated by periods, and here the choice of 1896 may be less compelling.

POLITICS IN AN INDUSTRIALIZING SOCIETY

Until 1860 the United States was overwhelmingly rural. Total population had grown at a rate that would never be matched again, but by 1860 only 10 percent of the population lived in cities of over fifty thousand. Between 1860 and 1900, however, urban population increased fivefold. In 1860 America had only one city of a million or more population. By 1900 three such cities together accounted for about 6.5 million inhabitants. In 1860 three people were employed in agricultural work for every two in nonagricultural work. By 1900 the ratio was almost reversed.[9]

Industrial enterprise had expanded before the Civil War, but the growth that now took place completely overshadowed it. According to one measure, manufacturing production was 4.4 times as great in 1890 as it had

[8]Eric L. McKitrick, "Party Politics and the Union and Confederate War Efforts," in *The American Party System: Stages of Political Development*, ed. William Chambers and Walter Dean Burnham (New York: Oxford University Press, 1967), pp. 117–151. Quotation on p. 142.

[9]Everett Carll Ladd, Jr., *American Political Parties* (New York: W. W. Norton & Company, Inc., 1970), p. 111.

been only thirty years earlier, even though population had only doubled.[10] Industrial output in 1860 was small by European standards, yet by the turn of the century the United States led the world in manufacturing. For example, American steel output exceeded that of Great Britain and Germany combined; the United States had twice as many telephones as *all of Europe*. The United States had a railroad network as early as 1850, and by 1871 there were five times as many miles of railroad track. Even so, the next twenty-nine years witnessed a new *threefold expansion* of track mileage as well as improvements in rail technology. Output of textiles, pig iron, agricultural implements, and clay products grew to enormous levels.

It was a period when politics seemed to be dwarfed by economic changes and when industrialization dominated all aspects of American life. Big business was in the vanguard. Its political objectives met some opposition, but it usually prevailed. The earlier preoccupation with the status of blacks almost totally receded.

The Republican party of 1868 was quite different from the party of a decade earlier. The earlier Republican party had been a party of reform— even crusading reform. Now, however, business triumphantly established itself in the Republican party. Although the platform endorsed radical reconstruction, the presidential nominee, Ulysses S. Grant, was not a radical. Industrialists contributed heavily to his campaign, and like most people of his time, Grant was deferential to men of wealth.

Financial success tended to be the main criterion of achievement in these years, and businessmen were the natural leaders of the time. For example, Richard Morris's excellent *Encyclopedia of American History* contains biographies of twenty notable business leaders. Two were most active before 1835, and five were especially prominent between 1835 and 1868. Between 1868 and 1896 no fewer than eleven made their most significant mark: Andrew Carnegie, Jay Cooke, James B. Duke, Marshall Field, Marcus Hanna, James J. Hill, J. Pierpont Morgan, John D. Rockefeller, Leland Stanford, Cornelius Vanderbilt, and Aaron Montgomery Ward.

By way of contrast, political figures of the period evoke no magic. Grover Cleveland, Horace Greeley, Samuel Tilden, Chester Arthur, Carl Schurz, and John Altgeld had considerable talents, but, fairly or not, none of them enjoyed the stature of the great public figures of the preceding or subsequent period.[11]

The scandals of the Grant administration reflected both the vigor and audacity of the era. An attempt by Jay Gould and "Jubilee Jim" Fisk to corner gold led to pressure on Grant's brother-in-law to prevent the government from selling gold. When the treasury did sell gold on September 24, 1869 ("Black Friday"), and the price plunged, many speculators were ruined. Gould later became a fabulously successful railroad promoter. In 1872 a *New York Times* exposé revealed that New York's Tweed ring was

---

[10]U.S. Bureau of the Census, *Historical Statistics of the United States* (Washington, D.C.: U.S. Government Printing Office, 1975), II, 667.

[11]Altgeld was Governor of Illinois 1893–1897; Schurz was a man of many talents who served as senator from Missouri 1869–1875.

plundering the city on a vast scale. Another series of articles in the *New York Sun* focused on a railroad construction company called the Credit Mobilier, set up in 1864 by the original promoters of the Union Pacific to divert profits from building the line to themselves. When it appeared that Congress might investigate in 1868, a stockholder sold Credit Mobilier shares to key public officials at prices far below their value. Investigations finally led to the censure of two U.S. representatives in 1873.

Two years later a conspiracy by revenue officials and distillers to defraud the government of the internal revenue tax led to the indictment of Grant's private secretary, and shortly afterwards the House impeached Secretary of War William Belknap for receiving bribes in the sale of trading posts in the Indian territory. The disputed election of 1876 brought vote manipulation on both sides. Modern authorities believe that Tilden would have won a fair election—thus modifying the older view that the Democrats stole the election in the first place and then the Republicans stole it back.

Party competition appears close when one examines voting statistics for the third party system. However, the general Republican advantage was greater than the figures in Table 2-1 would suggest. Republicans maintained high morale, while Democrats were strongest in the region that had espoused a discredited cause. Intimidation of black voters in the South accounted for some of the Democratic strength at the polls. Republican attitudes meshed more easily with ascendant business values, and the party had a strong sense of patriotic mission.

There were a number of important issues in this period, and Republicans usually took the leading positions. The party generally favored high protective tariffs, which benefited eastern business but were less pleasing to agrarian interests in the South and West. Republicans also got some mileage out of linking Democrats to the Southern secession—"waving the bloody shirt" in the language of the period.

Table 2-1
Competitive Politics in the Third Party System

	Presidential Plurality[a]	Voter Participation	Percentage of Competitive States[b]
1868	5.3% (R)	78.1%	33.3%
1872	9.8 (R)	71.3	45.9
1876	3.0 (D)[a]	81.8	45.9
1880	0.02 (R)	79.4	50.0
1884	0.25 (D)	77.5	52.6
1888	0.8 (D)[a]	79.3	52.6
1892	3.1 (D)	74.7	66.7

[a] Republicans won the presidential elections of 1876 and 1888 despite the Democratic edge in popular vote.
[b] States with presidential victory margins of 10 percent or less.
Sources: Voter participation figures computed by Walter Dean Burnham and reported in *Historical Statistics*, II, 1071–1072. Other percentages are based on data in Congressional Quarterly, *Guide to U.S. Elections*, 273–279.

Republicans bestowed huge grants of land on the railroads (an area that finally was almost as large as Texas) and reaped a continuing advantage from the Homestead Act, a measure they had passed in 1862 when the South was absent from the union. Southerners in Congress had opposed the Homestead Act in the prewar period because they had feared it would give the North an important advantage in the new territories. Sound money and generous veterans' pensions (Union soldiers only) complete the list of essential Republican appeals.

Democrats had few, if any, effective issue positions that were general to the period. Nevertheless, they obtained majorities in at least one house of Congress in eight elections out of fourteen. A bad depression in 1873 worked to their advantage, as did continuing scandal during Grant's administration. Declines in agricultural prices in 1884 helped account for Grover Cleveland's election that year, and the economic depression of 1890 also hurt the GOP. In fact, Democrats enjoyed a two-to-one advantage in the House of Representatives after 1890 and 1894.

Ethnic Groups and Machine Politics

For many ethnic groups, the post–Civil War years were an age of exploitation. Those who accumulated enormous fortunes extracted some of their wealth from elements of society less fortunately situated, and individual losers in the scramble to get ahead fared badly in all groups. Most groups, however, improved their material position somewhat (despite many adversities) because of the enormous expansion of America's material output.

Never assimilated in significant numbers, Indians had been steadily driven back for more than two centuries. In the prewar era, the dominant policy had been "removal" from settled areas. Nevertheless, the plains Indians were still free to roam half the continental domain as late as 1860. By 1884 senseless slaughter of the buffalo had reduced the herds to extinction, shattering the economy of the plains Indians. Survivors were penned up on two reservations. Legislation in 1887 sought to make the Indians citizen-farmers without tribal connections. Although well intended, this policy brought further disastrous effects, and it was not officially reversed until 1934.

As a group, blacks did not suffer as much as the Indians, but their plight was severe, and they constituted a much larger proportion of the population. Until World War I, blacks remained heavily concentrated in the South. Constitutional amendments passed between 1865 and 1870 outlawed slavery, extended citizenship to all persons born in the United States, and prohibited the denial of voting rights on the basis of race. Radical state governments, however, enjoyed only a mixed record in integrating the freedmen into the economic and political life of the region. Wealthy merchants and planters turned against the radical government by the mid-1870s. Despite terror and intimidation against blacks in the South, northern voters were less supportive of a military presence to protect black rights. In the aftermath of the disputed election of 1876, Democrats and ex-Whigs of the South tacitly acquiesced in Hayes's election victory in return for regional autonomy. The president withdrew the troops and established a sectional truce that had the effect of placing most blacks in a form of second-class citizenship or even peonage.

Despite the fearful cost of the conflict that had ended slavery, Americans of all sorts seemed indifferent to the human rights of blacks. Violent repression of the 1870s was followed in the 1890s with systematic disfranchisement via poll taxes and literacy tests. The late nineteenth century probably saw more lynchings in the South than any other period of American history.[12]

Many other ethnic minorities became an important part of American society in this period. A careful look at Table 2–2 shows some of the main tendencies. Note that total immigration had expanded greatly in the 1840s and 1850s. This was partly because steamships made the ocean crossing safer and cheaper than before. Economic hardship in Europe was always a significant "push" factor, and crop failures in the 1840s and 1850s brought many Irish and German immigrants. In the latter nineteenth century, a world market of cheap wheat and a spreading industrial revolution created severe hardship in the agricultural economies of southern and eastern Europe. The extraordinary industrial growth of the United States was, of course, an almost continuous "pull" factor.

The natural stresses of immigration depend on the number, location, outlooks, and social distance of the incoming groups. In proportion to total population, immigration was highest in the decade of the 1850s. In those years, significant antiforeign agitation centered in the Know-Nothing movement. Nativism also ran strong in the 1880s and from 1900 to 1910—decades when the proportional impact of immigration was almost as great.

Ethnic conflicts complicated industrial antagonisms of the period. Thus, chronic labor unrest in the coal fields of eastern Pennsylvania had produced a secret organization of miners called the "Molly Maguires." Authorities convicted ten members of murder and hanged them in 1875. Since the Molly Maguires were an outgrowth of the Ancient Order of Hibernians, the incident encouraged the public to blame "alien agitators" for increasing industrial violence. The Haymarket "Massacre" of 1886 reinforced the stereotype. In this incident, seven Anarcho-Communists were (unjustly) convicted of murder after somebody threw a bomb into the ranks of police who had broken up a protest meeting in Haymarket Square, Chicago. The most powerful nativist organization of the period, the American Protective Association, emerged the following year.

Cultures represented by new immigrants from central and southern Europe were less familiar to most Americans, and this encouraged the newer groups to be somewhat more clannish. Most of the good farming land was by now beyond their means. Urban transportation systems and multiunit

---

[12]For a discussion of lynching statistics, see Gerald M. Pomper, *Elections in America* (New York: Dodd, Mead & Company, 1975), pp. 216–220.

Table 2-2
Voluntary Migration[a] to the United States from All Countries

	Total in Millions	Percent of Total Population[b]	Irish	Percentage: Other Northern European[c]	Other European[d]
1820–1829	.1	1.0%	40.2%	34.5%	3.4%
1830–1839	.5	3.9	31.7	45.8	1.2
1840–1849	1.4	8.2	46.0	49.6	.3
1850–1859	2.8	12.1	36.6	55.8	.7
1860–1869	2.1	6.7	20.7	68.9	1.3
1870–1879	2.8	7.3	15.4	60.3	5.2
1880–1889	5.3	10.6	12.9	59.0	15.9
1890–1899	3.9	6.2	10.4	36.1	50.6
1900–1909	8.2	10.8	4.2	17.9	71.0
1910–1919[e]	6.4	7.0	2.6	15.0	62.2[e]
1920–1929[e]	4.3	4.1	4.8	24.9	28.2[e]

[a] All immigrants to the United States except blacks sold into slavery. One estimate is that about 400,000 slaves were imported into North America between 1701 and 1870. All but about 51,000 of these persons came before 1811. Phillip D. Curtin, *The Atlantic Slave Trade* (Madison, Wisc.: University of Wisconsin Press, 1969). All of the figures in this table are subject to possible error because of rounding, imperfect records, uncertain allowances for return migration, European boundary changes, and so forth.

[b] Total immigration for the decade as a percentage of U.S. population in the first year of the decade.

[c] Great Britain, Germany, Scandinavia, other northwestern Europe.

[d] Central Europe, Russia and the Baltic States, other eastern Europe, Italy, other southern Europe.

[e] In the period from 1911 to 1930, 1.6 million Canadians emigrated to the U.S., as well as 0.7 million Mexicans. See Morris, *Encyclopedia of American History*, p. 655.

Source: Adapted from Ladd, *American Political Parties* pp. 76, 141.

dwellings made cities economically attractive sites for work and residence, and ethnic neighborhoods of Italians, Poles, Hungarians, Russian Jews, Slavs, and other groups became common in the larger cities.

Initially, most new groups experienced social exclusion as well as arduous working conditions without effective unions. Nevertheless, they fared better than blacks for several reasons: First, they worked in a more dynamic setting (urban and nonsouthern); second, they came to America from personal choice; third, skin color did not preclude their admission to the dominant culture by the second or third generation; and finally, they arrived in America at a later period, when egalitarianism was stronger.

The lot of Chinese and Japanese immigrants probably fell somewhere between that of the blacks and the new European immigrants. About 300,000 Chinese immigrated before 1900, mostly as coolie railroad workers from 1868 to 1882, the year congressional legislation excluded Chinese laborers. By 1950 almost two-thirds as many Japanese had immigrated, but the period of largest influx for Japanese was from 1901 to 1920. In the latter year, state laws limited rights of Japanese to own or lease farm lands.

Bosses and machines became a conspicuous feature of the urban scene. Although the beginning of America's political machines are lost in the mists of time, politics in this country had always been localistic. In the 1760s John Adams had discovered a smoke-filled room operating in Boston where a "caucus club" regularly chose "selectmen, assessors, collectors, fire wards, and representatives before they are chosen in town." One can assume that such operations had always been common. Jacksonianism, with its embrace of the spoils system, glorification of the common man, and the bedsheet ballot, probably gave an assist to the machines.

In an industrial age, it was natural for a party organization to stress material inducements and to become, in effect, "a business organization in a particular field of business—getting votes and winning elections."[13] The machines organized disciplined phalanxes in which each rank of party work carried increasingly well-understood duties and privileges. At the top of the structure was the "boss," an individual who wielded power by negotiations and who used personal contacts to cut through the formal procedures of government. The United States Senate could also be an extension of boss influence in the Gilded Age. Since state legislatures chose the senators until passage of the Seventeenth Amendment in 1913, machine politicians were in a good position to obtain senatorial appointment and with it leverage over federal patronage.

As cities grew, political insiders could exploit lucrative traction, paving, and utility contracts. Advance knowledge about site improvements could result in "honest graft." On the positive side, machine power may have reduced tensions among different immigrant cultures. New immigrants received personal attention and party favors in exchange for their votes. The machine gave positions to representatives of ethnic communities, and it became a channel for personal advancement.

A Business-Centered Power Structure

The era we have been describing lends itself more easily than any other to the theory that American society is illegitimately controlled by a small class centering on big business. Big businessmen of the period accumulated enormous wealth, and they were free to use it as they wished (even to purchase public officials and political machines). Organizations that could check big business were weak or nonexistent, and governmental policy did not restrain the search for ever greater profits. Neither the Democratic nor the Republican party organized disadvantaged groups around their (presumably) vital interests, and neither party challenged business.

The central position of business in this period cannot be denied. However, a test of the legitimacy and extent of its power needs more evidence and analysis than space allows. To be convincing, a theory of *illegiti-*

---

[13]Edward C. Banfield and James Q. Wilson, *City Politics* (New York: Vintage Books, 1966), p. 115. The quotation refers to machines in general, not just to machines in the period under discussion.

mate business *control* must confront the pervasive admiration of business success and the popularity of wealthy men in these years. Numerous groups stood in actual or potential opposition to the industrial barons: sweatshop labor, farmers gouged by discriminatory pricing, and residents of areas that became appendages to industrial capital. Nevertheless, the nation's commitment to business values was authentic, not engineered by business leaders. Although industrial workers probably did not receive their fair share of the increase in wealth, they may well have improved their position as a class in material and other terms. The rising voices of dissatisfaction and social criticism must be balanced against a strand of continuing optimism about the future.

THE FOURTH PARTY SYSTEM: CONSERVATISM
TEMPERED BY PROGRESSIVISM

Processes centering on the election of 1896 transformed the third party system. Although no one had successfully challenged the power of business, agrarian discontent was building. Agricultural prices persistently declined after the Civil War, and farmers felt less appreciated as the society became more cosmopolitan.

In the late 1880s a severe agricultural depression (worst in Kansas, Nebraska, and the Dakotas) led to an upsurge of agrarian radicalism. Farmers' clubs increased their memberships and joined in state and regional "alliances." These organizations discovered some common grievances (low farm prices, high transportation costs, inadequate credit) that came to a focus in the 1890 elections. Alliance victories in the South that year included four governors, eight state legislatures, forty-four U.S. representatives, and three U.S. senators. Similar successes in the prairie states, plus support from the Knights of Labor, produced a new national party in 1892—the Populists.

Among other things, Populists called for national ownership of railroads, a graduated income tax, an increase in the money supply, and an eight-hour day for industrial workers. In the 1892 elections Populist campaigners in the South tried to unite white and black farmers against the conservative Democratic party leaders. In the Northwest, they berated the "bankers' conspiracy."

The movement was less successful in 1892 than it had been two years earlier. The attempt to unite white and black farmers in the South aroused conservative Democrats. Significant labor support failed to materialize; the only statewide sweep was in Kansas. Although Populist candidate James Weaver polled about a million votes, none of the basic elements in the attempted radical alliance effectively reinforced each other.

The country's worst financial depression—usually called the Panic of 1893—came one year later, bringing bank closings, commercial failures, a stock market crash, and a large loss in gold reserves. The following spring four hundred unemployed men ("Coxey's army") marched on Washington, where they were dispersed by club-wielding policemen. The Populist vote in the 1894 congressional elections increased by 42 percent. As the election of 1896 approached, the mood among people of property was unusually tense. Protesting farmers had demonstrated considerable political prowess, and industrial workers had resorted to strikes, which often became violent.

The first large industrial conflict in American history had occurred in 1877. After four railroads jointly announced a 10 percent wage cut, a badly organized general strike led to rioting in every large industrial center in the country. There were pitched battles between militia and mobs in more than half a dozen cities. Rioting destroyed major rail facilities in Pittsburgh and led to scores of deaths.

Another major encounter that had erupted in 1892 was still fresh in the public's memory. After strikers at the Carnegie Steel Company in Homestead, Pennsylvania, fired on river barges, strikebreakers and the state militia moved in. Seven people were killed, and a Russian-born anarchist shot and stabbed the company manager. In 1894 the American Railway Union boycotted Pullman cars in Chicago. Federal troops smashed this action over the objection of the governor of Illinois, and the magnetic leader of the union, Eugene Debs, went to prison, where he began to study socialism. Although some of the worst industrial violence was yet to come, the country lacked the benefit of long experience in dealing with such conflicts. The specter of class warfare seemed quite real in 1896—especially in the centers of the new industrial order.

The main issue in the campaign was money, with the Populists urging unlimited coinage of silver. After Federal legislation in 1873 demonitized silver, inflationists and silver miners demanded a return to bimetallism; conservatives resisted. Compromise measures permitting limited government purchases of silver tended to satisfy no one.

When the Democrats decided on a free silver platform and nominated William Jennings Bryan, the Populists endorsed him, as did a free silver group that had bolted the Republican convention. Although the Democrats also had their bolting minority (the gold Democrats), this group did not endorse McKinley.

The pattern of independent and secessionist actions had apparently strengthened Bryan and weakened McKinley. For the first time since the Civil War, the party battle offered a challenge to business domination. With both sides campaigning effectively, voter interest was high. Bryan castigated "the money power" while Republicans portrayed Bryan as an anarchist and a revolutionist.

McKinley's success gave the Republicans their broadest popular support in a quarter of a century and represented the most strategically important victory ever achieved by conservatives in an American election. A number of reasons help explain the result, despite the potency of Bryan's appeal. For one thing, hard times had begun in 1893, during a Democratic administration. Also, Bryan had greater appeal to the rural than the urban elements of his potential coalition. Urban labor had little to gain from inflationary money, and Bryan's statements about the relative importance of farms and cities were unrealistic in the new industrial era.[14] Bryan also had the misfortune to be opposed by a politician who was possibly the most skillful Republican candidate since Lincoln. The campaign waged by McKinley's close friend, Mark Hanna, was a masterpiece of fund raising, planning, and press relations.

The hotly contested election and the economic upswing that followed set a new political pattern that endured for decades. Major contrasts with the earlier period can be understood by comparing Table 2-3 with Table 2-1. Republican victories had been narrow, now they were huge. Indeed, the one Democratic president of the period, Woodrow Wilson, obtained office only because of a temporary split in the Republican party. Voter participation had been consistently high, but it now declined precipitously. Politics in the earlier period brought close party competition to an increasing number of states, but after 1896 one-party control existed in most states. Major segments of labor and the middle class in the Northeast and the Midwest defected to the Republican party. In the southern states, where the Democratic party had been strong since the 1880s, conservatives forged a one-party monopoly.[15]

Table 2-3
Republican Ascendancy and Sectional Politics in the Fourth Party System

	Presidential Plurality	Voter Participation	Percentage of Competitive States[b]
1896	4.3% (R)	79.3%	31.1%
1900	6.2 (R)	73.2	33.3
1904	18.8 (R)	65.2	8.9
1908	8.5 (R)	65.4	30.4
1912	14.4 (D)[a]	58.8	45.8
1916	3.1 (D)	61.6	47.9
1920	26.1 (R)	49.2	6.3
1924	25.3 (R)	48.9	27.1
1928	17.4 (R)	56.9	20.8

[a]Wilson's plurality over Roosevelt. If Taft and Roosevelt votes are combined, the plurality for the combination is 8.7 percent Republican.

[b]States with presidential victory margins of 10 percent of less.

Sources: Voter participation figures computed by Walter Dean Burnham and reported in *Historical Statistics*, II, 1071–1072. Other percentages are based on data in Congressional Quarterly, *Guide to U.S. Elections*, 273–279.

[14]"Burn down your cities and leave our farms, and your cities will spring up again as if by magic. But destroy our farms and the grass will grow in the streets of every city in the country." Professor Burnham suggests that Bryan's nostalgia for Jacksonian democracy made him a reactionary figure for the urban immigrants. Walter Dean Burnham, "The Changing Shape of the American Political Universe," *American Political Science Review*, 59 (1965), 227.

[15]V. O. Key, Jr., *Southern Politics* (New York: Alfred A. Knopf, Inc., 1950), p. 542

The sectional cast of American politics in the fourth period carried profoundly conservative implications. The sharp decline in turnout reduced the electoral influence of low-income groups. A Republican party of business dominated politics in the North, and a Democratic party of white supremacy asserted hegemony in the South. The opposition party in each region was extremely weak. Conservatives disfranchised the southern radical constituency and prevented it from combining with radicals in western states. Although western Republican insurgents launched some effective local movements, they had no place to go in national politics.[16] Industrial workers in the big cities usually found little reason to prefer Democratic presidential candidates during the fourth period.

Despite the conservative pattern described above, the dominant tone of national public policy until 1916 was "progressive." This was partly a matter of chance: The two most notable figures in the progressive movement were accidental presidents. The assassination of McKinley in September 1901 elevated Theodore Roosevelt from the vice presidency, and the natural successor to McKinley, Mark Hanna, died in February of 1904. It is unlikely that Theodore Roosevelt would have received a Republican nomination in the normal course of events. Woodrow Wilson's victory in 1912 would have been inconceivable without the Republican party split that year.

Nevertheless, the progressive movement would have left a significant mark even without Roosevelt and Wilson. Leading elements in the urban middle class wanted government measures that would correct business and political abuses. Although big business was generally hostile to government intervention, the affected interests often sought regulation in particular areas.[17] Business still enjoyed enormous prestige and success, but new developments qualified its power in the following ways:

1. Government regulation limited the sphere of purely "private" decision making. Thus the Elkins Act (1903) prohibited railroad rebates, and the Hepburn Act (1906) sharply restricted the granting of free railroad passes.
2. Opponents of big business achieved important objectives or received important concessions. The Populists had agitated for the graduated income tax, direct election of U.S. senators, an elastic national currency, and restrictions on immigration. They obtained all of them: two by constitutional amendments ratified in 1913, the others by legislation.
3. The feeling grew that business practices should include consideration of one's opponents and that business interests should be in harmony with the community. Although this sometimes meant simple rationalization of the business interest, there was a greater tendency to assume that wealthy people had civic obligations.

[16]E. E. Schattschneider, *The Semisovereign People* (Hinsdale, Ill.: Dryden Press, 1960), pp. 77–78.

[17]Gabriel Kolko goes much further than this. He argues that the big industrial mergers were not notably successful in curbing competition, that big business led the struggle for federal economic regulation, and that the legislation was designed in most cases by the regulated interest to meet its own needs and not those of the public or commonwealth. Gabriel Kolko, *The Triumph of Conservatism* (New York: The Free Press, 1963), pp. 28, 58, 59. The implication is that business was more powerful than ever. It seems plausible to me to view the period 1900–1932 as one of more limited business power than the preceding period.

During this period investigative reporters (who took the insulting term "muckraker" as a badge of honor) examined business methods more closely. The ultimate dependence of business on public opinion was implied by Hanna when he said of Pullman's refusal to arbitrate in 1894: "A man who won't meet his men half way is a God-damn fool."[18]

The progressive movement drew from several sources: the fight against governmental corruption and inefficiency going back at least to the liberal Republicans of 1872; Granger and Populist efforts to control big business; and the activity of settlement house workers and other urban reformers such as Jane Addams. Concern about the growth of large impersonal organizations had been increasing. The new corporate order had threatened established and moderately prosperous businessmen, professionals, pastors, and educated persons with a loss of their former position as tycoons and political bosses pushed their way to the fore.[19]

Progressivism bore a moralistic strain. It tried to purify American life by arousing decent people (usually the middle class) to social responsibilities. The movement did not challenge the fundamental principles of capitalism; it was moderate rather than radical in its goals. It tended to be paternalistic toward the poor and infirm, hostile toward new immigrants, and insensitive to the plight of blacks. By reflecting distrust of politicians and political organization and approval of businesslike methods, the movement gave modern reform its characteristic style and objectives. Progressivism sought to eliminate special influence in favor of more responsive government, and it approved of governmental actions that would relieve social distress.[20]

Except for the years when Woodrow Wilson was in the White House, and despite the conservative victory of 1896, the Republican party seemed to be the better vehicle for political reform. To progressive leaders like Herbert Croly, the Democratic party seemed too provincial and backward-looking. Even in the 1920s, when progressivism had lost its force at the national level, one could argue that the candidacy of Herbert Hoover offered a more sophisticated understanding of modern industrial society than that of Al Smith.[21]

Retrospect

We think of the present as an era of unprecedented change. Yet, a case can be made that the country changed more in the half century that centered

---

[18]Thomas Beer, *Hanna* (New York: 1929), as cited by Binkley, *American Political Parties,* p. 331. "What could capitalists think of a politician from their own ranks who wanted to know why the government should not run power plants?" Ibid., p. 332.

[19]Garraty, *A Short History,* pp. 360–361.

[20]Ibid., p. 363. The objectives were stated by Benjamin Parke DeWitt in 1915. See Arthur Mann, ed., *The Progressive Era: Liberal Renaissance or Liberal Failure?* (New York: Holt, Rinehart & Winston, 1963), p. 2. For a discussion of local reform, see Thomas R. Dye, *Politics in States and Communities,* 3rd ed. (Englewood Cliffs, N.J.: Prentice-Hall, Inc., 1977), pp. 255–261.

[21]In his campaign of 1928, Hoover called for a shorter workday, higher wages, and collective bargaining. Smith insisted that government should interfere as little as possible with business. Ladd, *American Political Parties,* pp. 154–156.

on 1896. With expanded industrial activity, the population had tripled, reaching 106 million by 1920. The automobile industry, practically unknown in 1900, had built 26 million cars by 1929. The country's first commercial broadcasting station went on the air in 1920; within a decade more than 10 million Americans owned radios. Electric lighting was virtually unknown before 1879, yet thirty years later much of middle class urban America had not only electric lights but also central heating and hot and cold indoor water. Medicine made immense strides between 1860 and 1920.

Many of these changes took place in all Western nations; most were expected and eagerly awaited (unlike some that have occurred in our own time). According to John Lukacs, expanded life spans, electric lights, self-propelled cars, underground railways, and skyscrapers were accepted images of the future by 1870.[22] The dominant impulses of progressivism and standpat conservatism each reflected the buoyant optimism of American society.

AMERICA'S FIFTH PARTY SYSTEM
AND THE NEW DEAL COALITION

The collapse of the stock market, October 1929, signaled America's most serious economic crisis. By spring of the next year, business was in disarray with banks failing by the hundreds. A spiraling effect took hold: Business cutbacks increased unemployment; this curtailed economic demand and led to still further declines in output. The industrial production index declined from 125 in June 1929 to 59 four years later. By 1932 one-third of the population of Pennsylvania found itself on relief; 40 percent of the Chicago work force was jobless.

Of course, collapse of stock market values was a symptom rather than a cause of the crisis. The more important causes include high tariff policies of the 1920s, which weakened European economies and curtailed foreign demand; overproduction of goods (especially automobiles) relative to effective demand; unequally distributed wealth, which kept effective demand low; and credit and tax policies that tended to reinforce inequality and overproduction.

The Great Depression had worldwide repercussions. American consumption of foreign goods shriveled, and the flow of loans to Europe stopped. As industrial nations of Western Europe found themselves cut off from their American market, they lowered their agricultural imports from eastern Europe, with catastrophic results for the people of that area. German economic recovery had been especially dependent on American capital. The huge rise in German unemployment starting in 1929 contributed mightily to Hitler's rise in January 1933.

The 1932 election proved to be another pivotal point of electoral change in American politics. Voters naturally turn against the party in power during hard times, and this was the worst depression in our history. The

[22]John Lukacs, *The Passing of the Modern Age* (New York: Harper & Row, Publishers, Inc., 1970), pp. 6–7, 73–74.

Republican party's association with big business was especially pronounced. Presidents Harding and Coolidge had enthusiastically espoused the business viewpoint during uninterrupted Republican control from 1920 to 1930. Multimillionaire Andrew Mellon had been secretary of the treasury from 1921 to 1932, and Herbert Hoover had been secretary of commerce for seven years prior to his election as president in 1928.

In 1932, after four years in the White House, Hoover called for the free expansion of private enterprise, predicting that if the New Deal politicians came to power, "the grass will grow in the streets of a hundred cities, a thousand towns; the weeds will overrun the fields of millions of farms. . . ." According to E. E. Schattschneider, the defeat of the Republicans was "much more than the defeat of a political party; it was something very much like the overthrow of a ruling class."[23]

Some general social tendencies help explain the durability of the new political alignment. Many of the most recent immigrants had settled in the big cities; they were joined by rural people who began streaming to the cities during World War I. The agricultural malaise of the 1920s kept them coming by the hundreds of thousands. These urban have nots had little reason to support the Republicans. The Republican philosophy of rugged individualism was reasonably compatible with middle-class American life in rural areas and small towns, but it did not resonate too well with slums, sweatshop labor, and other realities of working and lower-class life in the cities. Higher birthrates among the urban segment made them increasingly important as the years went by, and Democrats reaped the political advantage. In the twelve largest cities Republican strength in presidential elections declined steadily after 1920.

Actually, the Democrats first carried these cities in 1928, *not* 1932, though by only a small margin. Al Smith, a Catholic, was the first Democratic candidate with a cultural affinity to the urban underclasses. With his brown derby and rasping East Side accent, he was unmistakably a man of the city. Moreover, as governor of New York, he had fought to improve factory conditions and reduce working hours for women. Bryan had been at the other cultural extreme—a Protestant fundamentalist from the prairies. (Other Democratic nominees had been almost as remote: Woodrow Wilson, a patrician intellectual; James M. Cox, an Ohio publisher; and John W. Davis, a Wall Street lawyer.)

Smith's candidacy broke into the sectional alignment that had dominated American politics since McKinley. Several southern states went for Hoover, and in the North many counties went Democratic for the first time in decades. Smith's candidacy catalyzed growing cultural and status cleavages in the American electorate. Between 1928 and 1932 Democratic pluralities in the big cities became substantial, and between 1932 and 1936 they grew to overwhelming proportions.[24]

---

[23]Schattschneider, *The Semisovereign People,* p. 84. Compare Hoover's rhetoric with that of Bryan cited above.

[24]The interpretation of this and the preceding two paragraphs draws heavily on Samuel Lubell, *The Future of American Politics* (New York: Harper & Row, Publishers, Inc., 1952), pp. 28–41.

In his acceptance speech at the 1932 Democratic convention, Roosevelt pledged "a new deal for the American people." As president, he embarked on a number of vigorous experiments in public policy—especially during the first hundred days. He took the country off the gold standard, opened the banks under Treasury licenses, used government to guarantee bank deposits, put people to work via Civilian Conservation Corps and the Federal Emergency Relief Administration, established industrywide production codes via the National Recovery Administration, helped agriculture through the Agricultural Adjustment Act, and launched the Tennessee Valley Authority (TVA).

The second "hundred days" in 1935 saw equally important New Deal programs: the National Labor Relations Act, the Social Security Act, the Public Utility Holding Company Act, the Rural Electrification Administration, and the Wealth Tax Act. This phase of the New Deal generated growing opposition from businessmen and conservatives, who no longer exerted much of an influence on Roosevelt. In the 1936 campaign, Roosevelt denounced "economic royalists" and appealed more directly to the underprivileged.

A broad medley of underdog groups formed the heart of the "Roosevelt coalition." As we have seen, native newcomers to the city joined the latest immigrants from Europe. Of course, neither group was solidly Democratic, nor were all of the underdog groups in the cities. People who stayed behind in the shanties, small farms, mines, and hill country and immigrants who settled in rural areas also received tangible benefits from New Deal programs.

The Roosevelt coalition was not confined to underdog groups. Roosevelt maintained the electoral support of most southern leaders, even though the balance of power in the party was shifting away from the South. Writers, artists, and intellectuals found the innovations of the New Deal exciting. Roosevelt attracted some middle-class elements and a smattering of support from the social upper crust to which he himself belonged. Leadership echelons in agriculture and labor organizations tended to support Roosevelt, as did important leaders of some big-city machines.

The flow of power to the Democrats from 1928 to 1937 constituted the most astonishing political success since Jefferson's rout of the Federalists:

	Percent Democratic in Given Presidential Election	*Number of Democratic Seats following Election of Given Year*	
		House	Senate
1928	40.8%	167	39
1930		220	47
1932	57.4	310	60
1934		319	69
1936	60.8	331	76

The only serious obstacle to the New Deal was the Supreme Court. The Roosevelt coalition had captured two of the three government branches, but the third eluded its grasp. Conservative justices dominated the Court, and it had declared several important pieces of New Deal legislation unconstitutional. The flow of power finally overcame this barrier in the spring of 1937. During the period that Roosevelt proposed to "pack the Court," Justices Charles Evans Hughes and Owen Roberts started to side with the liberal justices. In May of 1937 one of the conservatives, Willis Van Devanter, resigned, enabling Roosevelt to make his first Court appointment—the liberal, Hugo Black. Since then, the Supreme Court has rarely invalidated federal attempts to regulate the economy.

Lacking a consistent body of doctrines, New Deal administrators often seemed to have conflicting philosophies and approaches. Many special interest groups battled for influence. Although larger and more diverse than big business, these groups were not representative of the unorganized majority. Still there was some economic recovery, and the New Deal radiated a new sense of energy, experimentation, and hope.[25] The New Deal, however, did not bring about full employment and restore prosperity. The war accomplished this, beginning in 1939, well before the Japanese attack on Pearl Harbor.

The larger importance of the New Deal derives from its enlargement (in the public mind) of the national government's appropriate responsibilities. Power shifted dramatically away from the states towards Washington. Federal activity increased substantially as the government moved into new regulatory, promotional, and managerial fields. The Republic began to abandon the old belief that the Constitution constrained the government in Washington to act within narrow limits. Citizenship began to include new "rights"—to a job, a good education, adequate medical care, fair pay, and a decent home. Most of the basic measures of the New Deal have never been repealed.

Post-New Deal Politics

World War II and the cold war reinforced the country's accommodation to big government. The war proved that the government could capably direct an enormous economic effort, and Washington administrators acquired experience in complex planning and regulatory activity.

Roosevelt died on April 12, 1945, only five months after being elected to a fourth term. Germany surrendered in May and Japan in August. President Harry Truman's first year in office was mainly preoccupied with terminating the war, guiding the transition to peace, and dealing with new international realities—matters that were all interrelated because of the atom bomb and the perceived threat of Soviet expansionism.

Truman's political situation proved extremely difficult. Like most men elected to the vice presidency, he had few obvious qualifications for the presidency. He had received the nomination in 1944 as a noncontroversial border-state politician, his public image in sharp contrast to Roosevelt's. At

[25]Garraty, *A Short History,* pp. 421–422.

first he seemed inadequate, cocky, and yet dwarfed by his awesome responsibilities. Moreover, the public seemed to be demanding the impossible: a return to normalcy and a relaxation of controls without inflation.

When the Republicans won control of the House and Senate in 1946 for the first time in fourteen years, many viewed this as a repudiation of Truman's leadership. Senator Fulbright, a fellow Democrat, even advised the president to appoint a Republican as secretary of state and to resign from office. The Republican-controlled Eightieth Congress proceeded to reject Truman's major domestic legislative proposals and passed a number of measures he opposed.

Public opinion polls were now a more significant element in public life. The president's standing in the polls was at its lowest point when the Eightieth Congress was elected in November 1946. By the spring of 1947 his popularity had recovered substantially, but it declined fairly continuously during the next year. In December 1947 Henry Wallace (a New Dealer and former vice president whom Truman had dropped from the cabinet) announced that he was forming a new party. The president reacted by proposing a big new social welfare package plus a tax cut. In February 1948 he also promoted a far-reaching civil rights program and ordered an end to segregation in the armed forces.

In the spring of 1948 a coalition of notables pressed for General Dwight Eisenhower's nomination by the *Democratic* convention.[26] Without revealing his policy views or party preference, Eisenhower refused to consider seeking or accepting any nomination. The Republican convention then nominated Thomas E. Dewey. A brief Democratic effort to draft Supreme Court Justice William O. Douglas failed, and Truman received his party's nomination almost by default. Later that month rebellious southerners from thirteen states formed the States' Rights party (the "Dixiecrats") and nominated Governor Strom Thurmond of South Carolina for president. Henry Wallace received the Progressive party nomination later in July. The upshot was that both liberal and conservative segments of the Democratic party had temporarily deserted, thus destroying the normal Democratic majority and making a Republican victory appear inevitable.

However, Truman mounted an effective campaign and scored an upset victory that demonstrated the durability of the New Deal coalition. It embittered Republicans and provided a further demonstration of the declining importance of the Old South in the Democratic party. In essential ways Truman had modernized the New Deal appeals, especially in civil rights, immigration policy, and health care. Since 1948 the Republicans have controlled Congress only once, from 1953 to 1955.

Truman had thrived on controversy and activism, but when Eisenhower came into office in 1952, he endeavored to be above politics and to limit government domestic policy initiatives. The new president, very much

[26]The coalition included states' rights Southerners, Chicago leader Jacob Arvey, the mayors of New York and Jersey City, spokesmen for the ADA and CIO, and other liberals including James Roosevelt, Hubert Humphrey, Chester Bowles, and Claude Pepper. *Congress and the Nation 1945–1964* (Washington, D.C.: Congressional Quarterly Service, 1965), p. 5.

of an unknown quantity in politics before taking office, turned out to be extremely conservative for his time, despite slogans like "modern Republicanism." He disliked politics, tried to leave legislation to Congress as much as possible, preferred to associate with businessmen, and often appointed to regulatory commissions men who did not believe in regulation. Also, he was comfortable with Richard Nixon as his running mate, regretted his appointment of Earl Warren as chief justice of the Supreme Court, refused to endorse the Court's landmark desegregation decision in 1954, and felt that TVA was "creeping socialism."

Republicans fashioned some moderately liberal measures in housing, social security extension, civil rights, admission of Alaska and Hawaii, construction of the St. Lawrence Seaway, and other matters. Moreover, the party found it either difficult or undesirable to repudiate the New Deal measures.

Beneath its relatively placid surface, the country was changing in important ways during the Eisenhower years. Despite occasional recessions, real family income was in an unprecedented upswing. America had always been relatively better off than the rest of the world, but incomes had now reached the point where real economic privation was a minority rather than a majority concern. Indeed, middle America was enjoying a living standard without historical precedent. John Kenneth Galbraith and other liberal intellectuals spread the word that the country was *affluent.*

Most liberals of the time thought that affluence would lead to conservatism, that as more people obtained a stake in society, they would lose interest in helping deprived groups that remained and be more inclined to view deprivation as the result of insufficient effort. It was noted that union workers were moving to the suburbs. Many suspected that once they got there they would start voting Republican. Everyone seemed to want middle-class status. Catholics, Jews, and immigrants seemed to be losing their distinctive cultures and disappearing into a big grey middle class. This middle class in turn appeared less interested in public life. Some liberal intellectuals thought the middle class was glutting itself with private amenities while it starved essential public services.

Long-run effects of affluence were quite different, yet there is enough truth in the liberal perceptions of the time to make one wonder why the Republican party did not thrive in the 1950s. That it did not prosper is evident in the election results:

Number of Republicans after Elections of Given Year

	U.S. Senators	U.S. Representatives	Governors
1952	48	221	30
1954	47	203	29
1956	47	200	21
1958	34	154	15
1960	36	174	16
1962	32	176	16

The answer lies partly in the durability of old voting habits: Eisenhower's personal appeal could override partisan preferences, but it could not change them. If large segments of the American public were giving politics a rest, they were still maintaining their old party loyalties. Nor was this too surprising: In the past, widespread changes in party loyalties had only occurred in times of stress.

The political quietude of the 1950s should not be exaggerated. The international scene remained tense, and it took the new concern with domestic communism a long time to subside. The Senate condemned Joseph McCarthy in December of 1954, but efforts to modify relatively liberal Supreme Court decisions in the internal security field lost by close votes in the summer of 1958. The House Un-American Activities Committee became less active, but its mandate remained intact until 1969, and it was not abolished until 1975. The decade also witnessed a snowballing civil rights movement: the pathbreaking Supreme Court decision in 1954, Martin Luther King, Jr.'s Montgomery, Alabama, bus boycott a year or so later, and, in 1960, the beginning of "sit-ins" and "freedom rides."

Noteworthy population changes also took place. As recently as 1945, demographers had expected total population to level off at about 150 million. Instead, between 1950 and 1960, the population expanded from 151 million to 179 million—an increase of 18.5 percent. The proportion of young people began to rise dramatically just as the proportion seeking higher education increased. As a result, policy makers in the 1950s experienced tremendous pressure to expand the country's educational facilities. By 1956, 30 percent of those between eighteen and twenty-one were enrolled in college or university classes. Growth of the educational establishment continued well beyond the 1950s, with far-reaching effects on American politics.

Between 1955 and 1960, the number of cars in use increased more than two and a half times as rapidly as the population, and domestic passengers carried by airlines increased 47.4 percent. This growth in automotive and air travel was to continue as railroad transportation declined, affecting nearly every aspect of American life. A constantly mobile population shifted markedly towards the South and West, producing heavy concentrations of people in Florida and California by the end of the decade.[27] Another movement pulled people into the suburban fringes of expanding metropolitan regions.

The America of 1960 was in many ways similar to that of today. Through it, even older outlooks have continued to affect our political actions. The events since 1960, to which we now turn, were admittedly extraordinary. Yet they may have been only an extension of a longer story, even more remarkable when viewed as a whole, and no less fateful.

---

[27]The combined populations of these two states were 8.8 million in 1940, 13.4 million in 1950, and 20.7 million in 1960. This last figure meant that more than one in ten Americans lived in these two states.

3

Developments since 1960

All beginnings are arbitrary, but the election of John F. Kennedy in 1960 seems to mark a new phase in American politics. The Kennedy approach was new, and it contrasted in interesting ways with that of Richard Nixon. Taken together, this odd pairing leads directly and consciously to the "new politics" of the 1960s and the sense in both parties of a sharp break with the "old politics." After 1960 personalities of candidates assumed a new significance, style received as much or more emphasis as substance, tangible power of the parties declined, and mass media became even more significant in politics. The 1960s in many ways feel contemporary; the 1950s seem impossibly distant. Continuous change and a sense of perpetual crisis have made it difficult to gain perspective on the period as a whole.[1]

The parties as such are not the main protagonists in the following account, and I will return to them in Chapter 5 for a summary on the nature of party change. You will recall from last chapter that the duration of the fifth party system is in doubt, and we may now be in a transition period. It is not inconceivable that we have even passed into a new kind of party system whose essential characteristics will be apparent only at some time in the future.

Some clever person has noticed that yesterday's history is the most forgotten, but the history of day before yesterday the least well known. If true, a chronology of recent events can even be valuable to persons old enough to remember them. Younger readers will be no less amazed. Young

---

[1]The accounts of Theodore White have been a rich and valuable resource for the pages to follow: *The Making of the President 1960* (New York: Atheneum Publishers, 1961); *The Making of the President 1964* (New York: New American Library, 1965); *The Making of the President 1968* (New York: Pocket Books, 1970); and *The Making of the President 1972* (New York: Bantam Books, Inc., 1973).

or old, those who cannot absorb what happened to the United States after 1960 may draw consolation from the fact that hardly anybody else can either.

KENNEDY AND NIXON

John F. Kennedy represented a family that showed every sign of becoming a political dynasty. Unlike the other great families of American politics (such as the Livingstons, the Tafts, the Adamses, the Harrisons, the Longs, or the Roosevelts), the Kennedys were Irish Catholic to the core. Both grandfathers had been active in Boston politics. His father, Joseph P. Kennedy, supported Roosevelt for the nomination in 1932 at a time when most of the Boston politicians wanted Al Smith. The elder Kennedy's reward was appointment first to head the Securities and Exchange Commission and then later to be Ambassador to Great Britain. Unlike most successful, self-made men, Kennedy led his sons away from his business and into public service. After making a huge fortune in movies, the stock market, liquor, and real estate, he set up trust funds of about $10 million for each of his nine children.[2]

The family's hopes rested most strongly on Joe, Jr., the eldest of the children and a strong influence on the character of all the others. With this young man's death in a World War II bombing raid, the next oldest son, John, took the lead. He began his political career by winning election to Congress in 1946 in a district that included the former strongholds of both grandfathers. At twenty-nine, Jack was the youngest U.S. representative from Massachusetts in the twentieth century. In 1952, he won a seat in the U.S. Senate, and in the following year his younger brother Robert came to Washington as the new associate counsel on Senator Joe McCarthy's Permanent Investigations Subcommittee.

The skill of Kennedy campaign operations made all party rivals in the early 1960s seem dull or out of touch. The candidate image was young, understated, athletic, and sophisticated. It suggested a political independence from the professional politicians, and it was made to symbolize a new political generation coming into its own. The enormous wealth of the family was never a political liability. After all, John F. Kennedy had performed bravely in the war as a PT boat commander. He and his brother Robert wrote books. These were qualities that money could not account for, and touch football was not the sport of aristocrats. (The golf that Jack Kennedy also enjoyed was successfully deemphasized.) Their father had taught them that winning is more important than how you play the game. This idea is neither moral nor aristocratic, but it endorses success in a way shared by many Americans. The Kennedys put their whole heart into winning, and in true egalitarian style, used the advantages they had.

[2]Stephen Hess, *America's Political Dynasties* (New York: Doubleday & Co., Inc., 1966), pp. 493, 496.

Richard Nixon was only four years Kennedy's senior and, like Kennedy, had also been elected to Congress, his first elective office, in 1946. Nixon had been a Navy officer in the war. His vehement campaign style reflected the rootless, incessantly changing California scene where politics was already under the strong imprint of professional public relations and where party organization was weak and chaotic.

Nixon's father had been a streetcar conductor in Columbus, Ohio, before migrating to southern California, where he managed a grocery store and service station. The family was closeknit but often felt the pinch of hardship. Nixon was a poor boy growing up in a middle-class Quaker community.[3] He distinguished himself in debate and oratory, worked in the store afternoons while in high school, won a scholarship to Duke University Law School, and finished third in his class in 1937. He practiced law in Whittier, California, from 1937 to 1942, including a stint as assistant city attorney. In Congress, Nixon made a name for himself as an ardent anticommunist.

Eisenhower chose Nixon as his running mate in 1952 on the recommendation of a "strategy board" in which he himself did not participate. One of those present is reported to have said, "We took Dick Nixon not because he was right wing or left wing—but because we were tired and he came from California."[4] In September, Nixon almost lost his place on the ticket after the public learned that he had accepted an $18,000 special fund raised by southern California businessmen. However, he defended his action in an effective, if sentimental, televised defense (the "Checkers" speech) and remained on the ticket after a massive outpouring of popular support. During Eisenhower's second term, Nixon gave unstintingly of his time to Republican candidates and organizational leaders across the country while Eisenhower remained aloof from the party.

A notable feature of the 1960 campaign was the series of televised debates between Kennedy and Nixon. In their first encounter Nixon was tired from campaigning and from a leg injury that had hospitalized him for twelve days. In resuming his campaign, Nixon overextended himself and developed a fever. On camera, he seemed defensive, and he addressed himself to Kennedy instead of the national audience. Before the debates, Nixon was generally considered the most likely winner and Kennedy the underdog. By their conclusion, this image had been completely erased.

The Kennedy campaign also had some problems, especially at the beginning. Until September 1, Kennedy was trapped in Washington by roll call votes at a special session of Congress; meanwhile, his opponent was getting an early lead in the polls. Kennedy also began in bad voice from the exhausting spring primaries. The well-oiled Kennedy political machine seemed intimidated by the size of the country in which the campaign had to be fought.

---

[3]White, *1968*, p. 399.
[4]White, *1960*, pp. 66, 206.

The First Catholic President

Kennedy's victory margin was a thin 115,000 votes out of more than 68.3 million. Subsequent analysis suggested that his religion hurt him in the total popular vote. However, the defection was most severe in the South; in many northern states, Kennedy's religion seems to have been an advantage.[5] Because Democrats actually lost seats in both the House and Senate, Kennedy's political position was weak. However, prejudice against a Catholic in the White House soon vanished.

In the midterm elections (usually adverse to the incumbent party) Democrats actually gained four Senate seats (including that of thirty-year-old Ted Kennedy) and only lost five House seats. Richard Nixon failed in his attempt to unseat California governor Edmund G. (Pat) Brown. The next day, ignoring efforts of aides to restrain him, he stormed at the press: "You won't have Nixon to kick around any more, because, gentlemen, this is my last press conference."

Kennedy's legislative accomplishments were rather meager as conservative Southern Democrats often joined Republicans to oppose his policy initiatives. Kennedy's more notable achievements were symbolic and administrative. The Kennedy talent search attracted able people to top administrative positions. White House functions took on a glamorous "Camelot" aura peopled by celebrities, artists, intellectuals, and theatrical figures. Kennedy launched the Peace Corps to channel the energies of young people, and in May 1961 he urged a national commitment to the ten-year goal of landing a man on the moon and returning him safely to earth. The president also threw his support behind Court efforts to achieve racial desegregation of public facilities.

Assassination

In addition to the immediate shock it caused, the assassination of the president in November 1963 left a persistent sense of incompleteness. John F. Kennedy had held the office for too short a time to permit a fair judgment of his achievements, and his goals awaited fulfillment. He was, of course, dead beyond recall, but an important segment would long for another Kennedy presidency.

The American public's skepticism of the Warren Commission's investigation of his death has added to the sense of incompleteness. The commission's findings have been challenged in books and articles, and congressional inquiries in 1975 raised new doubts. In that year an FBI spokesman acknowledged to a House subcommittee that Oswald had visited its Dallas office in November 1963 and left a threatening note. Moreover, the note was destroyed two hours after Jack Ruby killed Lee Harvey Oswald, and no record of the note or Oswald's visit appeared in FBI files.

By 1975 general disenchantment following the Watergate scandal (dis-

[5]Herbert Asher, *Presidential Elections and American Politics* (Homewood, Ill.: The Dorsey Press, 1976), pp. 143–144.

cussed below) was reinforcing doubts about the Warren Commission's investigation and intensifying the distrust of government so noticeable in the 1970s. A report issued by the Church committee in 1976 stated that Kennedy's death might have been in retaliation for CIA attempts on the life of Fidel Castro. The report claimed that the FBI and CIA had never turned over to the Warren Commission evidence pointing to this conclusion and that these might have been conscious decisions not to disclose important information.[6] The House Assassinations Committee concluded in its final report in 1979 that Oswald had not acted alone and suggested a conspiracy involving organized crime figures. Author Edward Jay Epstein was reported to be skeptical. His own investigations revealed extensive connections between Oswald and the Soviet KGB, but he told an interviewer that Americans would never know with certainty whether Oswald had acted alone. His investigations had never uncovered any evidence that Oswald had acted other than alone, and his own belief was that it was Oswald who had determined that the president must be killed.[7]

TIME OF TROUBLES

When Johnson moved into the White House, Kennedy measures mired down in Congress could move more easily. Among the more important was the Civil Rights Act of 1964. It passed after mounting civil rights demonstrations that came to a climax in August 1963 with a march of 200,000 on Washington. Johnson also called for a "War on Poverty," and Congress delivered the Economic Opportunity Act a year later.

Lyndon Johnson became the inevitable Democratic nominee for president in 1964, although Robert Kennedy received significant support in the polls. In July 1964 Johnson announced publicly that he would not consider any cabinet member or official in regular attendance at cabinet meetings for vice president. Designed to exclude Kennedy, the action also eliminated Robert McNamara, Adlai Stevenson, Sargent Shriver, Orville Freeman, and others. "I'm sorry I took so many nice fellows over the side with me," said Bobby, who resigned from the cabinet, moved to Long Island, and became New York's new Democratic senator in the fall election.

Even before John Kennedy was assassinated, Republicans had approached 1964 in an unusually dispirited mood. After their party failed to make a comeback in either 1960 or 1962, its moderate and conservative wings came into unusually bitter conflict. The main hope of the moderates was Nelson Rockefeller. He had secured reelection as governor of New York in a dry year for Republicans and expanded his staff with new talent. However, he went through a divorce in 1961 and quickly remarried. By the end of May, Goldwater led Rockefeller by five points in the polls, a sharp reversal

[6]*Congressional Quarterly Almanac 1975*, pp. 408–409. *Congressional Quarterly Almanac 1976*, pp. 300–309. *New York Times Index 1975*, pp. 1176–1177.

[7]Paul Krueger, Copley News Service, *Terre Haute Star*, March 12, 1979. Edward Jay Epstein, *Legend: the Secret World of Lee Harvey Oswald* (New York: McGraw Hill Book Company, 1978).

of previous polls in which Rockefeller had led Goldwater by seventeen points.

Conservatives in the party had been pushing for Goldwater since the 1960 convention. Dismayed by the erosion of traditional values, and infuriated by an accommodation between Nixon and Rockefeller in 1960, a loosely knit group of volunteers worked effectively for Goldwater's nomination without his support. By August 1963 volunteers had formal organizations in thirty-two states, and several states were firmly for Goldwater.

The hero of the conservatives fared badly in the New Hampshire primary. In his encounters with the press, he tended to drop conversational bombshells that often received more coverage than his formal policy statements.

> In New Hampshire, Goldwater would say exactly what he thought, as he had always thought it—then shake with fury at its quotation. . . . He was offering New Hampshire the gospel of the true faith, hard money and individual rights. . . . And yet . . . when he read of himself in the papers, it was another Goldwater he was reading about, a wild man seeking to abolish Social Security and go to war with Russia.[8]

Fortunately for Goldwater, Henry Cabot Lodge's strength in New Hampshire dramatized Rockefeller's electoral weakness more than Goldwater's. The New Yorker's candidacy turned into a futile "stop Goldwater" exercise in the Oregon and California primaries, and the Goldwater forces triumphed at the convention. In his acceptance speech, Goldwater asserted, "Extremism in the defense of liberty is no vice, and moderation in the pursuit of justice is no virtue."

Johnson, after his unanimous nomination at the Democratic convention, chose Hubert Humphrey as his running mate. In the campaign that followed, Johnson made the broadest possible appeals as Goldwater defended himself against charges of extremism.

The 1964 election produced the biggest Democratic victory since 1936. Although Johnson's margin of Democratic preponderance in Congress was somewhat less than Roosevelt's in 1936, conservative Southern Democrats were a much weaker force than they had been in the 1930s. As a result an extraordinary number of liberal measures could be passed, including the first large-scale program of aid to schools, a strong voting rights law, rent supplements to low-income families, Medicare, elimination of national origins quotas from the immigration laws, antipollution laws for air and water, federal scholarships, highway safety and model cities acts, and creation of the Department of Transportation.

These and other items formed a notable body of legislation, but they failed to exhilarate the nation. Many of the new laws embodied ideas that had been around for years. Follow-through on the new programs was often deficient, and the war in Vietnam competed for attention and funds. A rising tide of discontent seemed to eclipse these liberal measures.

[8]White, *1964*, p. 131.

New Political Movements

The 1960s were years when existing institutions and orthodoxies of all sorts came under attack. A new radical-sounding rhetoric emerged. *Confrontation* was preferred to *discussion* (although *dialogue* enjoyed a certain vogue). *Goals* became *demands*, *discrimination* became *genocide*, and *freedom* became *liberation*. Paralleling the new rhetoric was new militancy: protests, marches, disruptions, sieges, and various free-form political activities. Political spectaculars were often media events, and televised dissemination of protest politics greatly magnified its impact. Primary discontents concerned the place of blacks in American society and the Vietnam War. Women, Chicanos, homosexuals, American Indians, and other groups also sought liberation, recognition, or respect. Intermingled with such claims were the values of a "counterculture" (centered on college campuses) that seemed to conspicuously reject achievement and clean living in favor of bad grooming and drug-induced turn-ons.

Yet, reaction was not as strong as might have been expected, partly because children of the establishment were in the forefront of much of the protest. Lower-middle-class and working-class opposition centered on "law and order." Even if the FBI figures and claims about crime were suspect, crime was rising. By 1965 people were telling pollsters that crime was the country's number one or two problem. By 1968 poll evidence suggested that half of the husbands in America had wives who were afraid to go out at night.[9]

Black militancy passed a critical threshold in 1963, the year when blacks seeking to integrate public facilities in Birmingham, Alabama, were met with water hoses and police dogs. A plausible theory about the timing of black militancy proposes that serious uprisings are most likely to occur "when a prolonged period of rising expectations and rising gratifications is followed by a short period of sharp reversal, during which the gap between expectations and gratifications quickly widens and becomes intolerable."[10] In this view, blacks had been too close to "the flat plane of survival" to be militant until about 1941, when Franklin Roosevelt ordered an end to discriminatory hiring in defense industries. By the end of the war, 2 million blacks had jobs in war industries, many of them through the efforts of the Fair Employment Practices Commission. After the war, black employment continued to advance; gains in housing, entry into unions, and some desegregation in the armed forces and education also began to take effect. By 1950 lynch-mob violence had practically ceased.

In 1952, however, new violence by whites against blacks began in the South, resulting in 530 cases of violence between 1954 and 1958. It obstructed the lawful efforts of blacks to achieve approved goals and thus led, the theory continues, to direct action by blacks in a reciprocal violence that

[9]Richard Scammon and Ben Wattenberg, *The Real Majority* (New York: Coward, McCann & Geohegan, Inc., 1970), p. 95.

[10]James C. Davies, "The J-Curve of Rising and Declining Satisfactions as a Cause of Some Great Revolutions and a Contained Rebellion," in *The History of Violence in America*, ed. Hugh Graham and Ted Gurr (New York: Bantam Books, 1969), p. 690.

peaked in 1965–1967. In other words, the events of 1963 reflected a sudden increase in violence against blacks, quickly frustrating rising expectations generated by slow and steady progress since 1940.[11]

In 1964 the twenty-three-year-old Stokely Carmichael became a field organizer for the Student Nonviolent Coordinating Committee (SNCC) in Mississippi. After registering more blacks in Lowndes County than there were whites, he organized a county party that took a snarling black panther as its ballot symbol. In 1966 he was shouting "black power" to Mississippi share croppers. The Black Panther party, founded in 1966 by Huey Newton and Bobby Seale, took Stokely Carmichael as its prime minister (and Eldridge Cleaver as its minister of information). Chapters sprang up in many cities between 1966 and 1969, and despite the guns and leather jackets, the rhetoric of revolutionary struggle, and the police hostility, the organization often concentrated on constructive ghetto programs like children's lunch programs and antidrug clinics. There were, of course, other important leaders, too numerous to discuss here, who called for a new posture of racial assertion.

Campus protest, the antiwar sentiment, and new black demands were loosely allied. Students who took part in the freedom rides of the late 1950s helped to mobilize the campuses. Blacks pushed hard for a better recognition by the universities of their contributions to American society. Blacks did their fair share of the fighting in Vietnam (and perhaps took more than their fair share of battle casualties). The stature of Martin Luther King, Jr., helped to link racial causes to the peace movement.

Distinctive changes were also occurring among whites. American affluence, already notable in the 1950s, expanded still further in the 1960s, raising family income 27.9 percent over the decade. But affluence, instead of being a conservatizing influence, as expected, seemed to generate new demands and expectations. In the view of one scholar, white campus dissidents tended to come from prosperous families, "bathed in affluence" and (unlike their parents) having no experience of anything else. He believes that "Affluence . . . increases dissatisfactions, and thus conflict, by contributing to a mentality of demand, an inordinately expanded set of expectations concerning what is one's due, a diminished tolerance of conditions less than ideal."[12]

Universities had traditionally been hospitable to social criticism; in the setting of the 1960s they stimulated new thinking about ecology and personal expression. By 1964 the college population included large numbers of talented people clustered at places where they could easily organize.

In retrospect, it seems entirely natural that university students provided the major opposition to the Vietnam War. These people instinctively felt that the war resulted from deficient policies and priorities. Then too, they were vulnerable in a self-interested way. After all, they or their friends might be drafted and *killed* in the war. Draft deferments to continue one's

---

[11]Ibid., pp. 716–723.
[12]Everett Carll Ladd, Jr., *American Political Parties* (New York: W. W. Norton & Company, Inc., 1970), pp. 255–256.

education could instill feelings of guilt, reverse attitudes towards dropping out, and feed resentment of "the system." Many college youth were proud of their freedom from compromised outlooks. Despite their shortcomings, they were sensitive to the war's evils and showed that they had not lost the capacity to feel strongly about it.

Women's liberation was in part a spin-off from other protest movements and in part a response to new patterns of living. It had a special affinity to war protest. (One of the few reliable attitudinal differences between women and men as groups is that women tend to be more opposed to the use of force.[13]) Members of feminist organizations were typically middle class, white, and urban. Like other causes of the 1960s, women's lib had an important international dimension. Thus Simone de Beauvoir's book *The Second Sex* quickly put her in the hot center of the movement along with Betty Friedan, Ti-Grace Atkinson, Kathie Sarachild, Robin Morgan, and Gloria Steinem. By 1970 at least, women's liberation was a political force, particularly in the sectors of American life most affected by the national media.

The radicalism of all these movements should not, however, be exaggerated. Whether antiwar, black protest, or women's liberation, few individuals in the 1960s seem to have undertaken a long-term commitment to fundamental change. Some of the radicalism amounted to playful posturing with an eye to media coverage. Moderates of this era who became active in mainstream politics often shared the disaffections felt by their "radical" counterparts.

Deepening Conflict

As the 1968 elections approached, the nation's political difficulties were mounting. Sporadic antiwar parades of a year or so earlier had culminated in a march of 55,000 on the Pentagon, where the marchers encountered lines of troops with fixed bayonets. January of 1968 had brought the Tet offensive in Vietnam and an apparent military setback. Casualties were mounting, as were the number of draftees killed in action.

	U.S. Forces in Vietnam	*Americans Killed and Wounded*	*Percent Killed Who Were Draftees*
1965	184,300	4,677	16%
1966	385,300	21,534	21
1967	485,600	41,749	34
1968	536,100	61,391	34
1969	475,200	42,354	40
1970	334,600	19,432	43

Source: U.S. Bureau of the Census, *Statistical Abstract of the United States* (Washington, D.C.: U.S. Government Printing Office, 1972), p. 260.

[13]Gerald Pomper, *Voters' Choice* (New York: Harper & Row, Publishers, Inc., 1975), p. 87. "When issues of war and social coercion are raised, the truly gentler sex is particularly likely to be on the side of pacific settlement."

Between 1965 and 1968 racial violence erupted in many northern cities. Some of the worst rioting broke out in Newark and Detroit in the summer of 1967. The National Advisory Commission on Civil Disorders reported in February of 1968 that "white racism" was the main cause of the black violence. A month later, the assassination of Martin Luther King, Jr., brought new riots in scores of cities and eliminated the constructive influence of one of America's noblest citizens and most talented political leaders.

Television dramatized the racial riots, making the violence more contagious and fraying the emotions of millions of people who were not directly affected. Television coverage played a similar role in antiwar protest. Symbolic violence, such as the pouring of blood on draft records, the unwashed clothes and the dirty talk, the mass meetings, and the occupations of university offices were natural "media events." Disturbances reinforced each other and escalated; protest leaders and constituents seemed determined to outpace the older liberalism that Johnson's programs expressed.

Lyndon Johnson became the target of Democratic opposition to the war via the candidacies of Eugene McCarthy and Robert Kennedy. McCarthy, like Vice President Hubert Humphrey, was a product of Minnesota's liberal political tradition. Unlike Humphrey (whose sunny disposition was a liability in 1968) McCarthy was aloof, witty, intellectual; his statements were eminently quotable: "Escalation is a word that has no point of interruption. By the time you raise the question the flag has gone by." Or, when asked how he would deal with the Pentagon if president: "I would go to the Pentagon. If not, I would at least try to get diplomatic representation there."[14] McCarthy had a magical appeal to college students in 1968, and they hitchhiked to his primary battles by the thousands. The media were so impressed by the "children's crusade" in New Hampshire that they interpreted the result as a McCarthy "victory" even though Lyndon Johnson received more votes and even though all of them were write-ins.[15]

Robert Kennedy announced his candidacy three days after the New Hampshire primary. He wanted, of course, to resume the Kennedy imperium. He also felt quite simply that McCarthy would make a bad president. His announcement came after a vain effort to get Johnson to appoint a special commission to review Vietnam policy.[16]

On March 31, Johnson startled the nation by announcing that he would neither seek nor accept renomination. The president also proclaimed a unilateral halt of air and naval bombardment and called on Hanoi to begin negotiations. North Vietnam agreed on April 3, and the leaders of the peace movement felt that they had scored a major victory. With these developments the campaign entered a new phase. Kennedy and McCarthy had the nation moving towards a negotiated peace, and political pressure no longer seemed as necessary. Humphrey announced his candidacy in April. He

[14]White, *1968,* p. 102.
[15]For this and other 1968 New Hampshire anomalies, see Scammon and Wattenberg, *The Real Majority,* pp. 85–92.
[16]Johnson did appoint a commission a few days later, and it marked a turning point in policy. However, it was summoned on his own initiative, and the people on it had the status of presidential advisors. White, *1968,* p. 205.

appealed to older liberals, but not the new activists. He did not enter any primaries—partly because his candidacy was so late and partly because he already had strong support from traditional segments in the party.

Kennedy received more votes than McCarthy in the Indiana, Nebraska, California, and South Dakota primaries. Only in Oregon did McCarthy defeat his opponent. In states where write-ins could be compared, Kennedy received more support than Humphrey each time. The second Kennedy assassination on June 4 came about one month after the murder of Martin Luther King, Jr., and two and a half months before the Democratic convention in Chicago.

Again the country went into shock. Campaign operations came to a virtual standstill for weeks; millions experienced numbness and despair. Robert Kennedy had been the torchbearer of a romantic cause symbolized by his martyred brother. In some respects he had assumed Martin Luther King's political legacy. More prosaically, he was an energetic and able person who would now not have a chance to test his support in the party or his talents in governance.

We have no way of knowing what would have happened if Robert Kennedy had not been killed. Theodore White felt that he would have received the Democratic nomination. However, Humphrey led in the polls from the time of his announcement until Kennedy's death. If Robert Kennedy had received the nomination, possibly the Republicans would have chosen Nelson Rockefeller instead of Richard Nixon. In that event, America's subsequent political history would have been dramatically different.

The Democratic convention was suffused with emotionalism and vio-lence in the streets. Hubert Humphrey was by now the expected candidate, but he found himself in an extremely difficult position. Exploration of a possible Ted Kennedy candidacy was almost inevitable, especially since polls suggested that Humphrey might not be able to win the election. Mayor Daley, who controlled the Illinois delegation, withheld his support from Humphrey for forty-eight hours while he conferred with Jess Unruh, leader of the California delegation. A Kennedy draft might have developed if McCarthy had supported it wholeheartedly, but Kennedy's representatives felt McCarthy had too many reservations.[17] Also, the southern delegates (and Lyndon Johnson) decided that they preferred Humphrey to Kennedy. Humphrey found himself in a delicate balancing act as he tried to conciliate Johnson (who as president still controlled basic convention arrangements) and liberals who wanted to abolish the unit rule and incorporate a strong plank against the war in the platform.

For the viewing audience on TV, Humphrey's nomination was jux-taposed with images of the Chicago police clubbing demonstrators on Mich-igan Avenue and shots of a scowling Mayor Daley. A major party convention can often be a confusing affair; this one seemed to have lurched out of control. Important segments of the Kennedy and McCarthy campaigns now fused into an insurgency against the political establishment. They saw Mayor Daley and his club-wielding police as symbols of establishment evils,

[17]Ibid., p. 354.

and since Humphrey had received his nomination from the establishment, he too was seen as at least slightly suspect.

NIXON AGAIN

On the Republican side, events moved steadily in Richard Nixon's favor. Political obituaries following his 1962 defeat had proven to be distinctly premature: Nixon became bored with California, moved to New York, developed a lucrative law practice, made new acquaintances, and kept his options open. In 1964 he had strong support in the polls but could not push for the nomination. In 1965 and 1966 he mended fences with Goldwaterites and campaigned for Republicans across the country. By 1968 Nixon had strong support among Republican voters and organization people.

After initial hesitancy, Rockefeller became an active candidate, and he even won the Massachusetts primary on a write-in vote. Following this initial good fortune, however, the cause of Republican liberals experienced little success. Nixon had most of the delegate commitments, and Rockefeller's barnstorming could not pry them loose. The New York governor was very strong in polls of the entire electorate, but by June two out of three Republicans were for Nixon.[18] Richard Nixon won the nomination on the first ballot.

Nixon surprised the convention by choosing Spiro Agnew as his running mate. In Theodore White's account, a series of conferences had boiled the alternatives down to John Volpe (governor of Massachusetts), Spiro Agnew (then governor of Maryland), and Robert Finch (an old Nixon friend). In the final conference, Finch was the choice, but he "refused" for reasons that are not clear. The group then decided that Agnew was more impressive than Volpe, and so it was decided.[19]

Wallace and Humphrey

The independent candidacy of George C. Wallace complicated the 1968 election. When elected governor of Alabama in 1962 Wallace had proclaimed in his inaugural address: "Segregation now . . . segregation tomorrow . . . and segregation forever." In June 1963 national television showed him standing in the door of the University of Alabama administration building, defying the United States government to admit blacks. Almost instantly, Wallace became a national figure. A sarcastic and demagogic politician, Wallace appealed to the darker side of southern politics. He also specialized in deprecating the "pointy-head" officials of the federal government, "guideline writers," and "theoreticians." Wallace had entered some northern primaries in 1964; he won by 33.9 percent in Wisconsin, 29.9 percent in Indiana, and 42.7 percent in Maryland. Some of this astonishing vote clearly represented a backlash against gains made by blacks. In stopping short of a direct push for the presidency, Wallace had deferred to

[18]Scammon and Wattenberg, *The Real Majority,* p. 327.
[19]White, *1968,* pp. 314–315.

Lyndon Johnson's apparent strength and to the distinctly conservative candidacy of Barry Goldwater.

In 1968, however, he mounted a skillful presidential campaign, eventually achieving the remarkable feat of getting his name on the ballot in all fifty states, usually under the rubric of the American Independent party. After Robert Kennedy was shot, Wallace began to rise in the polls. For almost a year, no poll had shown him with more than 10 percent, but now, his fortunes began to rise, peaking at about 21 percent in mid-September.

Hubert Humphrey's position was strong early in the year. However, Nixon received a natural boost from the Republican convention while Humphrey was hurt by the disarray of the Democratic convention. The convention had been scheduled very late, Humphrey had not been in a position to be very active politically in the spring, and it was now difficult for him to pull together an effective campaign. Furthermore, Humphrey was desperately short of campaign funds, and hecklers dogged many of his appearances. His opponent rolled out a well-oiled media campaign, while Humphrey could not afford a nationwide telecast until the Salt Lake City speech of September 30. He now dissociated himself to some degree from the president's Vietnam policies and began to receive a steady resurgence of support. Yet Humphrey was never able to regain the level of approval he had enjoyed in the spring. Subsequent studies indicated that if Wallace had not run, Nixon's victory would have been greater.[20] Nevertheless, the Democrats lost only a handful of seats in the Congress. Wallace received 13.5 percent of the popular vote and won the electoral votes of five states.

The Nixon Presidency

Richard Nixon began his presidency in an extremely weak political position. Although the GOP held thirty governorships, the opposition party controlled both houses of Congress. Nixon's margin over Humphrey was a mere half million votes, and he had difficulty getting the people he wanted to serve in his administration.[21] His approval rating in the Gallup poll began at 59 percent in January 1969; it rose to its highest level, 68 percent, in November of that year. This was the lowest "high" of any president since polling had begun. (Eisenhower's maximum, for example, was 79 percent; Kennedy's, 83 percent; and Johnson's, 80 percent.)

The new president's first eight or nine months in office brought a sense of relaxation and reconciliation. For the first time in several years, there was no large scale racial rioting (although shootouts between police and Black Panthers occurred in Los Angeles and Chicago). A lottery system replaced the old arbitrary draft categories, and in July the first successful walk on the moon produced a temporary euphoria.

However, the problem of Vietnam was not yet resolved. Withdrawal from Vietnam proceeded slowly, and massive antiwar demonstrations took

[20]Asher, *Presidential Elections and American Politics,* pp. 175–176.
[21]According to Theodore White, Hubert Humphrey turned down the UN; Henry Jackson spurned Defense; David Rockefeller rejected Defense and Treasury; Scranton refused to be secretary of state. White, *1972,* pp. 361–362.

place in October and November. On November 16, 1969, the first press reports of the My Lai massacre (which had ocurred in March of 1968) appeared. And Spiro Agnew, the man who had been a distinct liability in the 1968 campaign, now blossomed forth against opponents of the administration. Agnew charged that the moratorium day war protests had been "encouraged by an effete corps of impudent snobs who characterize themselves as intellectuals." He also lashed out at the power of network television, the *New York Times,* and the *Washington Post.*

In 1970 Nixon managed to temporarily neutralize Vietnam as a political issue by increasing the pace of staged troop withdrawals. However, an incursion against sanctuaries in Cambodia beginning April 30 led to unprecedented levels of campus protest. At Kent State University, national guardsmen killed four students in early May. A massive demonstration in Washington and an intensive antiwar lobbying campaign aimed at Congress followed. There were sharp increases in terrorist bombings, apparently by the Weathermen underground, and court martial proceedings against Lt. William Calley for his role in the My Lai atrocities kept the Vietnam War at the focus of attention.

In 1971, after important setbacks from the Democratically controlled Senate, Nixon seized the initiative with remarkable new steps in public policy. On August 15 he announced a ninety day freeze on wages, prices, and rents under the authority of the Economic Stabilization Act of 1970. At the end of the year, he took the United States off the gold standard and freed the dollar for devaluation against other currencies. He stated that the "postwar order of international relations is gone," and with it, "the conditions which have determined . . . United States foreign policy since 1945." With this came the announcement of the presidential visits to Peking and Moscow that took place the following year. The American presence in Vietnam continued to wind down, and the tide of antiwar protest diminished. Again the country was spared extensive racial rioting in the cities. However, on July 1, the *New York Times* began printing the *Pentagon Papers,* a classified history of United States involvement in Vietnam through 1968. The Supreme Court had denied injunctions against the *Times,* and authorities had indicted Daniel Ellsberg, a former Defense Department aide, for theft of government property and leaking classified documents.

The 1972 Election

As the 1972 election approached, Richard Nixon maintained a remarkably consistent level of support in the polls: a high of 68 percent balanced by a low of 48 percent. By June of 1972 his trips to Moscow and Peking had raised his rating to a healthy 60 percent. The Watergate break-in, which occurred June 17, 1972, did not have any significant impact on the election.[22]

The Democrats, meanwhile, were reacting to difficulties in their convention procedures. The 1968 convention had taken unprecedented steps to seat black delegates. It also adopted two important reports on future

[22]*Gallup Opinion Index,* July 1972, p. 3.

delegate selection, stipulating that at the 1972 convention delegates would have to be selected in a way permitting full and timely opportunities for participation. "All feasible efforts" would be taken to assure open participation within the calendar year in which the convention was to be held. Furthermore, the chairman of the Democratic National Committee was urged to establish special committees to implement the reports.

The defeated candidate for president, Hubert Humphrey, appointed the new chairman of the Democratic National Committee, Senator Fred Harris. Harris in turn, with Humphrey's approval, appointed George McGovern to head up the Commission on Party Structure and Reform. A young liberal staff infused with the idealism of the 1968 insurgency dominated the commission and hearings held around the country often bypassed the regular party organizations in favor of blacks, Chicanos, women, and insurgent groups.

The commission required that in convention states at least 75 percent of a state's delegation be chosen from districts and not by the convention at large. The commission did not, however, outlaw winner-take-all primaries in states such as California (and this is one reason why more states held presidential primaries in 1972). New rules stipulated that state parties could not appoint public or party officials as delegates by virtue of their official positions, and party committees could not choose more than 10 percent of all delegates.[23] In other words, all delegates had to be specially selected, and in most cases the process had to be open to widespread participation.

In an even more drastic step the commission required state Democratic parties to take "affirmative steps to encourage" representation of "minority groups," "women," and "young people" (defined as people not more than thirty nor less than eighteen years of age) in the national convention delegation "in reasonable relationship to the group's presence in the population of the states."[24] Although Chicanos, blacks, young people, and women were present in approximately correct statistical proportions at the 1972 convention, older ethnic groups, working-class people, and the elderly —some of whom had been bulwarks of the Democratic party—were underrepresented.

George McGovern had appeared as a late and minor candidate for the Democratic nomination in 1968. Although he was one of the insurgents, he campaigned for Humphrey in the fall. In 1969 he decided to run again and rather quickly assumed leadership of the causes associated with the insurgency. There were many more contenders than usual in 1972, the major figures (besides McGovern) being Ted Kennedy, Edmund Muskie, Hubert Humphrey, George Wallace, Henry Jackson, and John Lindsay.

In July 1969 Ted Kennedy took a wrong turn on a dark road, and in the subsequent accident the young woman with him drowned beneath the Chappaquiddick bridge. Kennedy's conduct in the incident and the judicial proceedings that followed were widely criticized. The Kennedy magic was

[23]Donald Johnson, *The Politics of Delegate Selection* (New York: Robert A. Taft Institute of Government, 1976), p. 9.
[24]White, *1972*, pp. 38–39.

such that skilled observers believed he could have received the 1972 Democratic nomination for the asking, but he firmly decided against running.

Edmund Muskie was the early frontrunner but fared badly in the early primaries and quit the race late in April. John Lindsay received a crippling blow in the Florida primary where, despite maximum effort in a large field of candidates, he received only 7 percent of the vote. (The low-key McGovern effort came in with 6.2 percent but, by staking much less on the outcome, had damaged the main rival on the left.) George Wallace won in the Florida primary with 42 percent and came in second in Wisconsin, but a madman's bullet took him out of the process on May 15. This was a more moderate Wallace than the one the country had witnessed in 1964 and 1968, and he received genuine sympathy from all parts of the political spectrum.

Of all the campaigns McGovern's operation was best able to take advantage of changes in nominating procedures. Old party organizational structures could no longer deliver convention votes in a reliable manner, and McGovern's network of enthusiastic volunteers became a major force in both primary and nonprimary states. In the latter, so few eligible Democrats normally participated in delegate selection that an intelligent and well-planned volunteer effort could reap a rich harvest of delegates.

In the election itself, however, the McGovern candidacy was a political disaster. Polls taken just before the convention showed that McGovern was the preferred candidate among Democratic voters, but his margin was small and the party far from united. McGovern needed support from traditional leaders, and they had to be courted. Early in the year he had espoused huge cuts in defense spending, "demogrants," and absolute limits on the value of inheritances. Press scrutiny of these positions made them appear simplistic, inadequately prepared, and bereft of necessary detail. McGovern found himself on the defensive before the contest with Nixon began.

Soon after the Democratic convention in Miami Beach (July 10–13), reporters discovered that Senator Thomas Eagleton from Missouri, McGovern's running mate, had been hospitalized three times for psychiatric disorders. An embarrassing sequel followed Eagleton's withdrawal; six prominent Democrats apparently refusing McGovern's offer of his spot on the ticket before R. Sargent Shriver was finally in place on August 8. There had also been a painful failure to assert control in the choice of party chairman: Larry O'Brien had been first beseeched to take the position, but when he accepted, the McGovern forces rejected him in favor of Joan Westwood.

McGovern's campaign organization had shown extraordinary prowess in winning the nomination, but it now seemed leaderless and inept. By mid-October, McGovern's pollster, Pat Caddell, claimed he felt like "the recreation director on the Titanic." The Democratic nominee apparently lost the respect of his own activist supporters.[25]

Nixon's election victory in 1972 was as one-sided as Johnson's win in 1964. To some observers, these outcomes suggested that both parties were

[25]Ibid., pp. 429, 454. Says White, "He had failed them not in honor or devotion—but in craftsmanship."

vulnerable to ideological candidacies with little support in the general electorate. Unlike 1964, however, the partisan composition of Congress showed
little change in 1972. Despite the large number of Democrats in the previous
House and Senate, Republicans made a net gain of only twelve House seats.
In the Senate, the GOP suffered a net *loss* of two seats.

Watergate

The next two years brought increasing reverberations from the break-
in at Democratic headquarters in the Watergate complex. "Watergate" was
an enormously complex affair, and it seemed to take on a life of its own as
it impacted the American political process.

Prior to November 1972 press secretary Ronald Ziegler had referred
to the break-in as a "third-rate burglary," and on August 29 Nixon had
stated that he could "categorically" affirm that a probe by his own staff
indicated that "no one in the White House staff, no one in this administration presently employed was involved in this very bizarre incident." Then
in September and October *Washington Post* reporters Robert Woodward and
Carl Bernstein revealed that a secret fund had financed spying and sabotage
operations against Democratic primary campaigns. Ziegler accused the *Post*
of character assassination and shoddy journalism. Television networks did
not emphasize the story in their election coverage, and McGovern's claim
that he was opposing the most corrupt administration in history came across
as political desperation.

However, at the January 1973 trial of the Watergate Seven, Judge John
Sirica read a letter from one of the defendants, James McCord, charging that
others had been involved, that defendants had been pressured to plead
guilty, and that perjury had been committed. On April 17 the president read
a brief statement at a news conference and refused to answer any questions.
The statement said in part, "On March 21, as a result of serious charges
which came to my attention, some of which were publicly reported, I began
extensive new inquiries into this whole matter." Press secretary Ziegler now
stated that all previous White House statements were "inoperative." On
April 27, in Los Angeles, U.S. District Judge William Byrne released a
Justice Department memorandum stating that two Watergate defendants
had burglarized the files of a psychiatrist with the intention of stealing
Daniel Ellsberg's medical records. On April 30 Nixon announced the resignations of Robert Haldeman and John Erlichman, his most important aides,
and Richard Kleindienst, his attorney general. Nixon conceded the possibility of a White House cover-up in a televised address that evening but
emphasized that until March 1973 he "remained convinced that the denials
were true and the charges of involvement by members of the White House
staff were false."

Televised hearings of the special Senate committee, chaired by Sam
Ervin, that summer were a political sensation. John Dean, former counsel
to the president, submitted a set of documents that included lists of "enemies" singled out by the "White House" for harassment. The documents
indicated that audits by the Internal Revenue Service and denial of federal
grants had been proposed as weapons. Dean asserted that the president had

been party to the Watergate cover-up for eight months, and he implicated the president in offers of executive clemency to the burglary defendants. On July 16 the Senate committee learned that Nixon *secretly* tape-recorded *all* his conversations in the White House and Executive Office Building. The gravity of this appalling action was often forgotten in the swirl of events that followed. A complex battle for possession of the tapes led on October 20 to Nixon's forcing the resignation of Attorney General Elliot Richardson, and his deputy, William Ruckelshaus, after they refused to dismiss special Watergate prosecutor Archibald Cox (the "Saturday Night Massacre"). Solicitor General Robert Bork then became acting attorney general and fired Cox. FBI agents proceeded to seal off the offices of Richardson, Ruckelshaus, and Cox.

As if all this was not astonishing enough, Vice President Agnew resigned on October 10, and a few hours later pleaded no contest to a charge of federal income tax evasion. His resignation was part of a plea bargain that included publication of grand jury information against Agnew, citing his acceptance of payoffs while governor of Maryland and vice president. (Agnew got off lightly because the prosecutors wanted to avoid any possibility of Agnew's succeeding to the presidency, were Nixon to resign or be impeached.) Following the requirements of the Twenty-fifth Amendment, Nixon nominated House Minority Leader Gerald Ford to be the new vice president; he was confirmed by the Senate on November 27 and by the House December 6.

In the wake of protest over the "Saturday Night Massacre," the president agreed to obey Sirica's order to surrender the tapes, and eighty-four representatives sponsored impeachment resolutions in the House of Representatives. The House Judiciary Committee began preliminary impeachment investigations October 30. Nationally televised deliberations of the House Judiciary Committee in July preceded the committee's recommendation of three articles of impeachment. Article II received the strongest voting support on the committee: In effect it charged the president with a persistent effort to abuse the power of the office referring specifically to attempts to obtain confidential information in tax returns for unauthorized purposes, misuse of the FBI and other executive branch personnel, and many other matters.

A few days later Nixon released transcripts of three tapes for June 23, 1972, which showed that he had been aware of a cover-up long before March 21, 1973, and that he had personally ordered a halt to an FBI investigation of the Watergate break-in. His remaining support in Congress now crumbled. All eleven Republicans who had voted against the first article of impeachment considered the new evidence enough to support that charge: obstruction of the investigation into the Watergate break-in, the cover-up, and the protecting of those responsible.

It was now clear that Nixon would be convicted if the impeachment proceedings went forward, and the president resigned on August 8, 1974.

Gerald Ford immediately became the nation's first unelected president and his successful nomination of Nelson Rockefeller gave the country its second unelected vice president. Ford made his most controversial decision a month after he was sworn in: He unconditionally pardoned Nixon for all federal crimes that he committed or might have committed. Nixon admitted to mistakes but did not confess guilt. A torrent of criticism followed the pardon, and Ford's standing in the polls dropped twenty points.[26] Early in 1975, Robert Haldeman, John Erlichman, and John Mitchell each received sentences of two and a half to eight years in prison for conspiracy, obstruction of justice, and perjury. The conspiracy charge concerned payment of $429,000 in hush money to the Watergate seven, destruction of documents, offers of presidential clemency, and schemes to obstruct investigations. By this time, twenty-four Nixon aides had received convictions or had pleaded guilty to Watergate-related crimes.

Political factors in Watergate. As facts about Watergate surfaced, Democrats naturally tended to be critical of the president and Republicans tended to give him the benefit of the doubt. However, Watergate reflected partisan antagonisms only to a limited degree. Some of the other political elements in the affair reflected a psychology of aggressive insecurity. The president had shown a tendency towards resentful isolation. The opposition party controlled Congress, and even within his own party Nixon had not been very successful in enlisting the support of congressional leaders. Conflicts with Congress were institutional as well as partisan. They had become especially acute because of controversy over the extent of presidential authority to impound congressional appropriations. Nixon's campaign techniques isolated him from the working press, and his long-standing grievance against liberal elements in the press and television had deepened into bitter hostility. Over the years he had developed the style of a loner. He preferred to make his important decisions by himself, and he preferred a staffing pattern that gave few people direct access to him.

Important changes in political attitudes and practices caught Nixon on the trailing edge. In moving away from the cold war era, America found national security a less compelling rationale for presidential discretion. Laws governing campaign finance—historically, often inadequate in their intentions and effects—were also undergoing important modification. Campaign costs in the television era had risen dramatically, aggravating the problem of money in politics, and the Federal Election Campaign Act of 1971 represented the first new approach in forty-six years. The act detailed spending limits and disclosure procedures. It took effect in the midst of the 1972 political season, causing many problems in informing political activists and obtaining compliance. Nixon had vetoed a 1970 bill, and reform forces in Congress had made a strong attempt to override the veto. Heightened sensitivity to the issue made manipulations of money by his reelection committee (CREEP) seem particularly repellant. By August 1973 at least six corporations had voluntarily disclosed illegal corporate contributions to the

[26]In response to the Gallup poll question, "Do you approve or disapprove of the way Ford is handling his job as President?" In August, 71 percent approved; by late September only 50 percent approved. His highest rating after January 1975 was 51 percent. *Public Opinion,* 1 (March/April 1978), 28–29.

Nixon campaign. Elaborate efforts to "launder" campaign funds had come to the public's attention quite early in the Woodward and Bernstein reports.

With the failure in Vietnam, pressure against presidential prerogatives had also been building. Impoundment had been a weapon in the president's armory for years, but after Nixon impounded unusually large sums of appropriated money in 1972 and 1973, the administration lost more than twenty federal court challenges. Distrust of the "imperial presidency" was not aimed specifically at Nixon, yet he managed to make himself the symbol of it as Watergate unfolded. Privilege in high places also came under attack. Nixon's difficulties deepened when the public learned that more than $10 million of public funds had been spent to secure the grounds at his estates in Florida and California. In April 1974 the Joint Committee on Internal Revenue Taxation reported that Nixon owed $476,531 in back taxes and interest.

LIGHT AT THE END OF THE TUNNEL

Watergate certainly registered a significant impact on public opinion, but it was not really an obsession at the mass level. Gallup polls, for example, showed that throughout 1973 and 1974, most people mentioned inflation, the high cost of living, or the energy crisis as the most important problem facing the country. The nation was importing an increasing percentage of its petroleum, and total energy use continued to climb. Energy scarcity fed inflation, and deficits in the balance of payments tended to aggravate unemployment. Price levels increased 5.9 percent in 1970, 6.2 percent in 1973, and 11.0 percent in 1974. Unemployment reached 8.1 percent in 1975 and 7.3 percent in 1976.

The 1974 elections brought an important group of newcomers to Congress. The House had slightly more freshmen representatives than usual, and (more important) they broke sharply with past congressional practice by caucusing against congressional elders. The Democrats, of course, made significant gains—forty-three House seats, three Senate seats, and four governorships. Among the new faces were Edmund G. Brown, Jr., governor of California, Ella Grasso, governor of Connecticut, and Gary Hart, McGovern's main political strategist in 1972. The insurgency was still an important force in Democratic politics, and many newcomers had outlooks similar to persons first elected in 1972. In that year, fewer incumbent senators and representatives than usual sought reelection. All in all, more than a third of all House members in the Ninety-fourth Congress (which served in 1975 and 1976) were first elected in 1972 or 1974.

An important legacy of Watergate was the comprehensive investigation into intelligence agencies triggered by press reports in 1974 that focused on CIA abuses. During 1975 and 1976 the Rockefeller commission on the CIA, the Church committee in the Senate, and the Pike committee in the House brought frightening new information before the public. Despite earlier denials, the CIA had conducted extensive actions in Chile aimed at overthrowing the government of the late Salvador Allende. This agency had also plotted the assassination of Fidel Castro of Cuba and Patrice Lumumba of the Congo. Under J. Edgar Hoover, the FBI had compiled derogatory information on elected officials to be used in the bureau's dealings with Congress. It engaged in extensive activities to disrupt protest groups over a twenty-year period and in 1963 launched a campaign against Martin Luther King, Jr. (In one instance they placed bugs in his hotel rooms and sent him an anonymous letter, accompanied by transcripts from the bugs, recommending suicide.[27]) An executive reorganization of intelligence operations followed these revelations, and both houses created permanent committees to oversee the intelligence agencies.

Politics under New Rules

New developments that would affect the 1976 presidential election were also taking place. Legislation in 1974 provided public financing for presidential elections and set limits on political contributions and campaign spending for candidates in federal elections. The Democrats held a miniconvention in Kansas City in 1974 to approve a new party charter and new delegate selection rules for 1976. Each state party would have the option of selecting a fourth of its delegates by the state Democratic committee or by a committee consisting of all publicly elected convention delegates. Although this would assure most state party leaders of a free ride to the convention, it would by no means permit party insiders to control the convention. Nearly three-fourths of all delegates to the convention would be chosen directly by voters in presidential primaries. Anybody who aspired to be a Democratic convention delegate, whether via primaries or caucuses, would have to declare his or her presidential preference. Moreover, a principle of proportional representation in delegate selection (in primary as well as convention states) would enable candidates to pick up delegates even in states where they were weak. The same principle would also make it difficult for power brokers to move unified blocks of delegates from one candidate to another.[28] The rules barred "mandatory quotas," but each state had to take "affirmative action" to assure full participation for women and minorities.

The Democratic party had become something of a national association instead of a league of state and local organizations. The rules were not all decided upon at once, and there was widespread confusion and uncertainty. However, it was clear that many Democrats would be encouraged to make a try for the nomination.

"Fat cats" could no longer carry the full load of money raising. To obtain a large federal subsidy to meet expenses of the nomination campaign, a presidential candidate would have to accept spending limits and raise at least $5,000 in contributions of $250 or less in each of twenty states. The events of 1976 suggested that presidential politics had become in part a matter of starting very early and enduring all of the many obstacles that lay in the path of the nomination.

[27] *Congressional Quarterly Almanac 1975*, pp. 387, 410.
[28] Ibid., pp. 6–7.

The Road to 1976

James Earl (Jimmy) Carter, Jr., won the 1976 nomination in part because he had a political base and perhaps because he wanted it more than anybody else. He had first tried to become governor of Georgia in 1966 (with the help of Hamilton Jordan, Robert Lipshutz, and Gerald Rafshoon). Following his defeat, Carter spent the next four years working the state "like a migrant worker hustling for harvest work, putting in a regular day at the family's peanut plant, then driving to all corners of Georgia to speak and meet voters."[29] Following his victory in 1970, Carter's moves to open Georgia government to women and blacks brought him national attention as an exemplar of the "New South."

The twenty-seven-year-old Jordan prepared a detailed blueprint for Carter's national effort that was ready November 4, 1972. The Georgia governorship was used to full advantage. The state established Georgia trade missions so that Carter could travel to each of the continents of the world. The Carters systematically invited political and press luminaries who happened to be in the state to the governor's mansion. One such invitation brought Carter together with Robert Strauss, the recently appointed Democratic National Chairman. In a few days they were working out the details of how Carter would run the Democratic National Committee's 1974 campaign for senators, governors, mayors, and representatives.[30] As he worked tirelessly for candidates across the country, Carter forged wide-ranging contacts that would later be invaluable. He also became a familiar figure with Democratic leaders who met at the national committee and in regional meetings. Carter did not formally announce his candidacy until December 1974, after he had completed this campaign activity.

Carter's game plan assumed an Edward Kennedy effort, and he was one of the only Democrats who intended to challenge Kennedy for the nomination if it came to that. However, Kennedy made an unequivocal declaration of his noncandidacy in September 1974. Two months later, after spending a year and $100,000 exploring the possibilities, Walter Mondale withdrew from the race, stating that he did not "have the overwhelming desire to be president which is essential for the kind of campaign that is required."

Others who sought the nomination may not have grasped as well as Carter the import of the new political rules—the need to campaign in many states rather than a few, the need to start very early and not depend on older power groups, and the need to stress personal organization rather than expensive mass media appeals. Carter was so little known that he appeared unrecognized on "What's My Line?" in 1973. Because of his obscurity, early successes would have strong impact. These came in the Iowa caucuses and in New Hampshire. Carter emphasized personal qualities that would restore faith and trust in government. He had many specific issue stands, but he did not stress them in his campaign—an approach that was quite compatible with the post-Watergate political mood.

An arresting characteristic was Carter's unequivocal identification as

[29]Jules Witcover, *Marathon* (New York: The Viking Press, 1977), p. 105.
[30]Ibid., p. 117.

69

a "born-again Christian." Carter in fact was the first evangelical Christian
to be elected president in the twentieth century. In the early 1970s the
"Jesus movement" and the growth in fundamentalist and evangelical denominations were significant trends in America. Mysticism and the occult
were in vogue, and people were concerned about "mind control techniques" attributed to Reverend Moon's Unification Church and other cults.
The apparent resurgence of interest in and confusion about religion in
America may have benefited Carter politically. A Gallup poll taken in 1976
stated that 34 percent of those interviewed claimed a "born-again" experience, and about 40 percent believed that the Bible should be taken literally.[31]

However, the religious issue also posed difficulties. It tended to raise
the question of what Hamilton Jordan referred to as "the weirdo factor."
Carter was careful to emphasize that he believed in a complete separation
of church and state, that his religious experiences mainly involved "a quiet
feeling that was reassuring," not a "blinding flash of light or voices of God,"
that he did not consider himself to be better than other people, and that no
religious revelation would instruct him on the performance of his public
duties.[32]

Perhaps his most important success on the route to the nomination
came when he defeated Wallace in the Florida and North Carolina primaries. The principle of proportional representation meant that Carter kept
accumulating delegate support, even in states where he did not run particularly well. His opponents were divided, and they found his early lead insur-
mountable. He began to lead in the polls, and by the Ohio primary on June
8, he was the obvious winner.

On the Republican side, polls suggested that the decline in President
Ford's political standing following the Nixon pardon had bottomed out by
January 1975 and gradually improved thereafter. In running close to or
ahead of potential Democratic nominees in the polls, Ford may have benefited from a climate of diminished expectations following Watergate. However, Ronald Reagan mounted a strong challenge.

In his early years, Reagan had been a radio sportscaster and then a
Hollywood motion picture actor. When his acting career began to stagnate
after World War II, he spent eight years as master of ceremonies for the
General Electric Theater on television. The experience seems to have developed his political interests and projected them to a wider audience. General
Electric apparently broke the connection when his views became too controversial. Reagan had become nationally prominent in Republican circles
when he developed an especially effective speech for fund raisers in 1964
that was finally televised nationally in the latter part of the Goldwater campaign. In 1966, at a time when few believed that conservative Republicans
could carry major states, Reagan beat Edmund G. Brown by a million votes
in the race for California governor. In 1967 a Reagan push for the presidential nomination had been derailed by a homosexual scandal involving mem-

---

[31] *Encyclopedia Americana Annual 1977.*
[32] Witcover, *Marathon,* pp. 270–272, 330, 562–570.

bers of the governor's personal staff.[33] Even so, Reagan had entered the battle for nomination at the eleventh hour, doing surprisingly well. In 1970 he ran for a second term, beating Jess Unruh by a half million votes. There had been no presidential prospects for Reagan in 1972 because Nixon's claims on the nomination were unassailable.

The natural advantage usually lies with the incumbent president, but in 1976 the new rules and Ford's peculiar status reduced that advantage somewhat. Reagan qualified for public financing, and as an unelected president, Ford could not avoid the primaries. Primary voting was surprisingly close, and a small number of uncommitted delegates ultimately decided the nomination for Ford. The Reagan entourage, encouraged by its showing at Kansas City, began laying the groundwork for 1980.

Verdict at the Polls

Issues emphasized in the contest between Carter and Ford reflected a return to familiar contrasts between the two major parties. The most important domestic issues were high inflation and high unemployment. Ford (and the Republican platform) predictably emphasized the dangers of inflation and urged a reduction in government spending. Republicans minimized the government's role in stimulating employment, and Democrats just as predictably argued that the way to reduce inflation was to put people back to work.

Superficially, interview data suggested that the first southerner since the Civil War to be elected absolutely in his own right would not have won without black votes. However, in a close election any group can claim to provide the critical margin of victory. Carter ran much stronger among southern white Protestants than any Democratic nominee since 1960, and these voters may have provided the essential support that he needed.[34] In contrast to 1972 the election was marked by a reassertion of class and party preferences. But low turnout and other evidence suggest that neither candidate aroused the enthusiasm of the electorate.

The 1976 election produced little net change in the makeup of Congress—a gain of two Democratic seats in the House and no net change in the Senate. However, seventy-nine Democratic first-term members of Congress were reelected. For the Ninety-sixth Congress (serving 1977 and 1978) more than half entered office as a result of the 1972 or later elections. The Senate had unusually high turnover in 1976. Fewer senators than usual sought reelection, and of this group only 64 percent won reelection. Congress thus had more new members than at any time since 1948.[35]

[33]Like the hapless Rockefeller effort, and the tragedy of Robert Kennedy's assassination, this may have been a fateful event in the 1968 contests. One wonders what would have happened if Reagan had been nominated in 1968 instead of Nixon. See White, *1968,* pp. 42–43. For background on Reagan, see the special report in *Newsweek,* July 21, 1980.

[34]Richard Scammon and Ben Wattenberg, "Jimmy Carter's Problem," *Public Opinion,* 1 (March/April 1978), 3–8. Pomper, *The Election of 1976,* pp. 73–76.

[35]Charles Jacob, "The Congressional Elections and Outlook," *The Election of 1976,* ed. Gerald Pomper et al. (New York: David McKay Co., Inc., 1977), pp. 83–105.

CARTER'S PRESIDENCY AND THE 1980 ELECTION

During the Carter years, difficulties facing the Republic mounted and deepened. Rather than a restoration of normalcy following Vietnam and Watergate, the country experienced declining morale and a growing sense of insecurity. Entire sectors of the society were implicated in the failure to mount creative responses to the difficult choices posed by an interdependent yet increasingly inharmonious world. In November 1979 historian Henry Steele Commager spoke of a rapid descent to mediocrity and a crisis of leadership in all walks of American life.[36] As Table 3–1 indicates, many may have concurred with the latter judgment.

Yet the country took some important steps under the Carter administration. Operational features of American foreign policy began to include

Table 3–1
Trends in Leadership Assessment by the Mass Public

	Percent Having "A Great Deal of Confidence" in Particular Sectors		
	1977	1973	1966
Governmental Sectors			
The White House	31%	18%	n.a.
U.S. Supreme Court	29	33	50%
The Military	27	40	62
Executive Branch Federal			
Government	23	19	41
State Government	18	24	n.a.
Local Government	18	28	n.a.
Congress	17	29	42
Nongovernmental Sectors			
Medicine	43%	57%	73%
Higher Education	37	44	61
Organized Religion	29	36	41
Television News	28	41	25
Major Companies	20	29	55
The Press	18	30	29
Organized Labor	14	20	22
Law Firms	14	24	n.a.
Advertising Agencies	7	11	21

Based on responses to the following question: "As far as people in charge of running (read list) are concerned, would you say you have a great deal of confidence, only some confidence or hardly any confidence at all in them?"

Source: The Harris Poll, February 1–7, 1977, as reported in *Current Opinion*, 5 (April 1977).

[36]Talks given at Indiana State University and reported in the *Terre Haute Tribune,* Nov. 17, 1979.

a new concern for human rights which, however limited and controversial, is not likely to be scrapped entirely. Carter's limited pardon of Vietnam war resisters in January of 1977 seemed to ease recriminations over amnesty and point the way to eventual release from the trauma of Vietnam. The president established full diplomatic relations with China in 1979 and obtained Senate ratification of the Panama Canal treaties in 1978. Another significant achievement was the Civil Service Reform Act of 1978, which terminated the Civil Service Commission and called for the creation of a Senior Executive Service.[37]

The president's efforts to fashion an adequate energy policy had the highest initial priority, but legislative results were slow in coming. Within ninety days of inauguration a small team of energy planners, headed by James Schlesinger and working closely with the president, had constructed a comprehensive energy program. The country was importing more than half of the oil it consumed; only seven years earlier, in 1969, its oil imports had been 33 percent. The Arab oil embargo of 1973–1974 had produced some fear and even panic, but at its conclusion the nation returned to its wasteful ways. Before Carter, no president had faced the energy problem head on.[38] Worldwide energy consumption was growing faster than available supplies, and in the view of some energy specialists, substantial conservation would be necessary to avert devastating shortages sometime between 1985 and 2000.[39]

Carter's initial proposals were a complex mix of regulatory and tax measures that emphasized tighter standards of energy efficiency in industrial products, permissible lists of industrial fuels, programs to encourage owners to insulate buildings, taxes on low-mileage automobiles, and taxes against purchases of domestically produced oil. Carter gave three evening television addresses to the nation in 1977 and each time spoke of energy. In the only speech he made that year to a joint session of Congress he again spoke of energy. His advocacy of a comprehensive energy program came after the coldest winter in American history and sporadic energy shortages. The Speaker of the House and the Senate majority leader gave Carter's energy program top priority, and cabinet members criss-crossed the country defending it.

Congress finally provided energy legislation in October of 1978, but it contained only remnants of Carter's original plan. Polls taken in 1978 showed that about half of the nation refused to take the energy crisis very seriously, and this probably increased the program's vulnerability to opposition lobbyists.[40]

In January and February of 1979, the flight of the Shah and subsequent

---

[37]For a brief discussion, see George E. Berkley, *The Craft of Public Administration*, 3rd ed. (Boston: Allyn & Bacon, Inc., 1981), pp. 154–156.

[38]Haynes Johnson, *In the Absence of Power* (New York: The Viking Press, 1980), pp. 185–187. *BP Statistical Review of the World Oil Industry 1979* (London: British Petroleum Company Ltd.), pp. 19, 21.

[39]*1977 Congressional Quarterly Almanac*, p. 708.

[40]The 1978 legislation is too complex to summarize here. See *1978 Congressional Quarterly Almanac* for specifics.

developments in Iran lowered Iran's oil exports. Gasoline prices passed the dollar-a-gallon mark for the first time in U.S. history. On March 28, a nuclear accident occurred at Three Mile Island near Harrisburg, Pennsylvania; more than $800 million would eventually be spent to clean up the damages. In June an oil well blew out of control in the Gulf of Campeche, creating the largest oil spill in history. In California and some eastern states, brief gasoline shortages tended to magnify into long lines of waiting cars.

In the wake of these developments, Carter proposed two new energy programs. The one announced in April called for new thermostat settings: a phased-in decontrol of oil prices; and a windfall profits tax on oil production, with proceeds going to lower-income families, mass transportation funding, and other purposes. In July Carter asked for a massive commitment to the development of America's alternative sources of fuel. At year's end the legislation needed to implement the windfall profits tax and energy mobilization board was tied up in conference committees. Congress cleared the windfall profits tax in March of 1980, and it was expected to yield more than $227 billion in revenue over the next decade. In June the conference report on the energy mobilization board went down to defeat but a multibillion dollar synfuels bill passed.

It is too soon to evaluate the significance of these legislative measures, but they may well come to be regarded as important steps taken under highly difficult circumstances. Toward the end of the Carter years, the public began to perceive the reality of the energy crisis. The future (if any) of nuclear energy appeared uncertain despite official optimism, and there was no widely shared sense of urgency. Fundamental adaptations in mass transit and urban design had not yet begun. However, by 1980 one seldom heard any longer that the energy crisis was all a plot by the big oil companies.

Many other issues, of course, crowded to the fore. In 1977 human rights initiatives produced visible rifts with South Africa and the Soviet Union. In June Carter announced his opposition to production of the B–1 bomber. Indiana's ratification of the Equal Rights Amendment meant that support from only three more states was needed for passage; however, the measure remained in limbo as a string of defeats followed, and Representative Elizabeth Holtzman introduced legislation that successfully extended the deadline. In September Carter's old friend Bert Lance resigned as budget director in the wake of a controversy over his personal financial dealings. That same month, there was a widely heralded summit meeting between Begin and Sadat at Camp David, and with it agreement on a framework for a peace treaty between Israel and Egypt.

Perhaps the most noteworthy political news of 1978 was the overwhelming approval California's voters gave to Proposition 13 in the June primary. This measure required cuts of 57 percent in California's property taxes, and it sent waves of alarm through the nation's liberal community. In November tax-cutting initiatives appeared on the ballots of twenty-six states. Although these had less impact than Proposition 13, momentum generated by the California measure tended to color evaluations of the off-year elections. The GOP gained three Senate seats, twelve House seats, and six governorships. There were also some important Republican gains in the state legislatures.

Many observers discerned a shift to the right. Charles Percy claimed that the message from the voters was too much government spending, too much government regulation, and too much taxation. Ronald Reagan said "There were no liberals in this campaign," and *Newsweek* sensed a new politics in which Democrats would have to talk like Republicans to survive. Carter and members of his family campaigned hard for many fellow Democrats, but they came home with little more than plaudits for trying—often in lost causes.[41] Carter had spoken of the need for fiscal prudence in the 1976 campaign, and his proclaimed compatibility with the new political mood was not implausible.

Economic problems and foreign policy issues loomed large as the nation moved toward the 1980 election. In 1979 Carter initiated measures to admit large numbers of Indochinese refugees—more than 405,000 projected by the end of 1981. In June Carter and Brezhnev met in Vienna to sign a new strategic arms limitation treaty (SALT II), and the question of Senate ratification became an important issue in the 1980 election. A number of antinuclear demonstrations in the U.S. and other countries came on the heels of the Three Mile Island incident.

On the domestic front, the consumer price index increased 13.5 percent in 1979, and the Federal Reserve Board's tight-money policies led to the highest interest rates the country had ever experienced. These in turn seriously hurt the housing markets and greatly complicated emerging problems in the American automobile industry. Chrysler and U.S. Steel were in difficulty, and Congress passed a controversial $1.5 billion in federal loan guarantees for Chrysler. In June 1979, in the midst of sporadic gasoline shortages and a strike of independent truck drivers, Carter's approval ratings in the polls sank to the lowest level (25 percent) ever recorded by a major polling organization for any American president.

Carter's difficulties were compounded when an ill-planned cabinet shake-up in July 1979 robbed his most important speech of much of its impact. On July 15, after elaborate consultations and mounting suspense, Carter had spoken of "a fundamental threat to American democracy, the erosion of our confidence in the future" and had called for major steps to deal with the energy crisis. But two days later, press secretary Jody Powell announced, without explanation, that all of Carter's cabinet officers had offered the president their resignations. Four days later, five cabinet officers had lost their jobs, and Hamilton Jordan had been appointed White House Chief of Staff. In Haynes Johnson's account, the available rationales suggested that the president had placed political loyalty over independence and competence. In some departments the work pace slowed drastically, and in a few days George McGovern and Henry Jackson suggested that Carter might well abandon hope for a second term in favor of Edward Kennedy. The president's poll ratings had risen 9 points after his speech, but they soon returned once again to record low levels.[42]

[41]*Newsweek*, November 20, 1978, pp. 44, 46.
[42]Johnson, *In the Absence of Power*, pp. 314–315.

Carter's low level of popularity encouraged many candidates to seek a major party nomination, and this got the election season off to an early start. The sense that the 1980 election campaigns would never end was also fortified by the November 1979 seizure of embassy personnel in Teheran. This event accented the general mood of insecurity. Awareness that the militants' action might significantly (perhaps deliberately) affect the course of the campaign generated anger and resentment.

On the Democratic side, Carter's only significant rivals for the nomination were Edward Kennedy and Edmund G. Brown, Jr. The latter soon withdrew after disappointing performances in the New Hampshire and Massachusetts primaries. Kennedy's campaign suffered from initial campaign gaffes and from widespread sympathy for the president generated by the hostage crisis. Throughout the first phase of the nominating season, ending in mid-April, Kennedy continuously trailed Carter by a substantial margin as the preferred Democratic candidate of Democrats and Independents. In the first thirteen primaries, Carter won 54 percent of the total vote, Kennedy 30 percent. Carter did even better in the second-phase contests, ending May 27. Yet, Carter's political appeal declined thereafter, and in the "super Tuesday" primaries of June 3 he received 4 percent fewer votes than Kennedy. A week before the Democratic convention, Gallup reported that only 39 percent of Democrats preferred Carter as their nominee; 52 percent preferred someone else. Even so, Carter did better in the polls than any alternative candidate, including Kennedy. Fifty-five percent of polled Democrats approved of Carter releasing his delegates from their commitments and allowing them to vote for whomever they wished.[43]

At the Democratic convention, Kennedy supporters failed to overturn a proposed rule binding all delegates to their previous commitments on the first ballot. Kennedy then announced that his name would not be placed in nomination, and Carter won the nomination on the first ballot.

On the Republican side, Carter's apparent weakness and Gerald Ford's reluctance to seek the nomination brought forward a number of plausible contestants. In addition to Ronald Reagan and George Bush, John Anderson, Howard Baker, Philip Crane, and John Connally made major efforts to obtain delegate support. Bush scored impressively in the Iowa caucuses in January but thereafter was usually bested by Reagan. Reagan increased his lead over Bush in each successive phase of the primary season, and (aside from Anderson) support for other contestants was never large enough to be significant. Bush somewhat improved his share of the total primary vote in the second-phase primaries, but by "super Tuesday" he had withdrawn.

On April 24, after disappointing showings in some of the early primaries, John Anderson withdrew his quest for the Republican nomination and began to mount an independent bid for the presidency. The Illinois congressman portrayed himself as a unity candidate, with supporters in each of the major parties. He explicitly disavowed any intention of forming a new

---

[43] *Indianapolis Star,* August 7, 1980.

party. Anderson sought to portray himself as the provider of straight answers to tough questions, especially via his advocacy of a fifty cents per gallon tax on gasoline to be fully rebated through reductions in payroll and social security taxes. His campaign struck a liberal note on such issues as abortion, ratification of ERA, and prayer in the schools. On taxing and spending questions, however, Anderson seemed more conservative.[44]

Gerald Ford did not enter any of the primaries, but he considered a push of his own for the presidency early in the year, at a time when Reagan appeared to lack broad electoral appeal. However, on March 15, after a number of public statements and high-level consultations, Ford announced his decision not to run.

Reagan's nomination was a foregone conclusion by the time of the Republican convention in Detroit's Joe Louis Arena. However, the vice presidential nomination was still open. At first it appeared as though Ford would occupy the second spot. The possibility was explored in some detail, and in interviews with Walter Cronkite and Barbara Walters, Ford speculated about the basis of a possible interest. However, Reagan broke with tradition by visiting the convention at 12:15 A.M. on July 17 to announce that Bush was his choice. Ford's addition to the ticket might have strengthened it, but he would have been the first former president to run for vice president. His apparent interest in defining unusual vice presidential responsibilities via convention negotiations raised difficult political and constitutional questions.

The Final Rounds

Some of the contours of the 1980 election can be gleaned from Figure 3–1. Both Carter and Reagan enjoyed a marked upsurge in the polls after receiving major party nominations, and the level of Anderson's support simultaneously declined. Note also how Carter's support declined from mid-May to early August. In May the president was experiencing great difficulty with the boatloads of Cuban exiles who were coming into Florida. In June unemployment rose to 7.8 percent while prime interest rates remained at a high 12 percent. In July a Carter proclamation required 4 million men to register for a possible future draft, and the country learned that Japan had become the world's largest producer of cars and trucks. Also in July the Senate set up a special panel to investigate questionable and embarrassing dealings with Libya by the president's brother Billy.

In late June Reagan overtook Carter in the polls and widened the gap rather consistently up until the Democratic convention. There was apparently some fluctuation in the last month and a half, but many pollsters seemed to believe that the election was too close to call. Like his Democratic opponent, Reagan brought an effective presence to the television screen. As election day approached (and as the mass electorate became more involved

[44]Anderson had some appeal to Kennedy supporters, and some of them crossed over and voted for him in some of the March primaries. Even after he declared as an independent candidate, Anderson remained on the Republican primary ballot in a number of states. Indeed, in the District of Columbia, Oregon, and New Mexico he got better than 10 percent of the Republican primary vote. *Congressional Quarterly Weekly Report,* July 5, 1980, p. 1871.

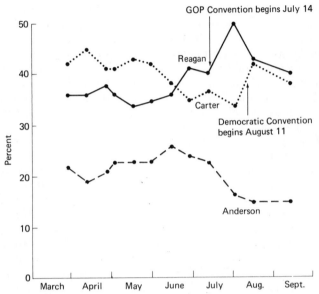

Question: "If President Jimmy Carter were the Democratic candidate
running against Ronald Reagan, the Republican candidate, and John
Anderson, the Independent candidate, which would you like to see win?"
(Those who named another person or who were undecided were asked:
"As of today, do you lean more to Carter, the Democrat, to Reagan,
the Republican, or to Anderson, the Independent?")

FIGURE 3–1 Carter, Reagan, and Anderson in the Gallup
Poll, 1980

Source: Public Opinion, October/November 1980, p. 21. Published
by American Enterprise Institute.

with its prospective choice) Reagan appeared to moderate or disregard
extremely conservative positions taken earlier in his career and during the
primary season. In a televised debate, staged a week or so before the election, he successfully countered Carter's attempts to have him perceived as
an advocate of risky economic and defense doctrines. Mounting difficulties
of the Carter years, an apparent shift towards conservatism in the larger
society, and Reagan's skill as a campaigner all figured in the final result.

Although Ronald Reagan had been active in American politics for
many years, the attentive public received him as something of a fresh personality in 1980. In the total popular vote it was Reagan 51 percent, Carter
41 percent, and Anderson 7 percent—an impressive victory, though not a
landslide.[45]

Only time would tell whether 1980 marked the beginning of a major
new phase of American politics. Some signs encouraged this view: A conser-

[45]These are rounded percentages, based on five-way unofficial counts that include votes
for Ed Clark (Libertarian) and Barry Commoner (Citizen). *Congressional Quarterly Weekly Report,*
November 8, 1980, p. 3299.

vative trend that had begun at least as early as 1978 was still running, and the Republicans achieved the remarkable feat of winning control of the Senate for the first time since 1955. Also, later analyses might show that some groups were shifting their political loyalty. For example, Reagan did well enough with blue-collar workers to carry all of the big industrial states. Some former Democrats, now labeled "neoconservatives," seemed to be well on their way to a home in the Republican party. There was also a good deal of speculation late in 1980 about the possibility of restructuring the Republic's constitutional and political practices.[46]

On the other hand, there was considerable negativism in the 1980 election. One often heard that voters were faced with choosing "the lesser of two evils." Although one could easily interpret the results in partisan terms, special interest groups and candidate organizations contributed the most conspicuous campaign support activity, not Democratic or Republican regulars as such. Also, turnout was down for the fifth consecutive time in presidential elections. That the Republicans had an opportunity to become a strong new majority party was entirely possible. Whether they would make the most of that opportunity, only time would tell.

---

[46]Kevin Phillips, "An American Parliament," *Harper's,* November 1980, pp. 14–21.

4

Social Forces

Sometimes particular societies take on energies that give them an influence entirely disproportionate to their size. Greece, Rome, and Great Britain are the most familiar examples from the past. Sweden today is inward-looking and peaceful, but in the seventeenth century, Swedes rallied behind an expansionist monarchy and for a time the country was a major European power. The Mongols provide an even less familiar example. This obscure community in central Asia developed an advanced military machine late in the twelfth century and used it to spread in all directions. By 1256, after the death of Genghis Khan, Mongols had established tributary relationships over a land mass much larger than the Roman Empire at its greatest: It included most of the territory governed today by China, the Soviet Union, Iran, Afghanistan, and Pakistan. However, military force could not sustain Mongol power, and by 1300 the empire was disintegrating.

The dynamism of American society will not last forever, but we can hope that the total American experience will be more instructive than that of the Mongols. American influence has cultural and organizational dimensions as well as a military one. This country has profoundly influenced the world's ideas of liberty and self-government. Its novel forms of mass culture, leisure, and consumer tastes have penetrated societies around the globe.

The United States is a complex amalgam of many groups. If not a "melting pot," its people have been less homogeneous than the Mongols and probably more anxious about their common identity. The United States pioneered mass participation in politics, economics, and culture. Forces of idealism, self-interest, and change continue to shape the nation's politics. American idealism is distinctive and often pervasive in its practical effects. Science and technology have been engines of change, and a gospel of individualism, coupled with the particular circumstances of American life, have shaped people's notions of their self-interest.

NATURE OF MODERN LIFE

The later stages of modernization have produced a society never foreseen in earlier periods. New modes of production and technology, new capacities for communication and movement have brought exciting modifications in the way people relate to work, family, local community, and government. However, the changes have also been unsettling. The workings of society have become ever more puzzling, and nobody is sure of where the changes will lead. Basic understandings about how the individual relates to other human beings seem increasingly uncertain. Intellectuals have proposed different concepts—some quite pessimistic—to explain the modern condition.

Mass Society

Party politics goes hand in hand with mass politics, and mass politics is presumably a reflection of what might be called a mass society. In its actual usage, however, *mass society* has almost always been a loaded term. Sigmund Neumann noted many years ago that "the masses" are often referred to "with a moral undercurrent: the canaille [rabble or riffraff], the great unwashed, the rebellious masses, the eager masses, etc."[1] An important strand of twentieth-century thought stresses the impersonality of modern life and its tendency to make the individual a standardized item of mass culture and mass marketing. In this context, "mass" is likely to mean an aggregate whose members do not differ significantly in group or individual terms.[2]

Images of mass society often include the bureaucratic element in modern life. Early in this century Max Weber considered standardized bureaucratic practices to be superior to the piecemeal, often corrupt, administrative arrangements of earlier aristocratic regimes. He also believed that modern bureaucracy and social equality reinforced each other. Bureaucracy tended to support social leveling in the interest of recruiting people on a wider scale. Social leveling tended to support bureaucracy because it eliminated arbitrary privileges that had often limited administrative efficiency in the past. For him, leveling and bureaucratization were complementary aspects of "modern mass democracy."[3]

The critic of mass society can be either for or against "the masses," and the term can therefore be used with either "left" or "right" political

[1]Sigmund Neumann, *Permanent Revolution* (New York: Harper & Row, Inc., 1942), p. 102.
[2]William Kornhauser, "Mass Society," in *International Encyclopedia of the Social Sciences,* ed. David L. Sills (New York: Macmillan Inc., and The Free Press, 1968), X, 58. See also Kornhauser's *The Politics of Mass Society* (New York: The Free Press, 1959). For an extended critique of mass society concepts, see Daniel Bell, "America as a Mass Society," in *The End of Ideology,* rev. ed., ed. Daniel Bell (New York: Collier Books, 1962), pp. 21–38.
[3]H. H. Gerth and C. Wright Mills, eds., *From Max Weber: Essays in Sociology* (London: Kegan Paul, Trench, Trubner & Co., Ltd., 1947), pp. 224–248.

connotations. Antidemocratic conservatives have sometimes believed that the masses were fundamentally incompetent. Ortega y Gasset, for example, likened them to spoiled children, who in displacing their betters, had rejected all models or standards from the past. However, those sympathetic to the masses often feared that they would be the victims of modern politics. Thus, C. Wright Mills stated that "the classic community of publics" was being transformed into a "society of masses." That is, most people were less and less likely to find themselves in a situation where they could express opinions, answer back, find outlets for effective action, and maintain their privacy against governmental intrusion.[4]

William Kornhauser has combined the viewpoints of the "left" and "right" into a single theory. He argues that the key element common to both is that mass society leaves the individual naked to the larger society, regardless of the individual's social position. Authentic groups that mediate between the individual and society become weak; elites as well as masses become vulnerable to each other. If such tendencies are well advanced, social standards may become both uniform and fluid, and people may become susceptible to movements that promise to restore the lost sense of community and legitimate authority.

In any of its versions, the notion of mass society can easily induce melancholy thoughts about the possibilities of modern electoral politics. To some it may imply that equal voting rights merely reflect false standards of numerical superiority. Just as audience size tends to be the debasing standard of mass culture, so the numerical weight of opinion may become the inappropriate criterion for what is acceptable in politics. One may wonder if public opinion is not merely the end result of propaganda, and in substance little more than a slogan for whatever is considered popular. As meaningful deliberation and discussion disappear, and as individuals in the society lose a sense of authentic participation, one may expect that people will come to feel alienated. Perhaps those who can mobilize large numbers of supporters, usually leaders of mass parties, can develop great power in some cases. In other cases one suspects that bureaucratic structures retain power, with the rest of the system perpetuating symbols of democracy that have lost their substance.[5]

The mass society idea contains important elements of truth. But in the United States at least, there are a number of counterconsiderations.

1. The twentieth century has improved the quality of life enjoyed by most Americans. Although this is most conspicuously true with respect to creature comforts, it is also true with respect to art, literature, and music. Significant numbers of people read books, attend concerts, and go to plays. People will turn out for classical ballet and modern dance not only in New

[4]C. Wright Mills, *The Power Elite* (New York: Oxford University Press, 1957), pp. 302–304; Jose Ortega y Gasset, *The Revolt of the Masses* (London: George Allen & Unwin, Ltd., 1932), pp. 11–29, 63–64. This work was first published in Spanish in 1930.

[5]Some of these ideas appear in a slightly less pessimistic form in Kornhauser, "Mass Society," pp. 60, 63.

York and San Francisco, but also in Sandusky, Wilkes-Barre, Terre Haute, and Des Moines. Even though ethics have become secularized, the general sensitivity to ethical issues may be greater than in earlier times.

2. Administrative coordination has obviously increased in many aspects of American life, and most people are vulnerable to bureaucratic influence. However, an unprecedented increase in leisure time permits more people than ever before to live beyond the immediate control of the administered work place. Also, organizational discipline seems to be getting weaker rather than stronger, with a variety of work patterns replacing chain-of-command relationships. Work in modern, complex organizations can even have liberating effects rather than the deadening influences sometimes attributed to Weber's concept.

3. There is no evidence that ordinary people are inferior, and the notion that ruling aristocrats were better than ordinary people can be dismissed as simple prejudice. Jefferson's views on eighteenth-century European monarchs are instructive:

> Louis XVI was a fool, of my own knowledge. . . . The King of Spain was a fool, and of Naples the same. . . . The King of Sardinia was a fool. All these were Bourbons. The queen of Portugal, a Braganza, was an idiot by nature. And so was the King of Denmark. The King of Prussia . . . was a mere hog in body as well as mind. Gustavus of Sweden and Joseph of Austria, were really crazy, and George of England, you know, was in a straight waistcoat.[6]

4. American society may not be as impersonal as some have thought. Even in urban areas, close-knit neighborhoods can still be found, and kin relationships are often very important. Friendship groups are nearly universal, and a substantial minority of urban dwellers attend church at least once a month. Leisure activities frequently involve small groups. The notion of mass society does not prepare us for the enormous relaxation of conformity that has occurred in recent years or for the vitality of modern American society.

5. For ordinary people, the close-knit communities of times past may have been qualitatively inferior to the more cosmopolitan and stimulating modern communities of today. Modern urban life undoubtedly does produce some alienation, but it also offers privacy and freedom.

6. Mass society theorists warn us against equating democracy with government by public opinion. However, American democracy does not act simply on the basis of mass opinion. Decisions of government are so numerous and complex that popular opinion can guide only a few of them. Our governmental system includes the strongest deliberative body in the world,

---

[6] *Thomas Jefferson on Democracy,* selected and arranged by Saul K. Padover (New York: Penguin Books, 1946), p. 26, as cited by Robert A. Dahl, *Democracy in the United States,* 3rd ed. (Chicago: Rand McNally College Publishing Company, 1976), pp. 125–126.

and it must be responsible to a complex network of group associations. Constitutional freedoms continue to be strongly emphasized in American politics.

Mass opinion is not necessarily the inauthentic product of propaganda; in fact, there may be inherent limits on the effectiveness of propaganda campaigns in a modern multigroup society. Messages available to the mass public are becoming more diverse rather than more similar, and the danger of fragmentation may well be greater than the danger of uniform opinions.[7]

The fact that public officials and major policies must attract some measure of popularity if they are to succeed may well offer the best long-run prospects for stable government. If elections are free, it is difficult to imagine a fairer or more reliable test of one's right to exercise authority than the ability to get more votes than one's opponents. To be successful, politicians must be able to get reelected, and for this momentary popularity is not enough. In this respect modern politics is different from some aspects of mass culture in which performers obtain only temporary recognition. Mass parties are adjuncts to authentic democracy in the modern era and, as such, need to be analyzed on their own terms, not prejudged on some assumption that makes democracy impossible.

It is not my intention to have you leave this topic thinking that it has been neatly disposed of. Although one can defend the quality of modern life in a fair comparison with earlier conditions, we cannot ignore troubling features that mass society notions help us to understand better. The insistence on judging the quality of culture and social institutions is valuable, and the theory of mass society plausibly indicates how authentic democracy might be lost.

Postindustrial Society

A somewhat more optimistic prospect is that of the postindustrial society. If mass society carries with it the pessimistic associations of standardized factory routines, postindustrial society centers on the freer life of the information-processing institutions—universities, think tanks, and the like. This concept accommodates some of the deficiencies of the mass society idea and opens up new questions about the direction of modern life. The ideas received their main exposition in a book by Daniel Bell published in 1973, and the term still enjoys a certain cachet in American social science.[8]

In Bell's discussion, postindustrial society is the sequel to earlier agrarian and industrial societies; it differs from them in its economic system, characteristics of the population, and dominant social values. Professional, technical, and managerial work tasks dominate the postindustrial economy, and theoretical knowledge plays a central role in it. Technology and research come to be more important than physical capital. The population enjoys unprecedented affluence and leisure, and a college education

[7]For an optimistic view of democratic prospects in modern society, see Robert E. Lane, *Political Ideology* (New York: The Free Press, 1962).

[8]Daniel Bell, *The Coming of Post-Industrial Society: A Venture in Social Forecasting* (New York: Basic Books, 1973).

becomes a general norm. Values cease to be centered on work and come to embrace quality-of-life concerns.

In contrast to mass society, postindustrial society easily accommodates the existence of complex organizations and thus alows us to be skeptical of the ability of organizations to exert comprehensive bureaucratic control. The postindustrial image implies more varied forms of individual expression than seem likely in the advent of a homogeneous mass. It also offers the hope of purposive change spearheaded by advances in theoretical knowledge.

Apparently, postindustrial society has no specifically political component. Reasonable people could draw various political implications from the elements cited. For example, the growing weakness of political parties and the rise of single-issue concerns in the 1970s are compatible with the theory, but on the other hand higher educational levels and the prevailing mood of political disenchantment could as easily account for these trends. At one point, Bell seemed to suggest that scientists and research men displace businessmen as dominant figures in the postindustrial scheme of stratification and power.[9] But he did not press this notion and in the 1980s it is difficult to conceive of scientists and researchers as a ruling class.

A study based on survey data from a number of Western European democracies indicates a shift in values toward quality-of-life concerns among younger age groups. Its author believes that larger proportions of the Western publics are developing the political skills necessary to participate in political decisions. There is also, he thinks, a new emphasis on belonging, esteem, and self-realization. His analysis suggests that the joint impact of these trends is affecting politics in profound ways. Concerns centered on personal choices are becoming more apparent than concerns about class or occupational interest. Nation-states find declining support, and localistic "tribal" loyalties on the one hand and transnational or supernational affiliations on the other loom larger. Stated differently, important segments have a heightened interest in the autonomy of local cultural areas, such as the Basques in Spain and the Welsh in England, but these same segments also find the notion of a united Europe (or even a united world) more appealing. Persons in authority are experiencing a declining ability to channel popular demands, and groups concerned with new issues are challenging them.

Those on the leading edge of these changes are "postmaterialists." When interviewed these people place greater emphasis on "protecting freedom of expression" and "giving people more say in government decisions," than on "maintenance of law and order," and "fighting rising prices." Even though postmaterialists appear in the interviews in limited numbers, their skills may enable them to exert a multiplier effect. Compared to other people, postmaterialists are much more likely to favor social change and to desire a less impersonal society. In choosing a job, they seek a "feeling of accomplishment" and "working with people they like." The author of this study sees such values as essentially positive in their effects. He acknowl-

[9]Ibid., p. 359.

edges that the trend could be disastrous if pursued to excess but believes that so far postmaterialism has represented an essentially healthy redressment of balance.[10]

Others do not find the political implications so reassuring. In one view, such a society drastically increases demands on government without improving its capacity to govern effectively. Too much popular interest and participation can produce a political stalemate; it can result in a persisting gap between perceived and actual possibilities of governmental action and, therefore, widespread frustration. This scholar foresees more intense conflicts and wonders whether postindustrial societies will be capable of pursuing foreign policy goals that require military force.[11]

Individualistic Society

Individualism cuts across both the mass society and the postindustrial portraits. One might even say that as social critiques these are only updated versions of concerns first expressed in Greece in the fifth century B.C. It is the apparent loss of individualism that is the main point of the mass society idea. And it is the possible enhancement of individualism that accounts for at least part of the appeal of the postindustrial prospect.

Individualism espouses the idea that the interests of the individual are or ought to be paramount. American culture has a strong tendency to stress this in distinctive ways. To a remarkable degree, Americans assume that family, group, class, community—from the smallest to the most inclusive—exist to serve individuals. People are not only permitted to be independent of such entities, they are expected to be.

For Alexis de Tocqueville (one of the first to use the term), *individualism* is a disposition to live somewhat apart from society in the circle of one's friends and family, leaving the society at large to itself.[12] This remarkable observer of the American scene of the 1830s was not certain that he approved of America's individualism. Although his appraisal was balanced, Tocqueville feared that people who were engrossed in private matters might in the long run be vulnerable to the forces of conformity and despotic government.

Compared to the social apartness Tocqueville properly emphasized, other possible aspects of individualism may be more positive. These include:

Autonomy—the capacity of individuals to make their own choices without being subject to threats or internalized compulsions

Competence—the capacity of individuals to influence as well as be influenced by their environment

Privacy—the capacity of individuals to be free from surveillance by groups, communities, or government

---

[10]Ronald Inglehart, *The Silent Revolution* (Princeton, N.J.: Princeton University Press, 1977), pp. 5, 392.

[11]Samuel P. Huntington, "Postindustrial Politics: How Benign Will It Be?" *Comparative Politics*, 6 (January 1974), 163–191.

[12]A. D. Lindsay, "Individualism," in *Encyclopedia of the Social Sciences* (New York: Macmillan, Inc., 1932), VII, 674.

Variety—the capacity of individuals to develop along lines uniquely suited to their personal nature

Unfortunately, these more desirable aspects of individualism may reflect optimistic hopes rather than real social possibilities. Can the individual who hopes to be independent achieve this in a society of increasing interdependence? Is it realistic to suppose that the single individual can significantly influence his or her environment without the assistance of others? To what extent are ordinary people willing to assert their need to be different?

Traditionally, it was the privileged few who enjoyed such values, and the question of whether it is possible for large numbers of people to share them is still open. The larger question turns on claims ordinary people now make to all kinds of objects, services, and experiences that may be in limited supply. Some tend to be devalued as more people enjoy them—a crowded beach or camping site, for example. Power may be another example. If a few people share power, each individual member of the ruling group may experience a real sense of possessing it. If power is distributed widely, however, nobody may feel influential.

Not all things are debased when they are enjoyed by larger numbers of people. Many people can enjoy a Beethoven quartet originally composed for a small circle of aristocratic patrons, if they are willing to give it patient attention. Even the more esoteric contemporary art and literature, with its private meanings and avoidance of mass appeal, imposes no *numerical* limitation on those who may enjoy it without damaging it. Indeed, a middle-income American today may be in a position to enjoy more objects and experiences of genuine value than the most wealthy potentates of earlier times. Then too, some things (such as an efficient system of roads) cannot be enjoyed by anybody unless they are also available to large numbers of people, or even everybody.

The American commitment to individualism is so natural and pervasive that it is difficult for us to view the key ideas with detachment. The chief weakness of individualism is that it stands in an uneasy relation to the needs of society. People may think of society as nothing but a collection of individuals. Or they may feel that there can be no compromise between individualism and collectivism. In truth, each of us has important personal characteristics deriving from the society we live in. The individual and his or her society interact and depend on each other. By avoiding this truer notion, extreme individualism does a disservice to both the individual and the society. It takes the desired characteristics of individualism as something innate rather than something to be achieved, and it makes insufficient allowance for the fact that the society has tasks that require coordinated action for the good of all.

Individualism can also degenerate into self-indulgence. Thus, Christopher Lasch argues that competitive individualism and the self-awareness movement (among other things) have reached a dead end characterized by increasingly narcissistic traits. The narcissistic culture, says Lasch, is disinterested in the past and imagines this disinterest to be progressive and optimistic. In reality, however, this attitude masks "the despair of a society that cannot face the future." The new narcissist "demands immediate gratification, and lives in a state of restless, perpetually unsatisfied desire."[13] Since it is so disturbing, one may hope that Lasch's portrayal exaggerates the recent loss of purpose in American society.

Individualism may produce a widespread reluctance to collaborate with others in political activity. Except for the few who are active in election campaigns, many people wish to do little more than vote. Citizen-initiated attempts to pool votes are rare, and many citizens feel that their candidate and party choices are private—not a platform from which to influence others or to seek purposive control of the government. These tendencies are very strong, and they award considerable power to election professionals willing to garner votes. At the same time, they weaken support for political organization from the mass electorate. Lasch's book may be something of an example of this. In asking that we get hold of ourselves, he properly emphasizes the need to restore a concern for the past. He also suggests that we renew the moral discipline of work while divorcing it from the defense of property rights. However, Lasch appears to be in flight from the more important arenas of politics. His political program consists of vague gestures in the direction of "localism, self-help, and community action."[14]

THE DEMOGRAPHY OF AMERICAN POLITICS

Politicians and academic analysts alike try to comprehend the mysteries of politics by looking at people's age, sex, region, ethnic background, residence, occupation, and so forth. These basic population characteristics often shape people's experiences and thus reveal a good deal about forces of attraction and repulsion in politics. The new social conditions, under whatever label, change things somewhat, but one should not exaggerate their effects. In any community, there may be some "narcissists," but many more people are probably struggling in unexotic ways with the tasks of ordinary living. Chances are that the young computer programmer down the block has not read Daniel Bell; his "postmaterialism" may not be as striking as his tendency to think about politics in ways that are predictable from his social background.

Class

Politics is sometimes a battle between haves and have nots. The things people can "have" are quite varied, but social class is often taken to center on money, education, and occupational status. American society places considerable emphasis on achievement and materialistic standards of evaluation. In such a society, money can perhaps buy other valued things—up to a point, even things like respect and affection.

Astute observers have recognized from the beginning the potential for conflict between haves and have nots in American society. Alexander Hamil-

[13]Christopher Lasch, *The Culture of Narcissism: American Life in an Age of Diminishing Expectation* (New York: W. W. Norton & Co., Inc., 1978), pp. xvi, xviii.
[14]Ibid., pp. 235–236.

ton stated in the Constitutional Convention that "all communities divide themselves into the few and the many. The first are the rich and well born, and the other the mass of the people." In *Federalist Paper No. 10* James Madison wrote that "the most common and durable source of factions has been the various and unequal distribution of property."

Economic inequality in the United States tends to be insufficiently appreciated because modern Americans (unlike the framers of the Constitution) tend to stress distribution of *income,* rather than distribution of *property.* Although property ownership is much more concentrated today than it was in the late eighteenth century, the average person thinks of property as tangible possessions, such as one's house, car, and furniture, and overlooks property represented by commercial real estate, corporate stock, bonds, and demand deposits. Holders of considerable wealth do, of course, own a greater share of the ordinary objects thought of as property. But their most startling economic advantage is in the holding of intangible assets. Thus, in 1972 the best estimate was that the top 0.5 percent of wealth holders possessed 49.3 percent of all corporate stock, and 52.2 percent of all bonds. This group of one million persons also owned 10.1 percent of all real estate (commercial as well as personal) and 8.5 percent of all personally held cash and demand deposits.[15]

It is true that ownership no longer constitutes control of America's giant corporate enterprises. The dissatisfied stockholder simply sells his securities and invests elsewhere while control stays with corporate management. However, there are many family-owned businesses and other small units, far from penury, in which ownership does constitute control. (Many local newspapers fall in this category.) Moreover, corporate managers often belong to the top property-owning group, either initially or after working their way up the corporate ladder.

Income derived from large property holdings has many advantages over income from salaries or wages. The income is more secure over the long run if the property is managed with a reasonable degree of prudence.

Table 4-1
Top Shares of Income and Wealth in the United States

	1950[a]	1955[b]	1960[c]	1965	1972[d]
Percent of Family Income Earned by Top Five Percent	17.3%	16.4%	15.9%	15.5%	15.5%
Percent of Personal Wealth Held by Top One Percent	20.8%	24.0%	23.8%	23.4%	20.7%

[a]Personal wealth value for 1949. [b]Personal wealth value for 1954.
[c]Personal wealth value for 1958. [d]Family income value for 1973.
Source: Bureau of the Census, *Statistical Abstract 1977,* pp. 443, 464.

[15]U.S. Census, *Statistical Abstract of the United States 1977,* p. 464.

Since property can often be shifted about, the owner is better able to take advantage of tax loopholes. Those with substantial wealth have more free time to devote to political and other interests, are not physically tied to a limited geographic area, and can engage in political activities without fear of economic constraints from employers or customers.

Have nots are not as easily pinpointed as the large wealth holders. The group can be defined arbitrarily, of course, by taking any given percentage of lowest income earners. If one thinks of the have nots as the lowest fifth of income earners (usually receiving only about 5 percent of all income), the category includes some persons who are poor in a relative rather than an absolute sense. Even the poorest Americans of today may be better off than the poor of earlier times, and estimates of what constitutes poverty vary widely. In 1978 the Social Security Administration estimated that 25 million Americans earned too little to cover the necessities of life. However, a Portland State University economist claimed that 7.7 million were poor, and the Congressional Budget Office estimated their numbers at about 15.2 million.[16]

Again, wealth is only one of many desired values. Have nots could be defined as those short on affection, health, enlightenment, and capacity to sacrifice for the future. To some extent, low income correlates with illness, lack of self-respect, and other undesired characteristics. Whatever their actual number, the have nots are a heterogeneous group. Some poor people are simply victims of racial and ethnic discrimination. Others are poor because they are handicapped, lack parents, lack children, are blind, old, ill, neglected, or in jail. The poor are quite numerous, even in the most conservative estimate, but their condition and lack of political resources has usually prevented them from having an important impact on electoral politics.

Theories that emphasize the importance of class conflict must contend with the real possibility that the middle class, not the upper class, dominates American life. The matter is further complicated by the presence of a "working class" as well as a "middle class."

"If you were asked to use one of four names for your social class, which would you say you belong in?"

"Lower class"	4.8%
"Working class"	47.3
"Middle class"	44.6
"Upper class"	2.7
Don't know or no answer	.6
TOTAL	100.0%
	(N = 8,369)

Source: National Opinion Research Center (NORC), *General Social Survey, 1972–1977*, cumulative codebook, question 126, p. 120.

[16]Robert J. Wagman, "Number of America's Poor is Exaggerated," *Indianapolis Star,* April 5, 1978, p. 25.

The middle class is much more influential than the working class. It staffs educational establishments, sciences, professions, media, and middle-management positions in government and business. In its upper reaches, the American middle class also constitutes a very important part of the property-owning group. The haves are, as we have seen, quite a small segment of society. Nevertheless, in 1972, 78.9 percent of all assets held by persons with a gross estate of $60,000 or more was held by those whose gross estate values were between $60,000 and $200,000.[17] Although such individuals were far from being the widows and orphans extolled by Chambers of Commerce, they were not really rich—at least not as that term is understood by Americans.

America's middle class has been under pressure for at least a generation. Postmodern values often seem to deprecate the good qualities associated with the middle class—moderation, sobriety, hard work, desire to achieve, thrift, and prudence—almost as much as such less desirable qualities as materialism, anti-intellectualism, and complacency. For many Americans, the term *middle class* has a negative connotation. The inner torments of American life reflected in unprecedented divorce rates and rebellious children appear to be centered in the middle class. The increasing role of large bureaucratic organizations may well be generating pervasive insecurity in its midst. Ruinous inflation threatens the middle class, and its members are oppressed by a sense of pervasive waste in government programs aimed at health, education, welfare, and urban areas. The middle class pays the bulk of the bills for government services, and it does so over a steeply progressive range of the federal income tax schedule.

Although those identifying with the working class are still slightly more numerous than those in the middle class, working-class ranks are gradually declining as patterns of education and occupational choice change. Working-class people have blue-collar occupations for the most part. They tend to invest less heavily in the future and to place a lower value on privacy and self-expression. The life cycle tends to be shorter, with first job, marriage, first child, and old age coming sooner than in the middle class. Working-class people also tend to join fewer organizations and to participate in all forms of political activity to a lesser degree. The differences between working-class and middle-class people must be stated as tendencies rather than uniformities, but they are very real. Work roles and education are involved as much as income, and they affect many aspects of life.

If we make our counts within national categories, we tend to blur the reality of social class in the United States. Class alignments are most tangible in small towns, where a high degree of consensus often sorts and grades individuals into specific categories associated with particular residential areas and behaviors. Aggregating by class is probably most meaningful where the haves are concerned. Large wealth holders are acutely conscious of their small numbers, stand out from the run of ordinary people in all parts of the United States, and are highly aware of each other. This awareness and

---

[17]U.S. Census, *Statistical Abstract of the United States 1977*, p. 463.

sense of mutuality are especially pronounced among wealth holders of established families.

Regional disparities in the United States have traditionally reinforced the conflict potential of economic differences. However, regional differences are on the decline. Since the Civil War, people in the Northeast have enjoyed higher per capita incomes than any other of the standard regions delineated by the census. The northeastern states led America's nineteenth-century industrial expansion and forged its railroad, banking, commercial, and cultural muscle. The Civil War reversed relative standings of the South and Midwest. Between the Civil War and 1940, the South assumed the role of a semicolonial area in a nation dominated by the economic might of the Northeast. The Midwest improved its relative position in these years, and net differences in wealth between Northeast and Midwest are now rather slight. The South's disadvantage vis à vis the Northeast, though still substantial, is no greater than *before* the Civil War. As Table 4–2 indicates, the distribution of both population and income in the United States has evened out over the years.

Table 4–2
Regional Income Disparities in American History

	1840	1880	1920	1940	1960	1970
Northeast						
Income Disparity	134	141	129	122	112	110
Population Share	39.2%	28.9%	28.0%	27.2%	24.9%	24.1%
Midwest						
Income Disparity	71	96	98	98	100	100
Population Share	19.9%	34.7%	32.1%	30.3%	28.8%	27.9%
West						
Income Disparity	n.a.	186	118	115	107	100
Population Share	n.a.	3.6%	8.7%	10.9%	15.7%	17.1%
South						
Income Disparity	96	52	61	65	76	82
Population Share	40.9%	32.9%	31.2%	31.5%	30.7%	30.9%
Total United States						
Income Disparity	100	100	100	100	100	100
Population Share	100%	100%	100%	100%	100%	100%

Note: Income disparity is an index of per capita income in a region to U.S. per capita income. Figures presented here for the Northeast, Midwest, and South consist of unweighted averages of standard census subregions presented in the source. *Northeast* consists of Maine, New Hampshire, Vermont, Massachusetts, Rhode Island, Connecticut, New York, New Jersey, and Pennsylvania. *Midwest* consists of Ohio, Indiana, Illinois, Michigan, Wisconsin, Minnesota, Iowa, Missouri, North Dakota, South Dakota, Nebraska, and Kansas. *West* consists of Washington, Oregon, California, Alaska, Hawaii, Montana, Idaho, Wyoming, Colorado, New Mexico, Arizona, Utah, and Nevada. *South* consists of Delaware, Maryland, Washington, D.C., Virginia, West Virginia, North Carolina, South Carolina, Georgia, Florida, Kentucky, Tennessee, Alabama, Mississippi, Arkansas, Louisiana, Oklahoma, and Texas.

Source: Bureau of the Census, *Historical Statistics of the United States*, Washington, D.C., 1975, Part I, pp. 22, 242.

It would appear that class differences, while very real in the United States, are not homogeneous enough to create a deeply divided national society. The have-not lower class has the most to gain from agitation of class-related issues, but it is the least unified. Two very large classes interpose themselves between the haves and have nots and provide a buffer. The middle class and working class have conflicts of their own, but there is a weaker objective basis for those conflicts since both classes share many of the benefits of the American economy. Also, class viewpoints do not always converge with economic interest. Many upper-class people are liberal in their willingness to help the have nots through public and private channels. One even hears occasionally of a liberal alliance of upper and lower orders against the conservative middle. The affluence of American society has helped prevent the framers' fears of an alliance of all the ordinary people against the property-owning class from being realized.

Ethnicity and Culture

Ethnic groups bond people through a common race, language, religion, or combination of these factors. The United States is not unique in having many different ethnic groups. The world's ethnic communities are much more numerous than the number of nation-states, and most nations are therefore multiethnic. What distinguishes America's ethnic situation is the fact that the country was settled by immigrants who, with few exceptions, made a decisive break with their ancestral cultures. Once in the United States, the members of most groups continued to move about: They tended to cluster in particular neighborhoods, but no one region became the preserve of the particular ethnic group. Most newcomers "voluntarily" accepted English as the national language, and a definitive American version came to be spoken with only minor variations in accent and dialect.

There are exceptions, of course, to this general picture. Hispanic Americans maintain closer ties with the parent culture, and their language differences may persist indefinitely. Some areas of Indian settlement are large enough to perhaps be considered regions. A few Americans speak French, Italian, Polish, and many other languages within local community groupings. In general, however, immigrant cultures have been broadly diffused throughout the country. America's religious groups have shown similar patterns. Even among America's Jews, the most concentrated of the major religious groups, only about a third live in New York City, where they comprise at most about 25 percent of the city's population. Most Jews live outside New York City, and those within tend to congregate in different residential areas. One of these areas, the borough of Manhattan, has very mixed residential patterns, with the exception of Washington Heights.

The general diffusion of immigrant cultures has had mixed effects on social conflict in America. On the one hand, most people have shed many outward signs of their traditional culture, and this has surely lowered the potential for conflict. On the other hand, ethnic identifications have persisted to a surprising degree. The National Opinion Research Center surveys asked, "From what countries or part of the world did your ancestors come?" Only 21.7 percent of the respondents cannot be assigned unambiguously to one nation, to "Africa," or to the "American Indian" category. Almost half of those who cannot be assigned name *two* areas and cannot choose between them. One might have expected a much greater loss of ethnic identity, if only through intermarriage among white ethnic groups.

Diffusion of cultures probably *increases* the potential for ethnic conflict in some respects. Diffusion reduces the amount of difference between groups, but it increases the number of friction points at personal, neighborhood, and community levels. We have seen above that one loses touch with social class in the United States by aggregating within broad national categories. A similar point can be made about cultural differences. At the community and neighborhood level, ethnic differences are often palpable, especially in the eastern part of the nation. This undoubtedly accounts for some of the country's high level of crime and violence.

On balance, however, geographic diffusion has worked against segmental divisions on cultural lines. Localized tensions do not easily add up to national cleavages. The geographical expanse of the country is large, and the number of groups involved is too great.

Differences in education, occupation, and income among ethnic groups tend to be linked to class position. However, these linkages are only partial, and you should be alert to exceptions. Thus, at least until recently, Jews have enjoyed lower status in American society, yet their average wealth is greater than many other groups. Contrary to popular impression, most of this wealth does not come from positions in major commercial or financial institutions. Jewish wealth is to a large extent derived from small businesses or professional positions. In "Elmtown," Hollingshead found that many people of the lowest class (Class V) were of "American stock" that had come to the community before the Civil War. Yet Class V also included distinct Irish, Norwegian, and Polish residential areas.[18]

Religion can to some extent divide ethnic groups that might otherwise be more unified. White Americans of English and northern European cultural origins have historically tended to enjoy higher status and influence than those of eastern and southern European origins. However, some of these white "Anglo-Saxon" Americans are Catholic. Those who are Protestant (or WASP) divide among different denominations that are often accompanied by status distinctions. When religion defines the group, as with America's Jews, differences in national origin can be quite significant.

The conflict potential of religious differences in America should not be overemphasized. Religious separatism was a major source of political conflict in sixteenth- and seventeenth-century America. However, the feeling began to grow quite early that the various Christian confessions were not separate sects but rather members of a single family. An evangelical fervor that began in the eighteenth century tended to bring the denominations together. Although a demogagic strain in nineteenth-century American Protestantism may have fortified hostility towards Catholics, the more

[18]August B. Hollingshead, *Elmtown's Youth and Elmtown Revisited* (New York: John Wiley & Sons, Inc., 1975), pp. 80–81; Nathan Glazer and Daniel Patrick Moynihan, *Beyond the Melting Pot* (Cambridge, Mass.: The M.I.T. Press, 1970), pp. 147–153.

united Protestantism seems to have reached out in important ways towards Indians and Negroes.[19] Despite a recent resurgence of evangelical religion, American society has been mostly preoccupied with secular concerns. Protestantism may have contributed to stress on material achievement, but if so the effects have not been limited to Protestant Americans. Conflict between Catholics and Protestants, often virulent in the past, today seems to be largely restricted to the issues of aid to parochial schools and abortion. Even here, the cleavages are really specific to the issues—by no means a simple matter of Protestant versus Catholic.

There has also been a self-amused and buoyant liberation from older pecking orders. The WASP is distinctly dull and passé in American popular culture, and ethnicity is "in." Even so, the exclusion of certain groups persists in corporate circles and among the property-owning class. Major political offices have become accessible to all only at a rather slow rate, and some ethnic minorities, particularly Hispanics and Indians, continue to experience great difficulty.

Historically, America's deepest divisions were between South and non-South, and between whites and blacks. The two conflicts were intertwined, and our failure to manage them produced a struggle that ranks as the eighth most violent quarrel to occur in any part of the world since 1820.[20]

Over the past century South/non-South antagonism has eroded practically to the vanishing point. Concentration of blacks in the South has been declining overall (see Table 4-3), and economic development is making the region more like the rest of the country. Caste distinctions are still evident between whites and blacks in the South, but the apparatus of official repression has been largely dismantled. Blacks now constitute an important segment of the southern electorate. Their level of voting approaches that of whites at similar economic levels, and they have elected many black officials. The power of white southern politicians to prevent federal support of civil rights policies ended in the 1950s and 1960s. A distinctive southern culture no longer serves as a major obstacle to the cause of black advancement.

In some respects, the potential for black/white conflict is still great. Unlike Latin American countries, which recognize gradations of racial mixture, the perception of race in the United States tends to be polarized: One is either black or white; blacks retain outward signs of ethnic difference that have become blurred among other ethnic groups. Relative improvement of blacks' economic, social, and political position has not necessarily lessened the potential for conflict between the races. Black gains are vulnerable to economic fluctuations, and a stubborn residue of significant disadvantage persists. Eliminating it may require increased assertiveness that could easily be channeled into racial conflict. In the years since 1915 massive migrations have produced a significantly more urban black population in both southern and nonsouthern regions. This has undoubtedly tended to stimulate racial

[19]On these matters, see Timothy Smith, "Congregation, State and Denomination," *William and Mary Quarterly,* 25 (April 1968), P 156–176; and Sidney Mead, "Denominationalism; The Shape of Protestantism in America," *Church History,* 23 (1954), 291–320.
[20]Lewis F. Richardson, *Statistics of Deadly Quarrels* (Pittsburgh, Pa.: Boxwood Press, 1960).

Table 4-3
Residential Location of Blacks and Whites

	1970 Black Population in Millions	1970 White Population in Millions
Non-South		
Central City Metropolitan	8.1	34.3
Metropolitan Ring	1.7	53.9
Nonmetropolitan	.7	39.8
South		
Central City Metropolitan	4.5	10.8
Metropolitan Ring	1.8	14.7
Nonmetropolitan	5.9	23.9
TOTAL	22.8	177.4

Source: Census data presented by Karl and Alma Tauber, "The Black Population of the United States," in *The Black American Reference Book*, ed. Mabel Smythe (Englewood Cliffs, N.J.: Prentice-Hall, Inc., 1976), p. 187. Numbers may not add to total due to rounding.

consciousness and mobilization for political action. Discrimination creates special injustices in a market economy based on free choice. Thus, despite lower incomes, blacks probably have to pay more for equivalent housing because most black housing is still heavily segregated. Housing choices determine neighborhood services and schools, and most black children must attend schools in which per capita school expenditures are lower. Blacks continue to obtain poorer jobs than whites with comparable levels of education, and they continue to receive lower pay than whites with similar educations and occupations.[21] Blacks also face other socially derived problems, including teen-age unemployment, high levels of incarceration, and high levels of victimization by criminals.

Nevertheless, racial conflict in the United States could turn out to be manageable well short of violence. Further changes in the geographic spread of blacks throughout the nation can be expected, even if the change is not on the scale of the past sixty years. Relative to whites, the black population is still skewed toward young age groups. But fertility rates may be converging, and this could lessen the age differences in another twenty years or so. Such a development could ease tensions related to teen-age unemployment, school dropouts, and street crime. In the past generation, gaps between the two races have narrowed, and the white majority is more accepting of black rights. Dissatisfaction with remaining racial discrimination will doubtless increase, but blacks today have a larger stake in the society than they once did. If there is no retrograde shift in white racial attitudes, and if the nation can sustain reasonable economic growth, violent racial conflict will probably not occur on a large scale.

[21]Karl and Alma Tauber, "The Black Population of the United States," *The Black American Reference Book*, ed. Mabel Smythe (Englewood Cliffs, N. J.: Prentice-Hall, Inc., 1976), p. 197.

Age and Gender

American women have always been more socially active than their counterparts in most other societies. Interviews conducted in five nations in 1959 and 1960 revealed that the relatively greater propensity of Americans to belong to organizations (compared to the British and Germans) depended primarily on the high rate of organizational membership among American women. Moreover, American women were most likely to report that they had been *officers* of organizations than the women of the other nations; they even exceeded American *men* in this respect.[22]

Numerous studies from more than a dozen countries support the proposition that men have been more likely to participate in politics than women. However, the gap in participation rates between the sexes is usually smaller among high-status people than among those of low status. In the South sex differences are more pronounced among blacks than whites, and in India the more modernized states have higher levels of female voting than the less modernized ones.[23]

Table 4–4 shows that younger American women have now caught up with, and even surpassed, American men in voting turnout. Notice that by 1976, the relatively higher levels of female voting had spread to an older age bracket. Careful analysis by Gerald Pomper mostly confirms a traditional view that political differences between men and women at the mass level are not attributable to gender alone. He reasons that for political differences to

Table 4–4
Spread between Male and Female Voting in Different Age Groups

	1972	1976	
18–20	−1.1%	−3.3%	
21–24	−2.0	−1.7	
25–29	−.4	−2.3	
30–34	+.4	−.7	
35–44	−.8	−1.6	
45–54	+2.1	no difference	Male turnout
			greater below
55–64	+3.2	+3.9	this line
65–74	+8.9	+7.9	
75+	+16.8	+12.8	

Positive percentages indicate greater male turnout; negative percentages indicate greater female turnout. Numbers are based on interviews conducted with large samples after the elections.

Source: U.S. Census, *Current Population Reports*, Series P-20, No. 304, December 1976.

[22]Gabriel Almond and Sidney Verba, *The Civic Culture* (Boston, Mass.: Little, Brown & Company, 1965), pp. 247, 249. The authors speculate that the women's high rates relative to men may have resulted from women belonging to smaller organizations.
[23]Lester Milbrath and M. L. Goel, *Political Participation,* 2nd ed. (Chicago, Ill.: Rand McNally & Company, 1977), pp. 116–118.

occur, there would have to be a differentiation of some sort that would permit men and women to be affected in different ways by the same policy. Even though the women's liberation movement has had pervasive effects, the differentiations are now much *smaller* than before.

> The economic division of labor between the sexes is narrowing, not increasing, as women leave the drudgeries of housework for schools and for jobs similar to those of men. The sexes are not segregating themselves, but coming together—in sports, college, on the job, and in their leisure.[24]

Sex-related differences in attitudes between men and women are neither large nor consistent. Even on abortion, men tend to favor the practice more than women, and more men than women express favorable attitudes towards ERA.

The only substantial and consistent difference Pomper could discover between women and men centered on the use of force in social relations. Women were more likely to view entry into the two worlds wars as mistakes, and they were more dovish on both the Korean and Vietnam wars. Women have tended to approve gentler approaches to urban unrest than men, and women have been more willing to support gun control. In speculating about the political implications of these findings, Pomper suggests that the differences are consistent enough (among "liberated" and "nonliberated" alike) to have a political impact.[25] Women, of course, outnumber men to a slight degree in nearly every age bracket over eighteen, and the disparity tends to increase in older groups.

It should be repeated, however, that these mass level differences are confined for the most part to general opinions and voting turnout. In some forms of political participation, women still appear to operate under serious handicaps of the traditional sort. Thus, only seventeen women served in Congress in 1979, one senator and sixteen representatives. Moreover, men may still have more political efficacy and confidence than women.

Speculation about differences among political generations has long intrigued observers of modern societies. Each new generation may grow up in a distinctive period and be shaped by the political events of its most receptive years. Thus one might expect depressions to make their greatest impression on people just entering the job market, and wars their greatest impression on those who fight in them. Moreover, rapid social change would add to the generation gap. Those who are twenty years old today have no personal memories of World War II or the Korean War; those in their late fifties do. This older group, of course, is in the better position to have greatest impact on political decisions. Outlooks of younger groups have probably been shaped to a greater degree by the themes of television and the values of postindustrial society.

Plausible theory concerning political generations can easily outrun rigorous evidence, and interpretation of available data can be tricky. However, sophisticated analysis of surveys taken over many years do permit

[24]Gerald Pomper, *Voter's Choice* (New York: Harper & Row Publishers, Inc. 1975), p. 68.
[25]Ibid., pp. 68–71, 81–83, 87.

some reliable comparisons. An ingenious analysis by Kristi Anderson suggests that the shift to a Democratic majority in the New Deal occurred mainly because of the new groups that entered the active electorate between 1920 and 1936; the conversion of long-time Republicans played a far less significant role.[26]

Today's youth seem to be responding to the nature of the times rather than the impulses associated with their chronological age. Pomper's careful analysis, for example, contains the following findings:

1. In 1972 young voters were more likely than older ones to be ideological liberals, regardless of party. They were more inclined to define themselves in liberal terms, and they took consistent stands on the issues conventionally associated with liberalism. Generational differences were, however, confined to "life-style" issues rather than to views on economic programs. Such findings were quite marked even among persons with no college education.
2. Younger people with higher education were more inclined in 1972 to want to avoid politics, to reject the idea of a citizen duty to vote, and to feel cynical about the government. (Education has usually been an indicator of more positive feelings.)
3. Vietnam had an especially strong impact on young voters in 1972. Compared to older voters, partisanship affected them less, and policy issues influenced them more.[27]

As social change accelerates, the succession of generations may occur more rapidly. Thus, today's young voters may well be of a different political generation than those only a few years older—Vietnam only a dim memory, Watergate fading, and America's current economic performance a clear and pressing concern. The potential for a changed political system through generational succession is very great, since young people can quickly move into positions of influence in various sectors of American society.

As a major force in American electoral politics, however, the accelerated succession of generations is working against declining birthrates and persistently lower levels of political participation among younger people. For example, in 1976 there were almost 1 million more people in the 18–29 age bracket than in the 45–64 category. Yet, there were almost 5 million more *voters* in the older age group. The U.S. Census projects that by 1990 there will be 3 million fewer people in the 18–24 category than in 1976, and almost 1 million *more* people aged 45–64.[28]

    [26]Kristi Anderson, "Generation, Partisan Shift, and Realignment: A Glance Back to the New Deal," in *The Changing American Voter*, ed. Norman Nie, Sidney Verba, and John Petrocik (Cambridge, Mass.: Harvard University Press, 1976), p. 75. She pooled the results of eight election surveys between 1952 and 1972 which contained items on past party identification and made estimates of party adherence after correcting for changes in the age composition of the population.
    [27]Pomper, *Voter's Choice*, pp. 106, 114–115. For interesting thoughts on the effects of the 1946–1964 "baby boom" see Richard A. Easterlin, *The Impact of Numbers on Personal Welfare* (New York: Basic Books, 1981).
    [28]U.S. Census, Current Population Reports, Series P-20, No. 304, December 1976; U.S. Census, *Statistical Abstract of the United States 1977*, pp. 6–7.

There are also some constraints that limit the influence of young activists. Admittedly, congressional and campaign staff personnel have tended to be astonishingly young in recent years. The weakness of party organization has shifted influence away from the "boss" (usually middle-aged or older) to the young campaign managers, polling experts, media consultants, and field agents. Even in presidential politics very young people have left their mark. However, careers in elective offices often take time to unfold. One study indicated that the age of greatest achievement in politics came a good deal later in life than in other fields.[29] As birthrates decline and life spans increase, the slower pace of traditional American politics could reassert itself.

IMPACT OF TELEVISION

Modern technology occupies a prominent place in all notions of contemporary society, and it has undoubtedly affected politics in profound ways. Yet effects attributable to technological innovations are not of one piece. Artificial satellites have spawned an enormous expansion of wide-area message exchange that may be shifting political perceptions and loyalties in new directions. Jet travel has changed the ambience and itineraries of presidential politics. Computers have helped shape the more sophisticated modern campaign techniques and are beginning to change the way votes are tabulated in some areas. Yet, of all the recent technological innovations, television has an importance that seems to place it in a category by itself.

One can approach the power of television by examining the attempts of certain people to use it as a vehicle of propaganda. Alternatively, one can emphasize the unprecedented nature of the medium itself. Like the hydrogen bomb, the fact that television exists may be more important than the question of who "controls" it. However, the medium does not exist in a vacuum. Organized human activity determines what is available on television, creates a distinctive television style, and exploits only a small part of the medium's total potential. It is the *combination* of television as such plus its organizational setting that constitutes the medium as we have known it.

The impact of television, while difficult to overstate, is just as difficult to document in a reliable fashion. An enthusiast convinced of the medium's political power might argue that television elected Kennedy in 1960; developed the "imperial presidency" by providing a presidential megaphone; dramatically increased American acceptance of racial integration between 1960 and 1964; shifted political frustrations towards Washington; forced American withdrawal from Vietnam; escalated the impact of campus radicalism and urban riots in the 1960s; forced Lyndon Johnson's "abdication"; made it impossible for Hubert Humphrey to win in 1968; turned the national party conventions into appendages of the media; produced socially "liberal" public attitudes with respect to sex, divorce, women's roles, and

[29]Harvey Lehman, *Age and Achievement* (Princeton, N.J.: Princeton University Press, 1953).

interracial personal relations; amplified public attitudes of pessimism and alienation; and took over the role of "loyal opposition" from the party out of power.[30]

We cannot, of course, prove that television has actually had such pervasive influence. Modern social science envisages a world of multiple causes and multiple effects. One could list the factors that led to Kennedy's victory in 1960, or the U.S. withdrawal from Vietnam, or indeed any of the other events mentioned. The more one learns about any of them, the more "factors" one uncovers to explain them.

Michael Robinson has suggested that the effects of television have become so pervasive that they are difficult to document with the correlational techniques of social science. The 1972 election may be a good example. Patterson and McClure carefully studied the effects of television on voter attitudes in four waves of interviews beginning early in September. They found that television network news coverage did not change voters' images of the candidates. Televised political commercials added significantly to general knowledge of where Nixon and McGovern stood on issues but had little influence on voter preferences.[31]

The subtitle of Patterson and McClure's book—*The Myth of Television Power in National Elections*—suggests that television power had little to do with the outcome of the 1972 election. But is that really true? After all, a superb television performance twenty years earlier probably saved Nixon's political career. George McGovern obtained the 1972 nomination in part because of his position in the Democratic insurgency, and in part because of unusual weakness in the regular sectors of the party. Television probably contributed heavily to the weakness of the party and the strength of the insurgency. Television put McGovern under enormous pressure in the Eagleton affair, even if it did not create the problem or bring about Eagleton's being "dumped" from the ticket.[32] Admittedly, television did not directly determine the outcome of the 1972 election, but it was an extremely important contextual element.

One can, of course, advance counterarguments to the television enthusiast. The parties began to weaken many years before television became pervasive, and other considerations of equal or greater significance can account for their decline (we note these more fully in Chapter 5). Even those who assign great influence to television may discount the importance of political advertising in the medium. Michael Robinson notes that the more Richard Nixon spent in 1968 (in a campaign that was almost totally media-oriented), the worse he did in the polls. In 1972 McGovern lost even though he outspent his opponent on television ads.

One should also note that television programming anticipates the reactions of the audience. By giving the audience what it wants, a program's

[30]Michael Robinson argues many of these propositions very persuasively. See "Television and American Politics: 1956–1976," *Public Interest* (Summer 1977), pp. 3–39.

[31]Thomas Patterson and Robert McClure, *The Unseeing Eye: The Myth of Television Power in National Elections* (New York: G. P. Putnam's Sons, 1976).

[32]For an account that comes close to claiming this, see David Altheide, *Creating Reality* (Beverley Hills, Calif.: Sage Publications, Inc., 1976), pp. 142–155.

rating soars, and the tinkling of precious metals gladdens the hearts of producers and sponsors. But by catering to what it perceives as the tastes of the audience, television may be reflecting and perpetuating rather than creating the predominant attitudes of the society.

Some aspects of television influence are fairly obvious. Practical application of the technology is still very new, and society's adjustment to it is as yet incomplete. Television's technical achievement is remarkable, but its power to command attention is astonishing. As early as 1959, poll evidence suggests that Americans considered it the most important electrical appliance in the home. Surveys by the Roper organization showed that hours of viewing increased steadily and stood at a median of just over three hours per day in 1974. The people Roper interviewed said that television was an important source of political information at all levels of government, and they increasingly relied on it more than newspapers in evaluating the higher levels of the political system. By 1974 more than a third of those interviewed indicated that they relied exclusively on television in obtaining "news about what's going on in the world today." On the question of which medium was most *believable*, television outranked newspapers by more than two to one.[33]

A bit less obvious is the fact that network television has been truly a *mass* medium of political information. Books, magazines, music, art, movies, and newspapers exist for all tastes, but the networks have taken aim at a single mass audience and have rarely made subcultural programming available.[34] With few exceptions, newspapers have always been local institutions with a local audience and a localistic stance towards the news. The largest weekly news magazines (*Time* and *Newsweek*) sell as many as 5 million copies a week, but 40 million Americans usually watch network news *every night.* According to Michael Robinson, this audience is largely inadvertent. They watch because the news is on or they stay tuned in because the news leads into or out of something else. Thus, they are exposed to the news on a nonselective basis. Unlike all other news audiences, this one is drawn disproportionately from the lower-status levels of the population. He believes that such a group is extraordinarily vulnerable to the messages it receives.[35]

Television seems to heighten the importance of personality in politics. Although the medium has undoubtedly raised significant issue concerns, critics complain that campaign coverage rarely provides useful issue interpretation. Television seems to focus on campaign hoopla and campaign prediction instead. The candidate is a more natural object of camera interest than the serious issues, which tend to be abstract and require time to present adequately. And although television advertising may have lost some of its punch in national politics, its importance in primary and state-level contests may persist. Among the thousands of minor-league offices, where television advertising is infrequently used, there is every reason to believe that it can be decisive in individual cases.

[33]R. H. Bruskin Associates, May 1975, as reported in *Current Opinion*, November 1975, p. 107; *Changing Public Attitudes Toward Television and Other Mass Media 1959–1974* (The Roper Organization, Inc., 1975), pp. 3–6.
[34]Muriel Cantor, review of *Popular Culture and High Culture*, by Herbert Gans. *Public Opinion Quarterly*, 39 (Winter 1975–1976), 586–587.
[35]Robinson, "Television and American Politics," p. 15.

Television Bias

One can approach television news bias as propaganda or as an aspect of the "television news perspective." Both approaches raise intriguing questions, but the latter may be more pervasive in its significance and less fully appreciated. If we examine the bias as propaganda, we seek to understand the deliberate shaping of program content to inculcate values that reflect the personal preferences of the communicator as owner, manager, sponsor, or commentator. One scholar argues that the intention and result of network programming is to foster the positions of a liberal elite. He feels that America's institutional leadership in commerce, government, and civic life is already generally liberal, but that the newsmakers are even more liberal than the other elite segments. For him, such values "do *not* foster attitudes of exploitation, but rather of public service and do-goodism." The elite philosophy is not widely shared among the masses, and since elite values are "functional for the preservation of the American political and economic system," they may be self-serving rather than humanitarian.[36]

Another analyst stresses a television news perspective centered in corporate profit making. Programming appeals to the lowest common national denominator, and advertisers buy viewers like cattle on the hoof. This violates the notion of local broadcasting that was supposed to rule when federal regulation began. Individual programmers are unable to introduce new forms and ideas even though they are not under the direct control of local stations and network officials. This programming stance reinforces the status quo, with tendencies toward a general uniformity of thought. Television not only buries dissent, "It buries the possibility that new ideas may emerge. The conditions under which the broadcasting industry flourishes make a farce of the notion that the United States encourages a free marketplace of ideas."[37]

Personal views of the communicators may be less important than practices that have emerged in a television system based mainly on profit. A study by Edward Epstein some years ago described a number of distinctive stylistic and organizational traits in network news: investing news stories with attributes of fiction or drama, for example, and a tendency to select news pictures for their symbolic value.[38] Epstein was also impressed with the degree of composition and editing that went into newscasts and with the strong pressures against following an independent line of coverage. He found that producers and executives tended to compare their program content with what was being produced by other networks and reported in the major newspapers.

His research noted some crucial differences between television and newspaper journalism. Newspapers could increase circulation by investing

[36]Thomas Dye, *Who's Running America?* (Englewood Cliffs, N.J.: Prentice-Hall, Inc., 1976), pp. 93, 170.
[37]Gaye Tuchman, ed., *The TV Establishment* (Englewood Cliffs, N.J.: Prentice-Hall, Inc., 1974), pp. 5, 38–39.
[38]"The real child and its real crying become symbols of all children." Reuven Frank as quoted in Edward J. Epstein, *News From Nowhere* (New York: Random House, Inc. 1973), p. 5.

in the quality of their product. Television, however, operated on the belief that to increase the size of the news audience, it was necessary to invest in programs that preceded the news. Newspapers could expand their editions without sacrificing advertising; television news could not. Newspapers could add to circulation by including items of interest to special groups, but television operated on the notion that each item had to be of some interest to everyone who watched, or the audience would shrink.

Political neutrality and suspicion of politicians were especially noteworthy characteristics of network news operations. Television journalists deliberately maintained an "outsider's" stance toward the news, and executives rotated correspondents from story to story. This lessened reporters' control over their stories, as Epstein saw it, and made it difficult for them to resist control by producers or executives over news themes and content. Epstein's informants told him that when they recruited new correspondents, the networks carefully weeded out people with pronounced ideas or with political commitment to anything. There was a great fear of having an advocate report the news, because such a person could pose problems with the Fairness Doctrine, draw complaints from local affiliates, and so forth. The newspeople Epstein interviewed claimed to be almost totally nonpolitical in their prenetwork careers. Almost all of them held politicians and public office holders in low esteem.[39]

Epstein believed that such characteristics may distort television news more dangerously than the simple operation of personal bias ever could. Whether he was right about that or not it does seem clear that the television medium, along with the rest of the press, is engaged in making the news as well as reporting it. Television's claim that it is just a mirror of reality is not consistent with the facts. A recent (and particularly questionable) example of this occurred in coverage of Iranian demonstrations in front of the Teheran embassy after militants took American embassy personnel hostage in 1979. Although the television news reporters knew that many of the demonstrators were inactive until the television cameras showed up, this essential fact was rarely reported when the filmed footage appeared on the evening news. Television producers seemed indifferent to the question of whether it was in the general interest to amplify emotions that the demonstrators attempted to project.

It is possible that the concentrated political power of television will not be as great in the future as it was in the medium's salad days. Public broadcasting and cable and subscription television may bring increased choice and diversity. Home viewers can now purchase devices that tape programs for replay, and use of videotape cassettes is becoming common. Games that use television sets are also becoming popular. Audience evaluation tech-

---

[39]Ibid., pp. 37–43, 152, 206–208, 215. A recent study by Herbert Gans is much more sympathetic to TV. Gans suggests that people are hired on the basis of journalistic skill and that there is no deliberate effort to exclude "ideologically committed journalists." However, in his account, conformity pressures operate to drive out "ideologists as well as other nonconformists." *Deciding What's News* (New York: Pantheon Books, 1979), p. 192.

niques that consider factors other than sheer audience size are now available. One of these, according to a December 1979 Associated Press story, permits the viewer to report ten different evaluations of programs being viewed. Some evidence indicates that audiences are evaluating what they see on TV more critically. One study reported positive attitudes toward television among the public, but also some guilt feelings over spending so many hours watching a medium they despised.[40] A poll taken in December 1979 by Peter Hart Associates found that twice as many people were satisfied with public television as with television as a whole. Nearly half felt that commercial television was too simpleminded, and 80 percent said they watched at least some public television.[41] As people and institutions adjust to the medium and as useful knowledge of television operations expands, the medium's capacity to produce significant new change may decrease or may be channeled in more specialized directions. At some point people may even begin to spend less time watching television.

Other media. A very real tendency in examining the effects of media on politics is to overemphasize television and neglect the other media. Face-to-face communication, radio, and newspapers are probably much more important than television at the local level, where the greatest number of electoral contests occur, where party organization is often strongest, and where most politicians begin their careers. It also seems that in the world of professional journalism major print reporters are more highly regarded than television journalists. David Broder tells us that about twenty-five Washington reporters (representing *The New York Times, The Washington Post,* the *Washington Evening Star,* the *Los Angeles Times,* the *Christian Science Monitor,* the *Baltimore Sun,* the major chains, and a few syndicated columnists) constitute an informal but highly potent "screening committee" that regularly examines the qualifications of individuals who seek the presidency.[42]

Print communication can be both efficient and potent. One can evaluate information in a good book much more easily than the equivalent information in moving pictures of persons and objects. The closer one gets to the locus of political decision making, the greater the volume of print information that is necessary. This, too, is the lifeblood of partisan politics. Congress, for example, produces a staggering volume of written information every year to facilitate its operations. Where communication must control behavior in a specific way, as with constitutions, laws, administrative regulations, judicial operations, auditing, and budget systems, words and numbers reign supreme.

[40]Paul Ashdown, review of *The Tin Kazoo* by Edwin Diamond, *Public Opinion Quarterly,* 40 (Fall 1976), pp. 413–441. The study referred to is Robert Bower, *Television and the Public* (New York: Holt, Rinehart & Winston, 1973).
[41]United Press International, December 29, 1979.
[42]David Broder, "Political Reporters in Presidential Politics," in *Inside the System,* 3rd ed., ed. Charles Peters and James Fallows (New York: Holt, Rinehart & Winston, 1976), pp. 216–218.

POLITICAL IDEALS IN A MODERN WORLD

Electoral politics is profoundly affected by the society and culture in which it operates. To understand politics, we must be alert to connections between political and social spheres. Conflict is the essence of polities, but large-scale conflicts require bonds that link people together as allies, as well as interests that divide them as opponents. Depictions of modern society discussed in this chapter encourage us to look for patternings among elements that are themselves rather complex and problematical. As the example of television illustrates, individual elements also require attention in their own right.

The topics we have pursued are loosely related, but the human condition in modern society is to some extent a unifying theme. In comparison to any earlier eras modern life is so novel that we should not be surprised by its many puzzles. The old question of the individual's relation to other human beings and to society is as pressing as ever, but today many more matters must be taken into account. Democratic ideals address modern conditions with difficulty, but perhaps this is true of other valued legacies as well. It may even turn out that the modern era (and eras yet to come) will provide the best examples of a practicing democracy. The age of mass participation is still very young.

One of our main difficulties in politics may well turn out to be simple impatience—expecting that which is eventually possible to take place impossibly soon. Samuel Huntington warns us that democratic societies can generate more political demands than can be satisfied by government. If he is right, and if we wish to preserve our democratic institutions, perhaps we must learn to restrain our demands. American individualism places a premium on improvisation, and this too will be an essential skill in the years ahead.

5

Parties
as Institutions

It is not easy to place American political parties in clear focus. A major party involves many different relationships, and those who created the parties seem to have done so in a less than fully deliberate manner. Jefferson, for example, once said that if he could not go to heaven but with a party, he would not go there at all. The Republican party in the standard view began spontaneously in 1856 without the assistance of any outstanding leader.[1] American party *systems* are even less the result of explicit intention. They are byproducts of standing preferences or specific activities, not arrangements that certain people created at a particular time in a deliberate way.

Analysts usually think of the parties as organizations or groups, but neither term is entirely appropriate in the American context. Maybe parties are better thought of as institutions—"complex normative patterns governing behavior in certain fundamental and recurring situations."[2] "Normative patterns" in this case center on the search for power, and "recurring situations" refer mainly to elections. The concept of *institution* is not very precise, but it helps us to understand the diffuse nature of parties. If parties are institutions we shall not be surprised to find that they resist precise description. The same would be true of such major social phenomena as *property, marriage,* and *religion.*

American parties include workers, auxiliaries, group allies, leaders, activists, savants, financial contributors, and floating professionals, but not *members* in the ordinary sense. Even persons who hold official positions do

---

[1]William Safire, *Safire's Political Dictionary* (New York: Random House, Inc., 1978), p. 466; Wilfred E. Binkley, *American Political Parties* (New York: Alfred A. Knopf, Inc., 1954), p. 207.

[2]Bernard Berelson and Gary Steiner, *Human Behavior: An Inventory of Scientific Findings* (New York: Harcourt Brace Jovanovich, Inc., 1964), p. 384.

not carry Republican or Democratic membership cards or pay party dues. There are several reasons for this odd state of affairs. For one, partisanship in the United States implies unrestricted rights of participation. Anybody is supposed to be able to participate in a party of his or her choice; nobody is supposed to be excluded. The individual's sense of self-interest is the only criterion. In such an association, membership may have little meaning.

Then too, American politicians learned at an early stage to rely on patronage rather than large groups of enrolled members. When the time came to distribute the spoils of office, they recognized the advantage to them of limiting effective participation in party activity. Finally, most Americans have shown little interest in party membership. Only a tiny proportion has ever sought to be active in party affairs. Those who wanted close associations with other people could find them more easily by joining civic, religious, and fraternal organizations.

The situation is ironic and ambiguous. Although our parties are completely nonexclusive, they are almost impossible to "join." The public has little interest in party activity, yet it insists on unlimited rights of participation in them.

ESSENTIAL CHARACTERISTICS

In some respects, political contests resemble athletic events. Winning is very important. The players readily forgive minor violations of the rules; in fact, they expect them to go unnoticed. "Political hardball" is accepted, but the public sometimes frowns on "dirty tricks." Bear in mind, however, that politics is slower and more complex than a football game. Leaders of party coalitions are quite happy to wield whatever advantages they possess and may be most content when not effectively opposed.

In the United States, the norms of party competition took about forty years to become established—from 1800, when parties began, to 1840 when competition was fully in place. Rivalry between the parties produced similarities that derived from the preferences of the electorate, the nature of the offices being sought, and the cost-efficient practices appropriate to winning American elections.

Localism and Antiparty Attitudes

American parties are highly decentralized. They not only began as localistic entities, but have remained so. Most elected officials represent small constituencies, and the parties quite naturally focus most of their attention on local elections. Most laws regulating party activity are state rather than federal statutes. National party leaders lack authority over local party officials and can neither appoint nor remove them. Senators and representatives are often more dependent on local party officials than the other way around.

In an era of instant global communication, the localism of America's parties is quite remarkable. Methods of local party organizations have been slow to change. These center on appeals in terms of party label, the potency of closed caucuses, and the lure of patronage to reward party faithful. In hundreds of local communities local party operations are almost invisible to the national media and only dimly understood by many local residents. About the only significant offset to the localism of the parties is the integrative power of the presidency.

These characteristics of political parties are closely related to the public's persistent distrust of them. Divisions within the parties are the rule rather than the exception, and neither the Republicans nor the Democrats present a strong front at the national level, where most important issues are decided. Antiparty attitudes have resulted in nonpartisan local government in many parts of the United States. Moreover, the shift of the population in much of this century has been away from the older parts of the nation where partisanship has deeper roots and toward these newer, nonpartisan areas.

In many respects, California epitomizes these tendencies. A continuous influx from other parts of the country brought the population to over 20 million by 1970. Dynamic change, diversity, and rootlessness hindered the development of local machines, and hostility towards partisan politics probably had greater effect here than anywhere else. California's local elections are all nonpartisan, and for many years partisan office seekers could cross-file in both the Democratic and Republican primaries. Most Californians indicate a party affiliation when they register for voting, but ticket splitting is the rule rather than the exception. Formal party organizations cannot legally endorse candidates in the primaries, and extraofficial auxiliaries such as the California Democratic Council do most of the effective party work.

The Two-Party Mold

A two-party system may be more firmly established in the United States than anywhere else. For example, in 1979 this nation had a smaller proportion of national legislators who were not in one of the two major parties than Britain, Canada, Australia, or New Zealand. The comparative world view in Chapter 1 did not pinpoint the "causes" of the two-party system; when we restrict our view to the United States, we still cannot be certain about them. Many have supposed that the uniquely indivisible nature of the American presidency creates a two-party system. A president holds all of the executive power. His executive power is not shared with the cabinet and thus cannot be parceled out to different parties.

However, the two-party system may have perpetuated the indivisible presidency rather than the other way round. It is not inconceivable that political history could have evolved in a way that required the sharing of executive power with Congress or the cabinet. Political theories of the Whigs tended strongly in that direction. If enough politicians had desired such an arrangement, they could have amended the Constitution, if necessary.

Also frequently mentioned as promoting a two-party system are consensus on fundamental issues, the persistence of an initial twofold division in the debate over Constitutional ratification, and winner-take-all election systems. Yet, interesting as all the explanations are, they fall somewhat short of being fully persuasive. Whatever its cause, the American two-party system demonstrated great staying power once it became established. Until recently at least, the system introduced new generations to its practices and tended to assimilate new movements, new population groups, and new causes.

Party Change in Historical Perspective

Before moving on, it may be useful to discuss general changes in the American party system that have occurred over the entire sweep of American history. Some political scientists have asked whether such changes constitute "development" in any meaningful sense. A related question is whether the parties have initiated major changes or simply tended to respond to change.

If we think back to the historical accounts of Chapters 2 and 3, the direction of party change seems clearest when we compare the first and second party systems. One could say that the position of the parties in the second system improved in just about every respect: They became more legitimate, more reliably competitive, better organized, more flexible, and more capable of generating mass electoral support. The change from the second to the third party system appears almost as clear-cut, if not as great in degree. The basic form of party politics carried over from the second to the third system. Electoral support increased somewhat, but not as much as before. The implications of the full flowering of the machines during the third party system were more ambiguous. Machines undoubtedly increased the organizational strength of the parties, and they probably helped new ethnic groups move toward fuller participation in American life. However, the machines' unsavory methods threatened the legitimacy of parties and led to a reformist reaction that weakened them in the next period.

Indeed, the transition from the third to the fourth party system seems somewhat retrogressive in terms of party development. The secret ballot and mass-circulation newspapers gave citizens opportunities to become independent of the parties. Turnout declined and reformers pursued their attack on parties via direct primaries, nonpartisan elections, and other means. The parties became less competitive at both the state and national levels. However, a more favorable interpretation of this period would be that the country was moving away from a politics of regimented partisanship toward a politics of individualistic partisanship. In the changing circumstances of American democracy at least some of these changes were desirable.

In comparing the fourth with the fifth party system (to about 1964) one senses a partial resurgence of party capability. Levels of voting generally rose from 1924 to 1960. Nationalizing tendencies began to offset the traditional localism of the parties and the lack of competition at the state level. Although the Republican party began to show serious weaknesses in 1948, the New Deal seemed to have brought new groups, especially unskilled workers, into effective activity in partisan politics.

The final comparison between the 1932–1960 period and the period since 1960 is hardest to judge. The choice of 1960 or any other year as a line of demarkation is somewhat arbitrary, and we are still too close to the events of the past generation to have a good perspective on them. However, it seems clear that the parties became much weaker as split-ticket voting increased and the potency of local party organizations declined. Developments in polling and the media tended to personalize politics as never before, and the affluent society spawned new types of political activism that could rival electioneering activity. Voter participation declined steadily, as did trust in leadership of all sorts. Political reform was given extraordinary emphasis, but the reforms had neither the purpose nor effect of increasing the organizational capacities of the parties.

Everett Ladd has argued persuasively that the American parties have usually responded to social change and that they have rarely initiated it.[3] He believes that much of our history reflects changes in technology and economic life and that these usually produced a steady increase in our "capacity to harness or dominate the physical environment." One could imagine this producing larger-scale party operations, lessening parochialism in the parties, and increasing bureaucracy in party organization. Had such changes occurred, we would have seen genuine party development. However, the history of the party systems, in Ladd's opinion, shows little evidence of such responses. He argues that the American parties never had to effect sweeping social change and that the impetus for change came largely from outside the government. Moreover, the parties have frequently been slow to respond to social change. Although this has often helped them perform "a 'peacemaking' or 'reconciling' function," when change is especially rapid (as it is today), the relative passivity of the parties tends to add to a general picture of their political unresponsiveness.[4]

The issue of party development is difficult to resolve without an extended analysis of development concepts. One suspects that ultimately *development* is a controversial item on the political agenda. Richard Jensen, for example, points out that much of American political history involved a "search for modern values" (such as progress, science, roads, banks, canals, upgrading of morals), with the Republicans often the party of modernization and the Democrats frequently in resistance as a party of traditionalism (small farming, traditional folkways, job security, and so forth). Today, there is important support for what he refers to as a "loose set of postmodern values" pioneered by the well-educated youth of the 1950s and 1960s. Those who espouse such values tend to reject particular items in the modern value repertoire or to be lukewarm to them.[5]

[3]Everett Carll Ladd, Jr., *American Political Parties* (New York: W. W. Norton & Co., Inc., 1970), Introduction and Chap. 2.
[4]Ibid., pp. 9–10, 45, 307–308.
[5]Richard Jensen, "Party Coalitions and the Search for Modern Values: 1820–1970," in *Emerging Coalitions in American Politics*, ed. Seymour M. Lipset (San Francisco: Institute for Contemporary Studies, 1978), pp. 11–41. Jensen believes the postmodern values have a greater affinity to traditionalism and that the affected people therefore gravitated to the Democratic party. However, with respect to such matters as pot, abortion, sexual experimentation, and rejection of patriotism, the new norms may be at odds with traditionalism in important ways.

MINOR PARTIES

The annals of presidential elections list many candidates other than those nominated by the major parties. In most cases they received few votes, and the nature of the partisan support was obscure. Of more interest are the parties that polled 10,000 to 50,000 votes in more than one election. The Socialist Labor party (SLP), for example, achieved this level of support in every election from 1892 through 1940. Yet in prewar radical politics the SLP was no match for the Communists when that party chose to offer candidates in presidential elections. In 1924 the Communists got half again more votes than the SLP and in 1936 outpolled that party by better than six to one.

Even with the Communists, however, we have not reached the level where minor party votes make much of an impression. For example, in 1936 (the party's best year at the polls) it received less than 0.2 percent of the popular vote. The Socialist party outpolled them better than two to one in what was far from their best year. More normal for the Socialists was the 402,489 votes they received in 1904—more than five times the Communist vote of 1936. Yet, like most of the parties listed in Table 5-1, the Socialist party formed in order to propagate particular doctrines and had little hope of winning many national offices. The 6 percent of popular vote that the Socialists received in 1912 represents the peak strength of these parties. In a more normal year this would have attracted considerable attention, but 1912 was highly unusual: The larger commotion of Theodore Roosevelt's defection from the Republican party overshadowed the Socialist's cause. The electoral vote system makes it difficult for small parties to play a pivotal role as broker between two larger, evenly matched parties, and few of them seem to have made the attempt. Indeed, with the exception of the States' Righters, none of the election efforts in Table 5-1 received a single electoral vote.

The electoral impact of the parties in Table 5-1 was less important than the underlying sentiments they expressed. The Liberty party was an important step in the evolution of effective opposition to slavery. The Greenback party rose as the fortunes of the Grange ebbed, the party tactic to a degree displacing the pressure-group tactic. Prohibitionism was strong enough to amend the Constitution, but it was the bipartisan effort of the Anti-Saloon League, not the Prohibition party, that achieved this objective. The influence of socialist ideas has been much more important than the efforts of the Socialist party.[6]

The most conspicuous minor parties have sought national influence without a strong underpinning of state and local organization. There have, however, been a few exceptions. The former Farmer-Labor party in Minnesota, the Wisconsin Progressive party, the American Labor party in New York, and the Nonpartisan League in some of the prairie states are the main examples, and most of them left their mark in an earlier, pre-1950 era. All

[6]V. O. Key, Jr., *Politics, Parties, and Pressure Groups,* 5th ed. (New York: Thomas Y. Crowell Company, Inc., 1964), p. 268.

Table 5-1
Minor Parties or Candidates Polling 1–6 Percent in Presidential Elections, 1828–1972

Party	Year	Percentage of Total Votes Cast
Liberty	1844	2.3%
Greenback	1880	3.3
	1884	1.7
Prohibition	1884	1.5
	1888	2.2
	1892	2.3
	1900	1.5
	1904	1.9
	1908	1.7
	1916	1.2
Socialist	1904	3.0
	1908	2.8
	1912	6.0
	1916	3.2
	1920	3.4
	1932	2.2
Union	1936	2.0
States' Rights	1948	2.4
Wallace Progressive	1948	2.4

This table lists only those years in which the given party received at least 1 percent of the vote. The Free Soil party of 1852 and American party of 1972 are excluded because they received more than 6 percent of the vote in other elections.

Source: *Congressional Quarterly's Guide to U.S. Elections* (Washington, D.C.: 1976).

of these associations faced formidable competition from the major parties and either became attached to them in some fashion or disappeared. Some, however, have left an important legacy in the politics of a particular state. Because of the greater nationalization of political life and the apparent ascendance of antiparty outlooks, such local parties are increasingly rare.[7]

Parties of Crisis

One can say, with a few qualifications, that the formations discussed so far operated outside the two-party system. Those in Table 5-2, however, seem to have been intimately connected with it. Daniel Mazmanian's recent study argues persuasively that significant minor party voting occurs during periods of crisis

[7]For information on such parties, see ibid., pp. 273–278.

when a few issues become highly controversial; when one or more of the issues generates an intense minority; when the major parties ignore or attack—in either case alienate—the minority; and when an individual or group of political entrepreneurs then mobilizes the minority behind a third party.[8]

Mazmanian takes the 1968 Wallace candidacy as the prototype of the party of crisis. In his analysis, the American Independent party was a response to intensely held minority views on race, the related issue of "urban unrest," and Vietnam. He notes that by 1968, 15 percent of the public still favored segregation, and 18 percent would not support candidates who wanted to deescalate the war in Vietnam. Another poll indicated that 20 percent favored "use of all available force" in dealing with urban unrest. These minority views overlapped somewhat, and they found no significant support in the major parties. (In the formulation quoted above, major parties "ignored" the minority positions even though they did not "attack" them.) Thus it was that a party of crisis formed just when observers had begun to wonder whether important minor parties might be a thing of the past. The efforts of 1948 had come to naught, and 1952, 1956, 1960, and 1964 had brought unusually small numbers of votes for any but the two major-party candidates.

Mazmanian applies his theory to each of the elections in Table 5-2, but limitations of space do not permit us to do justice to that part of his analysis. We should mention, however, that two periods of crisis have failed to produce any significant minor party activity—the reconstruction era and the period of the Great Depression. Mazmanian reasons that during reconstruction the Democrats provided an umbrella for dissidents as the crisis came to a head in the election of 1876. In the case of the Great Depression, the

Table 5-2
Parties of Crisis: Most Significant Minor Parties

Party (Candidate)	Year	Percentage of Total Votes Cast
Anti-Mason (William Wirt)	1832	8.0%
Free Soil (Martin Van Buren)	1848	10.1
American (Millard Fillmore)	1856	21.4
Southern Democrat (John C. Breckinridge)	1860	18.2
Constitutional Union (John Bell)	1860	12.6
Populist (James B. Weaver)	1892	8.5
Progressive (Theodore Roosevelt)	1912	27.4
Progressive (Robert M. La Follette)	1924	16.6
American Independent (George C. Wallace)	1968	13.5

Minor parties receiving more than 6 percent of the presidential vote 1828–1972.

Source: Daniel A. Mazmanian, *Third Parties in Presidential Elections* (Washington, D.C.: The Brookings Institution, 1974), p. 5.

[8]Daniel A. Mazmanian, *Third Parties in Presidential Elections* (Washington, D.C.: The Brookings Institution, 1974), p. 5.

crisis came on very suddenly. Its effects were so pervasive that the Democratic party could take advantage of quickly developing opposition and lead it. By 1936 the two major parties offered starkly contrasting views about what the government should do about the economy.

Mazmanian's analysis helps to deepen our understanding of major party alignment and realignment. The "alignment" of a two-party system is based on major issues and social groupings that differentiate (to a degree) the major parties. A "realignment" occurs when the pattern of party attachments within the electorate undergoes a durable change. In the three examples so far (the 1850s, the 1890s, and the 1930s) "the line of party cleavage sliced through the electorate in a new direction, shifting the party structure on its axis. When things settled down, the changes had been so profound that . . . a new party system can be seen to have replaced the old."[9] In this view, realignments occur when a major new issue dominates debate, polarizes the community, and cuts across the existing line of party cleavage. The new issue competes with older ones that underlie the existing system. Both parties tend to straddle it, but in each party groups who are more concerned about the new issue than about their party's electoral success emerge at each pole. If the new issue retains its momentum, both parties may persist in their straddle, or either or both may come under the control of forces opposed to the issue. If so, some of the polar elements supporting the issue may form a third party while others remain in the major parties. The precise nature of the realignment is rather complex, and the role of the third party in it can take a number of forms.[10]

Clearly, some minor parties or candidacies can play an important part in the career of the two-party system, which is why even those favoring a two-party system may have an interest in preventing undue difficulties for minor-party challenges. Mazmanian advocates a federal election code that would standardize electoral procedures among the states. The code would keep petition requirements for access to the ballot from being burdensome, eliminate large differences in filing deadlines, and ensure that such deadlines were not earlier than two months before the election. Beyond that, he favors publicly sponsored television time for minor parties and (apparently) modification of antiraiding and antifusion statutes so that important third parties could participate more continuously, in the manner of the New York Liberal and Conservative parties. Some supporters of the two-party system might question this latter proposal.[11]

---

[9]James L. Sundquist, *Dynamics of the Party System* (Washington, D.C.: The Brookings Institution, 1973), p. 7.
[10]Ibid., Chap. 13.
[11]In 1960 Kennedy got some of the votes he needed to win the presidency on the Liberal line in New York. Under a unique arrangement, New York's minor parties are permitted to nominate candidates of major parties (with their permission), and the candidate's name appears on each of the relevant lines on the ballot. Most other states have antifusion statutes that prohibit the appearance of a candidate's name in more than one place. Party-raiding statutes require that a candidate be a member of the party that nominates him. Ibid., pp. 117–119; Key, *Politics Parties, and Pressure Groups*, p. 276.

MAIN ELEMENTS OF THE MAJOR PARTIES

I have emphasized that a major American party obtains support from many different groups and from state and local units. We can also think of parties as having three main segments: organization, officeholders, and supporters. *Organization* as used here really means its *extragovernmental* organization—units composed of party officials and workers rather than governmental officials. Officeholders turn up for further examination in a later chapter, and this book considers supporters in many contexts. As long as we remember that the division is somewhat artificial, it is useful to examine the three segments separately.

Each segment is only loosely related to the others, and people in them tend to have different perspectives. Thus supporters, many of whom do little more than vote, may regard party organization people as unnecessary intermediaries between themselves and candidates. Supporters are also apt to be less localistic in their political outlooks. Organization people may feel misunderstood by voters and insufficiently appreciated by the officeholders they feel they have elected. Officeholders, in turn, are the only sector of the party that becomes intimately familiar with the day-to-day realities of public policy and administration.[12]

Organization

The organizational sector of American parties is the least well-known sphere. Every state still has a more or less elaborate hierarchy of party caucuses, committees, conventions, and the like. Although these arrangements are prescribed by state law, their variety and complexity have discouraged comprehensive academic descriptions in recent years. Formal structures laid out in the statutes, while not irrelevant, should never be taken at face value. The essence of party politics is an indifference to formalities and an instinctive reticence about essential matters of strategy and policy. The informal behavior that may breathe life into official forms is not easily uncovered. Despite political scientists' long-standing interest in American parties, there are still relatively few detailed descriptions of particular state or local party organizations, in part because researchers have had higher priority tasks to attend to.[13] To understand the politics of any large city, for example, one must examine the role of many types of actors, and the parties are only one type. In smaller communities, researchers have often focused on the nature of community "power structures." The literature on these topics is, of course, quite extensive.[14]

[12]The threefold division receives an especially good treatment in Frank Sorauf, *Party Politics in America*, 4th ed. (Boston: Little, Brown & Company, 1980).

[13]Perhaps the most notable recent example is Samuel Eldersveld, *Political Parties* (Chicago: Rand McNally & Company, 1964). Raymond Wolfinger, *The Politics of Progress* (Englewood Cliffs, N.J.: Prentice-Hall, Inc., 1974) describes New Haven in the 1950s. See also Edward Banfield, *Political Influence* (New York: The Free Press, 1961).

[14]For an introduction to the main topics and issues, see Thomas R. Dye, *Politics in States and Communities*, 3rd ed. (Englewood Cliffs, N.J.: Prentice-Hall, Inc., 1977), esp. Chaps. 8–16. See also Edward Banfield's many works, especially *City Politics* (with James Q. Wilson) (Cambridge, Mass.: Harvard University Press, 1963), and *Big City Politics* (Cambridge, Mass.: Harvard University Press, 1965).

A major theme in discussions of contemporary party organization is decline of machines—today a ghostly remnant, but once a palpable reality. James Bryce, writing in 1888, referred to the "vast and intricate political machine which lies outside the Constitution" and bemoaned the total absence of impartial written accounts of its daily workings or "the influences which sway the men by whom this machine has been constructed and daily manipulated."[15]

Even in their prime, the machines were not uniformly distributed. According to an early authority, they were strongest in the states of New York, Pennsylvania, New Jersey, Maryland, Ohio, and Illinois; in the cities of the midwest; and in San Francisco and New Orleans.[16] Bosses such as Huey Long in Louisiana, Harry F. Byrd in Virginia, and J. H. Roraback in Connecticut occasionally extended their power to entire states, but no national boss ever emerged. Perhaps there were inherent limitations of scale in the informal style characteristic of machine politics. The machine's strength lay in the personal networks of politicians and in their ability to offer specific material inducements to supporters within a neighborhood. Even so, machines formed a larger pattern that gave professional politics a distinctively national flavor. The various local operations were similar in many ways, and they developed political outlooks common over wide areas. The language of Bryce invites one to think of American party politics in the 1880s as a single vast machine. For many years, efforts to eliminate machines through programs of civic reform enjoyed only limited success.

Why did the machines persist? Robert K. Merton, in one of the more systematic explanations of the machine's persistence, points to latent functions that were not adequately fulfilled by approved social patterns and structures. (By *latent functions*, he meant observed consequences of machine activity that make for adaptation or adjustment but that are neither intended nor recognized as such.) In somewhat simplified terms, these latent functions of the machine were

1. *Political integration.* The boss and the machine acted as an antidote to the dispersion of power in the official structure of American government. A capacity for action was needed, and the official structure was too fragmented to supply it. Therefore, an unofficial structure came into being "to fulfill existing needs somewhat more effectively."[17]

2. *Humanizing of government.* The machine forged links with people at the neighborhood level, dispensing all manner of help with personal problems. Official assistance agencies with their cold, professional manner could not compete with a precinct worker who was "an understanding friend in need." Personal relationships of the machine counteracted the legalism of the official order.

3. *Satisfying group needs.* The machine helped deprived groups as well as licit and

[15]*The American Commonwealth,* ed. Louis Hacker (New York: G. P. Putnam's Sons, 1959), I, 135. This work first appeared in 1888.

[16]Mosei Ostrogorski, *Democracy and the Party System in the United States,* p. 266, as cited by Robert Brooks, *Political Parties and Electoral Problems* (New York: Harper & Row, Publishers, Inc., 1933), pp. 193–194.

[17]Robert K. Merton, *Social Theory and Social Structure* (New York: The Free Press, 1968), pp. 126–136. Merton's account of the machine treated it as a continuing entity and was written in the present tense.

illicit businesses. Those down on their luck got assistance with a minimum of red tape, condescension, or questions. The machine organized economic activity in a way that was unofficial and therefore acceptable to business. Those having little access to socially approved goals of success through money and power could experience upward social mobility through advancement in the machine. Illegitimate businesses (vice, crime, and rackets) enjoyed a constant demand for their services, and they could be protected from undue governmental interference, just as the legitimate businesses were.

The power of the machines was something of an anomaly. Bossism seemed to place real power in the hands of persons who were not supposed to be powerful. If the key issue is who had decisive power, there is good reason to believe that business actually held it in the period when the machines operated at peak efficiency. In the gilded age, it may have been easier to deplore moral laxity in the machine than to confront the questionable ethical practices of big business. Business power may have possessed a legitimacy that machine power lacked.

Machines have had their apologists. One scholar regarded "the traditional politician" as a specialist in human relations who adjusted social conflicts in nonviolent ways. "Our great cities have been racial jungles for generations," he said. "The politician takes the pieces at hand, whether good, bad or indifferent. . . . His product is no better than his materials."[18]

Daniel Patrick Moynihan's affectionate portrait of the New York Irish is also pertinent. He notes an indifference to Yankee proprieties: "The Irish brought to America a settled tradition of regarding the formal government as illegitimate and the informal one as bearing the true impress of popular sovereignty." He likens Tammany Hall to an Irish village transferred to Manhattan and notes that "To the Irish, stealing an election was rascally, not to be approved, but neither quite to be abhorred."[19]

Although machines have not disappeared entirely, machine power and the machine style have definitely faded. This should not be surprising if we recall the categories of Merton's analysis and note profound changes in the way American society is now organized to meet human needs. Official structures today provide elaborate benefits to many groups, and stronger executives at each level of government mean that unofficial structures no longer perform at a relative advantage. In today's society fewer people are at a serious economic disadvantage. The official structures acknowledge their needs; labor unions, work training programs, and welfare assistance can help them far more than a local machine. Furthermore, racial and religious discrimination has declined, and most ethnic groups have made enough gains so that they no longer can derive status satisfactions from a career in the machine. Crime and the rackets operate with new sophistication and on a larger scale. Like big business, they are more sensitive than ever to actions and policies of the federal government.

[18]Pendleton Herring, *The Politics of Democracy* (New York: W. W. Norton & Co., Inc., 1940), pp. 135–136, 139–140.
[19]Nathan Glazer and Daniel Patrick Moynihan, *Beyond the Melting Pot* (Cambridge, Mass.: The M.I.T. Press, 1970), pp. 224, 226.

In the contemporary era it is society that tends to be cold and impersonal, not the political and governmental order. Political machines cannot humanize life on the freeways, in the suburbs, or in the large shopping centers. (If they could, they might be worth reviving.)

A trend towards organizational weakness in the parties is clear enough, but the extent of the weakness is as yet unclear. In particular, we lack good studies and measures of patronage. Although patronage is generally assumed to have declined, Jewell and Olson urge caution in drawing sweeping conclusions. They note that some patronage-based parties have been dispersed and fragmented, and they warn against stereotyping the setting in which patronage operates.

> In California, which we will use as an example of a progressive and reformed state supposedly free of patronage, the governor has about 170 appointments to make of heads and administrators of agencies, including several important regulatory boards. Another 2,200 appointments are made as part-time members of over 300 commissions and councils within state government. The governor also appoints, in the average four-year term, about 160 persons to judicial positions (about 16 percent of all judicial positions). Finally, the governor fills vacancies to otherwise elective positions (e.g., Lt. Governor, U.S. Senator) not only at the state level, but also on boards of county supervisors. Some 40 percent of Los Angeles County's Board of Supervisors were originally appointed by Governor Reagan, as one example.[20]

Jewell and Olson acknowledge that patronage has eroded as a major motivation for party work, but this does not necessarily mean that patronage itself has declined. Instead, patronage is controlled by the individual officeholder or government official, frequently without any coordination by a governor, mayor, or political party. They think that white-collar patronage (financial and contract patronage, judicial patronage, election system work, and so forth) is actually increasing, even if blue-collar patronage is not.[21]

Even the decline of the machine should not be exaggerated. According to one authority, Pennsylvania is still to some extent a machine state, and machines hum away in practically all of Indiana's county courthouses. Another study cites machines or machinelike remnants in Buffalo, Baltimore, the New York City boroughs of the Bronx, Brooklyn, and Queens, Albany, Plaquemines Parish in Louisiana, Duval County in Texas, Kansas City, Boston, St. Louis, Cleveland, Cincinatti, and Jersey City. These writers believe that the machine may only be in a temporarily dormant phase.[22]

Officeholders

Elected officeholders of a major American party may not be a governing formation, but they do constitute an important community of partisans.

[20]Malcolm E. Jewell and David M. Olson, *American State Political Parties and Elections* (Homewood, Ill.: The Dorsey Press, 1978), pp. 79–80.

[21]Ibid., p. 83.

[22]Michael Barone, Grant Ujifusa, and Douglas Matthews, *The Almanac of American Politics* (New York: E. P. Dutton, 1977), p. 262; Ruth K. Scott and Ronald J. Hrebenar, *Parties in Crisis* (New York: John Wiley & Sons, Inc., 1979), p. 101.

The community is tenuous and diverse. The ties that bind are gossamer thin, but nonetheless they do bind. Mutual recognition as a fellow Democrat or Republican in office normally carries with it obligations and calls for expected kinds of behavior. Many legislative bodies organize themselves along two-party lines. A surge of electoral strength towards candidates for particularly visible offices, especially the executive offices, can boost the fortunes of lesser candidates. Ticket splitting can reduce such effects, but one must keep in mind that most elected officials occupy minor offices, where ticket splitting may be less likely to occur. With the decline of strong extragovernmental party organization, officeholders have become dominant elements in each party. They are expected to uphold party views to a much greater degree than ordinary partisans.

Other things being equal, it is to the advantage of each officeholder to help the others in the party. The community therefore tends to serve as a gigantic mutual aid society. To the extent that it is effective, it compensates in part for weaknesses in the organizational sector.

There are limits, of course, to the mutual help. No officeholder is expected to jeopardize his or her own reelection prospects. A liberal Democratic senator is not required to campaign for a conservative Democrat. Major officeholders may discourage an unpopular president of their party from visibly assisting in their reelection efforts. The community encourages candidates to concentrate on their own races, so as not to accumulate the enemies of other candidates or officeholders.

Candidates usually do not expect help from fellow partisans of the same or lower levels beyond their immediate district or state. However, higher level officeholders may be expected to give more assistance. Without putting themselves to great inconvenience, fellow officeholders can supply a candidate with useful tips on campaigning, research on issues, personnel from their political staff, encouragement, and even financial support.

A number of variables condition the closeness of party ties. In our governmental system elective offices are widely distributed at different levels and serve different functions. Although this arrangement keeps the community of officeholders divided and weak, it offers compensations. A community thus dispersed has extraordinary potential as a communication net. Also, the fragmentation minimizes mutual interference and reduces the scale of political rivalries. As a mutual aid society designed to assure reelection to the same offices, things are often harmonious. However, many representatives would like to be senators or governors, even if members of their own party already hold these offices. Political ambition is practically universal in each community, and the perpetual rivalry it produces can lead to disunity.

Certain aspects of the political structure tend to limit such rivalries. Residence rules keep most officeholders from casting covetous glances at higher offices in other states; at the level of minor officeholding such rules operate with great severity. Moreover, differences in terms make it difficult for those with congressional seats to contest Senate seats. Residence rules confine them to their own state; their two-year terms mean they cannot make a try for the Senate without forgoing reelection to the House; and a Senate contest normally occurs in only two out of three election years in any given state.

Constituency differences are another source of disunity within each community. Democrats from downstate Illinois are a different breed from their Cook County fellows. Northern Florida is Deep South terrain, but Dade County is urban and ethnic. Dade County's congressman, William Lehman, is a former used car dealer with a reputation for honesty and a strong rating from the liberal Americans for Democratic Action (ADA). He is of a very different political species from fellow Democrat Don Fuqua of the state's second district in northern Florida. Fuqua strongly supports military spending and receives low ratings from the ADA.[23]

In the past generation or so, partisan ties among major officeholders have weakened substantially. The presidency seems to have become politically detached from its partisan counterparts in Congress, in part because of the personalism of recent presidential nominating and electoral contests. Presidents are no longer as dependent as they once were on the community of partisans for either their nomination or their success in winning.

In congressional contests we currently find a high proportion of incumbents being reelected by heavy margins. The reasons for this are elusive, but simple name recognition may have become the dominant cue for many voters. (The incumbent, of course, is much more likely to have a recognizable name.) With the increased advantage of incumbency, the House has become much less sensitive to partisan swings in the vote.[24] In 1980, for example, the Republicans gained less than 10 percent of the seats in the House, despite the size of Reagan's victory margin. To the extent that House members are less dependent on the electoral fortunes of the president, they have much less incentive to work with him.

An analogous partisan separation among president, governors, and senators may also have occurred. Senators usually have greater political visibility than House members—enough perhaps so that voters are less dependent on name recognition in voting. A smaller proportion of Senate incumbents regularly succeed in getting reelected, and Senate races occasionally draw enough publicity to become personality contests. In 1976 especially, the voters exhibited extensive ticket splitting between presidential and senatorial choices. Expensive candidate organizations have become more prominent in recent gubernatorial campaigns, suggesting that here too the voters are making individual rather than partisan choices. Adding to the dissociation among offices is the fact that governors have been less important figures at national conventions in the past twenty-five years. Also, some states have changed their election calendars so that fewer governorships are decided in presidential election years.[25]

[23]Barone, Ujifusa, and Matthews, *Almanac of American Politics 1978,* pp. 165–166, 181–182.

[24]Albert D. Cover and David R. Mayhew, draft of chapter for Lawrence C. Dodd and Bruce I. Oppenheimer, eds., *Congress Reconsidered* (Washington, D. C.: Congressional Quarterly Press, 1981).

[25]Nelson W. Polsby and Aaron Wildavsky, *Presidential Elections,* 5th ed. (New York: Charles Scribner's Sons, 1980), pp. 108–109.

In sum, the interlocking of state and national voting that once characterized American politics in the higher offices has eroded considerably. In the older politics—especially before 1960—one could say that "the presidential result, the elections to the House of Representatives, and the choices of governors tend to move in the same direction."[26] Today, at least for the time being, the presidency integrates the political ambitions of all major partisans, but neither it nor the nominating convention seems to link the others to a common electoral fate.

Supporters

Who should be included among the supporters of an American party? If parties had members, possession of a membership card might be the test. Since this is not possible in the American case, we can define supporters as those who are officially *registered* with the party. The difficulty here is that registration concepts and procedures vary and will not yield comparable results. Still another possibility is to consider those who regularly *vote* for all or most of a party's nominees as the party's supporters. This also produces a less than precise definition since states differ in the particular offices that are elective, the officeholders who are to be chosen concurrently, and in the format of their ballots.

Defining party support by either registration or by straight-ticket voting may understate the importance of the party as a *national* association. If the test is merely support of the party's presidential nominee, however, one is then faced with the fact that a voter's party adherence does not necessarily determine his or her vote. Thus in 1952 Eisenhower sought and obtained the votes of Democrats who "liked Ike." A vote for Eisenhower did not mean that the individual who cast it had become a Republican. One party's supporters are always fair game for the appeals of the opposition candidates.

Because of such difficulties, political scientists usually employ the concept of "party identification" when they want to think about party adherents or supporters in the most inclusive terms. Party identification is a person's sense of attachment to a political party, and it is discovered by asking the person: "Generally speaking, do you usually think of yourself as a Republican, a Democrat, an independent, or what?"[27] The pattern of answers over the years is presented in Table 5-3.

Party identification may not be a perfect indicator of party support. It assumes that partisanship is comparable across local areas, it relies exclusively on how people think about the parties, and it does not attempt to incorporate what people do. Party identification is not a membership concept, either. However, psychological attachment to a party is important in its own right, and we now have a series of high-quality data spanning many years.

[26]V. O. Key, Jr., *Politics, Parties, and Pressure Groups,* 5th ed. (New York: Thomas Y. Crowell, 1964), pp. 304–305.

[27]Persons answering Republican or Democrat may then be asked: "Would you call yourself a strong (Republican) (Democrat) or a not very strong (Republican) (Democrat)?" Persons who answer "independent" on the first question may be asked: "Do you think of yourself as closer to the Republican or Democratic party?"

Table 5-3
Party Identification, 1952-1978

Election Year	Democrat Strong	Democrat Weak	Independent	Independent	Republican Independent	Republican Weak	Republican Strong	Other
1952	22%	25%	10%	6%	7%	14%	14%	3%
1954	22	26	9	7	6	14	13	4
1956	21	23	6	9	8	14	15	4
1958	27	22	7	7	5	17	11	4
1960	20	25	6	10	7	14	16	3
1962	23	23	7	8	6	16	12	4
1964	27	25	9	8	6	14	11	1
1966	18	28	9	12	7	15	10	1
1968	20	25	10	11	9	15	10	1
1970	20	24	10	13	8	15	9	1
1972	15	26	11	13	11	13	10	1
1974	18	21	13	15	9	14	8	3
1976	15	25	12	15	10	14	9	1
1978	15	24	14	14	10	13	8	3
1980	18	23	11	13	10	14	9	2

Source: American National Election Studies, Center for Political Studies, University of Michigan. For wording of questions, see text.

Perhaps the most significant findings to be gleaned from Table 5-3 are the following:

1. *Decreasing strength of party attachments.* The proportion of "hard-core" independents has increased markedly since 1952. The proportion of strong identifiers (both parties) has dropped from 36 percent to 27 percent.

Other findings corroborate this trend towards weaker party attachments. More people who identify with one party have voted for the other party's candidates in recent years, and fewer of them have mentioned a candidate's party affiliation as a reason for their choice. In counts of what people like or dislike about each of the parties, those who give more negative than positive evaluations to both parties have shown a sharp increase since 1960—from 29 percent in 1960 rising steadily to 51 percent by 1972. The proportion of those who say they voted a split ticket has also sharply increased: 32 percent in 1960, rising to 65 percent by 1972.[28] Because of such tendencies, contemporary politics may be moving in the direction of "*de*alignment" rather than the "realignment." Partisan feeling in the mass electorate seems to have been eroding for a long time and may be partly responsible for a long-term decline in voter turnout.

2. *Extraordinary scope of party identification.* Even so, only moderate portions of those interviewed do not readily classify themselves as Democrats

[28]Norman H. Nie, Sidney Verba, and John R. Petrocik, *The Changing American Voter* (Cambridge, Mass.: Harvard University Press, 1976), pp. 51, 53, 56, 58.

or Republicans. The term "independent" carries high social approval (except among political scientists), and it can mean different things. Some independents are closet partisans. Others may "vote the man, not the party," yet confine themselves to Republicans or Democrats. For still others, "independent" is a socially approved way of saying "apolitical—no politics please."[29]

3. *Stability of party identification.* The distributions change very little from year to year, and, at least until recently, this has not resulted from a large number of opposite changes. Historically, most people retained their party attachments for many years. Generations of children have picked up their party attachments from their parents, and this has sometimes produced voting patterns in the modern era that go back to the Civil War. Thus, in Indiana, except for eight highly urban counties, the counties of greatest Democratic strength in elections between 1932 and 1960 were for the most part the same counties as in the election of 1860.

4. *Persisting weakness of the Republican party.* By 1976 strong and weak Democrats outnumbered strong and weak Republicans 40 percent to 23 percent. If one included independent partisans, the Democrats led by 52 percent to 33 percent. A study published in 1978 argued that Republicans lacked any secure turf of their own. Even though the GOP had increased its southern support since 1964, it still had less ability to compete for House seats in that region than anywhere else in the country. Outside the South, Republicans had lost an enormous amount of ground over the preceding fifteen years. By 1976, there was only one state where the party controlled the governorship and both houses of the legislature.[30] The 1980 election was favorable to the Republicans, but they still had a good deal of ground to cover before they would overcome the Democratic advantage, or even match it. The GOP was still fifty-one seats short of controlling the House, and it held only 39 percent of the nation's state legislative seats. Republican governors occupied only twenty-one of the nation's fifty statehouses.

Taking Stock

Growing debility in the American party system troubles many of this country's most knowledgeable political observers. Political scientists and historians have often thought of party politics as integral to the entire democratic enterprise. In the opening words of an older book: "No America without democracy, no democracy without politics, no politics without parties, no parties without compromise and moderation. So runs the string of assumptions on which hangs this exposition of the politics of American

---

[29]It is interesting to consider other identifications of similar scope. For example, take the question: "What is your religious preference? Is it Protestant, Catholic, Jewish, some other religion, or no religion?" The distribution of answers is 64.2 percent Protestant, 25.3 percent Catholic, 2.5 percent Jewish, 6.6 percent no religion, 1.3 percent some other religion. (NORC, six pooled surveys, 1972–1977, N=9,120). Note that the question does not offer a socially approved option comparable to *independent.*

[30]Everett Carll Ladd, Jr., *Where Have All the Voters Gone?* (New York: W. W. Norton & Co., Inc., 1978), pp. 1–17.

democracy."[31] Proparty scholars differ in some respects, and not all of them would agree with this statement. However, most proparty scholars believe that when parties are weak, important tasks tend to be performed by other groups or institutions in a less satisfactory manner, performed badly, or not performed at all.

At a minimum, one can say that party activities have centered on selecting candidates, contesting elections, promoting a party program, and guiding elected officeholders.[32] When one goes beyond these minimal tasks, the contributions of parties become more speculative. For example, a textbook published in 1949 spoke of the "function" of party as a "nationalizing and educating agency," and as "intermediation between individual and government."[33] Speculative or not, these notions have since appeared in one guise or another with great frequency in the political science literature. Many political scientists believe that party weakness has led to personalism in electoral politics, made it more difficult for elected officials to engage in responsible policy making, and diminished the opportunities for meaningful mass participation.

However, scholars disagree somewhat about party functions and the degree to which parties share them with other types of association. Furthermore, an important group of "minimalist" scholars tend to believe that the contributions of parties have been exaggerated and that other types of associations are likely to be just as valuable or important.[34]

Some reservations. Even though parties are now very weak, it is important not to assume that they no longer count in electoral politics. Figure 5–1 shows a powerful relationship between party identification and presidential vote in 1976. Note especially that independent partisans played as important a role as weak partisans in that election.[35] We can assume that debility has proceeded furthest in the organizational sector of the parties. However, old-style precinct organization may not be as necessary to a viable party as it once was. The modern electorate may be largely self-organized, and the increased power of elected executives at the state and local level may compensate somewhat for organizational weakness.

Perhaps we should also note a slight resurgence of partisanship in the state that has been a harbinger of antipartyism in this century. California

---

[31]Clinton Rossiter, *Parties and Politics in America* (Ithaca, N.Y.: Cornell University Press, 1960), p. 1.

[32]Frank Sorauf, *Party Politics in America,* 4th ed. (Boston: Little, Brown & Company, 1980), p. 11.

[33]Charles E. Merriam and Harold F. Gosnell, *The American Party System* (New York: Macmillan, Inc., 1949), p. 470. Similar functions appeared in the 1923 edition of this book by Charles E. Merriam. See Howard A. Scarrow, *Comparative Political Analysis* (New York: Harper & Row, Publishers, 1969), p. 81.

[34]See Jeff Fishel, ed., *Parties and Elections in an Anti-Party Age* (Bloomington: Indiana University Press, 1978), Introduction, for a good discussion.

[35]This fact is somewhat inconvenient from a technical point of view. When gradations of strength and weakness do not follow in logical order, one may doubt the validity of the concept. It should also be noted that some recent research has discovered short-run shifting on the order of 16 percent among the categories Democrat, Republican, and Independent over a four-year period. Ibid., pp. xx–xxi.

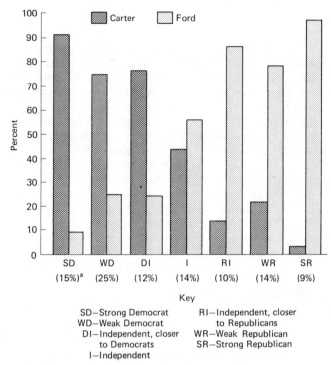

FIGURE 5–1 Vote by Party Identification, 1976

Source: Arthur H. Miller, "The Majority Party Reunited?" In Jeff Fishel, ed., *Parties and Elections in an Anti-Party Age* (Bloomington, Ind.: Indiana University Press, 1978), p. 128.

[a]The percentage distribution for party identification does not add to 100 percent because "apolitical," who comprise 1 percent, have been excluded.

required candidates to list their party affiliation on primary ballots in 1954, and five years later the legislature eliminated cross-filing. Democrats have enjoyed a consistent edge in registrations, and these developments rebounded to their advantage. One study notes that the period from 1958 to 1966 was one of increasing partisanship among voters and in the state legislature. Another study notes considerable partisan gerrymandering and claims that "A highly competitive two-party system is alive and well in California today and seems likely to remain that way."[36]

PARTIES AT THE NATIONAL LEVEL

The three segments of the parties—the officeholders, supporters, and party organization—may be less associated and less unified at the national level than at any other. Wide-ranging change has been taking place in recent

[36]Neil R. Peirce, *The Megastates of America* (New York: W. W. Norton & Co., Inc., 1972), p. 586; Clyde E. Jacobs and Alvin D. Sokolow, *California Government,* 2nd ed. (Toronto, Ontario: Macmillan, Inc., 1970), pp. 103–104.

years, and much of it can be approached via themes of the preceding pages. Antipartyism, weakness, and ambiguity are the hallmarks of the present situation. The basic units of national party organization are the national conventions and national committees. The convention has usually taken a minimal view of its responsibilities, and its four main functions have been realized only to a limited extent. These functions are

1. To nominate presidential and vice presidential candidates
2. To draft a platform
3. To serve as a campaign rally
4. To serve as a governing body of the party.[37]

In nominating a president, the real opportunities of the national convention, although important, are limited. By the time the convention meets, only a few potential candidates are in real contention. Nor should the importance of the platform be exaggerated, although platforms are more informative than many believe. Moreover, one suspects that the campaign rally function matters most when it fails to come off, as happened in Chicago in 1968. More often, the convention-as-rally provides a useful opportunity for activists to be recognized, meet with others, and be sociable. Display of a party in final agreement can be a unifying ritual.

Traditionally, the convention's governing function was least important. Basic rules of the convention's composition and procedure jelled in the early years, but state and local leaders had fashioned them to meet their own needs, not to provide for a real governing body. The congressional caucus, which nominated the party's candidates until 1824, had been an instrument of centralized party control despite its serious imperfections. With its dismantling, state and local politicians won an important victory. When these politicians first began to organize national conventions in the 1830s, they established convention procedures that would maintain parties on a decentralized basis.[38]

It quickly became understood that the convention would decide *how many* convention votes each state party would have, but the state parties themselves would determine how delegates casting those votes would be chosen. In apportioning delegates, the major criterion was always the size of a state's congressional delegation. In other words, it was thought appropriate to represent the states in accordance with the electoral vote formula. Beginning in 1852 the Democrats permitted more delegates than votes and the corresponding use of fractional votes. The Republicans never adopted this practice.

Apportionment of delegates often posed difficulties because the distribution of a party's strength among the voters was rarely uniform. The Republican debacle of 1912 dramatized the nature of the problem: South-

[37]Paul T. David, Ralph M. Goldman, and Richard C. Bain, *The Politics of National Nominating Conventions* (Washington, D.C.: The Brookings Institution, 1960), p. 29.
[38]Austin Ranney, *Curing the Mischiefs of Faction* (Berkeley: University of California Press, 1975), pp. 172–174.

ern delegates at the convention had gone solidly for Taft, and their overrepresentation in convention largely accounted for Roosevelt's failure to get the nomination and his subsequent defection.[39] In 1916 the Republicans therefore adopted provisions for bonus votes from areas where the party had done well in 1908 or 1914. The Democratic party began to develop its version of the bonus vote idea in 1940.

From the beginning Democratic conventions allowed each state delegation to decide whether it would use the "unit rule." This meant that if a state wished to cast its delegation's entire vote as a majority of the delegation wished, the convention would enforce it. State parties often adopted the unit rule in order to maximize their weight in the convention. Moreover, if some large states adopted the unit rule, it was usually to the interests of all the other states to do likewise. As a safeguard to prevent a few states from using the unit rule to control the convention, the Democrats retained the 1832 requirement that *two-thirds* of all delegates voting were required to nominate a candidate for president. In other words, the two-thirds rule to some extent offset the unit rule. The unit rule reflected "states' rights" sentiments to which, until 1932, the Democratic party was hospitable. In the Republican party's formative years, "states' rights" was the slogan of secession. As a result, they never adopted the unit rule and never felt the need for the two-thirds rule. The Democrats kept the two-thirds rule (by actions of simple majorities) until 1936, and efforts to repeal the unit rule did not begin to succeed until 1968.

The first major-party national committee appeared in 1848, when the Democrats decided that they needed a more efficient means of coordinating arrangements for the presidential campaign. Republicans followed suit eight years later. Both parties took the same approach to its powers and composition: The national committee would consist of one member from each state, chosen by the respective state delegations, and the person designated would be accepted by the national committee without question. In 1920 both parties added a national committeewoman from each state.

Until recently, the national committees have shown little interest in realizing their opportunities for influence. Their main task has been to make arrangements for the convention and raise money for the presidential campaign. The president totally overshadows the national chairman of his party; the chairman of the other party is likely to have uncertain tenure. For both, the period of service has usually been short: Chairmen have often had other responsibilities, and they do not preside over the convention. The leading study of the national committees, published in 1964, emphasized their homelessness, impermanence, and lack of importance. The national committees were frequent rivals of partisan campaign committees in Congress, their members were little more than a categorical group, and those chair-

---

[39]The South had 23 percent of the delegate votes, but it accounted for less than 7 percent of the party's popular vote in 1908. David, Goldman, and Bain, *The National Conventions*, pp. 166–167; Ranney, *Mischiefs of Faction*, p. 110.

men who tried to apply their talents were usually frustrated, opposed, and derided.[40]

Despite continuing weaknesses of the national committees, important changes have been occurring. Most of them seem to have begun with the abolition of the two-thirds rule in 1936, which limited the power of the South in the Democratic party. Although the move may have led indirectly to the Dixiecrat rebellion in 1948, the party's northern strength proved sufficient to win that election.

In the 1950s the Democratic National Committee (DNC) was able to punish two southern actions in a way that gave it modest but unprecedented control over its own membership. When the national committeeman from Texas, Wright Morrow, supported Eisenhower rather than Stevenson in 1952, Chairman Stephen Mitchell interpreted Morrow's account of his actions as a letter of resignation from the DNC. The DNC backed him up, and Texas finally appointed an acceptable committeeman. In 1958 Chairman Paul Butler refused to let Louisiana remove its national committeeman, Camille Gravel, Jr., and successfully asserted that Gravel would remain on the committee unless the DNC removed him by a two-thirds vote.[41]

These events seem to have facilitated even more significant actions by the Democratic national convention. In 1964, that body adopted the rule that in selecting delegates, it was understood that a state party would undertake to assure that voters of the state have an opportunity to participate fully in party affairs, regardless of race. In 1968 a convention marked by disarray enforced this rule by denying seats to the "regular" Mississippi delegation and instead seating a rival delegation that had been selected on a nondiscriminatory basis.[42]

It is hard to imagine any of these events occurring in a Democratic party operating under the two-thirds rule. Yet abolition of that rule also led to a sequence of events with different implications. As Keech and Matthews have noted, 1936 nominations were not only the first ones made by a simple majority, they were also the first to benefit from public opinion polls that measured the popularity of potential candidates.[43] Symbolically and practically, abandonment of the two-thirds rule made it possible for convention choices to reflect judgments of the public as expressed in polls. Polling gave delegates a new basis for their nominating decisions that made the two-thirds rule inappropriate. Polling also made old rules of thumb about "availability" increasingly irrelevant. Under traditional practices, a man was not usually "available" for presidential nomination if he was too closely identified with a special interest, too antagonistic toward an important sector of his party, a Catholic, or too unconventional in his family life. (The system

---

[40]Cornelius P. Cotter and Bernard C. Hennessy, *Politics Without Power* (New York: Atherton Press, 1964), p. 63.
[41]Ranney, *Mischiefs of Faction*, pp. 180–181.
[42]Ibid., pp. 180–184.
[43]William R. Keech and Donald R. Matthews, *The Party's Choice* (Washington, D.C.: The Brookings Institution, 1976), p. 4.

operated on the assumption that only men could be elected; women, therefore, were "unavailable.")

As reliable methods of assessing an individual's standing with the electorate developed, the convention's authority as a "deliberative" body probably declined. Keech and Matthews note that since 1936, with only one clear exception, the candidates preferred by their fellow partisans in the final preconvention polls received their party's nomination.[44] Television's increasing influence in presidential politics interacted with polling. Thus, if a person had to demonstrate some standing in the polls before he could even be considered for the nomination, he would have to woo the public as much or more than the convention delegates. To get public attention, the aspiring candidate needed television coverage and in searching for ways to obtain it, discovered the presidential primaries to be prime political opportunities.

Prior to 1952, presidential primaries had been in a semidormant state for almost a quarter of a century. Only about fifteen states held them, and they usually generated little public interest. Important national candidates were often reluctant to enter a primary against a "favorite son"—a state political leader who entered a primary to retain control of his delegation.[45] However, once television turned its attention to the primaries, they became significant national events. Television ignored favorite sons, and fewer of them entered the fray.

By the 1950s presidential politics was already becoming more candidate-centered. Individual candidate organizations would increasingly become the principal vehicles by which media and polling expertise would be put to deliberate political use. Visible costs of campaigning would rise sharply and eventually lead to public subsidies and restrictions on spending.

Although the national party organizations increased their influence relative to state and local units, in the 1960s and 1970s they would, by the logic of events now in motion, be overshadowed by the organizations and followings of particular candidates. It is difficult to assess the significance of more recent changes, but they derive some of their meaning from trends already described. New rules on delegate selection have been especially noteworthy.

Reforms in the Nominating Process

On the surface, the McGovern-Fraser guidelines of 1970 presented us for the first time with a vigorous, comprehensive, and successful effort by a national party to control the delegate selection process. As a total package, the guidelines were complex; they demanded much from the state party organizations. That the state organizations complied almost totally is thus an important fact in itself. However, the national committee may have won

---

[44]Estes Kefauver had a decisive lead in the 1952 polls but lost out to Adlai Stevenson. In 1940 and 1964 it was not entirely clear which Republican was favored in the polls. Ibid., p. 8.

[45]James W. Davis, *Presidential Primaries* (New York: Thomas Y. Crowell Company, Inc., 1967), pp. 140–142.

a hollow victory in an important sense. The state and local leaders had usually been more interested in the contests for state and local offices. Faced with complex new delegate selection requirements and an electorate increasingly inclined toward split-ticket voting, many of them may have simply surrendered national nominating politics to the new activists.

Technically, the new guidelines applied only to the 1972 convention. However, successor commissions for the 1976 and 1980 conventions (Mikulski and Winograd) made minor modifications that continued the basic thrust. Indeed, adjusting the delegate selection rules became a more or less continuous activity, and as of 1980 no early end appeared to be in sight. The question of whether national party committees would be able to deal effectively with their newly discovered powers remained unanswered.

Among the more important elements of the Democratic party reforms were these:

1. *Greater representation for young people, women, and minorities.* In 1972 this goal was widely interpreted as requiring quotas, but the emphasis has since shifted to affirmative action. There is also extensive language in the rules prohibiting discrimination on the basis of race, sex, age, color, creed, national origin, religion, ethnic identity, or economic status at any level of the party.

2. *Limiting the role of party regulars.* The original guidelines prohibited ex officio delegates and limited to 10 percent the proportion of a state's delegation that could be appointed by a party committee. The 1980 rules continued the prohibition against ex officio delegates and specified that 10 percent of the voting delegates would be party leaders and elected officials. However, these rules also stated that governors, senators, and representatives who were not voting delegates would have "privileges except voting rights." As it turned out, many Democratic senators and representatives did not attend their party's 1980 convention.

3. *Fairness, openness, and "timeliness."* State parties must publish detailed rules at least ninety days prior to the first step in the delegate selection process, and all steps must take place within the calendar year of the election. Other rules deal with quorum requirements, petitions, proxies (no more than three at a time for any person), and other procedural matters. The 1980 rules restricted participation in primaries or caucuses to declared Democrats.

4. *Individualism and proportionality.* Use of the unit rule at any stage of the delegate selection process in any party unit or delegation is forbidden. Nor can any law or party rule mandate a delegate to vote against his or her choice at the time of selection.[46] Large portions of a state's delegates must be selected at the congressional district level or in smaller units, regardless of whether a caucus or primary system is employed.

The Republican party seems to have followed the major thrust of these reforms, but to a lesser degree. In 1969 the Republican national chairman appointed a Committee on Delegates and Organization (known as the "DO Committee"), which recommended objectives similar to those in the Demo-

[46] *Delegate Selection Rules for the 1980 Democratic National Convention* (Washington, D.C.: Democratic National Committee, June 9, 1978), 1A, 7D, 8C, 10B, 11G, 13, 14, 15, 16.

cratic guidelines. The 1972 convention made most of these effective for 1976. The Republican party was better organized, less affected by insurgent reform movements, and more committed to retaining party authority at the lower levels. The DO Committee made considerable progress, however, in making the Republicans more a "party of the open door."[47]

Several knowledgeable observers of the American political scene have critized reforms initiated by the McGovern-Fraser Commission for promoting growing weakness in the parties. A major concern is that the reforms had the unintended result of increasing the number of presidential primaries—from seventeen in 1968 to twenty-two in 1972 to thirty in 1976 and to thirty-five in 1980. A presidential primary was the easiest way for a state to meet the complex demands of the rules, and in some cases it spared state leaders from having to compete with new political activists in caucuses.[48]

Jeane Kirkpatrick is concerned that new-style primaries can produce delegates and candidates who have never served an apprenticeship in the party. She also argues that the new rules have had undesirable results even in the nonprimary states:

> Under the new rules anyone willing to state that he is a Democrat (at least for the evening) can join the small group making decisions about the party's presidential nominee. The dynamics of participation . . . insures that turnout at these meetings will be relatively low and made up mainly of persons whose interest in politics is much more intense than that of the ordinary voter, and whose views are probably also more extreme. Opening the caucuses, in sum, has made them vulnerable to manipulation by candidate or issue enthusiasts who may or may not have a broad or long-term concern with the party.[49]

An allied view is that the reforms have advantaged the "new class" of young, college-educated professional and managerial types. Everett Ladd asserts that instead of benefiting "rank-and-file citizens," as claimed by McGovern, the rules have instead served the interests of the upper-middle-class elite, which participates to a much greater degree in open nomination processes.[50]

It is well to remind ourselves that the delegate selection process may be of limited importance. Presidential nominations seem to be strongly affected by the contestants' relative popularity with the voting public. Upheavals of the 1960s, television, the increased role of money in politics, demographic changes, and other factors have been at work in shaping our national nominations.[51] In defense of the reformers, one could say that it might be dangerous to exclude from participation persons who are deter-

[47]For details, see William J. Crotty, *Political Reform and the American Experiment* (New York: Thomas Y. Crowell Company, Inc., 1977), pp. 255–260.
[48]Austin Ranney, *The Federalization of Primaries* (Washington, D.C.: The American Enterprise Institute for Public Policy Research, 1978), p. 3; Jeane Kirkpatrick, *Dismantling the Parties* (Washington, D.C.: American Enterprise Institute for Public Policy Research, 1978), p. 8.
[49]Kirkpatrick, *Dismantling the Parties*, p. 8.
[50]Everett Carll Ladd, Jr., *Where Have All the Voters Gone?* (New York: W. W. Norton & Co., Inc., 1978), p. 59.
[51]Keech and Matthews, *The Party's Choice*, pp. 229, 237.

mined to be active. One might also argue that if traditional politicians had the skills their supporters sometimes imply, they would not have been so easily driven from the field of presidential nominating politics.

We should not expect any system of nominations to produce ideal candidates. Yet many wonder whether or not post-reform candidates will be *acceptable* to most Americans. The nomination of Goldwater in 1964 and McGovern in 1972 illustrates the problem. In each case, after enthusiasts for a particular candidate prevailed in the nominating process, their cause lost disastrously in the general election. Presidential nominating politics has continued to be centered in the efforts of candidate organizations, and the reforms promoted this development. However, self-destructive tendencies of the Goldwater/McGovern variety do not seem to have been at work in 1976 or 1980, even though the ability of organization politicians to control the nominations was practically nil. Good evidence indicates that on such issues as abortion, busing, and defense spending, delegates to the 1976 Democratic convention were much more "liberal" than Democrats in the electorate.[52] Yet this did not prevent them from nominating the moderate Jimmy Carter.

FUTURE PROSPECTS

On balance, it would seem that the McGovern-Fraser impetus was more symbolic of party weakness than of party strength. As the nation entered the 1980s the Democratic National Committee was still a wobbly and uncertain entity, its newfound authority something of an optical illusion. Key actors seemed to have their power base not in the DNC but rather in the entourage of particular people who wanted to be president, or in particular nonparty organizations and movements. Instead of being routed, it would be more accurate to say that the state organizations no longer cared as much about presidential nominations.[53] The revival of Republican fortunes in 1980 seemed likely to generate greater interest in that party's organizational arrangements.

Further changes in national party organization appeared imminent. Many felt that the presidential primaries were too chaotic, that they strained the health of the candidates and the patience of the electorate. The most frequently discussed proposals for further change would involve Congress in activities traditionally left to national party organizations. A direct national primary is the most extreme of these, and it currently enjoys strong support in the polls. In the version advocated by Representative Albert Quie, this would be a closed primary held in August. Contestants for president and vice president would file and be voted on separately. If no candidate received a majority, a runoff between the highest two would be held four weeks later. To get on the primary ballot, a candidate would have to

---

[52]Ladd, *Where Have All the Voters Gone?*, pp. 64–65.

[53] *The Winograd Report*, for example, noted that the state organizations have "taken more of an administrative role than a decision-making role in recent presidential nominations." It cited the decreasing importance of presidential coattails as the reason, p. 24.

file petitions with signatures equal to at least 1 percent of the popular vote in the most recent presidential election.[54]

Before deciding on the merits of such a measure, you may want to consider the relevant discussions in Chapter 8. The present system is admittedly complex, but it has some advantages. It permits many people to participate, and it gives long-shot candidates a chance to attract enough publicity to qualify for serious consideration. Long campaigns also tend to minimize distortions caused by particular campaign blunders or news events.

A national primary might strike a death blow at the only important national party organizations we have. Candidates would still begin their campaigns when they chose, and an early start could well be more important than ever. The desire to shorten campaigns is understandable, but it may not be easily accomplished without more significant changes in the constitutional system. Canada, for example, has short campaigns, but the timing of elections is flexible, as it is in most parliamentary regimes, and presumes well-structured party conflict prior to the calling of elections. Keep in mind that the campaign may not seem long to those who have not been paying attention. A significant proportion of the population does not get involved until the final weeks. Efforts to redesign the nominating process are not likely to achieve their aims unless they face up to the role of the media.[55]

Regardless of the merits of the national primary, the national parties clearly face unprecedented challenges. Nothing in sight appears likely to lessen the impact of candidate organizations on presidential politics, and the national parties are particularly vulnerable to their influence. Under the old politics, candidates wooed state delegations but left them intact as part of an integral state party system. Today, delegate selection has been largely separated from other state party affairs, and candidates are able to *take over* state delegations, thus determining the composition of much of the national committees. Present laws subsidize the national conventions, but most public money is channeled directly to the candidates.

It is not at all clear how free the parties will be to solve their own problems. Congress has always had unquestionable authority to regulate the national parties, but it has never done so. The courts also have been most reluctant (until very recently) to examine convention proceedings. Lacking an acknowledged place in the Constitution or the laws, the convention has nonetheless represented the final authority in the party.

Dominant elements in both parties believe that in the absence of congressional legislation, the national parties are private associations with the right to govern their affairs by their own rules, even if they conflict with state laws. However, some federal courts have been declaring that national

<hr />

[54]Austin Ranney, *The Federalization of Primaries* (Washington, D.C.: The American Enterprise Institute for Public Policy Research, 1978), pp. 7–8.

[55]William Crotty is strongly opposed to the national primary and suggests that an effort be made to rationalize and simplify nominating procedures without fundamentally changing them. *Political Reform and the American Experiment* (New York: Thomas Y. Crowell Company, Inc., 1977), p. 234. For a cogent analysis of proposals to have regional or clustered presidential primaries, see Austin Ranney, *The Federalization of Presidential Primaries* (Washington, D.C.: American Enterprise Institute for Public Policy Research, 1978).

party processes are integral parts of the presidential selection process and therefore subject to judicial review, and members of both parties have challenged party rules in the courts. The Supreme Court may ultimately decide what (if anything) the Constitution requires in the way of delegate apportionment among the states.[56]

[56]Ranney, *Mischiefs of Faction,* pp. 3, 85, 111.

6

Organized
Political
Influence

This chapter will briefly examine some general characteristics of interest group, business, and elite power in the United States. Political movements will also receive brief scrutiny. Actions of the mass electorate enable the parties to capture nominal control of elective offices, but modern governments also respond to the influence of smaller formations that both collaborate and compete with the parties. Taken together, such formations shape much of the environment in which electoral politics unfolds. The methods of the more exclusive entities vary, although they sometimes converge on what someone has referred to as the "golden rule" of politics.[1]

POLITICAL ELITES

In ordinary English, the word *elite* refers to the choice part or "flower" of society. Although three of the early political sociologists employed *elite* as a term of scientific realism, they also invested it with pessimistic and antidemocratic connotations. The term tends to retain these associations, inviting us to "see through" the democratic myth and to give it up as hopelessly naive. In the theories of Gaetano Mosca, Vilfredo Pareto, and Robert Michels, all governance boils down to a class that rules and the others who are ruled. In Mosca's words: "The first class, always the less numerous, performs all political functions, monopolizes power, and enjoys the advantages that power brings, whereas the second, the more numerous class, is directed and controlled by the first."[2]

[1]"He who has the gold makes the rules."
[2]Gaetano Mosca, *The Ruling Class (Elementi di Scienza Politica)*, trans. Hannah D. Hahn, (New York: McGraw-Hill, 1939), p. 50. This work was first published in 1896.

When we employ the term *elite* in our discussions, we should take care to divest it of its unnecessary meanings. Undoubtedly there are different kinds of elites. The one we are concerned with is the political (or power) elite. It includes those persons with the greatest influence over the policies and activities of the state. This definition makes no assumptions about the social composition, size, or quality of the elite. Nor does it imply anything about the overall distribution of influence in the society. All of these matters are open to investigation.[3]

A major difficulty with analysis of the elite is that the links between rulers and ruled are not well understood. Political power seems to be a two-way street, with the authority of rulers depending on empowering responses from the ruled. However, the precise nature of these relationships remains elusive. To conceive them as ones in which the elite monopolize power is to see but one side. Those who use the elite approach often tend to understate the importance of nonelites at middle and lower levels.[4]

Some concepts of elite power are compatible with a democratic order. In one influential view, democracy depends on the *relations* between elite and mass, not on the *absence* of an elite. Rule is libertarian "where initiative individuality and choice are widespread." It is juridical "where decisions are conditional and subject to challenge." And it assumes commonwealth form where "benefits of the power process are distributed throughout the body politic." Democracy then is a "libertarian, juridical commonwealth." Other characteristics of democracy are closely related: voluntarism rather than regimentation; absence of an elite as a closed caste; dispersed rather than concentrated rule. Pareto's statement that "every people is governed by an elite, by a chosen element in the population," need not be accepted unless it means simply that every people is ruled by rulers.[5]

Note that the quotation from Mosca assigns no importance to government as such. He placed power entirely in a social class and ignored the possibility that government itself might be an independent source of power. Disregard of government might be justified in the many instances where government is very weak. However, governmental institutions in a nation like the United States have been so powerful that a group unable to assert major influence on them could not possibly be regarded as an elite.

There is, however, a difference between formal influence based on a position in the government and influence with an outside base. We must be prepared to discover formal positions whose occupants have little power, and less conspicuous persons outside government who wield great influence. Even so, formal and informal authority are likely to converge at the top. As one scholar puts it, "The conduct of national affairs in the United States or the Soviet Union would be extremely difficult if institutionally

[3]The definition is adapted from Robert D. Putnam, *The Comparative Study of Political Elites* (Englewood Cliffs, N.J.: Prentice-Hall, Inc., 1976), p. 6.

[4]James A. Bill and Robert L. Hardgrave, Jr., *Comparative Politics* (Columbus, Ohio: Charles E. Merrill Publishing Company, 1973), p. 173.

[5]Harold D. Lasswell and Abraham Kaplan, *Power and Society* (New Haven, Conn.: Yale University Press, 1950), pp. 202, 228, 234.

designated leaders did not normally also possess effective power to make and enforce decisions."[6]

Group, elite, and class approaches tend to be related to and sometimes confused with each other. In the interests of clarity, let us define *group* as an organized aggregate consisting of any number of persons, ranging from small, face-to-face groups to entire nations. Any society may include a large number of such groups, and any given individual may have from none to many group memberships. *Classes*, on the other hand, reflect the distribution of some value or values (usually power, wealth, or prestige); the number of classes is relatively small. An individual can belong to only one class— the one corresponding to his or her share of the values in question—and the members of the class may or may not be organized; they may or may not exhibit "class consciousness." Notions of rank are usually inherent in class analysis, but group analysis tends to focus on patterns of cooperation and conflict with no necessary element of ranking. We may consider the *rulers* to be the most active and powerful members of the elite. If there is a ruling class, it is the one from which rulers are selected and in whose interest they exercise power. Such a class must also be defined in terms of all values important to the society.[7]

One can identify elite personnel in different ways: by the formal positions that are thought to influence the state; by perceptions of informed observers as to who is influential (the "reputation method"); and by study of how particular decisions have been made. Each of these techniques has its pitfalls, but as noted above there is a tendency for at least two of them to yield somewhat similar results at the national level.

Some Comparative Findings

Studies in different nations show that in every nation large proportions of political leaders grew up in families situated in higher levels of the society. Surprisingly, upward mobility into the political elite has been *less* marked in the United States than elsewhere. One study found that proportionately fewer national legislators in the United States came from families with manual occupations than in England, Italy, or West Germany. This situation has also changed less *over time* in the United States than in Europe. Although the preindustrial aristocracy remained significant for many years after the industrial revolution in Europe, by the 1860s middle-class and working-class social origins were becoming progressively more important. In the United States, limited evidence available suggests that national political leadership has fairly consistently come from the middle and upper-middle classes. Upper-class backgrounds declined in the pre–Civil War period, but no consistent pattern of working-class increases has appeared.[8]

---

[6] Putnam, *Comparative Political Elites*, p. 18. Putnam notes that divergence between formal and informal structures is likely to be greater in smaller systems and that much of the debate on this issue has community power as its context. For issues in the community power debate, see Thomas R. Dye, "Community Power Structures," in *Politics in States and Communities*, 3rd ed. (Englewood Cliffs, N.J.: Prentice-Hall, Inc., 1977).

[7] This discussion has been adapted from Bill and Hardgrave, *Comparative Politics*, pp. 187–195; and Lasswell and Kaplan, *Power and Society*, pp. 62–69, 29–55, 181, 200–206.

[8] Putnam, *Comparative Political Elites*, pp. 23, 178–179, 185.

In general, the higher the status of the political elite, the more conservative it is. In most nations, leaders of conservative parties are further removed in status from their voters than are leaders of left-wing parties. Again, the main exception is the United States. In this country, Democratic elites come from no less privileged backgrounds than Republican elites, which in large part explains the relatively low degree of upward mobility into the American political elite. The absence of a working-class or socialist party in the United States and the relative ease of upward mobility into the middle class are also undoubtedly part of the explanation.

What is the relation between electoral politics and elite power? Although the answer remains somewhat uncertain, the literature does suggest that elected rulers tend to be more representative of various population categories than those who are not elected. Elections may strengthen the hand of elite figures who are "traitors to their class"—that is, who hold views that serve the interests of nonelite strata. There is also some evidence that in Western democracies elites have been more committed to civil liberties and basic democratic practices than nonelites.[9] These commitments are thought to be much greater than in nondemocratic nations, and it is possible that democratic election systems are partly responsible.

Partisan differences among elites are usually related to other types of cleavage, and the patterns can vary widely from nation to nation. In some cases the rulers are more sharply divided on ideological or other lines than the mass public—for example, Democratic political leaders are usually more liberal than Democratic voters, and Republican political leaders are more conservative than Republican voters. This pattern exists in a number of democratic nations including, in recent years, the United States and Canada. However, countries with deep cultural cleavages at the mass level may avert widespread social conflict by deliberate efforts to minimize differences within the elites.

Those who emphasize the integration of the political elite usually feel that elections do not modify power relationships in any substantial way. Thus, in *The Power Elite*, published in 1957, C. Wright Mills insisted that corporation executives, top-level administrators in the federal government, and the top ranks of the military had means for exercising power that was without historical precedent. Such persons were at the summits of the decisive institutions and, as such, manned this society's command posts. They could transcend "the ordinary environments of ordinary men," and be "history makers." Professional politicians, Congress, pressure groups, and "old upper classes of town and city and region" only occupied middle levels of power. Mills thought that American society was relatively unified and powerful at the top and relatively fragmented and impotent at the bottom. For him, those in the middle neither expressed the will of those at the bottom nor determined the content of decisions made at the top.[10]

Others have found partisan cleavage among elites to be significant. In Britain and the United States especially, they report a tendency for elites of

[9]Ibid., pp. 38–39, 116–117; Peter Rossi, "Community Decision Making," *Administrative Science Quarterly*, 1 (March 1957), 415–443.
[10]C. Wright Mills, *The Power Elite* (New York: Oxford University Press, 1957), chap. 1.

the different parties to adhere to different ideologies. Party elites may have been similar in their social origins, but they have differed in their social connections and acted on the basis of contrasting priorities. Elite agreement on important matters has tended to reflect popular preferences. Partisan competition has offered voters valuable choices and has encouraged elites to conform to popular preferences.[11]

Implicitly or explicitly, analysts convinced of the overriding importance of elites have erected an in-depth defense against the notion that electoral politics might significantly modify the power equation. Each argument has some merit but can be easily overstated.

The initial contention is likely to be that constitutional forms fail to provide elected officials with effective control or even major influence over the state. If forced to concede that such officials do have at least major influence, elitists can then argue that elected officials are under the control of corporate power, economic dominants, or the upper class. In taking this position, they tend to downplay the corporate power's vulnerability to political interference and to minimize the pressures on decision making that come from within the government itself. Although the complexity of the federal establishment probably makes it difficult for *any* set of persons to control it, elitists are reluctant to concede that upper-level decision makers might be influenced by those at middle levels rather than by those outside the government. They prefer instead to perceive public administration as a set of hierarchies that give greater control to those at the top.

It is, of course, extremely difficult to document the manner in which privileged segments of the society might exert control over elected officials. One way to sidestep this problem is to suggest that elected officials do not need to be controlled because they themselves tend to come from upper status backgrounds. The latter part of the assertion has a good deal of truth to it, as we have seen. Even so, the situation falls far short of that required for a ruling class. About 18 percent of America's national legislators had fathers who were employed in manual occupations.[12] The privileged background has often been middle rather than upper class. More important, studies indicate that social background is a very poor predictor of individual policy preferences at the elite level. The notion that decision makers raised in a given stratum serve the interests of that stratum, though plausible at first sight, is not consistent with the best available evidence and analysis. The views of people who achieve elite positions may well not be typical of their class. Distinctive career experiences may be as relevant as their social background in shaping their outlooks. We could expect their face-to-face contacts to differ in significant ways from those of nonelite persons of the same social origins.

The next line of defense is the argument that elected officials do not represent masses in any meaningful sense. Elite strata can control the symbolic and propaganda environment of elections; they can use their financial resources to affect election outcomes, promote safe candidates, and so

[11]Putnam, *Comparative Political Elites*, p. 130.
[12]Ibid., p. 23.

forth. The electoral process is certainly imperfect, and the elitists could strike some heavy blows here. However, this terrain does not particularly interest them. Instead, they tend to fall back on the argument that ordinary citizens are so apathetic and uninformed that they are deceived about the real issues. The elite keep sensitive topics off the political agenda, and their true power therefore lies in the area of "nondecisions."[13] In part, this argument may amount to little more than the disappointment of some academic theoreticians that mass opinion does not conform to their own. The possibility that nondecisions reflect valid preferences of ordinary citizens, or even a social consensus, is not seriously entertained.

Again, all of these issues are important, and none of the arguments cited is entirely without merit. However, I am sure you are aware that excessive elite control is not necessarily our most serious problem. A crisis reflecting a reduced capacity of government to govern is also possible. Such a crisis can occur in different ways, including the following ones: if there is too little consensus in the society or too little diffuse support of government; if the power of officials to make decisions and obtain compliance falls below a certain level; or if the things people expect government to do become too difficult for it to achieve.

Lack of capacity to govern and unwarranted elite influence are not necessarily mutually exclusive possibilities, but there may be some rivalry between them as analytic concerns. I have the impression that analysts who are most convinced of the reality of unwarranted elite influence are not particularly interested in the possible crisis of governance. Some have been eager to portray allegedly pluralistic systems as actually dominated by elites, giving little weight to the possible weakness of political authorities and the possible loss of national unity. Conversely, those who fear that America is becoming ungovernable may feel that decision makers now enjoy too little authority rather than too much. Hierarchies of all sorts seem to have experienced some erosion. Perhaps this erosion is only temporary, but elitist theories have not come to grips with it.

POLITICAL INFLUENCE OF BIG BUSINESS

Thomas Dye's recent study of elite power in the United States gives us an interesting entry into the question of business power at the elite level. The study identifies 5,416 elite positions, 36 percent of which are in government, mass media, education, the foundations, law, and certain civic and cultural organizations. The other 64 percent are in the corporate sector; these include presidents and directors of corporations with the largest total assets in each of several categories: industrial; transportation, utilities, and communications; banking; and insurance. Disparities in the size of corporations are most impressive and reflect a high degree of concentration in the corporate sector. For example, although there are more than 200,000 industrial corporations in the United States, the largest 100 control more than half of

[13]Ibid., pp. 130–131.

all corporate industrial assets. Concentration in other parts of the corporate sector is even more marked.

Dye reports a moderate amount of "interlocking" within the elite. Four-fifths of elite individuals held only one position, but about 40 percent of all *positions* were interlocked because a few individuals held three or more positions. Much of the interlocking occurred within the corporate sector itself. The 4,101 *individuals* in the elite tended to hold many other economic, governmental, and civic positions below the top. Other channels of influence derived from leisure activities. Thus, almost half of the individuals in the elite belonged to at least one of forty exclusive clubs, and these memberships were especially noticeable in the corporate sector.

Although Dye found overrepresentation of upper-class backgrounds, he claims that the liberal values espoused by the elite differ from preferences of the mass public. The elites stress public service and do-goodism, which derive from upper-class attitudes shaped in the New Deal era. Some might take this as evidence of the elite's willingness to offer disinterested service and to transcend narrow self-interest. However, for Dye, elite liberalism is no cause for rejoicing. "Radical critics of American business who portray top corporate elites as reactionary, repressive, narrow-minded, or short-sighted vastly underestimate their chosen enemy."[14]

Dye's focus is not on business as such, but he obviously considers business to be a key element in America's power system. He is probably right that some of the social outlooks of the elite are not widely popular, even if "do-goodism" is too derisive a label. However, many of the specific policies that this elite allegedly favors have enjoyed substantial support at the mass level—especially when conceived in moderate terms: reducing poverty and discrimination, promoting higher employment, curtailing slums, reducing illness (especially expensive illness), extending opportunities for mass education. There is no evidence to suggest that the mass public would like to do away with the existing economic and social system. Indeed, on these findings, one wonders why it should. Dye concedes a number of differences within the elite, but he minimizes them as slight or as concerning means rather than ends.

Determining the proper size of the elite is a problem with no single good answer. Dye's elite is much larger than those suggested by C. Wright Mills or Floyd Hunter, but it may still be too small. Most comparative studies concentrate on small numbers of people in the visible parts of the governmental sector. Dye's elite is about midway between Deutsch's suggestion of fifty names per million for the "central elite," and five names per million for the "top elite."[15]

One can also easily quarrel with the proportions of positions in various categories, and Dye concedes that subjective judgments are involved. He includes only 227 posts in the combined executive, legislative, and judicial

[14]Thomas R. Dye, *Who's Running America,* 2nd ed. (Englewood Cliffs, N.J.: Prentice-Hall, Inc., 1979), pp. 13–15, 20–22, 47.

[15]Karl W. Deutsch, *Politics and Government* (Boston: Houghton Mifflin Company, 1974), p. 51. Deutsch also speaks of a midelite core consisting of 5 percent of the population.

branches of the federal government; the addition of military figures brings the governmental sector of his elite to only 286 positions. This includes only 29 representatives and senators, no governors, no mayors, and no judges except those on the U.S. Supreme Court. One can justify the absence of influential persons at the state and local level on the basis of maintaining a clear focus to the study. However, this is a dubious procedure if one also seeks to demonstrate a high degree of centralization and concentration of elite power. The same could be said of excluding middle echelons in public and private institutions. One could easily expand several segments of this elite by including more organizations in places other than Washington or New York.

An Organizational Approach

Another approach to the influence of big business focuses on organizational requirements of large corporations. Since organizational theory quickly disabuses us of any notion that control from the top is rigidly hierarchical or absolute, it makes the power of presidents and directors seem less formidable. Some of them may even be persons of formal rather than real power. However, the organizational approach does not suggest that big business is any less influential.

Profit making is the corporation's reason for being, but subgroups within it have differing perspectives on production, inventory, sales, and market-share objectives. Theories of business organization have stressed the importance of middle-management levels for many years. With his concept of the "technostructure," John Kenneth Galbraith gave this idea a new emphasis. He stated that effective corporate decision making typically requires contributions from a variety of specialists, and the chief vehicles have become the ad hoc committees that operate at many levels. A top official cannot safely reverse the deliberations of such a group because he lacks the knowledge to do so. As a result, "It is not the managers who decide. Effective power of decision is lodged deeply in the technical, planning, and other specialized staff."[16]

Nevertheless, subcoalitions within the large corporations are closely knit and share many political interests. Large corporations have more *incentives* to be politically active than smaller firms or ordinary citizens. Their share of the costs and benefits of public programs may be considerable. Unlike the small firm or private citizen, large corporations can garner tangible and direct rewards from their investments of time, energy, and resources in political activity. The distribution of political *resources* is also heavily skewed towards the large corporate actor, which has plenty of money, expertise, and access to government that the ordinary citizen cannot match. Large corporations can operate over wide geographic areas while coordinating operations from a single point. They can exploit a profusion of human

[16]John Kenneth Galbraith, *The New Industrial State* (Boston: Houghton Mifflin Company, 1967), pp. 69, 71. For a useful summary of organizational theories, see William R. Dill, "Business Organizations," in *Handbook of Organizations*, ed. James G. March (Chicago: Rand McNally & Company, 1965), pp. 1071–1114.

contacts with employees, shareholders, suppliers, and customers. Millions of blue-collar and white-collar workers are dependent on large corporations for their livelihoods. The corporation may develop patron-client relationships with states and localities, even though the corporation is legally a creature of the state, and politically delegated authority to subcontract can give large firms leverage over others.[17]

The Interest Group Approach

One traditional approach to business was to view it as part of the much larger firmament of interest group power in America. Sometimes this approach brought with it an unjustified tendency to view the interest group universe as more diverse than it was. Also, in stressing similarities among groups of different sorts, the extraordinary influence of big business may not have been fully appreciated. The group approach often stressed divisions within the business community: exporters vs. importers, railroads vs. truckers, steel vs. aluminum, retailer vs. wholesaler, southern businesses vs. northeastern businesses and so forth. Such differences may well mitigate to a degree the political capacity of business.

When used with restraint, the group approach to business power produces useful insights. V. O. Key, Jr., drew attention to an enormous diversity within business and described in detail the astonishing apparatus of organizations centered in the Chamber of Commerce, the National Association of Manufacturers, and the trade associations. Yet overriding all the differences was an important common denominator:

> . . . a network of common interest pulls the business community together on major issues when its security is threatened. Party lines, sectional lines, and religious lines rarely divide businessmen when their common interests are in peril. Within the business community powerful factors operate to bring conformity.[18]

Business and Electoral Politics

In the above paragraphs, we looked first at a small group of elite positions and then considered the large businesses as organizations. Then examination of a group approach led us to an image of the "business community." As one considers larger and larger slices of the business system, its electoral prowess becomes ever more formidable. The steady flow of government policy making can easily threaten the interests of the business community if it does not bring its influence to bear. Participation of business in all phases of politics is evident.

V. O. Key stressed the high degree of mobilization for political action within the business community. Conventions, committee sessions, staff conferences, board meetings, incessant travel funded by expense accounts knit

---

[17]Lester M. Salamon and John J. Siegfried, "Economic Power and Political Influence," *American Political Science Review,* 71 (September 1977), 1029; Edwin M. Epstein, *The Corporation in American Politics* (Englewood Cliffs, N.J.: Prentice-Hall, Inc., 1969), pp. 192–212.

[18]V. O. Key, Jr., *Politics, Parties, and Pressure Groups,* 5th ed. (New York: Thomas Y. Crowell Company, Inc., 1964), pp. 72–73.

the leadership together in what is very much like a continuous political caucus. Lacking the strength of numbers, business has had to engage in political activity on many fronts, including aggressive attempts to mold public opinion.[19]

Though small in numbers, the business community can put together a respectable number of votes, and the value of these votes may increase if turnout continues to decline. As one examines relations between business and government at increasingly inclusive levels, the basic issues remain similar: To what extent are the two domains separate from each other? How much conflict or disagreement pervades the relationship? Which domain has the upper hand? We should not expect easy answers to such questions, and we must not arbitrarily exclude other influential domains. One could argue that a tight interdependence exists between government and business and that the remaining distinctions between the two are eroding.

E. E. Schattschneider, on the other hand, emphasized the *tension* between business and government. By *business* he meant something even broader than the business community; we may call it the *institution* of business. Business in this perspective dominates the nongovernmental world today in a manner analogous to church domination in some earlier eras. Business is a system of power, attitudes, and social relations that begins to challenge the supremacy of government. Put another way, Schattschneider advised us that business has become so powerful that the only effective check on it is the incredible prowess of the most powerful institution of all: the government itself.[20]

This scholar felt certain that a divorce of these two power systems had been achieved. The business system, he said, is exclusive and fosters a high degree of inequality and concentration of power. It operates on the assumption that the public responsibility of business is limited. In contrast, the political and governmental system is broadly equalitarian and designed to invite the widest possible participation. Schattschneider offered a vivid description of the difference:

> Imagine a political system in which votes are bought and sold freely in the open market, a system in which it is taken for granted that people will buy all the votes they can afford and use their power to get more money in order to buy more votes, so that a single magnate might easily outvote a whole city. Imagine a situation in which elections have become a mere formality because one or a few individuals are owners of a controlling number of votes. Suppose that nine-tenths of the members of the community are unable to exert any appreciable influence. Suppose, moreover, that the minority is entitled to very little information about what is being done. That is what the political system would be like if it were run the way business is run.[21]

[19]Ibid., pp. 90–91.
[20]E. E. Schattschneider, *The Semisovereign People,* Introduction by David Adamany. (New York: Holt, Rinehart & Winston, 1960), pp. 118–124.
[21]Ibid., pp. 117–119. Copyright © 1968 by E. E. Schattschneider, © 1975 by E. E. Schattschneider and the Dryden Press, Inc. Reprinted by permission of Holt, Rinehart & Winston and E. E. Schattschneider.

The place of the Republican party in this conception of politics is worth noting. Schattschneider did not feel that the GOP was simply the captive of big business. It is true that business had been forced to form a political organization designed to win elections and thus compete for power in the widest arena. However, in a two-party system, business could not afford to be isolated, and it had nowhere else to go. The fact that the Republican party had to win popular majorities, plus the fact that business was a minority, gave the Republican party a real measure of independence in its relationship with business. Since the Republican party was a mediator between business and government, its prowess as a political actor was very great. Schattschneider thought that the entire arrangement represented a striking accomplishment of American democracy.[22]

In recent years, business seems to have substantially recovered from the losses of prestige it suffered in the 1930s. Increasing dissatisfaction with governmental performance has given free-enterprise thinking a new cachet. A strong current of "neoconservatism" is running in intellectual circles, and the popularity of various voter-initiated tax-cutting measures has placed government somewhat on the defensive.

Business scored a number of victories in the Ninety-fifth Congress. It defeated efforts to create a consumer protection agency, weakened clean-up schedules under amendments to the 1970 Clean Air Act, and defeated proposals to strengthen the Federal Trade Commission, to name just three. In citing these and other battles, one analyst claims that "American business is on a winning streak."[23] The focus of recent political action by the major business organizations hardly fits the philosophy of do-goodism. Instead, the concerns appear to be much the same as they always have been: freedom from governmental regulation (including that undertaken to protect the environment); subsidies and other benefits to business; opposition to organized labor; and getting the right people elected.

INTEREST GROUPS

An interest group (or pressure group) is an organized aggregate which, among other things, seeks to influence governmental policy. As noted in Chapter 1, parties and interest groups are first cousins, if not even closer political kin. Each is a type of political association that emerged in an era of powerful governments and expanded opportunities for participation. In democratic societies, both can give citizens opportunities to control government and make it responsive. A free election system is the cornerstone of democratic party activity; constitutionally guaranteed rights of assembly and petition are fundamental to democratic interest groups. Other basic freedoms, particularly speech and press, undergird both party and interest group activity.

[22]Ibid., pp. 42–43, 121.
[23]"Corporate Assertiveness," in *Editorial Research Reports 1978* (Washington, D.C.: Congressional Quarterly Inc., 1978), I, 463.

In the United States, parties and interest groups are interrelated. The two-party format may encourage a proliferation of groups with limited but specific objectives. Groups and parties must both adapt to a governmental structure based on divisions among branches, agencies, and levels. Such an arrangement scatters governmental authority and places it in many different hands. The independent authority of each particular fragment of government tends to isolate it and make it vulnerable to whatever groups seek to influence its particular policy decisions.

These same structural characteristics make it difficult for any political party to obtain control of the government: A party must win victories in many different arenas if it is to gain leverage over the entire political system. To be truly successful in this, a party would need an extraordinary majority willing to persist for many years in a common endeavor. In reality, a party at best has a formal majority, weakly organized and subject to continuous defections.

Variations in Size

In the era of mass politics, organization is the key to influence. The individual may be lucky enough to enjoy privacy and freedom in isolation but cannot realistically hope to be influential unless he or she collaborates with others. Such collaboration often arises naturally out of everyday relationships: A group of neighbors pesters city officials to repair a street. Three or four law school students have a few beers and decide, half seriously, to assist each other in their future political careers. Some caseworkers in a small town welfare operation conclude that the director is incompetent and (bravely) decide to make a protest at the next city council meeting. None of these groups has formal meetings or bylaws. If visible at all, they appear only momentarily. Except for the caseworkers, the effort required to promote group action is modest.

Organization increases influence exponentially. A group of 10 persons working together has influence equivalent to 10^2 or 10^3 persons working by themselves. Their actual influence depends, of course, on the group's objectives and the energy and resources its members can contribute. Even a small-scale collaboration can be surprisingly influential if it can employ a variety of resources. The exponential increase is produced by group reinforcement of attitudes and morale, efficiencies derived from division of labor within the group, ability of groups to make their goals seem practical or acceptable to the community, and the greater visibility of groups compared to individuals. Small groups of politically astute insiders may control larger organizations, and the processes are similar.

Small groups of the type so far considered are too numerous to count. Nevertheless, many people do not participate in them. Some cannot be stirred to activity having modest objectives. Others lack even the minimum skills needed to collaborate effectively with others for a controversial purpose. Still others do not have enough emotional or economic security to be comfortable in political roles. All of these detriments to group participation tend to be at least moderately correlated with social class. Even at middle or upper-middle levels, many people would rather spend their time in what they regard as more pleasurable ways. American society offers a profusion of leisure activities that can distract people from politics and enough material benefits to soften many grievances.

Large Groups

The patterns of interest group activity change as the scale of collaboration expands. In general, as the size of a group increases, its influence also increases. The larger group can draw on more resources and can organize for effective action in different governmental arenas. Yet the increase in influence is not usually *proportional* to size, and apathetic members swell the rolls of most larger groups. Some analysts cite overlapping membership to account for lack of commitment. A person with ties to a fraternal organization, church, and union, for example, might have relatively little commitment to any one of these groups, because intense loyalty to one would conflict with attachments to the others.

Recent theorizing suggests that membership apathy may also derive from "free-rider" motivations. If a group seeks benefits that cannot be restricted to its members (as is often the case), and if the efforts of a large group are necessary to obtain the benefit, a rational person who shares the interest may not even join the group.[24] He reasons that the success of the group is not likely to hinge on his contribution, and that he will enjoy its benefits whether he joins or not. Imagine, for example, a group organizing to increase speed limits on interstate highways. A large group is needed because federal policy is involved. If the speed limit is raised to seventy-five miles per hour, all motorists will "enjoy" the privilege of driving at the new speed limit, whether or not they belong to the group that instituted the change. If it cost anything to become a member, no rational person would join such a group, even if the person very much favored higher speed limits, unless there were other incentives.

Theoretically, large groups cope with the free-rider problem in one or both of two basic ways. One technique is to offer *selective benefits to members*. For example, our hypothetical group might provide its members with special automobile insurance and motel rates. The other technique is *compulsion*. Thus, to be eligible for many jobs one must join a union. Membership in the group is not strictly voluntary.

Please note, however, that this is coercion of a special kind. It is quite rational for a person to support an organization with limited coercive authority in order to obtain important collective benefits. This is why members of labor unions and trade associations strongly support their groups even when a certain amount of coercion is present. Indeed, government itself is a partly coercive arrangement that rational people support in order to enjoy collective benefits such as public safety, security from attack by a hostile power, and an integrated system of streets and roads. Nevertheless, it would be an exaggeration to say that people enjoy coercive arrangements or that all of the coercion they experience is actually to their advantage.

[24]For a rigorous discussion, see Robert H. Salisbury, "Interest Groups," in *Handbook of Political Science*, ed. Fred I. Greenstein and Nelson W. Polsby (Reading, Mass.: Addison-Wesley Publishing Company, Inc., 1975), IV, 192–196.

The above discussion applies mainly to groups that organize to obtain benefits from government or other groups. Some groups, however, are formed to serve other purposes. Members of many fraternal, civic, religious, and veterans organizations (such as American Legion, Elks, Kiwanis, Knights of Columbus) want to enjoy close associations with other people. Such groups may possess latent influence, but they often try to avoid controversy. Members of still other groups seek the rapport that comes from expressing common outlooks or sharing common experiences.

Although motivations for joining organizations are usually mixed, much of the membership in large groups tends to be either inactive or ineffective in a political sense. The potential free rider who has been induced or coerced into joining the organization will invest little psychic energy in it. Joiners who seek pleasant associations with other people do not want controversy to spoil their fun, yet political actions are inherently controversial.

Many people want group benefits with a minimum expenditure of effort. This implies that in large groups the small minority that *is* active can easily control group policies and activity agendas. Control by the active minority generally occurs in all sorts of large interest groups. Genuine contests for leadership, in which the rank and file make an authentic choice, are rare. People in expressive organizations essentially endorse the public positions taken by group leaders.

Sectors of Group Activity

The complexity of group life in a nation such as the United States is a response to rapid social change, growing interdependence, and economic development. Interest groups representing specialized occupations, for example, are legion. Whether an occupation is trying to improve its position or to merely protect gains already achieved, it will often seek governmental regulations that limit entry into the given calling. The result is a profusion of licensing, registration, and examining boards for beauticians, architects, watch repairmen, speech pathologists, auctioneers, nurses, funeral directors, realtors, accountants, veterinarians, librarians, and many others. Often a given board is entirely a captive of the group, and state authority is, in effect, delegated to it.

Some groups organize their affairs in ways that adapt to the democratic expectations of the community. They elect officers, vest authority in conventions, and submit referenda to the membership. Usually, of course, the active minority is able to retain control, despite such devices. Other groups have made no pretense that members would control the organization. Members of Common Cause, for example, can support the organization, but according to one analyst, a self-perpetuating board of directors determines policy.[25]

Groups may exist at three organizational levels. At the first level, individuals are members, and the organizations they join serve the needs of those individuals. If such organizations are in turn members of a larger

[25]Ibid., p. 186.

organization, we have a second-order group. Thus, a union local may belong to an international union, and a corporation may belong to a trade association. At a third level is the peak association, which covers (or hopes to cover) all organizations in a particular sector. The AFL-CIO (a federation of international unions) is an example in the field of labor. The National Association of Manufacturers (NAM) has also been called a peak association. However, until recently it operated separately from the even more broadly based U.S. Chamber of Commerce. The NAM has about 12,000 corporations as members. The Chamber is a federation of state and local chambers of commerce, trade associations, and societies of businessowners not organized for private purposes. In 1973 the NAM moved its headquarters from New York to Washington and began to coordinate some important actions with its old rival, the Chamber of Commerce.

Agriculture. American agriculture has experienced a social and cultural transformation in this century. As recently as 1920, 30 percent of the American people lived on farms. By 1971, the proportion had shrunk to 5 percent. America as an agrarian society is becoming a memory. Station wagons and pickup trucks, household appliances, consolidated school districts, and television sets now integrate most farm families into a novel type of urban culture.

More than half of all farm land is now held in units of more than one thousand acres, and most farm organizations tend to be dominated by the larger and more successful producers. Increasingly, farmers consider their enterprise as much a business as a way of life, and the astonishing success of American agriculture in business terms is making agrarian culture increasingly peripheral to the larger society.

In its early years the republic was overwhelmingly agricultural, and the entire political system naturally reflected small town and agrarian values. Organization of a significant agricultural political interest did not take place until the 1870s, when expanding markets made farmers vulnerable to price fluctuations, railroad rate determinations, and the growing consolidation in manufacturing and credit. Since farmers had weight of numbers they naturally concentrated on electoral politics. However, the political system that emerged from the election of 1896 largely negated the electoral effectiveness of the agrarian constituency at the national level.

As the proportion of people employed in agriculture declined, pressure group tactics offered a more practical avenue to political influence. Despite their reduced numbers, farmers have developed an impressive array of effective organizations—general purpose formations such as the Farm Bureau Federation (traditionally strongest in the Midwest and South) as well as specialized organizations for dairy producers, citrus growers, tobacco farmers, cattle owners, beet growers, and so forth.

Despite the decline in numbers, one should certainly not underestimate the political muscle of American agriculture. Farmers maintain wide-ranging contacts with government through the U.S. Department of Agriculture, the land-grant colleges, and specialized committees in Congress. Until the Supreme Court forced reapportionment in the 1960s, rural interests were overrepresented in most state legislatures and the U.S. House of Representatives. Even today, problems of grazing, forestry, crop infestation, parity formulas, and the like are staples of congressional concern. The *farm* population was only 5 percent in 1970, but the rural population was 26.5 percent. Many of these persons live in communities and hold jobs directly linked to the economic prospects of farmers.

Labor. The successes of organized labor have been more limited in the United States than in most other Western democracies. The AFL-CIO is probably weaker in relation to its affiliates than any of the major union confederations of the countries listed in Table 6–1. As you can see, the comparatively low levels of unionization in private white-collar occupations and among government workers accounts for much of the disparity.

One might suppose that the United States has much lower levels of public employee unionism because it has fewer nationalized industries. For example, in France, the United Kingdom, and West Germany, state ownership predominates in electricity, railways, telephone service, gas, and coal; in the United States private ownership prevails in all of these sectors of the economy. However, a leading authority discounts the importance of this factor in accounting for levels of public employee unionization. He believes that in the United States business interests have been more influential in affecting government policy, and employers have been unusually hostile to unions. He also believes that the popular election of many state and local officials and their tendency to appoint subordinates on the basis of spoils has meant that many American employees had little use for public employee unions.[26]

Table 6–1
Extent of Unionization in Six Nations

		Union Members as a Percentage of:		
	Labor Force	Private Blue Collar	Private White Collar	Public Employees
Australia	53%	56%	26%	77%
France	25	25	15	75
Sweden	87	95	71	95
United Kingdom	50	50	27	85
United States	28	53	9	28
West Germany	37	42	19	93

Data as of 1972 or 1973 in each nation. Caution is advised in making comparisons among these figures because of varying definitions and counting procedures.

Source: Hugh A. Clegg, *Trade Unionism Under Collective Bargaining* (Oxford: Basil Blackwell, 1976), p. 12.

[26]Hugh A. Clegg, *Trade Unionism Under Collective Bargaining* (Oxford: Basil Blackwell, 1976), pp. 26–27, 52.

Compared to other nations in Table 6–1, three other differences are distinctive characteristics of American trade unions:

1. Locals are much stronger in the United States, and much of the collective bargaining occurs plant by plant. Union power is decentralized for some of the same reasons that government is decentralized: the huge size of the country and the pervasiveness of federalism. The power of locals helps mitigate bossism in American unions, and it produces a good deal more factionalism within unions than exists in Europe.

2. Unions have been more bitterly opposed in this country. None of these other nations has a history of labor violence even remotely comparable to that of the United States. Levels of violence in labor disputes did not decline substantially and permanently until 1938. National legislation recognizing the legitimacy of unions was lacking until the passage of the Wagner Act in 1935. In Australia comparable legislative recognition dates from 1904, and by 1918 unions in Germany enjoyed legal rights that are broadly comparable to those of today's American unions.[27]

3. American unionism has been much less committed to doctrines of fundamental social change. Unlike their European counterparts, many American workers have either thought of themselves as middle class or expected their working-class status to be temporary. In the American workplace, the manager remains boss, no matter how much he is hedged in by agreements; moreover, American unionism has usually endorsed capitalism in principle as well as in practice. Relatively few union leaders have espoused socialism, and unions have had to fight off attempts by single taxers, anarchists, socialists, and communists to take over. Even so, many Americans have perceived union efforts to obtain "collective bargaining" (the phrase sounds faintly subversive) as a threat to private property.

Union membership in the United States has increased only slightly in the 1970s, and the percentage of nonagricultural workers who are unionized has been declining somewhat. At the same time, the proportion of union members in white-collar occupations has been increasing: from 12.2 percent in 1960 to 18.4 percent in 1976.[28] These figures suggest that unions are not gaining middle-class support rapidly enough to expand the overall scope of unionization in the society. Of course, the numbers can be deceptive; many white-collar professionals have associations that serve similar purposes. The American Medical Association and American Bar Association are leading examples.

The public sector appears to be crucial to the American labor movement, and there have been dramatic increases within it in recent years. By 1972, 50.4 percent of state and local government workers belonged to unions. Firefighters, police officers, teachers, and sanitation workers seem to have gone furthest in levels of unionization; lowest levels of unionization are found in rural areas, among the many thousand smaller units of govern-

[27]On the power of locals and legal rights, see ibid., pp. 14, 33, 44, 48; on violence, see Philip Taft and Philip Ross, "American Labor Violence: Its Causes, Character and Outcome," in *Violence in America,* ed. Hugh D. Graham and Ted R. Gurr (New York: Bantam Books, Inc., 1969), p. 361.
[28]U.S. Census, *Statistical Abstract of the United States 1978,* p. 430.

ment, and in the southern states. A 1962 executive order authorizing collective bargaining by government workers triggered unionization at the federal level, and by 1968, about 1.4 million federal employees belonged to unions. However, the numbers have since changed little.[29]

Some public sector unions have become quite active in electoral politics. For example, the National Education Association (NEA), the largest of the teacher organizations (its membership was 1.8 million members in 1977), claimed that candidates it backed won 229 of 282 House races in which it made endorsements in 1974. In 1976 the NEA endorsed a presidential candidate for the first time and claimed to be looking forward to a time when it would have more campaign resources than even the AFL-CIO. The NEA boasted 310 delegates at the 1980 Democratic convention and may have made the crucial difference in Carter's contest with Edward Kennedy. The NEA's prime objective in 1976 had been the formation of a Department of Education, and the organization worked hard in 1980 to retain the department by supporting Carter against a Republican opponent who had pledged to abolish it.[30]

Despite the great gains made by public employee unionism, popular acceptance may be fragile. Public employee bargaining does not find an easy niche in general outlooks towards politics and government in this country. More than ever before, the public-sector workplace is an area of contending values: professionalism, "sovereignty" of the elected official, spoils, revulsion against bureaucracy, and simple economic self-interest.

Like much else in American public life at this time, the overall significance of evolving arrangements remains elusive. Sunbelt states still lag significantly behind other regions in their acceptance of unions, and for that reason many firms have been moving south. A highly publicized effort by the AFL-CIO in 1977 to obtain major changes in federal legislation on collective bargaining was unsuccessful. At this time values associated with business seem much more ascendant than trade unionism. Opinion polls indicate that the public has even less confidence in "organized labor" than it does in "major companies," though neither element ranks high in public esteem.[31]

The Pressure System

Many groups do not fit neatly into the categories of business, labor, or agriculture. Some groups are occupational but choose not to be equated with "labor." Others represent particular positions at lower levels of gov-

[29]Neal R. Peirce, "Employment Report: Public Employee Unions Show Rise in Membership, Militancy," *National Journal*, August 30, 1975, pp. 1239–1240.
[30]The NEA is a union in everything but name. If its membership claims are true, it is the second largest union in the United States. Its rival, the American Federation of Teachers, ranked about fourteenth among national unions in 1975. Ibid., pp. 1239–1240, 1246. James W. Singer, "Organized Labor: Speaking in Accents Other Than the One from the Bronx," *National Journal*, March 12, 1977, p. 376. Bureau of Labor Statistics, *Directory of National Unions and Employee Associations 1975* (Washington, D.C.: U.S. Government Printing Office, 1977), p. 65. Stephen Chapman, "The Teachers' Coup," *The New Republic*, October 11, 1980, p. 9.
[31]The Harris Poll, February 1–7, as reported in *Current Opinion*, April 1977.

ernment and constitute an "intergovernmental lobby" of increasing impor-
tance. The U.S. Conference of Mayors, the National Institute of Municipal
Law Officers, the Conference of Chief Justices, and the Association of
School Boards are examples. Other organizations such as the National
League of Cities and the Council of State Governments are more general.
Groups exist to promote the welfare of ethnic groups such as blacks, Indians, Italian Americans, and Polish Americans and to promote or oppose
various causes: a treaty with Panama, ratification of ERA, right to life, civil
liberties, civil service reform, gay rights, laetrile, and many others.

Any attempt to survey all the existing groups could easily create the
impression that everybody is organized. Such a conclusion would be errone-
ous. A bias at work in the composition of many groups favors people from
advantaged backgrounds, and its effects may well be cumulative. Such people can often articulate interests and communicate them more effectively to
others. They also tend to have better organizational skills, be better situated
to take political initiatives, develop access, and be free of intimidation. The
higher their income and educational level, the better they understand the
need to have lawyers and to develop technically adequate presentations over
a long time span. They may also be more satisfied with the system as it is
and with the relatively minor adjustments to it that pressure politics is best
able to achieve. Tendencies such as these led E. E. Schattschneider to state
that probably 90 percent of the American people could not get into the
pressure system. He thought that membership lists of the most prominent
organized groups tended to be heavily weighted towards business and that
even nonbusiness organizations reflected "an upper class tendency."

> The notion that the pressure system is automatically representative of the
> whole community is a myth fostered by the universalizing tendency of modern
> group theories. *Pressure politics is a selective process* ill designed to serve diffuse
> interests. The system is skewed, loaded and unbalanced in favor of a fraction
> of a minority.[32]

A novel development of recent years has been the remarkable increase
in influence of public interest groups. The older political science for the
most part did not expect this to happen. Groups that organized to seek
benefits for themselves were supposed to be dominant and easily able to
shoulder aside organizations that sought benefits for the whole society
(whether or not one agreed with their idea of the public good).

Leading examples of public interest groups are the various operations
sponsored by Ralph Nader and Common Cause. Ralph Nader's formal
techniques have included lobbying, but he is probably better understood as
a crusader in the closely related movements of reformism, muckraking,
consumerism, public service professionalism, and environmentalism. A
graduate of Princeton in the early 1950s (where he is said to have waged an
unsuccessful campaign to prevent the trees from being sprayed with DDT)
Nader attended Harvard Law School—and later described it as a high-
priced tool factory that only prepared its students to serve a bank or corpo-

---

[32]Schattschneider, *Semisovereign People*, p. 35. Emphasis is in original.

ration. Nader's influence may stem from his ability to symbolize what everyman would like to be: a courageously effective *individual*, certain in his pursuit of moral objectives in a world of frustration and complexity. Even when Nader was unsuccessful, his failure was somewhat like the dissenting opinion of a Supreme Court Justice—a signpost pointing towards more enlightened policies in the future.

By the late 1970s Nader's energy had spawned more than a dozen Washington organizations financed by an annual budget of about $1 million in public donations. These included Congress Watch, Litigation Group, and the Center for Study of Responsive Law. He had taken on the automobile industry in the 1960s and, after achieving new safety legislation, turned to mine safety, control of oil and gas pipeline hazards, justice for Indians, and many other projects. He had a gift for choosing viable causes, dramatizing them, and putting formidable opponents on the defensive in public debate.

Nader experienced some setbacks in the late 1970s. His effort to get Congress to require federal chartering of large corporations did not succeed, and he lost an important battle for a Consumer Protection Agency. When he attacked his former colleague and friend, Joan Claybrook, the *Washington Post* described him as "embittered" and "reckless." Benjamin Rosenthal, an influential consumer advocate in Congress, stated: "Ralph is a dogmatic ideologue." These reverses did not necessarily mean that the causes Nader espoused were losing steam. A former ally serving as Assistant Secretary of Agriculture said: "I think he's started something that has become much larger than he is."[33]

Parties and the pressure system. The relationship between parties and interest groups in America contains elements of a pattern. The republic's traditional parties often appealed to broad categories of voters defined by section, urban/rural residence, religion, ethnic group, income level, and occupation. The parties rarely ignored any of the larger sectors, yet partisan coalitions represented some more strongly than others. However, this did not mean that parties incorporated organized groups and their leaders into their organizations.

We have seen that party "membership" is remarkably vague in the United States. Yet, whether we think of it as voter self-identification, straight-ticket voting, or whatever, the basic relationship is always between the party and the individual voter. American parties do not have *group memberships;* there is no formal counterpart here to the pattern in England where, for example, many unions can be members of the Labour party, cast votes at party conferences, and provide the bulk of the party's annual income.[34]

[33] *Time,* November 14, 1977, pp. 76–81; *U.S. News and World Report,* December 19, 1977, p. 18.

[34] Trade union members vote on whether or not the union should have membership in the Labour party. If the vote carries, each union member has to pay an additional fee, which goes to the party. The only way for a member to avoid paying the fee is by signing a statement declaring that he is unwilling to do so. This is referred to as "contracting out," and, as you might expect, relatively few union men do it. Socialist societies and cooperatives can also join the Labour party.

   In America, interest groups vary in the degree to which they side with a party. Most are not aligned to a significant degree, even if members lean to one party more than the other. The strategic assumption seems to be that it is in the group's best interest to be able to withhold support or even switch sides. Thus, soon after Carter's election, many leaders of black organizations were expressing alarm and issuing dire warnings, despite continuing high levels of Carter support by blacks in the polls.

   The AFL-CIO has usually endorsed Democratic presidential nominees, and the Democratic National Committee has often relied on this organization's political arm to generate campaign literature, money, and campaign volunteers. However, the AFL-CIO did not endorse McGovern in 1972; moreover, the ability of union leaders to deliver the votes of union members is questionable. Some union leaders have endorsed Republicans. Since unions do not hold organizational membership in a party, workers are pretty much free to vote as they wish without strong pressures being brought to bear. Many working-class families will vote Democratic anyway, without the urging of union leaders. In 1976, however, union support may have been vital to Carter's victory. A *New York Times* survey indicated that 62 percent of votes from union households went to Carter; 52 percent of votes from other households went to Ford. Union households supported Nixon in 1972, but not as heavily as nonunion households.[35]

   The closest relationship between organized labor and the Democratic party is to be found in Michigan, the second most highly unionized state in the nation. Before World War II the Democratic party in Michigan was conservative and patronage-ridden. In 1948, however, leaders of the United Automobile Workers (UAW) and other unions formed an alliance with well-to-do businessmen liberals such as Hicks Griffiths, Noel Fox, Hickman Price, and Neil Staebler. Labor continued to be very active in the party and helped G. Mennen Williams win repeatedly as governor over a twelve-year period.[36] The UAW has been one of the most dynamic of America's unions. Its involvement in Michigan politics has helped to produce a state party system that has been distinctly issue-oriented. Walter Reuther, president of the UAW until his death in 1970, pressed the auto workers into a wide spectrum of issue concerns. Neil Staebler served as state Democratic chairman from 1950 to 1961. He later served as a national committeeman and became a member of the Federal Elections Commission in 1975.

   Until 1964 big business was probably even more dependably Republican than organized labor was Democratic, although the Republican party was not simply a creature of big business. The intensity of business commitment to the Republican party has waned. In fact, the recent mild resurgence of business political influence is not strongly linked to the Republican party. A new set of conservative spokesmen in Congress appear to be challenging old conservative ideas. Most are Republicans, and they feel that too much

   [35] Gerald Pomper, Ross K. Baker, Charles E. Jacob, Wilson Carey McWilliams, and Henry A. Plotkin, *The Election of 1976* (New York: David McKay Co., Inc., 1977), p. 61.
   [36] Malcolm E. Jewell and David M. Olson, *American State Parties and Elections* (Homewood, Ill.: The Dorsey Press, 1978), p. 40; John H. Fenton, *Midwest Politics* (New York: Holt, Rinehart & Winston, 1966), pp. 12–20.

business money in 1976 went to support campaigns of liberal Democrats. They have spoken often of a low-tax economic climate but are more interested in helping small business than big business.[37]

Business alignments have been quite fluid, and incumbent Democrats have been able to take positions more favorable to business without fear of electoral punishment. For example, the mid-1970s witnessed an explosive growth of corporate political action committees (PACs) that channeled large sums into congressional campaigns after enactment of the 1974 amendments to the 1971 Federal Election Campaign Act failed to place limits on total corporate contributions to political campaigns. In 1976 business PACs gave $6.9 million to congressional candidates; labor PACs, including teacher associations, gave about $8.1 million. Studies by Common Cause indicated that only 69 percent of this business money went to Republicans, and that this source of campaign money favored Democratic incumbents over their Republican challengers by more than a two-to-one margin.[38]

The tendency to structure partisan conflict around the antagonism between business and labor seems to be eroding, and the rise of public interest groups suggests that these old adversaries are no longer as dominant in America's pressure system. Such changes may be related to the current weakness of our two-party system.

Weaker party organizations have enabled many interest groups to become more active on behalf of particular candidates and causes. An interest group can focus on a single issue; parties usually cannot—although in 1978 the pro-life forces qualified as a full-fledged political party on the New York ballot. Interest groups have also increasingly turned to the initiative process to bypass the legislative branch and party platforms. As a result, state governments have experienced a veritable renaissance of interest in direct democracy: In 1978, voters coped with some 350 policy items, including measures for compulsory tax reduction, spending curbs, pornography limitations, restrictions on smoking, discrimination against homosexuals and many others. In 1977 only last-minute maneuvering saved the voters of San Francisco from having to decide the color of police cars on election day. Corey Bush, press secretary to the mayor, said that he could put any measure on the California state ballot for $325,000.[39]

CHANGES IN PRESSURE POLITICS

Despite the burgeoning activities of organized groups, some mutations are occurring in American pressure politics, and not all of them favor interest group politics as we have known it.

To some extent, movement politics has displaced pressure politics. The concept of a political movement is quite slippery, and most political scientists are not comfortable using it to classify and analyze political behav-

---

[37]"The Right in Congress," *Congressional Quarterly Weekly Report*, August 5, 1978, p. 2025.
[38]*Congressional Quarterly Weekly Report*, April 8, 1978, p. 849.
[39]Les Ledbetter, New York Times News Service, November 1977.

ior. Movements are highly fluid. They operate on different fronts with ever-changing memberships, tactics, and goals. In the words of Lasswell and Kaplan, they are characterized by "a perspective which does not antecedently limit the goals, plans, and participants (so that a movement may change its direction or composition without losing its identity)."[40] Although movements possess elements of organization, the organizations within the movement may not be impressive in their own right. The more important influence derives from ideology, followership, and commitment.

Without unduly worrying about the appropriateness of labels, it seems likely that movements centered on feminism, youth, racial assertion, and ecology have left a greater mark on American society than any pressure groups in the past twenty years. When the work of pressure groups and movements has overlapped, the movement has seemingly counted for more. Of course, there are exceptions. A persistent campaign of litigation by the NAACP in the 1940s and 1950s was pressure politics of a sophisticated sort. It led to the Supreme Court's unanimous repudiation of segregation in education and paved the way for the more militant phases of black protest that came later.

The youth movement, on the other hand, had little interest in traditional pressure politics. It tended to operate directly on the universities, the mass culture, and the family system. It achieved political objectives through protests and appeared almost totally unconcerned with conventional political objectives, such as votes for eighteen-year-olds, a victory it won without effort or desire.

Of course, movement labels can be a cover for specific group associations. For example, the movement centered on racial assertion included the National Association for the Advancement of Colored People (NAACP), Congress of Racial Equality (CORE), Student Nonviolent Coordinating Committee (SNCC), Black Power, Black Panthers, Black Muslims, and others. Also, one should not insist that movements (any more than groups) explain everything. Undoubtedly, many patterned events of the 1960s were not produced by movements.

Nevertheless, key figures often used the term self-consciously, and in the 1960s the sense of being part of a movement clearly energized many people. The more important leaders were not much beholden to any organizations, and such hallmarks of movements as ideology, patron saints, myths, and the search for distinctive styles of behavior were clearly present. Of course, one could say that successful pressure politics is usually a holding action, and that interest groups were often successful in blocking many kinds of changes. Yet, the complexity of modern politics may be such that simple veto actions have become hazardous.

Questions of Legitimacy

A second important change is a possible decline in the legitimacy of pressure politics. The unexpected prominence of public interest groups is symptomatic of increased skepticism among communities of activists, among intellectuals, and among the mass publics.

[40]Lasswell and Kaplan, *Power and Society*, p. 241.

In political science, ideas predominant in the 1950s accepted pressure groups in a spirit of realism. Indeed, in one very influential view, the entire political process could best be understood as a patterning of organized interests centered on groups and their activities.[41] In reconciling such a notion with democratic ideals, political science has tended to accept pressure groups as essential intermediaries between people and government. But the consensus about this is diminishing.

Theodore Lowi, for example, has attacked "interest group liberalism," a stance that allegedly approves of policy change by small increments and that glorifies bargaining and compromise at the expense of formal democracy. By formal democracy Lowi means "a majority rule democracy limited only by the absolute requirement that government be run as closely as possible to the way it says it is run."[42] Lowi finds "an iron law of decadence" in the careers of organized groups. He believes that though they often begin as creative ways for people to associate voluntarily, they later degenerate into rigid maintenance operations.

According to Lowi, group power in the United States has encouraged massive delegations of power and the formation of an administrative state in the private sector. The trade association, widely misunderstood as being a pressure group, has as its main purpose, he says (along with peak associations, agricultural commodity organizations, and trade unions) the administration of life in the industrialized society. James Madison and Alexis de Tocqueville were correct in viewing voluntary associations as healthy features of the young republic. However, they were thinking of people in the process of forming groups—*not* of a society of formed groups. In the contemporary period, a place like Guilford, Connecticut, can have hundreds of groups and still be completely static.[43]

Let us note in passing that political movements are central to much of Lowi's thinking. Many observers have felt that movement politics was profoundly antidemocratic—contemptuous of the majorities it usually glorified, neglectful or abusive of the procedural requirements of a democratic order, opposed to "the system," yet unwilling to offer constructive alternatives. One of the interesting features of Lowi's thinking is his attempt to side with movements as creative elements in American politics and at the same time to make movement politics consistent with formal democracy.

Judicial Expansion

A third factor that may be downgrading the pressure system is the growth in judicial policy making. Courts have always been significant elements in the American political system, but even so, the recent expansion is quite startling. Courts are not immune to "pressure"; on the other hand, they are not especially accessible, either. In most of its recent breakthroughs in policy making (school desegregation, reapportionment, criminal justice

[41]David B. Truman, *The Governmental Process* (New York: Alfred A. Knopf, Inc., 1951).
[42]Theodore J. Lowi, *The Politics of Disorder* (New York: Basic Books, Inc., 1971), pp. xvii–xviii.
[43]Ibid., pp. 69–71, 32–34.

reform, obscenity, contraception, and abortion), the Supreme Court has *not* been acting in response to focused pressure or in anticipation of major political pressure or support. Desegregation is a major exception, but even here, basic and widely diffused beliefs seem to have been at least as important as the judicial campaigns of the NAACP.[44]

Judicial expansion is not merely a Supreme Court matter. A recent article in *Newsweek* referred to the increase in litigation as "one of the great unnoticed revolutions in U.S. history." The article noted that the number of civil suits filed in federal courts had doubled between 1960 and 1977, and that in twenty years the number of lawyers in the country had grown from 250,000 to 425,000.[45] The political implications are far from clear. However, even though bargaining is an element in judicial decision making, it may be that Americans prefer decisions by "disinterested" tribunals to decisions by representative officials subject to "pressure."

Issue Networks

A final element of change pertains to decision making in Washington. Many observers have been impressed with the increased influence of those with knowledge-based skills and with the continuing disarray of policy-making arrangements in the nation's capital. One interpretation of why this is occurring is of particular interest. Hugh Heclo believes that growth in the sheer mass of federal government activity has brought with it a "peculiar, loose-jointed play of influence" that is much more complex than the older interest group politics. One reason: In augmenting its regulatory and spending activity, Washington has been working through a vast array of intermediaries (such as state and local governments, third-party payers, consultants, and contractors) rather than through an expanded federal bureaucracy. Indeed, federal employment has increased very little in thirty years, but money expended and regulations issued have expanded greatly.

National government has become the truly decisive arena in a way it never was in the past. The result, says Heclo, has been a "blossoming of policy participants and kibitzers," and many of them have moved to Washington. A great urge for improvement has moved the federal government in new directions, causing it to become concerned with unfamiliar policy issues. These new and often puzzling matters have encouraged the government to mobilize more fluid groups, including intergovernmental lobbyists as well as new private and semiprivate organizations.

In this milieu, the key formation according to Heclo is not the interest group but rather the "issue network." Issue networks are loose aggregations of highly knowledgeable participants and policy watchers. They have become crucial mainly because of the extreme difficulty in determining the proper courses of action in Washington. Unlike interest groups (and the autonomous subgovernments that interest groups tend to produce), the

[44]Martin Shapiro, "The Supreme Court: From Warren to Burger," in *The New American Political System*, ed. Anthony King (Washington, D.C.: American Enterprise Institute for Public Policy Research, 1978), pp. 179–182.

[45]"Too Much Law?," *Newsweek*, January 10, 1977, pp. 42–47.

issue networks lack unity, stable participation, or a preponderant material interest. "The price of buying into one or another issue network is watching, reading, talking about, and trying to act on particular policy problems."[46]

People in a particular network tend to have a common base of information, but they may or may not act on the basis of shared action or belief. In such a context, power becomes obscure. According to Heclo, "for a host of policy initiatives undertaken in the last twenty years it is all but impossible to identify clearly who the dominant actors are." There is little distance between the networks and the political executives in government. Almost all of President Carter's initial cabinet secretaries "came out of or had a lasting affinity to particular issue networks." Very few of them were personal loyalists, representatives of party factions, or recognized interest group leaders.

Heclo finds some positive elements in the new situation. The networks are consistent with increasing technological sophistication in the larger society. They help to link Congress and the executive branch in ways that political parties no longer can, and they give political executives room to maneuver. However, his overall assessment is tinged with concern rather than optimism. The very expertness of the issue networks tends to make policy making less comprehensible to the larger public and tends to promote an "everything causes cancer" syndrome. Their expertise also poses problems in developing public understanding and support for national policies, and he fears that the networks have more of a stake in complicating policy choices than in simplifying them. Instead of developing necessary trade-offs, networks tend to elevate true believers to policy prominence. They seem more interested in continuous debate and critical analysis than in action. In arrangements dominated by intermediaries, this has meant that "goals are piled on top of each other without generating any commitment to the administrative wherewithal to achieve them."[47]

CONCLUSION

The unifying theme of this chapter is the multitude of ways that influence can be organized in American society. Everything discussed has an essential bearing on what ordinary Americans must struggle against as they try to gain control of their government. Change has been a constant, and one is impressed with the ambiguity and tentativeness of influence patterns in America. If this sense of the situation is accurate, its most hopeful aspect is that there may be many alternative ways of organizing influence in the future. The simplifications inherent in two-party politics pose genuine risks in an ever more complex society. Yet it may be necessary to incur them if we are to recover and maintain a sense of common purpose.

[46]Hugh Heclo, "Issue Networks and the Executive Establishment," in King, *The New American Political System*, pp. 88, 97, 102–103.
[47]Ibid., pp. 93, 102, 107–108, 118, 120–121.

7

Political
Participation

If we ask why people participate in most phases of modern life, we find answers with little difficulty. People attend school and frequent shopping centers because it is in their interest to do so. People who go to movies, attend rock concerts, or watch the "Muppet Show" do so because they enjoy them. The 27 percent who say they help others as volunteers in charities or social services obtain satisfactions of a different sort. Motives, of course, can vary. For some people, shopping is a form of recreation, and volunteer work can be a way of demonstrating or improving one's social status. In a sense, it is hard not to participate in modern society in some fashion. Even those who seek the inner life may find themselves caught up in a mass phenomenon such as yoga, transcendental meditation, or Bible study.[1]

THE INSCRUTABLE VOTER

If we ask why people should vote, we are likely to get two kinds of answers, one concerning values, the other, interests. The question has an almost inescapable moral thrust. To ask it is to suggest that voting is natural and good, and that nonvoting is not to be approved. In terms of values, we have the idea that people should vote because voting is an indispensable attribute of citizenship in a democratic society, or because voting affirms a conception of ourselves as a self-governing people. When people say "You can't complain if you don't vote," they are voicing an ethical principle of this sort.

[1]The 27 percent figure comes from a Gallup poll of August 1977. A Gallup poll of February 1978 indicates that 3 percent of Americans are involved with yoga, 2 percent with transcendental meditation, and 19 percent with Bible study groups.

Social scientists, however, tend to be uncomfortable with such reasons, partly because many prefer empirical questions to normative ones. They have also shown a tendency to hope that democratic participation could be based on self-interested behavior rather than altruism. Politics, after all, is basically a question of interests, and many of the interests are rather selfish. Even if people are not narrowly self-seeking, we expect (and want) their voting to be "purposive"—that is, we expect people to hear conflicting viewpoints, weigh them, and come to a conclusion. We tend to suppose that people want their views to prevail and that they seize on voting as an opportunity to further them.

Yet, from the very beginning of sophisticated survey research, investigators have come up against evidence that diverges markedly from these expectations. For example, a study of the 1940 presidential election in Erie County, Ohio, found that people who got to the polls tended to conform to group or segmental attachments. When these attachments pointed in inconsistent directions, this did *not* liberate the individual to make an independent choice: Instead, these inconsistencies tended to "cross-pressure" the voter and make him delay a decision or cause a loss of interest. The study dramatically contradicted the notion that voting is an act of individual assertion, a finding that surprised even the authors. The senior author had expected ballot behavior to be like consumer behavior—an individualistic act strongly affected by the mass media. This turned out to be all wrong, and media-based explanations of voting have faced tough sledding ever since.[2]

Sixteen years later William Buchanan's analysis of leading voting behavior studies suggested that half of the voting citizenry were either unconcerned about their influence on government policy or unaware of it. Surveys were showing that neither the level of political interest nor a belief that one's actions can influence government decisions ("sense of political efficacy") were strongly predictive of whether a person would vote. His own research indicated that voting was only a peripheral concern to the small minority of people who were purposive voters and that such persons usually had social advantages that enabled them to influence policy by nonelectoral means. Such findings implied that the result of a particular election could well "have little relation to what most people want from the government, if they want anything."[3]

The University of Michigan's landmark voting behavior study reflected similar puzzlement over why people vote. These researchers found that whether a person voted or not had relatively little to do with the strength of partisan attachments, degree of concern over the outcome of the election, or interest in the campaign. They found some relationship of the sort one

[2]Paul F. Lazarsfeld, Bernard Berelson, and Hazel Gaudet, *The People's Choice* (New York: Duell, Sloan and Pearce, 1944); Peter H. Rossi, "Four Landmarks in Voting Research," in *American Voting Behavior*, ed. Eugene Burdick and Arthur J. Brodbeck (New York: The Free Press, 1959), pp. 5–54.

[3]William Buchanan, "An Inquiry Into Purposive Voting," *Journal of Politics*, 18 (May 1956), 281-296. The quotation is on p. 285.

would expect on each of these variables, but not one strong enough to be compelling.[4]

Sense of Citizen Duty

The Michigan researchers also gathered data on possible altruistic motives for voting. If people do not go to the polls to further their enlightened or not so enlightened self-interests, perhaps they go out of civic idealism. The investigators probed for this kind of motivation with a measure called "sense of citizen duty," and the results are depicted in Table 7-1. At first glance, this approach seems to give us the explanation we are looking for. Thus, percentages in the top row of Table 7-1 show that voting increases substantially at each successively higher step on the citizen duty scale. However, you can also see from the bottom row that it accounts for very little of the nonvoting that occurred in 1956. Both voters and nonvoters tended to feel that voting was a civic responsibility.

This study remains the most rigorous and comprehensive investigation to date of American voting behavior. Yet these researchers could not explain why some people vote and others do not, even by *combining* measures of political involvement. On a scale that combined various measures of political involvement with sense of citizen duty, most persons interviewed

Table 7-1
Sense of Citizen Duty and Voter Turnout in 1956

	Sense of Citizen Duty Scale				
	Low				High
Voted	13%	42%	52%	74%	85%
Did not vote	87	58	48	26	15
	100%	100%	100%	100%	100%
Number of cases	89	78	146	639	812
Number of nonvoters	77	45	70	166	122

"Sense of Citizen Duty" combines negative responses to each of the following statements: (1) "It isn't so important to vote when you know your party doesn't have a chance to win" (2) "A good many local elections aren't important enough to bother with" (3) "So many other people vote in the national elections that it doesn't matter much to me whether I vote or not" (4) "If a person doesn't care how an election comes out he shouldn't vote in it."

Source: Adapted from Angus Campbell, Philip E. Converse, Warren E. Miller, Donald E. Stokes, *The American Voter* (Chicago: University of Chicago Press, 1976), p. 106. The number of nonvoters did not appear in the source, but has been supplied here from other numbers in the table.

[4]Angus Campbell, Philip E. Converse, Warren E. Miller, and Donald E. Stokes, *The American Voter* (Chicago: University of Chicago Press, 1976), Chap. 5. This study was originally published by John Wiley & Sons, Inc., in 1960.

scored middle to high (83 percent were step five through eight of a nine-point scale). However, only 63 to 87 percent of these moderately to highly involved persons voted. The authors found it especially noteworthy that more than a fifth of the persons with the very *lowest* involvement nevertheless voted. In their words, "the person we 'expect' *not* to vote yet who does —is somewhat more difficult to explain than is the person we expect to vote yet who fails to do so."[5]

American politics has changed substantially since 1956, but voter participation is still a puzzle. For example, in one recent study of nonvoting (which we discuss later in more detail), similarities between voters and nonvoters stood out, not differences. Most nonvoters interviewed felt bad about not voting, and 94 percent of them regarded voting as a moral obligation. Moreover, nonvoters were only slightly less happy and more cynical about politics than voters, and they were not notably less well educated, poorer, black, or southern.[6]

Self-Interested Voting

Explaining the decision to vote in terms of individual self-interest presents logical as well as empirical difficulties. After all, the chance of one ballot's deciding an election is negligible, even in very close contests. For example, in November 1978 Kenneth Cole and Donald Moul each received 8,551 votes in a race for a seat in the Pennsylvania legislature. Moul (the Democrat) won by only fourteen votes in a recount. A citizen of Pennsylvania might have had a better chance of being struck by lightning than of deciding this contest.

Keep in mind, too, that it may be difficult for the self-interested voter to determine which if any ballot choices actually favor his or her interests. Needed information may not be available, or it may not be put out in convenient form. Using one's vote to serve one's real interests may require brilliant political insight or comprehensive evaluations.

Nevertheless, it is possible to imagine a certain amount of purely self-interested voting. A voter who knows that a preferred candidate cannot win might want to vote for him anyway to help prevent the loss from looking like a rout. For example, if Cole had lost by several hundred votes, instead of by fourteen, people might have perceived the outcome differently.

It is somewhat unrealistic to regard voting as totally a matter of individual preference. The actual voting unit may be the family, neighborhood, or some other group. Clusters of votes (even very small ones) are often important to people seeking office at the local level. Urgings from larger communities of interest may discourage one from free-riding on the votes of others and thus be in a person's natural interest—not a social force that robs the individual of autonomy. Some people vote as a favor to a friend,

---

[5]Ninety-six percent of the most highly involved group voted, whereas only 78 percent of the least involved did *not* vote. Campbell, Converse, Miller, and Stokes, *The American Voter*, pp. 106–108. The quotation is on p. 90.

[6]Arthur T. Hadley, *The Empty Polling Booth* (Englewood Cliffs, N.J.: Prentice-Hall, Inc., 1978), pp. 16–39.

Table 7-2
Percent of Age Eligible Electorate Reporting That They Voted

	1968	1972	1976
Sex			
Male	69.8%	64.1%	59.6%
Female	66.0	62.0	58.8
Race			
White	69.1	64.5	60.9
Black	57.6	52.1	48.7
Hispanic	n.a.	37.4	31.8
Age			
18–20	n.a.	48.3	38.0
21–24	51.1	50.7	45.6
25–34	62.5	59.7	55.4
35–44	70.8	66.3	63.6
45–64	74.9	70.8	68.7
65+	65.8	63.5	62.2
Urbanization			
Metropolitan	68.0	64.3	59.2
Nonmetropolitan	67.3	59.4	59.1
Region			
South	60.1	55.4	54.9
Nonsouth	71.0	66.4	61.2
Education			
0–8	54.5	47.4	44.1
9–11	61.3	52.0	47.2
12	72.5	65.4	59.4
12+	81.2	78.8	73.5
Employment			
Employed	71.1	66.0	62.0
Unemployed	52.1	49.9	43.7

Source: U.S. Census, *Statistical Abstract of the United States 1978*, p. 520.

campaign worker, or candidate, and such behavior may be self-interested to a degree. However, a decline in the strength of such ties may help explain why a decline in voting has taken place.

VOTING AS PATTERNED BEHAVIOR

When one compares voters and nonvoters as groups, some reliable differences emerge. Whether these differences are viewed as large or small depends in part on why the comparisons are being made. As we have seen, knowing a person's social characteristics is of little help in predicting whether or not that particular person will vote. However, if we want to make inferences about political demands flowing into the political arena, then even modest differences can be telling. For example, the difference in turnout between whites and blacks is seldom greater than 12 percent, so race is not a good predictor of whether a particular person will vote. But because blacks are already a small proportion of the electorate, their relatively lower rate of participation may be an obstacle to their obtaining a government more responsive to them.

Voting is patterned behavior. Similar tendencies show up in every election and in many different contexts. For example, in 1968, 1972, and 1976, census data reveal very similar turnout differences with respect to employment, sex, race, age, residence, education, and employment. Other data indicate that turnout among Jews is usually better than among Catholics and that Catholics vote more frequently than Protestants. Variations relating to income, occupation, and union membership reflect greater participation at higher socioeconomic levels.

When states are compared, again some rather durable patterns appear. The particular states in Table 7–3 do not portray the extreme range of variation, and it would be easy to select other samples in which the patterns were just as pronounced. Note that the range between highest and lowest turnout is much smaller in 1976 than in 1944 or 1920. Looking across the rows from right to left, one can see that each state's percentage tended to rise from 1920 to 1960 and then drop. This means that shared changes over time obtrude on differences between states.

What accounts for interstate variations? There is no single factor. Indiana has a high turnout in part because of a remarkably competitive two-party system. Some differentials reflect practices in election administration to be discussed below. Nobody knows exactly how many persons are eligible to register, and problems of excluding aliens and other ineligibles may be more difficult in such states as California and New York. Economic disparities are part of the story, but they are little help in explaining interstate variations. For example, in 1976 the rank correlation between per capita income and voter turnout in the states listed in Table 7–3 was only +.31. On the basis of per capita income, Indiana and Utah have higher levels of voting and California and New York lower levels than one would expect. Relatively low income levels probably contribute to reduced electoral participation in southern states, but a distinctive southern subculture could well be more important than income.

Interstate comparisons merely scratch the surface. Patterning occurs within most states, between regions, counties, and even neighborhoods. Turnout in midterm elections is lower than in presidential years, and local elections draw fewer voters than national elections. Primary elections draw fewer voters than general elections, and primary participation reveals distinctive patterns of its own. For example, people with strong party identification are much more likely to vote in primaries than independents, and the primary of the weaker party in a particular area usually attracts very few participants. Social characteristics, political practices, cultural outlooks, and

Table 7-3
Turnout in Selected States over Five Decades

	1976	1960	1944	1920
Utah	69%	80%	76%	64%
Indiana	61	77	76	71
Illinois	61	76	79	53
New Jersey	58	72	71	48
Connecticut	62	77	70	44
Massachusetts	62	76	73	41
Delaware	58	74	69	70
Michigan	59	72	64	47
Ohio	55	71	70	57
Pennsylvania	55	71	64	37
California	51	67	63	41
New York	51	67	74	45
Florida	52	50	36	36
N. Carolina	44	54	43	45
Tennessee	50	50	31	35
RANK ORDER	+.94			
CORRELATIONS	+.70			
(SPEARMAN'S RHO)	+.46			

Percentage of age eligible electorate voting in presidential elections. Rank order correlations vary between plus one and minus one. They are very easy to calculate, and the reader may wish to compute the others. For the computing formula, see almost any elementary statistics book.

Sources: Lester Milbrath, "Individuals and Government," in Jacob and Vines, Politics in the American States, 2d ed., 1971, pp. 38–39; U.S. Census, Statistical Abstract 1978, p. 523.

psychological characteristics all tend to have some effect on voting participation.

Status Bias

If every eligible person always voted, there would be no group differences in turnout. Larger segments of the population would have more votes than smaller ones, but the level of voting in all groups would be the same —100 percent. Turnout is, of course, well below 100 percent. It is now approaching 50 percent even in presidential elections and is considerably below 50 percent at lower levels of government and in off-years. As a result, even moderate differences in rates of participation can change election outcomes. In more general terms, a significant increase or decrease in the number and kinds of people engaged in a conflict tends to alter the balance of power between the parties and to affect the way the conflict is resolved. Thus, differences in participation rates always tend to affect whether one side or the other will prevail.[7]

[7]E. E. Schattschneider, The Semisovereign People (Hinsdale, Ill.: The Dryden Press, 1975).

Perhaps the most pertinent group differences in participation reflect occupational position, formal education, wealth, or other indicators of status or social advantage. Although such advantages are especially pertinent to "harder" forms of participation, they also leave their mark on "easier" ones—including voting. Whether this results in a fundamentally biased political system is a somewhat complicated issue. It depends in part on the degree to which upper- and lower-status groups have interests that differ and can be reconciled. It also depends on the kinds of leaders lower-status groups need or want. It any case, the tendency for status to be associated with participation is probably universal, although the strength and import of the association may vary.

We can understand status-biased participation both in terms of *resources* and *incentives*. Resources enable people to be influential in politics. Incentives make political activity desirable, beneficial, or attractive to particular people. In Chapter 4, we have seen the importance of wealth in politics. People with money tend to have other valuable political resources, such as leisure time, flexible work routines, opportunities to develop skill in dealing with people, and social contacts. In some settings, such as big business, participants can use special channels of communication to identify and activate mutual interests quickly.

In examining resources we of course find exceptions and qualifications. Our indicators of status are by no means perfectly correlated, and there are a fair number of special situations. Lawyers tend to participate more than any other occupational group. Doctors generally enjoy high incomes and occupational prestige, but they often lack leisure time, and this may restrict their political activity. Blue-collar workers may have excellent channels of communication in large factories. Some socially advantaged persons may use their resources to escape from politics.

Incentives also tend to favor socially advantaged people. Higher-status people have an incentive to be politically effective since government often has a tangible impact on their lives. Business managers, for example, confront detailed government regulations that are less visible to workers or consumers. Moreover, the American political system rewards organized group activity, and such pursuits come more naturally to those at higher-status levels. Schools, press, and churches transmit values that correspond to middle-class rather than working- or lower-class outlooks.[8] Since America's lower class is now in the unusual historical position of being outnumbered, its members may lack an important incentive even to vote.

A person's time perspective can also enhance or diminish political incentives. Democratic politics moves slowly, and people who live on a short-term basis may not be willing to pursue its long-delayed results. Willingness to defer gratification to some distant future may be a crucial element of class-related outlooks. Even altruism as an incentive seems to vary some-

[8]Seymour M. Lipset, *Political Man* (Garden City, N.Y.: Anchor Books, Doubleday & Co., Inc., 1963), Chap. 6.

what with status: We expect "do gooders" to be upper-middle or upper class.[9]

Again, there are exceptions. Not all incentives to political action vary with status. Government employees, miners, and commercial crop farmers have incentives to be active, because government policies affect them directly. Solidarity seems to encourage participation and is not necessarily related to status. Thus, Jews generally have more group cohesion than Catholics, and Catholics more than Protestants. As a result, the order in which these segments turn out at the polls is the opposite of what one would suppose from their usual status order in American society.[10]

Status advantages in participation tend to be self-reinforcing and cumulative. If a person believes that his or her actions can influence government, the person is more likely to participate, regardless of social position. However, such views are more characteristic of advantaged people. Group memberships promote political activity by giving people political experience, providing them with information, and pressuring them to be active. But this does not help low-status people very much because they have fewer group affiliations and are usually less active in those groups they do join. Service in a base office like the state legislature may be a prerequisite for seeking higher offices, but most people with little education and low income would find it difficult to campaign successfully for such an office.

At the extremes the cumulative impact of social advantage is substantial. For example, one investigation turned up the data in Table 7–4. Even this array may not capture the extremes too well, since those of the highest status and those most politically active are defined in generous numerical terms.

A study of local participation in Wisconsin creates a similar impression of status differences. The top quarter or so who were most inclined to vote, most interested in local politics, most informed, and in most frequent attendance at meetings included 55 percent of those with some college education, a nonmanual occupation, and an income over $6,000 a year. In contrast, only 13 percent of those with no college education, a manual occupation, and an income of less than $6,000 were in the highly involved group. The authors are skeptical of the idea that anyone who wants to become involved can do so, and they suggest that community role expectations erect barriers to participation.[11]

Voting is much easier than many of the other things required of the political activist. Therefore, status differences between voters and nonvoters should be, and are, smaller than the extremes or semiextremes among

[9]Edward Banfield, *The Unheavenly City Revisited* (Boston: Little, Brown & Company, 1974), Chap. 3, esp. pp. 53–57.
[10]Lipset, *Political Man*, pp. 191–193; Lester W. Milbrath and M. L. Goel, *Political Participation*, 2nd ed. (Chicago: Rand McNally College Publishing Co., 1977), pp. 118–119.
[11]Robert R. Alford and Harry M. Scoble, "Sources of Local Political Involvement," *American Political Science Review*, 62 (December 1968), 1193, 1204, 1206.

Table 7–4
Relationship of Socioeconomic Status to Political Participation

	Composite Participation Scale					
	Least 1/6	2	3	4	5	Most 1/6
SES Scale						
Top Third	12%	29%	30%	38%	48%	55%
Middle Third	34	35	33	29	30 '	29
Bottom Third	54	36	37	33	22	17
TOTAL	100%	100%	100%	100%	100%	100%

SES (socioeconomic status) is measured here by education and income. Percentages may not total exactly to 100 due to rounding. The SES groupings are equal for the entire sample, but the proportions differ markedly at successive levels of participation.
Source: Norman H. Nie and Sidney Verba, "Political Participation," in Fred I. Greenstein and Nelson W. Polsby eds., *Handbook of Political Science*, Vol 4, p. 43.

participants noted above. For example, education and employment groups in Table 7–3 differ markedly, but not massively. In yet another investigation, educational differences were marked at the extremes, but 78 percent of the sample had at least a high school education, and the difference between high school and college educated groups was only about ten points. Income differences were quite modest.[12] To repeat a point suggested earlier, the similarities between voters and nonvoters may be more important than the differences, even with respect to status and despite the persistence of a good deal of patterning. Informal barriers to the more difficult forms of participation may exclude most people, but few are barred from voting. The vote is now available to almost all adult citizens, and it is peculiarly determinative.

These and other considerations suggest that voting is more than just one of many kinds of political activity. Perhaps it is more accurate to think of voting as the main channel that gives the mass of ordinary people a real chance to control, at least crudely, what happens in public life. To the extent that voting loses the substance and symbolism of being the sovereign political act in American politics, democracy as we have understood it is weakened. High levels of nonvoting in the modern era may represent a dangerous erosion of both symbol and substance.

TURNOUT COMPARISONS

Some comparisons may help sharpen our perspective on nonvoting. In the pages to follow we will contrast the United States to other nations and examine present turnout levels in relation to previous periods. In the pro-

[12]Hadley, *The Empty Polling Booth*, p. 150. Some of these comparisons involve recomputed percentages.

cess we will clear up some prevalent misconceptions and reach a better understanding of this highly important form of political activity. Voter turnout in the United States is lower than in many other nations. Among the seven countries in one cross-national comparison, only India and Nigeria had smaller proportions of respondents who said they voted regularly.[13] Mean turnout in America's national elections in the 1960s was about 25 percent lower than Australia's, 20 percent lower than West Germany's, and 10 to 15 percent lower than Canada's. Voting levels in Belgium, Denmark, Finland, France, Israel, Italy, New Zealand, Norway, Sweden, and the United Kingdom were all considerably higher than the United States during the same decade.[14]

There are many reasons for these differences, but a lack of political interest in the United States is not one of them. Americans are *not* more apathetic than the citizens of these other nations. In fact, research shows that Americans are more apt to believe that they can influence the government and more apt to believe that they have a responsibility to do so. Americans are also comparatively more likely to form organizations and work through them in influencing government.[15] In most European countries, the government has a responsibility to see that each eligible citizen is properly included in the election rolls. In the United States, registration is voluntary; it is usually up to the voter to take the initiative and register. Registration can thus be something of an obstacle to voting in the United States, and it is usually necessary to reregister with every change of residence.

The unusual propensity of Americans to move about frequently and the highly decentralized character of American election administration are closely related to many of these differences. Many Americans experience the situation of being newcomers in particular communities, not just once, but several times, and their unfamiliarity with local issues and candidates probably lowers their incentive to vote. The proportion of voters needing absentee ballots is relatively high, and the special procedures for absentee voting tend to lower turnout in every country.

The American election system enables voters to go to the polls with considerable frequency. Typically, elections are held three years out of every four (depending on the state) with primary elections held earlier in the year of each general election. Yet despite all this voting (or perhaps because of it), voters cannot easily institute major changes of government. Election choices occur in sequence, as well as in combination. Voters can act frequently, yet the entire electorate can never throw all of the "rascals"

[13]Norman H. Nie and Sidney Verba, "Political Participation," in *Handbook of Political Science*, ed. Fred I. Greenstein and Nelson W. Polsby (Reading, Mass.: Addison-Wesley Publishing Co., Inc., 1975), pp. 4, 24. The seven countries were India, United States, Yugoslavia, Austria, Japan, Netherlands, and Nigeria.

[14]The percentage differences cited in this paragraph are all based on voting age population. See Kevin P. Phillips and Paul H. Blackman, *Electoral Reform and Voter Participation* (Washington, D.C.: American Enterprise Institute for Public Policy Research, 1975), p. 25.

[15]Nie and Verba, "Political Participation," pp. 24–25; Gabriel Almond and Sidney S. Verba, *The Civic Culture* (Princeton, N.J.: Princeton University Press, 1963), pp. 148, 246–247, 251.

out in a single election. Fragmented political operations of Congress permit only tiny proportions of Americans to vote for particular individuals who are among the most important figures in Washington.

One should also note that voting is "compulsory" in some of the countries cited in our cross-national comparison. In Belgium, the government has the power to punish unexcused abstention with admonition, fines, and even loss of political rights. Although abstainers rarely feel the bite of such sanctions, their existence undoubtedly accounts for many blank and spoiled ballots in Belgian elections. In Australia, abstainers receive what is known as a " please explain letter" and a fine of two dollars if they are unable to state valid reasons for not voting. Compulsory voting in Australia also produces a fair number of "donkey voters"—people who mark their ballots by simply numbering candidates from top to bottom or left to right in alphabetical order.[16]

There is firm evidence that legal compulsion does raise turnout, even if sanctions are rarely applied. In Belgium, turnout usually exceeds 92 percent, although blank and invalid ballots have been on the rise since 1965. In Australia, turnout is always between 91 and 96 percent. In the Netherlands, voting was compulsory up through 1967 but has been voluntary since then. The drop in turnout between the elections of 1967 and 1970 was quite marked.[17] Other governments have encouraged participation in ways short of making it compulsory. Finland, for example, has automatic registration, balloting on two successive days and many polling stations, easy provision for voting in advance by mail, and routine procedures for voting in hospitals and on Finnish ships. Turnout in recent years has exceeded 80 percent.[18]

Comparisons over Time

Interpretation of voting trends is much more controversial than the comparisons of voting turnout between nations. Scholars disagree in particular in their interpretation of high turnout figures in the late nineteenth century. If this turnout reflected a period of ideal democracy, then the subsequent slump is naturally cause for concern. But if American society is now better and its political life more democratic, then decreases in voting are not as alarming. At issue, in other words, is not simply "low" voter participation of recent years, but also "high" participation of some earlier periods.

Table 7–5 gives only a crude indication of advances in voting during the pre–Civil War years. It is generally agreed that this was a period of two-party "development" that tended (until the 1850s) to offer voters dis-

[16]Richard Rose, ed., *Electoral Behavior: A Comparative Handbook* (New York: The Free Press, A Division of Macmillan Publishing Co., Inc., 1974), pp. 59, 440.

[17]Especially at low educational levels. Those with only elementary education dropped from 93 percent to 72 percent. Those in the highest educational category dropped from 97 percent to 87 percent. Galen Irwin, "Compulsory Voting Legislation," *Comparative Political Studies*, 7 (October 1974), 299. These data are available in Sidney S. Verba, Norman H. Nie, and Jae-On Kim, *Participation and Political Equality* (Cambridge: Cambridge University Press, 1978), p. 7.

[18]Rose, *Electoral Behavior*, pp. 275–276.

Table 7-5
Estimated Turnout in Presidential Elections

Period Averages	Turnout
1824–1836	49.9%
1840–1860[a]	76.9
1864–1884	77.0
1888–1896	77.8
1900–1908	67.9
1912–1920	56.5
1924–1932[a]	54.2
1936–1944	59.8
1948–1956	59.0
1960–1968	62.1
1972–1980	53.8

Recent Years	Turnout
1960	64.0%
1964	61.7
1968	60.6
1972	55.4
1976	54.3
1980	53.9

[a]Highest turnout in American political history was 1860. Lowest turnout in the years since the Civil War was 1924 with 48.9 percent. Total presidential vote as a percentage of estimated eligible electorate. There are a number of sources of possible error and computational difficulty. Variations in state practices makes it impossible to achieve precise statements of the eligible electorate. Interpolations of estimates for intercensal years pose some difficulties. Estimates of the number of aliens are impossible to secure before 1870, and are quite speculative from 1880 through 1890. In some states, aliens who had declared their intention to become citizens were permitted to vote. Women suffrage was extended piecemeal from 1893 on until universal enfranchisement in 1920.

Source: For 1824 to 1968, Walter Dean Burnham in U.S. Census, *Historical Statistics of the United States Colonial Times to 1970* (Washington, D.C.: 1975), Part 2, pp. 1067–1072. For 1972, 1976, and 1980 sources, see Figure 7–1.

tinctly structured alternatives and increasingly capable party organizations. Parallel with this was a powerful surge towards politics in the common mold symbolized by Jacksonianism. Attitudes encouraging more people to participate in politics were taking shape.

During the third party system, turnout peaked and then, beginning in about 1890, dropped dramatically. In the election of 1896 turnout was 79.3 percent; by 1924 it had dropped to only 48.9 percent. Changes in the party system were partly responsible for the downturn—as were the campaigns of black disfranchisement that accompanied these changes in the South.

How important were the peculiar features of the fourth party system in explaining this massive decline? Walter Dean Burnham believes these decreases represent an appalling "dissociation from politics" among ever larger portions of the electorate. He notes that reversal of the trend after 1932 was only moderate and believes that recent downturns indicate that dissociation is again on the rise. His researches show that as turnout declined, the differences in turnout between presidential and midterm voting tended to increase and larger proportions of the electorate failed to vote for lesser offices. In other words, presidential voting declined dramatically, but —equally noteworthy—fewer people who got to the polls were interested in voting for lesser offices and smaller proportions of these were willing to vote again two years later. He also points to the larger changes in the partisan share of the vote ("partisan swing") from one election to another and the increased split-ticket voting of recent years as evidence that an erosion of coherent political motivations accompanied the long-term decline in voting.[19]

In Burnham's view, elites have been the prime beneficiaries of these tendencies. During most of this century, elites have sought half-consciously "to eliminate the political from politics and where the mass electorate must be consulted at all, to convert its choices into the personalistic and ad hoc." Parties are no longer able to educate or persuade, and party alternatives are "only occasionally relevant to electoral choice."[20]

Other scholars view long-term trends quite differently. They remind us that for most of the later nineteenth century (until the Australian ballot took hold), parties printed the ballots and carefully differentiated them by color or design so that watchers could easily see how people voted. Under such a system, they claim, there was ample opportunity for elites to control voting during the years when turnout was highest. In the big cities swarms of repeaters moved from one urban polling place to another, casting and recasting their votes. The unwillingness of rural areas to institute tight registration requirements suggests that vote frauds were common outside the cities as well.[21]

Until the progressive era, it is possible that nonsouthern voters lived in a highly corrupt and partisan atmosphere. If voters were willing to let parties mobilize them under these circumstances, levels of political interest may have been rather low. Strong registration systems and the secret ballot may have eliminated many corrupt and disinterested voters, leaving a better educated, better informed electorate that was no longer controlled by party organizations.[22]

One should also note the possible effect of increasing numbers of

[19]Walter Dean Burnham, "The Changing Shape of the American Political Universe," *The American Political Science Review,* 59 (March 1965), 7–28.
[20]Walter Dean Burnham, review of *Choices and Echoes in Presidential Elections* by Benjamin I. Page, *The New Republic,* March 3, 1979, pp. 33–34.
[21]Philip E. Converse, "Change in the American Electorate," in *The Human Meaning of Social Change,* ed. Angus Campbell and Philip E. Converse (New York: Russell Sage Foundation, 1972), pp. 278–283.
[22]Gerrold G. Rusk, "Comment," *American Political Science Review,* 68 (September 1974), 1048–1049.

eligible voters. The enfranchisement of women added persons who would require many years before habits of voting would bring their participation level up to that of those accustomed to the franchise. Record numbers of immigrants at the turn of the century may be considered in a similar light. In the South systematic disfranchisement of blacks seems to have begun in earnest after 1890 and persisted until at least 1944.

Unless you wish to devote more study to this topic, it may be best to view the long-term voting slump in mixed terms. Peculiar characteristics of the fourth party system and retrograde disfranchisement of blacks certainly contributed to turnout declines. But in all probability imposition of personal registration, the adoption of a secret ballot, and the addition of newcomers to the suffrage also had their effect, and turnout levels of 1930 are about what they are today. Many thoughtful Americans would prefer stronger parties and higher levels of voter participation, but few would regard the late nineteenth century as a golden age of American politics.

Recent declines are another matter. The proportion of nonvoters is large, and if one looks at absolute numbers, their increase is prodigious. In fact, we must examine the data carefully if we are not to be misled. In 1976, 12.8 million more people voted than in 1960, but the number of people old enough to vote who did not do so *increased by 30 million.* Such numbers seem

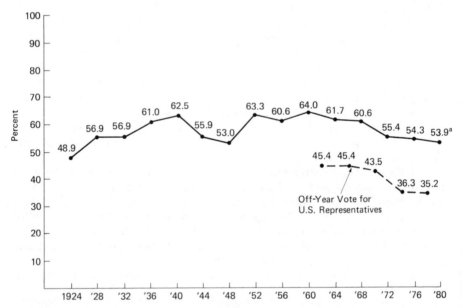

FIGURE 7–1 Percentage of Age Eligible Electorate Voting in Presidential Elections, 1924–1980

Source: 1924 to 1968 Burnham, *Historical Statistics*, p. 1071; 1972 and 1976, U. S. Census, *Statistical Abstract of the United States, 1978,* p. 520.

[a]*Congressional Quaterly,* October 25, 1980, p. 3193; and January 17, 1981, p. 138. If one assumes that an additional 1 percent voted, but not for president, and if one assumes about 4.5 million ineligibles in the voting age population, one comes to a turnout of 56 percent for 1980.

impressive because they are not compared with the expanding population of the United States. One can also dramatize the decline in voting by displaying only a segment of the scale used to measure it.

Use of a full percentage scale and a longer time span tells a more truthful story. We can see from Figure 7–1 that for the past half-century turnout for presidential elections has varied only moderately.

True, the decline from 1960 through 1980 is continuous but it is not notably different from preceding years. Some of the changes resulted from short-term factors. New Deal realignment and the growing familiarity of women with the suffrage may account for the steady upswing from 1924 to 1940. In 1944 many potential voters were either in the armed services or away from home working in centers of war manufacturing. Most people expected the elections of 1948, 1964, and 1972 to be one-sided, and this partly explains their being less well attended than immediately preceding contests.

Then too, the age composition of the electorate has constantly changed. Recently, the proportion of the population that is less likely to vote has expanded:

	1960	1970	1977
Percent of population age 35–64	33.5%	31.9%	31.1%
Percent of population age 18–24	8.7	11.7	13.1

Moreover, the eighteen- to twenty-year-olds became a significant part of the national electorate for the first time in 1972, and this gave these demographic changes added impact.[23]

Nevertheless, aspects of the recent downward trend are both puzzling and disturbing. All survey research shows that people at higher educational levels vote in greater proportions than those with less education. Yet, as we look back to an era when educational levels were much *lower,* we find that voting participation was much higher. Massive immigration relative to total population is now a phenomenon of the distant past, and women have had the vote for decades. By now these former newcomers should be fully adjusted to voting; indeed, we have seen that younger women were reporting higher rates of participation than men by the 1970s.

Significant obstacles to voting have disappeared. The Voting Rights Act of 1965 with the amendments of 1970 and 1975 removed discriminatory literacy tests in the South, and many more blacks have registered and voted. The Twenty-fourth Amendment, ratified in 1971, outlawed the poll tax, and the Supreme Court has struck down residence requirements in excess of thirty days.[24] The United States has not adopted "automatic" registration, but establishing eligibility is now quite easy in many localities. Some areas have effective door-to-door registration or permit registration by mail. States can no longer require prospective voters to register far ahead of an

[23]Data are from U.S. Census, *Statistical Abstract of the United States,* 1972 edition, p. 32; 1978 edition, p. 29.
[24]Dunn v. Blumstein, 405 U.S. 330 (1971).

election, and a few states even permit the voter to register on election day. Yet, despite obvious improvements in access to the polls and increases in levels of education, turnout has declined. Black voting has risen substantially, and with it the turnout level in much of the South. In the North, however, voting declined markedly between 1960 and 1978, and increasing proportions of the more highly educated people may be failing to vote.

Numerous possible explanations have been put forth for these declines, but many of them are difficult to test satisfactorily. A 1968 Buffalo study found that voting tended to cluster with patriotic sentiments such as "love my country," "pay all taxes," "respect the police" more than it clustered with party and campaign activity.[25] According to Milbrath and Goel, "This clustering indicates that voting is more an act by which the citizen affirms his loyalty to the system rather than an act by which he makes demands on the political system." Perhaps there has been a decline in the national idea, and with it both a loss of patriotic sentiment and an increased disposition to "think small." Although we may be deeply concerned about such possibilities, we should not indulge in too much speculation over what is basically a moderate decline in voting levels.

Where We Stand

Americans tend to attach great importance to voting. In moral terms, they regard it as the central democratic experience, not just another kind of participation. Nevertheless, no one has satisfactorily explained why some people vote and others do not. Neither theories based on altruism nor theories based on self-interest have enabled us to explain turnout levels. Even though voting is patterned behavior, none of the group differences explain the decision to vote at all adequately. Political participation tends to vary with social status, but status differences between voters and nonvoters are often unremarkable. Similarities between the two groups are in most respects more noteworthy than differences.

Many other nations have higher levels of voter participation than the United States, but this results from well-understood differences in the societies' political systems and political procedures; none of these differences indicate that Americans are less interested in politics or more negative about it. For the past half century, American voting has been substantially lower than it was in the late nineteenth century. The reasons for this and the implications that flow from it are in dispute. Post-1960 reduction in turnout has been continuous, but its magnitude is frequently exaggerated. Even so, the recent trend is even more puzzling and unexpected and may possibly be substantial among important subgroups.

Levels of voting in the past fifty years fall considerably short of what most of us would prefer. In due course, we will consider whether and how they might be raised. But before doing so we should examine the relationship between voting and other modes of political participation.

[25]Milbrath and Goel, *Political Participation*, p. 12.

Recent research suggests that political participation is not all of a piece. To some extent, it can be thought of in terms of separate activity clusters rather than a single dimension. For example, one rather large clustering consists of people who vote regularly but who do nothing else. Two much smaller groups specialize in different activities. Those in one group vote regularly and take an active part in civic campaigns but avoid partisan campaign activity. The other includes those who are active in political campaigns and partisan electoral activity but who do not participate in civic community efforts. A third group, much smaller than either of these, specializes in contacting public officials about personal problems. A few people are highly active in *both* civic and partisan affairs.[26]

These three types of participation differ in their communication content, scope of the outcome, and in other ways. We can think of voting as a "blunt but powerful instrument" that exerts great pressure on leaders and has very broad consequences for all leaders and citizens. Yet, voting requires little initiative and does not transmit much information. The voter's choices are very limited, and people decide between candidates for reasons that the vote itself does not reveal. Partisan campaign activity expands the voter's influence beyond the single vote and, like voting, has the capacity to place officials under great pressure. But unlike ordinary voters, campaign activists can communicate a great deal of information about their preferences.

Contacting officials is very different from voting. If a person has a pothole in front of his house, he can call his city councilmember about it at a time of his own choosing and set his own "agenda." Cooperative civic activity has its own distinctive features. Since it often centers on particular problems, this kind of participation also transmits information. An effective United Way program or cancer fund drive can have more extensive consequences than the single citizen concerned about his street. However, civic activities do not affect as many people as an election.[27]

All of this suggests that alternative ways of participating are available to citizens and that the potentials of one mode may partly make up for limitations of others. In a complex modern society, citizens may need a variety of ways to influence government and make it responsive.

Citizens who want to do more than vote once every year or so and who are either repelled by partisan activity or sense that they cannot achieve much by engaging in it seem to be seeking other channels of expression. We could even say that a "citizen involvement movement" is abroad in the land. In 1979 the Filene Center for Citizenship and Public Affairs began publishing a magazine devoted to participation. In their first issue the editors stated

[26]Sidney Verba and Norman H. Nie, *Participation in America* (New York: Harper & Row, Publishers, Inc., 1972), pp. 79–81. The following two paragraphs are also adapted from this source.
[27]Ibid., pp. 44–45.

that citizens had decreased their involvement in voting and political parties, but had increased it in issue groups and government-sponsored participation groups. They expected these trends to continue through the 1980s and hoped that their magazine would help "those who want to see democracy work more effectively in its many forms."

> It is likely that citizen groups will seek greater power, networking among groups will grow, electoral and political party reform will be attempted, new political parties may arise, and government administrative agencies will strengthen their commitment to citizen involvement.[28]

Initial issues of *Citizen Participation* dealt with such topics as how to improve grassroots participation at the local level and how to get media coverage for citizen activities, with neighborhood councils in Independence, Missouri, and so forth. John Gardner and Ralph Nader received prominent and favorable attention. Some pieces were sympathetic to increased participation through the parties, but much of the emphasis was on alternative channels. An article by Mark Hatfield, for example, urged the adoption of a voter initiative amendment to the Constitution and claimed that it had overwhelming public support.[29]

Participation in bureaucratic affairs is also likely to become an increasingly important issue in the years ahead. Federal agencies are inviting some citizens to take part in their programs, and the idea that people have a right to participate directly in agency affairs is gaining ground. The trend is towards making agencies assume responsibility for securing participation and towards enhancing citizens' standing to sue public agencies.

According to one analyst, the "new participation" assumes that, in addition to the traditional legislative and judicial oversight, adversary relationships among participating groups are also necessary. He believes that moves in this direction may reflect attempts to legitimize government in a time when authority is increasingly delegated "to agencies whose use of that power constitutes policy-making without direct public mandate or control." He notes little rigorous evaluation of these efforts and states that participation requirements vary from one program to another. Tensions can easily arise, says the author, when the agency's desire to "sell" a program collides with opinions of participants. Media often focus on the most controversial cases and neglect the more usual instances where citizen involvement proceeds without litigation, confrontation, or disruption. Although citizen involvement in agency programs has acquired a certain chic, and can serve broad public purposes, it can also further agency interests and the middle class.[30]

Expansion of participatory opportunities may be praiseworthy, but voting should remain the sovereign political act for two reasons: First, those who participate in these alternative activities are small in numbers and

---

[28]*Citizen Participation*, September/October 1979, p. 2.
[29]"Direct Democracy Now," *Citizen Participation*, November/December 1979, p.5.
[30]Walter Rosenbaum, "Public Participation: Now It's Required, But Is It Important?" *Citizen Participation*, September/October 1979, p. 12.

unrepresentative of the larger public. Common Cause, for example, claims a membership of 200,000 or so—a miniscule proportion of the total population—and it is concentrated among middle-class professional people. The numbers who directly participate in federal agency programs may be large in absolute terms yet still constitute a negligible percentage of the mass public. For example, we would have no reason to expect those participating under the Strip Mining Control and Reclamation Act or the Noise Control Act to be either very numerous or very representative of Americans in general. Voting ought to take precedence over all these other activities because so many more people can—and do—vote.

Second, it seems likely that these other activities ultimately *depend* on voting for their effectiveness. If we did not have the power to elect officials with the greatest authority, they might have little reason to be *responsive* to us through other channels. The same applies to heads of administrative agencies, who must to some degree be concerned with their relations to elected legislative bodies and executives. This is not to say that elected officials are totally responsible to voters or that administrators are totally responsible to elected officials. Without elections, however, all government officials would lack an important reason for wanting to be responsive to citizens either directly or indirectly. Administrative participation might continue, but only as a way for administrators to consolidate their power.

Elections make it possible for us to select the persons who possess the only power stipulated in the Constitution.[31] Frequently, the other modes of influence can usefully supplement voting, but if we are forced to choose between government being *responsible* to the many or being *responsive* to the few that seek to influence it, the former should take precedence.

In part, the view being stated here turns on values rather than facts. As Americans, we are free to do as we wish in relation to our government. Yet, the choices we make will have consequences. Placing too much emphasis on specialized forms of participation and not enough on voting may make it more difficult for us to maintain overall control. The point should not be overstated: We live in a society where complex organizations are increasingly important and many decisions are of vital significance only to small groups of people. The degree to which elected officials can or should control bureaucratic organizations is a large topic, and we cannot adequately cover it in this book. The general public cannot hope to manage any but a few of the most important matters. Yet, the problem of control will not go away. If our elected representatives become unable or unwilling to determine the shape and direction of public decisions, we shall have traded representative government for something very different.

A recent book states that we have already traveled far in this direction. Although its subject is bureaucracy, not parties and elections, the authors

---

[31]The only legitimate exception to voter sovereignty under the Constitution is the Supreme Court. In the final analysis, we *permit* the Court to maintain its "sovereign" powers by generally supporting its decisions, by not using the power of Congress to significantly restrict its appellate jurisdiction, and by not amending the Constitution to deprive it of prerogatives such as judicial review that it has long asserted.

conclude with a discussion of voting that locates what we have called the sovereign political act at the center of a crisis of legitimacy. They regard voting as the most crucial form of participation and cite a 1973 survey in which 65 percent of those interviewed agreed with the statement that "The trouble with government is that elected officials have lost control over the bureaucrats who really run the country." They believe the bureaucratization of our political life is a major explanation of nonvoting.[32]

Taking Stock

This chapter began on a note of perplexity that it has not been possible to dispel. Research on voting behavior has an awkward way of frustrating our most natural expectations. As a further example of this, consider the widespread decline of confidence in leaders that is often reported in the polls. Surely, one would suppose that this "explains" lower turnout. Yet no investigator has successfully demonstrated that these attitudes are linked to nonvoting. Pollsters have also uncovered a huge decline in people's trust of government, but a leading study insists that this too is subtantially unrelated to levels of voting. According to Miller and Levitin, other measures of system support (sense of efficacy, interest in elections and public affairs, and concern over the outcome of elections) have not declined in recent years. They attribute lower turnout to a disproportionate withdrawal of the poorly educated citizens least able to cope with issue voting and the increasing number of young voters.[33]

I believe that it would be desirable for the American people to raise their level of voting. Yet the fact that such a value position has wide approval does not mean that it is correct or that one can point with assurance to specific benefits that would result from it. In fact, we can make no convincing demonstration that large turnouts produce good government; voting levels may well be symptomatic rather than causative. Perhaps turnout will go up as the proportion of young persons declines. Or perhaps a revival of allegiant sentiment and a decline in discord will send more people to the polls. Without an understanding of what leads people to vote in the first place, an endorsement of voting becomes an act of faith. Yet, the faith is crucial, and it has many adherents. It can be defended persuasively and movingly:

> Political man needs both bread and the word: socioeconomics and faith. By the act of voting we accept those traditions of service, common good, and public interest that historically were given by God to guide monarch or aristocracy. To vote is both a political act to get something and a moral act to accept

[32]David Nachmias and David H. Rosenbloom, *Bureaucratic Government USA* (New York: St. Martin's Press, 1980), pp. 239–251. The opinion data appear at p. 244.
      [33]Warren E. Miller and Teresa E. Levitin, *Leadership and Change* (Cambridge, Mass.: Winthrop Publishers, Inc., 1976), p. 228.

responsibility for the future. To vote is to accept choice. To choose is to be alive.[34]

Some people argue that a moderate level of participation is better than a high level of participation. This follows the excellent Socratic principle that one should be moderate in all things. In America's present situation, however, it is not a good argument against more widespread voting and more involvement in electoral politics. Polls and surveys sometimes convey a sense that participation is higher than it really is, in part because interviewing usually focuses on presidential elections where voting is heaviest. Also many people are inclined to report higher levels of participation than they actually engage in because participation is an approved form of behavior. Anyone who has had experience in electoral politics knows that very few people are interested in nonpresidential contests, even when important offices are involved. (Only 37 percent of the electorate voted for U.S. representatives in 1974.) The number of people who will go to the slightest trouble to help a candidate for a minor office is miniscule. In terms of the country's values and political arrangements, the level of mass involvement is not moderate, it is very low. One could take 90 percent of the American electorate and multiply its political activity tenfold before a modern Socrates would consider very many to be moderately involved in electoral politics.

A Recent Study of Nonvoting

Before moving to the question of how voting levels might be raised, we should examine more closely the findings of a study of nonvoters cited earlier in this chapter. Robert Teeter's Market Opinion Research Corporation began interviewing 2,006 people on the day Carter was elected in 1976. Arthur Hadley reinterviewed about 100, analyzed all the data, and published his results in 1978.[35] Using somewhat arbitrary methods, Hadley was able to classify nonvoters (*refrainers* in his terminology) into six different categories, as follows:

1. *Positive Apathetics* (35 percent). These people are happy, educated, and well-off. They are not miserable or dissatisfied, yet they do not vote.
2. *Bypassed* (13 percent). Here we have those of low education and low income who have missed out on most of what America has to offer. They are hard-core refrainers, not likely to vote under most circumstances.
3. *Politically Impotent* (22 percent). People in this category feel that nothing they can do will affect their government. They are not necessarily hostile towards government, and they are not notably low in education or income.
4. *Physically Disfranchised* (18 percent). These individuals could not vote for legal or physical reasons. Many said they were in bad health or could not meet residence requirements.

[34]Hadley, *The Empty Polling Booth*, pp. 113–114. © 1978 by Arthur T. Hadley. Reprinted by permission of Prentice Hall, Inc. and The Sterling Lord Agency, Inc.
[35]Ibid. Hadley is a Democrat, Teeter a Republican polling specialist.

5. *Naysayers* (6 percent). Refraining is a conscious choice for these nonvoters—even an act of defiance. They are very assertive and willing to explain their various reasons at length.

6. *Cross-Pressured* (5 percent). Persons in this category have political information and want to vote but cannot make up their minds.[36]

We can see from this array that Hadley identifies a large group of "positive apathetics"—people we would have expected to vote, but who did not. This group has a counterpart called the "vergers"—people whose low sense of political efficacy leads us to believe that they would not vote but who nevertheless do.[37] The vergers constituted 21 percent of those who reported voting. They tended to be much more cynical than other voters, less well educated, and not as happy. In thinking about ways to raise turnout, it would be important to maintain the voting habits of this group and not to take steps that would dissuade it from continuing to vote.

One of the more pronounced and interesting differences between voters and nonvoters is the greater tendency of nonvoters to believe in luck. To the question: "Do you think it's better to plan your life way ahead, or would you say life is too much a matter of luck to plan ahead?" Hadley found the following:

	Percent "Plan Ahead"[38]
All voters	57%
Voters other than vergers	60
Vergers	48
All nonvoters	37%
Positive Apathetics	48
All other nonvoters	31

Note that vergers and positive apathetics come out the same on this question, whereas large differences show up between all other groups.

Hadley's findings are interesting in a number of respects. Cross-pressured people accounted for little nonvoting, although the criteria for this group were admittedly rather stringent. The naysayers are small in number and far from agreeing among themselves on why they should not register or vote: Some have religious scruples; others have had a bad experience in politics; still others seem to be saying no as a habitual posture toward life. The research, therefore, does not support the notion that nonvoting is to any significant degree a deliberate political act—at least it was not in 1976.

[36]Ibid., pp. 39–41. The procedures used to develop this classification appear at pp. 139–141. Not all refrainers fit neatly into one category or the other.

[37]To qualify as a verger, the person interviewed had to be a voter who agreed with *each* of the following three statements: (1) "People like me don't have any say about what the government does"; (2) "Sometimes politics and government seems so complicated that a person like me can't really understand what's going on"; (3) "I don't think public officials care much what people like me think." Ibid., pp. 98, 167.

[38]Adapted from ibid., pp. 158, 168.

GETTING MORE PEOPLE TO VOTE

Dr. Samuel Johnson once said that nothing is more hopeless than a scheme of merriment. Perhaps well-intentioned efforts to improve politics are similarly doomed to failure. One might suppose that people will vote if they want to, either spontaneously or out of dutifulness.

One way to raise the level of voting would be to improve the performance of homely but essential tasks of election administration in the United States. All facets of election administration can be important, but especially significant are the ease with which a person may register, how close to the election he or she may register, the ready availability of absentee ballots (properly administered), and the provision of adequate information about registration and voting in the media. Much of what occurs within these realms defies summary description, and much of it occurs in a zone of indifference from the media and public.

America holds elections in thousands of small local jurisdictions, and practices vary widely. Districting arrangements for precincts and minor offices, absentee voting practices, voter registration procedures, ballot format, filing requirements, timing of state and local elections, and selection of personnel to work at the polls are "just details" to all but the working politicians and some activists. Undoubtedly many local effects either cancel each other out or become invisible when aggregated within a state or over the entire nation.

Disinterest of the larger public permits the few involved in these matters to have an impact at the precinct, neighborhood, ward, district, or county level. If no one is particularly interested, one or two persons can maintain established routines, with far from uniform results. Such persons are likely to be lifelong local residents who are not representative of the larger, geographically mobile part of the American population. They often constitute the bedrock element in the dominant political subcultures in this country's thousands of local communities.

We have noted that since American registration procedures are "voluntary," voting requires two tasks rather than one. Since many people are not strongly motivated to vote, and since registration may be inconvenient, "voluntary" registration lowers turnout. Notice how registration-based turnout changes the rankings and narrows the differences between states:

	Persons Voting in 1976 as a Percent of:	
	Voting Age Population	Voters Registered
Utah	69%	78%
Indiana	61	76
New York	51	81
California	51	82

Source: Figures in the first column are from Table 7–3. Figures in the second column are from U.S. Census, *Statistical Abstract of the United States 1978*, p. 524.

Requirements vary a good deal from state to state. North Dakota has no registration requirement, and several other states, mostly in the Midwest, have traditionally permitted rural jurisdictions to conduct elections without voter registration. Significant efforts have gone forward to facilitate registration in ways short of making it automatic. By 1976 Minnesota, Wisconsin, Maine, and Oregon permitted election-day registration in one form or another. Laws in California, Michigan, and Ohio enable state motor vehicle agencies to distribute voter registration forms.[39] Some of these arrangements may differ only in a technical sense from the registration-free system of North Dakota.

Election-day registration has produced some interesting effects.[40] Between 1972 and 1976 turnout increased by between 0.6 and 4.1 percent in each of the states that adopted it, despite a nationwide decline in turnout of about 1 percent. The turnout rankings changed as follows:

	State Turnout Rankings[40]	
	1972	1976
Maine	19	5
Minnesota	2	1
Oregon	18	11
Wisconsin	15	4

Election-day registration may have also produced some partisan effects. Democrats made significant gains in state legislative seats in each of these states. Republicans were reluctant to criticize the measures, and local polling officials were among the most vocal opponents. In Minnesota 454,000 people had to be registered on election day. In Wisconsin, the figure was 215,000.[41]

In 1977 President Carter recommended election-day registration as the centerpiece of a comprehensive election reform package. As in Minnesota, the plan contemplated having preregistered persons vouch for voters unable to produce proper identification. Local officials would continue to be responsible for registration, with federal funds helping to defray the

[39]Richard G. Smolka, "Election Legislation," in *The Book of the States 1978–1979* (Lexington, Ky.: Council of State Governments, 1978), pp. 231–232.

[40]North Dakota, the state with no registration requirement, ranked third in 1976. The second ranking state was Utah. Turnout in the Canadian election of 1972 (measured against voting age population) was about 5 percent higher than in America's highest ranking state in 1976 (Minnesota). U.S. Census, *Statistical Abstract of the United States 1978*, p. 524. For data on Canadian elections, see Kevin P. Phillips and Paul H. Blackman, *Electoral Reform and Voter Participation* (Washington, D.C.: American Enterprise Institute for Public Policy Research, 1979), pp. 24–27, 77–80.

[41]Rhodes Cook, "How Election Day Registration Has Worked Out So Far," *Congressional Quarterly Weekly Report,* May 14, 1977, pp. 912–915.

costs. The plan was to be mandatory for federal elections in all fifty states beginning in 1978, with further funding available for states that wished to extend the system to state and local elections and stiff penalties for fraudulent registration.

Among the reasons for the defeat of Carter's proposal was the drumfire of criticism it received from local election officials and the lack of strong incentives for any important group to give it high-priority support. Most members of Congress had little to gain by changing the rules under which they had been elected. A Gallup poll based on interviews taken in March 1977 indicated that 55 percent of the public opposed the measure. Republicans now found that they could safely criticize it, and many did so. Some critics conceded that the idea worked well in states that had tried it, but they had genuine fears about its effectiveness elsewhere. According to Steve Klein, chairman of Independent Voters of Illinois, it would mean that "every fire hydrant and tombstone in Chicago would end up with a phony I.D."[42]

A Census of Voters?

In his analysis of Carter's proposal, Kevin Phillips suggested a different approach to universal registration. The potential for large-scale fraud under Carter's proposal is real, he claimed, but it could be avoided by having the government take a special census at certain intervals or a number of months before each election, so that no registration burden would fall on the individual.[43]

It is not clear how such a system might cope with large numbers of bona fide address changes. The United States has many transients, and elections take place with great frequency. This problem is probably not nearly as great in countries such as Australia, Canada, and Britain, which have procedures of the sort he recommends. A census of voters implies a strong federal role in what has traditionally been a local matter and would be likely to diminish and uniformly redefine the role of local election officials. By eliminating registration as the basis of a political favor, the census of voters would undoubtedly weaken local party organizations. However, this would not necessarily be a bad thing, even from the perspective of those who want stronger parties.

Phillips's analysis properly suggested that contentious side issues would quickly emerge. Partisans in the controversies over illegal immigration or benefits eligibility in Chicano neighborhoods could make the census of voters a political football and thus disturb many liberals. Phillips indicated that some conservatives were not eager to see large increases in turnout, and he implied that the concern over possible voter fraud might conceal a deeper interest in biasing the electoral process towards higher-income brackets.

[42] *Newsweek*, April 4, 1977.
[43] Kevin Phillips, "Time for Voter Census," *Viewpoint*, Vol. 2, no. 10 for October 1977, Card No. 294, Accession No. 157.

Resources and Incentives

Broader issues come to the fore if we think about incentives for voting, the vote as a political resource, and people's capability of voting. If voting had more impact on government, the vote would become a more important political resource, and people would be more likely to want to use it. However, this would not help those who, for whatever reason, are truly incapable of voting.

We might want to reject some measures that would undoubtedly increase electoral participation. For example, compulsory voting augmented by fines can undoubtedly change the costs and benefits of voting and thus get more people to the polls. But unless it also improves people's desire to vote, it might simply lead to the American equivalent of "donkey voting." Discouraging the use of alternative channels of participation is undesirable on general grounds (though perhaps not in all specific instances).

Other desirable changes might be too difficult, too general, or too important in their own right to be considered simply as ways to improve voting turnout. For example, a more productive economy with less unemployment might reduce the number of the bypassed even if it had little impact on the positive apathetics. Many people think that voting levels would go up if the candidates were better or if those who were elected followed through on their campaign promises. A cohesive family system might place many older persons in a position where their political rights were better protected and provide family members with better opportunities to discover their political interests. If national feeling or patriotic sentiment increased, voting would probably go up. Even if one approves of all these things, they tend to beg the question: *How* does one get a better economy, more closely knit families, better candidates, and the rest?

Most people are already capable of voting. They are not subject to serious intimidation or threats, except perhaps those they create for themselves through the low value they place on their political rights. They have time to get to the polls, they have access to general information, and so forth. Admittedly, the few who do lack capability (many of the physically disfranchised and the bypassed) have very real needs. Perhaps Hadley overstates the proportion who are physically disfranchised (18 percent seems high, and the tendency of this group to believe that life is too much a matter of luck to plan ahead is somewhat suspicious). Some of those who are in poor health or bypassed may not wish to tell the interviewer that the procedures are inconvenient, that they feel isolated and vulnerable, or that they distrust the integrity of the absentee ballot.

Easier absentee ballot procedures would undoubtedly raise turnout, but the potential for abuse is real. Stronger local party organizations could also help by providing the person-to-person contacts some persons need. But such organizations enjoy little public support, and at the present few seem interested in building them up. All of the tasks of election administration could probably be accomplished more reliably under centralized direction, but the dangers here are equally obvious.

Hadley urges that we find ways to heighten the symbolic dignity of voting and suggests that we set aside a special holiday for it. He also warns against undue reliance on the methods of the marketplace. The contest between commercial techniques and civic values does seem at present to favor the former. An attack on this problem might well require changes in campaign finance and in the practices of new politics campaign professionals. At root though, excessive commercialism in politics probably reflects the enthronement of commercialism in American television.

What could we do to make the vote a more important political resource? One approach is Mark Hatfield's proposed voter initiative amendment, which would allow nationwide voting on important substantive issues. Sponsors would be required to collect signatures over an eighteen-month period and would need a number equal to at least 3 percent of the votes cast in the previous presidential election to have a measure placed on the ballot in all states. The measure would become a law if a majority of those voting on the question approved it. Its supporters hope that it would bring government closer to the people and stimulate wide-ranging discussion on the important issues.[44]

Although proponents may be underestimating the degree to which organized pressure groups could dominate initiative campaigns, one could argue that the measure would force pressure groups to deal with the mass public in a visible and formal way. Hatfield does not comment on the possibility that an initiative process might give further encouragement to single-issue politics, or that it would make it more difficult to compromise our political differences or consider the relationships among issues. Without impugning the popular intelligence, one can question whether the polling booth is the place to consider legislation. Many ordinary people are anything but "dumb," yet most have limited political interest and poor access to good information and analysis. The electorate as a whole is not in a good position to deliberate on technical questions and would not be even if everyone in it had the wisdom of a Solomon. Large numbers of abstainers on initiative propositions might subject the legitimacy of the process to considerable strain. Moreover, as a practical matter, a constitutional amendment of this sort might be almost impossible to repeal if it did not work satisfactorily.[45]

Some analysts argue that the vote is more valuable if there are *fewer* choices to be made, rather than more. Shortening the ballot, the argument goes, gives voters a chance to focus on important contests; making many

[44]Such a procedure is not available for constitutional amendments, and the proposal excludes declarations of war. Congress would not be able to repeal within two years, except by a two-thirds vote in both houses and presidential signature. Hatfield first introduced the amendment in 1977 and a number of national legislators and other persons in public life have endorsed it. Mark Hatfield, "Direct Democracy Now," *Citizen Participation,* November/December 1979, pp. 5f.

[45]For a more favorable assessment of the voter initiative amendment, which views it as part of a continuing "assault on the governing class of officials," see Michael Nelson, "Power to the People," *Saturday Review,* November 24, 1979, pp. 12–17.

elective positions appointive would add to the stature of elected officials who remain. The short-ballot idea goes with related "good government" doctrines such as consolidation of small local jurisdictions, elimination of overlapping authority, and so forth. These efforts, and the more ambitious efforts to move the country towards parliamentary democracy, are much more than devices designed to get more people to the polls. Even though moves towards a parliamentary system have usually lacked significant support, it may well be that such a system would promote higher levels of voting. As noted before, the American system of staggered terms and independent authorities makes it very difficult for the voters to "throw the rascals out."

The long-run value of voting may depend crucially on whether elected officials will maintain the ability to steer the course of the political system. Some observers are already skeptical about this, but the matter is much in need of further analysis. A prominent historian claims that for much of American history elected officials ran the government, but for the past half century voters have had considerably less influence. Until the early 1970s, the seniority system largely removed congressional decision making from voter influence, except through organized lobbies. Since the 1950s, federal judges and civil servants have become increasingly more dominant in policy making. As interest in electoral politics declines ("Fewer people vote and fewer people care"), elected officials may become less interested in expressing the popular will in their decisions.[46] There is also a tendency for activists who care about issues to avoid working through the voters. Instead, they go directly to the media to influence politicians. In so doing, they may increase feelings of voter powerlessness.[47]

There is a distinct possibility that elected officials are losing control of government. Earlier in this chapter, we cited evidence that the public believes that this is happening. Moreover, the authors who presented that finding believe the public's perception is accurate.

Do we really wish to break out of this situation? If so, how can we do it? The superorganized, yet fragmented and unproductive society we seem to be heading towards is a distinctly unsettling prospect. Let us hope that we will discover how to change course and somehow move towards a humane future without massive dislocations and without regressing to an even less desirable society.

To restore stronger control of government by elected officials, conventional wisdom suggests some requirements, possibilities, and problems. Apparently elected officials must be organized in a way that enables them to make controversial decisions and to persist in important courses of action over time. This implies a need for leadership and broad coalitions. The political parties once helped meet these needs; at the moment, they appear too weak to do so. If the American people turn away from the parties, they

---

[46]Richard Jensen, "Party Coalitions and the Search for Modern Values," in *Emerging Coalitions in American Politics,* ed. Seymour M. Lipset (San Francisco: Institute for Contemporary Studies, 1978), pp. 12, 27–28, 31–32, 40.
[47]Hadley, *Empty Polling Booth,* p. 112.

may either have to find a substitute to perform these functions or else forsake this objective. Perhaps new party arrangements can be devised that will eventually elicit broad public support.

If the people we elect lack adequate influence over the course of events, they are not going to recapture it by having each elected official go his or her own way. They will have to work together somehow, and this could impose real limits on the individual discretion of legislators (at least on important roll calls). The continuing need for agreement between executive and legislative branches and between House and Senate makes it more difficult to construct coalitions and lead them. Governing coalitions will have to attract stronger support than a bare majority—which may necessitate a much greater degree of consensus in our society. Stated differently, discord on many fronts may make it impossible for elected officials to govern. Unfortunately, recommendations to reduce discord, like the other "good things to do" mentioned earlier, are more easily made than implemented.

The doctrine of popular sovereignty is so strongly embedded in the United States that Americans are uncomfortable with the idea of "rulers." We need to be careful that this does not take an escapist direction that can eventually put unaccountable administrators firmly in control. Although millions of Americans work for government, Americans do not like bureaucracy and wish it would go away. Still, most agencies have the popular support they need, so dramatic reduction of the administrative establishment is not likely. Perhaps the role and structure of the bureaucracy should be dealt with as a constitutional matter. Certainly, if we are going to trade representative democracy for a bureaucratic regime, we should do so with our eyes open.

However, we should also recognize that in a constitutional democracy elected officials should not have total control over administrators. Legislators need to delegate many decisions to administrators, and administrative agencies must be able to resist improper political directives from elected officials. Administration needs support as well as surveillance. Lowi's investigations suggest that Congress is too prone to delegate legislative authority without clear legislative standards; the leading specialist in administrative law appears to disagree. The issue needs to be more thoroughly explored by political scientists.[48]

CONCLUSION

The overall picture of American political participation is somewhat mixed. Citizens have been searching for new ways to influence government. Our major argument has been that voting is the basic expression of popular sovereignty, even if we cannot find many purposive voters in the surveys.

[48]Theodore J. Lowi, *The End of Liberalism,* 2nd ed. (New York: W. W. Norton & Co., Inc., 1979), Chap. 5. The leading specialist in administrative law has been Kenneth Culp Davis. See his *Administrative Law and Government* (St. Paul, Minn.: West Publishing Co., 1960), Chap. 2.

More than any other form of participation, voting enables those who lack special advantages to count in the political process. All forms of political effort are easier for those who are socially advantaged, but status distinctions are less significant in voting than in activities requiring more time and organizational skill. Voting does not preclude the use of other techniques to control government; it probably even encourages them. Voting, however, "outranks" other modes of democratic participation both in a constitutional and logical sense.

Recent declines in turnout are often exaggerated, yet there are grounds for concern, and the matter could become quite serious if electoral contraction should continue through the 1980s. Trends aside, there is no basis for satisfaction with the mediocre levels of voting that have characterized the past half century. Our discussion of how more people might be encouraged to vote emphasizes the importance of mundane aspects of election administration and the coalitional and leadership roles that parties have played in the past. However, many other aspects of American society also affect political participation.

8

Political Ambition

Thomas Hobbes spoke of political ambition as forcefully as anyone when he said, "I put for a general inclination of all mankind a perpetual and restless desire of power after power that ceases only in death."[1] In this famous statement, the word *power* is used very broadly to convey a person's "present means to obtain some future apparent good." However, Hobbes and many others have thought that the most significant power derives from a society's political arrangements. In his words, "The greatest of human powers is that which is compounded of the powers of most men, united by consent in one person." The search for power may not be as universal as Hobbes supposed, but his thoughts are still pertinent three centuries later.

Of course, this should not suggest that every contemporary American naturally seeks elective political office. For one thing, elective offices that are easiest to win are not very powerful. Also, there are now (as in Hobbes's era) other means to power such as "success," "friends," "servants," "reputation of power," and "reputation of prudence." Wealth is still another means to power in Hobbes's sense.

In the United States, as elsewhere, "honest" political ambition is apt to be "naked." Americans think it is immoral to seek power, and they have divided government into many parts so that no one will have too much of it. The pursuit of wealth is much more acceptable, if the purpose is self-indulgence or service to others, rather than the pursuit of power. Indeed, Americans seem to have taken to heart Adam Smith's observation that "man is never more innocently engaged than in making money." This is actually a crucial idea (though whimsically expressed) in a body of thought that began with his *Wealth of Nations.*

[1]Thomas Hobbes, *Leviathan.*

There is no intellectual tradition of comparable stature that can convince us that political ambition is innocent. However, a functioning system of free elections does much to civilize the manner in which power is acquired and the scope of its exercise. Political ambition becomes a more prosaic subject in some ways, but the intricacies of elections impart a fascination of their own.

THE NOMINATING PROCESS

In this chapter, we will be looking at the search for political office from a number of points of view. Party nomination is usually a necessary preliminary, and our first task will be to examine the main features of the nominating process in the United States. Nomination is important simply because the number of names to choose from must be limited if voters are to have a practicable choice. In essence, the question is which people will be listed on the ballot with enough sponsorship to give them some chance of winning. The nomination process is, of course, a widespread phenomenon. The university that must select a new dean or the firm that wants to fill a newly created position will each confine their serious scrutiny to a small list of preselected persons.

Obviously, the calibre of person the electorate selects to fill an office is limited by the alternative candidates available to it on election day. Yet, the choices put before the voters in any election are always a negligible proportion of those who meet minimum statutory requirements for the position. Any number of ways could be devised to both guarantee a selection yet limit the number of alternatives. From the viewpoint of the ambitious politician, nomination is an essential step towards political success.

The Nonpartisan Approach

Although political parties are the main vehicles of nomination in the United States, it is easier to understand some aspects of the process if we begin by describing efforts to remove nominations from party control. The crux of a nonpartisan election (whether primary or general) is that candidates run without any party labels on the ballot. At least two-thirds of cities with over 25,000 inhabitants, most school boards, all county offices in several states, many state judicial elections, and the Nebraska State Legislature are nonpartisan.

The nominating process in such cases may require a preliminary contest (the primary) that is also nonpartisan and that determines which two candidates will run against each other in the general election. However, primary elections emerged as a uniquely American attempt to have ordinary citizens select party nominees.

If one stipulates that the general election is to be nonpartisan, the justification for a preliminary contest is less clearcut. Accordingly, the usual arrangement is a single round of balloting that, in effect, combines the primary and the election. In these cases, the individual with the most votes wins—even if he or she does not receive a majority.

Such a system, of course, leaves open the question of how to select nominees, and leaves unregulated the actual practices that are followed. In a sense, nonpartisanship is not a *system* of nominations as much as an attempt to detour or brush aside the whole process. Although state laws limit *partisan* primary arrangements to specific offices, no laws prevent party organizations from helping nonpartisan candidates, and as a result party activists sometimes play important roles in nonpartisan politics. In some places, such as Chicago and Boston, the nonpartisan ballot is little more than a formality, and party organizations do the nominating. At the other extreme (many school boards, for example) parties are not involved either formally or actually. Most observers believe that the nonpartisan ballot tends to weaken the political parties. Cities that have nonpartisan ballots are also more likely to have other political features, such as council manager form of government and separation of local from state and national elections, that tend to weaken party organizations.[2]

In very small nonpartisan cities, nominating politics may be highly informal. Elsewhere, organized groups urge particular persons to run and support their campaigns. The absence of procedural regulations of the sort imposed on political parties means that nonparty nominating groups are often unaccountable to the larger community. A newspaper, labor union, civic organization, ad hoc group, or business firm may perform nominating functions normally provided by a party. Candidates may lack any group support, or they may seek alliances on a personal basis with a wide variety of interests, including the local power structure.[3] Many of the lesser posts are not eagerly sought, and individuals often need some group encouragement before they will file for such offices.

Nonpartisan politics is an expression of middle-class values. Working-class individuals seldom achieve the prominence in private life that makes them appealing to the nonparty groups that nominate or endorse candidates in nonpartisan elections. Nonpartisanship reduces the participation of labor, low-income, ethnic, and Democratic voters. Turnout has been lower in nonpartisan elections than in contests where party labels are on the ballot, and important segments of the electorate seem to lack an incentive to vote when the party cue is not present. A recent study shows that the median percentage voting for mayor in partisan cities in 1975 was 39 percent; the comparable figure for nonpartisan cities was 30 percent.[4]

One scholar maintains that nonpartisan elections are a twentieth-century phenomenon and not an "individualistic anachronism."[5] In his view,

[2]Thomas R. Dye, *Politics in States and Communities,* 3rd ed. (Englewood Cliffs, N.J.: Prentice-Hall, Inc., 1977), p. 264; Albert K. Karnig and B. Oliver Walter, "Municipal Elections," *The Municipal Yearbook 1977* (Washington, D.C.: International City Managers Association, 1977), p. 70.

[3]Dye, *Politics in States and Communities,* pp. 266–267; Hugh A. Bone, *American Politics and the Party System,* 3rd ed. (New York: McGraw-Hill Book Company, 1965), p. 602.

[4]Karnig and Walter, "Municipal Elections," p. 69. The difference is much smaller where city elections are held at the same time as state or national contests. However, most nonpartisan cities hold city elections independently of all other elections. Ibid., p. 70.

[5]Leon D. Epstein, *Political Parties in Western Democracies* (New York: Frederick A. Praeger, 1967), p. 96.

the type of community that tends to favor nonpartisan politics is becoming more rather than less common. On the other hand, the independence of such communities from state and national authority may be declining. Except for judicial elections, nonpartisanship has not made any notable advance to higher offices in the United States. The Minnesota legislature, previously nonpartisan, reverted to partisan nomination in 1970. Nonpartisanship has been a notable feature of California politics, but its influence there may have crested. Ronald Reagan has been a more partisan figure than Earl Warren, and Jerry Brown has had to blend partisan and nonpartisan appeals. In an earlier era, California governors could not display evident interest in the presidency without appearing neglectful of state matters. Today, everyone assumes that California governors will pursue presidential ambitions, and their attempts to do so may well enhance partisanship in the nation's largest state.

Ballots for governors, United States senators, and United States representatives provide party labels in every state. Running as an independent may enable one to finesse many of the obstacles to getting a party nomination to these offices, but so few independents win that this strategy seldom offers much promise. Independents may have greater success in the future, but even independent candidates need sponsorship of some sort.

Of course, nonpartisan styles can operate in a partisan milieu. In some cases, this can be a protective adaptation of partisan politicians; in others the partisan ballot may be an empty formality. However, even where parties are weakest, there are always statutory requirements governing partisan nominations, which participants cannot ignore. One authority suggests that politicians must often choose between a career in partisan or nonpartisan politics. Most nonpartisan offices are already relatively minor, and such a separation could detract further from their overall importance.[6]

Evolution of Partisan Nominations

Nominating methods in the United States have tended to follow a sequence with its own internal logic. As the difficulties posed by one type of nominating system become noticeable, participants in the political process respond by creating new arrangements, which in turn create new problems and new adaptations. In broad outline, the Republic moved from caucuses of insiders to a system of delegate conventions; these in turn yielded to the system of direct primaries that is the dominant method in use today.

The simplest way to arrange for nominations is through informal activities of incumbent officeholders. Such persons usually have a significant interest in nominating decisions, and they can easily communicate with one another. Most nonpolitical organizations still use this method, although a nominating committee may recommend persons who are congenial to the current leaders. A closely related possibility is *cooptation*—the practice of having officeholders choose persons to fill vacancies among their own number as they occur. This takes place in many city councils when a member

---

[6]Bone, *American Politics*, p. 284.

dies, resigns, or leaves town; and English society traditionally used it as a major method of forming its local councils. Such informal activities are similar to arrangements followed in a predemocratic age, yet they remain in use even after systematic procedures for mass consultation have developed.

In some instances, nomination by insiders was an important reform of earlier practices. Thus, in the 1790s, open caucuses held in the state capital frequently made nominations for statewide offices. However, local residents usually dominated such meetings, and people soon came to look upon caucuses of state legislators as more equitable. Party legislators were more likely to be representative of the entire state, and as elected officials they could lay some claim to the confidence of the people.[7]

In Great Britain, "nomination" of the leader who becomes prime minister is still pretty much left to insiders in the dominant party. In this country, insider control of nominations has been less effective and less well accepted. The congressional caucus was our most notable experiment in insider control, and it failed to provide vigorous competition. The expanding geographic scale and participation of American society also worked against insider techniques. From the beginning, local communities had provided significant bases of power.

As we have indicated, the caucus of elected legislators at the state level was probably a democratic improvement over the earlier ways of nominating candidates for state offices. However, the state legislative caucus had an obvious defect: No party had representatives from every district in the state. It was natural then for the state legislative caucus to quickly evolve into a "mixed caucus," which admitted delegates from districts or areas held by the other party.[8]

The discrediting of the congressional caucus in 1824 tended to place comparable arrangements at the state level in jeopardy. As the parties groped their way towards a different method of nominating presidents, the national nominating conventions became natural models to follow in choosing candidates for state offices. As Jacksonian ideals and practices surged through the land, Americans gradually installed the convention system over the entire country. The convention was supposed to be an expression of the popular will. People viewed it as a way to transmit the wishes of party adherents to a central point so that these preferences could determine the choice of nominees.[9]

A variety of methods emerged for choosing delegates to state conventions. Usually there were basic gatherings of party members at "precinct conventions," "caucuses," or "primaries," and sometimes these meetings would choose delegates directly. More often, the process would be indirect: The basic gatherings would choose delegates to county conventions, and these in turn would select the state delegates. It was a relatively simple

[7]Austin Ranney, *Curing the Mischiefs of Faction* (Berkeley, Calif.: University of California Press, 1975), pp. 14, 63.

[8]V. O. Key, Jr., *Politics, Parties, and Pressure Groups,* 5th ed. (New York: Thomas Y. Crowell Company, Inc., 1964), 372.

[9]Ibid., p. 373.

matter to set up conventions for congressional districts, cities, or whatever electoral area was desired.[10]

As the convention system evolved in the years following the Civil War, it came to be regarded as a tool of the machine politicians. One may wonder whether the popular image of the convention was ever an accurate picture of political reality. Now, however, the contradiction between representative ideal and blatant manipulation became more apparent. Convention methods did not produce the machines, but the two developed together. Since the machines had to work through conventions to achieve control, critics tended to blame the convention system for machine abuses. Improper practices became commonplace: meetings called without adequate notice ("snap primaries"), intimidation by strong-arm squads, high-handed tactics by presiding officers, and so forth. Instead of celebrating grassroots representation, the conventions dramatized the arrogant power of unsavory people.[11] The initial reaction to these abuses was legal regulation, but the direct primary presented a more formidable challenge to the convention system.

The direct primary reflected long-standing attitudes towards rights of participation. It was also nourished by the ascendancy of progressivism and the new pattern of political competition after 1896. With the one-party domination of many states and localities characteristic of the fourth party system, popular elections for most offices would be rendered meaningless unless voters obtained a direct voice in nominations. The direct primary developed first in South Carolina in the 1890s, but through party rather than statutory action. Another noncompetitive state, Wisconsin, passed the first statewide direct primary law in 1903. By 1917 the direct primary was being used for most nominations in most states.[12]

In the past few years, the number of states using conventions for nomination to state offices has declined further. New York permitted conventions instead of a primary until 1970. Indiana used the state convention for all statewide offices (including U.S. senator) until 1976. As of this writing, Delaware remains the only state where both parties use conventions for statewide nominations to major offices.[13]

Although reformers began to advance proposals for a national presidential primary as early as 1911, the national conventions have so far survived the progressive onslaught. Some of the reasons are worth noting. First is the better balance between the parties over the nation as a whole than in any but a few of the individual states. Also, at the time when progressivism held its strongest appeal, people took the constitutional authority of the states quite seriously. Even now, a direct national primary in lieu of party conventions raises difficult technical questions. In 1913, when Woodrow Wilson proposed it, such an innovation would have been a substantial departure from previous constitutional and political practice, and it was easier to seek presidential primaries within the individual states. State presidential

[10]Ibid.

[11]Ibid., p. 374.

[12]Ibid., p. 375.

[13]Malcolm E. Jewell and David M. Olson, *American State Political Parties and Elections* (Homewood, Ill.: The Dorsey Press, 1978), p. 94.

primaries were not dramatically successful, and interest in a national primary faded. Interest has been revived in the past eight or ten years as general dissatisfaction with nominating procedures and the number of state presidential primaries have increased.

There can be little doubt that on balance primaries are associated with organizational weakness in the parties. However, the nature of that relationship is in dispute. One view claims that the direct primary *caused* parties to become weak. Conventions compelled leaders to negotiate with each other, but the primary forced individual politicians to cultivate the party rank and file. This tended to produce factions and cliques attached to the ambitions of individual leaders, making it difficult to maintain an organizational core devoted to the party as such. A different view is that the primaries were symptomatic of party weakness rather than causative. If in most parts of the United States people wanted weak party organizations, perhaps the primary was a way of achieving this objective. Since parties were usually not successful in their opposition to the adoption of primaries, parties may already have been losing strength when the nominating practices changed. Parties in some states were able to adapt to the primary and maintain considerable strength for many decades.[14]

Changes in nominating practices have proceeded as much by accretion as by displacement, with older devices continuing to coexist with the new. Informal party gatherings did not disappear when legislative caucuses assumed the lead in nominations. These caucuses in turn continued to operate as legislative associations, as they had previously. The convention came to be as much a symbol as an embodiment of the real party. The direct primary signified a weakness in both but did not totally eliminate either any more than nonpartisan ballots always or even usually eliminated partisan politics. The changes represented widespread adaptation to previously established practices. In recent decades the party system as a whole evolved not only toward greater weakness, but also toward greater complexity, ambiguity, and inconsistency. Nothing has been discarded completely—least of all the smoke-filled room where it all began.

Types of Primaries

Partisan primaries are customarily classified as open, closed, or blanket. A closed primary is supposed to exclude all voters who are not adherents of the given party. In an open primary, any registered voter can participate, and the voter's choice of ballot is neither known nor recorded. In the blanket primary (used only in Washington, Louisiana, and Alaska) the voter may choose, office by office, which party's primary he or she votes in. For example, the voter may choose among the Democratic nominees for one office and select among the Republican candidates for another, exercising this option through all of the contests on the ballot.

Those who favor open or blanket primaries feel that voters should be able to participate freely in the nominating process without revealing their

---

[14]Ranney summarizes the arguments on both sides in *Mischiefs of Faction*, pp. 129–130. See also Epstein, *Parties in Western Democracies*, pp. 209–211.

party affiliation. Defenders of the closed primary claim that a party is a voluntary association and, like other associations, has a right to make its own determinations. This approach is very natural for political scientists and organization politicians. However, many persons today do not think of themselves as adherents in this sense, do not think of the primary as a way to participate in *their* party, and feel that they should either have simultaneous rights in both parties, or that primaries should be nonpartisan.

Some critics contend that the open primary encourages "raiding," or that opponents will invade the primary so that the party will nominate weaker candidates. There is little evidence one way or the other on this, although cross-over voting certainly does occur. One analysis concludes that very few voters deliberately shift primaries to choose weaker candidates. According to the authors, voters are much more likely to cross-over "because they are particularly attracted to a candidate in the other party, or because the other party has closer, more interesting primary contests."[15]

Differences between open and closed primaries are not always clear-cut, and particular examples may be difficult to classify. In California, voters fill in a line relating to party on the affidavit at the time of registration if they wish to vote in a partisan primary. They may change their registration from one party to another if they do so more than fifty-four days before the primary. The primary is closed, and voters receive primary ballots containing only the names of the candidates of the party with which they are registered. In Indiana, voters do not enroll in a party at registration. Since they may request the ballot of any party at the primary election, the primary is open in an important sense. However, the ballot of the party they request is permanently recorded by their name, and they can be challenged by a worker of that party and required to sign a statement saying that they will support that party's candidates in the general election.

In open primary states, the primary ballot may contain a column for each party or the primary ballots of all the parties may be stapled together. In the first case, voters merely make their choices within the preferred column in the privacy of the polling booth. In the other, they detach the ballot they prefer and drop the others (again in the polling booth) in a box for discards. Minnesota traditionally employed the first technique, Wisconsin the second.[16] Where voting machines or other techniques of processing votes are used, it is a simple matter to adapt the technique used in Minnesota.

Nature of Primary Elections

A significant number of primaries are not contested. The probability of this happening increases when an incumbent is running for renomination or when it is thought that the party nominee will have no chance of winning the general election.[17] Neither of these tendencies is difficult to understand. Incumbents usually have name recognition and other advantages that make

[15]Jewell and Olson, *State Parties and Elections,* p. 128.
[16]Key, *Politics, Parties, and Pressure Groups,* p. 391.
[17]Ranney, *Mischiefs of Faction,* p. 127.

them hard to defeat, and party organizations are rarely sympathetic to those within the party who would unseat incumbents. The weaker party in an area can usually expect to lose any but the most highly publicized contests. Even then, the weaker party operates at a disadvantage, and getting anybody to run is usually difficult enough. Even the office of governor is frequently uncontested in the primary of the weaker party. Jewell and Olson calculated the percentage of nonsouthern gubernatorial primaries between 1946 and 1976 where both parties had contests. Kentucky, Missouri, and Washington were the only states that reached 100 percent. North Dakota, South Dakota, Arizona, Wisconsin, Massachusetts, Vermont, Rhode Island, Michigan, Iowa, and Colorado each had less than 60 percent.[18]

Level of participation. Undoubtedly, the advent of the direct primary broadened the scope of participation in nominating politics. More people will vote in a primary than will attend caucuses or party meetings. Yet turnout is usually much lower in primaries than in general elections, for many reasons. In most states, primaries receive much less publicity than general elections. Partisans of the weaker party often have few contests to attract them to the polls and may not wish to cross over even if the electoral procedures permit them to do so. Party leaders may prefer a small turnout so that they can more easily control the outcome. When Democrats run against Democrats and Republicans against Republicans, the element of partisan combat is absent, and party labels cannot cue the voters' choices. Many people shun controversy and "declaring your party" seems to place unbearable stress on their capacity for political assertion. Primary elections offer different kinds of choices, and in truth, many persons do not understand these choices well enough to participate with confidence.

One investigation found that the average turnout in gubernatorial and senatorial primaries in two-party states between 1962 and 1968 was 28 percent; by comparison, 61 percent turned out in the ensuing general elections. Another study reports a turnout of 31.3 percent for nonsouthern primaries in the period from 1946–1950 to 1976. The authors found much variation among the states, with West Virginia and New Jersey at the extremes with 46.7 and 16.9 percent, respectively. Their analysis indicates that states with low primary turnout tend to have closed primaries with long waiting periods for shifting registration. Higher turnout tends to occur in states with open primaries requiring no declaration of party and in the states with blanket primaries. Participation tends to increase when primaries are contested and to reflect the degree of voting in *general* elections.[19]

Southern primaries represent a special case. Traditionally, southern laws permitted the Republican party to hold conventions rather than primaries. The Democratic primary offered the only possibility of a real contest, and usually more Democrats voted in it than in the general election.

[18]For example, only 38.5 percent of Colorado's gubernatorial primaries in this period offered contests in both parties. Jewell and Olson, *State Parties and Elections,* p. 143.
[19]Ranney, *Mischiefs of Faction,* p. 127; Jewell and Olson, *State Parties and Elections,* pp. 142–143.

Another distinguishing feature of southern primaries is the runoff that occurs (except in Tennessee) when no candidate gets a majority. Turnout in the southern primaries varies considerably from state to state, with the lowest figures in states like Texas, North Carolina, and Virginia where the Republican party is somewhat stronger. The presence of a stronger than usual southern Republican party not only lessens the proportion of the state electorate that identifies with the Democrats, it also tends to shift the attention of the electorate somewhat more towards the general election. Texas and North Carolina have had a number of contested *Republican* primaries since the 1960s.[20]

Characteristics of primary voters. Available evidence indicates that a voter's education, income, occupation, and age affect primary participation to an even greater extent than participation in general elections. The strength of party identification (one or two states excepted) also has a greater effect on primary voting. According to one scholar, primary voters are richer, better educated, more interested in politics, and more likely to have strong political opinions.[21] These tendencies may be more reliable outside of the South.

Party Involvement in Primary Contests

The politician with serious ambitions must usually obtain a party nomination. In some cases he may hope to achieve this simply by filing for a particular office, assembling his own organization, and waging an effective campaign. At other times, the procedures are not so simple. The following discussion omits considerations that apply to specific offices because circumstances are so varied. Presidential nominations are a special case and are discussed later in the chapter.

As we have seen, Delaware is now the only state that relies exclusively on a state convention in both parties for statewide nominations. Most southern states make conventions optional, a fact of real significance for the Republican parties of those states. (States generally allow minor parties to nominate by convention in order to save work and expense.) In a fair number of states, party organizations are given important prerogatives through a party convention held before the primary.[22]

A variety of formal and informal arrangements give party organizations limited influence over nominations and control the number of candidates running in the primary so that one person can get a majority. Such arrangements are generally referred to as "preprimary endorsements."

The strongest formal party role occurs in states where the convention controls *access* to the statewide primary ballot. In Connecticut a candidate must obtain 20 percent of the convention votes to get on the ballot. In Utah the convention can designate two persons, but if one of these gets 70

---

[20]Jewell and Olson, *State Parties and Elections*, p. 150. Virginia's Republican party has continued to use the convention, apparently to prevent any Republican from running against Senator Harry F. Byrd, Jr. Ibid., pp. 94, 151.

[21]Ranney, *Mischiefs of Faction*, p. 128.

[22]Jewell and Olson, *State Parties and Elections*, pp. 93–94.

percent of the convention vote, he is declared the nominee. In Colorado any contestant with 20 percent of the convention vote gets on the ballot; a petition process is also available but very rarely used. The situation is similar in New York, but here the requirement is 25 percent and candidates have resorted to the petition route more frequently.[23] Other states such as Massachusetts and Rhode Island have endorsement procedures that do not give candidates favored by the party any advantage in getting on the ballot. In some—Minnesota, Illinois, Pennsylvania, and the Republicans in Wisconsin are examples—the endorsements are "informal" in nature; that is, they are public but do not have any legal standing. In California, a number of extralegal organizations make "unofficial" endorsements. Where statutes specify endorsement procedures, the favored candidate may have a special designation on the ballot. In Connecticut and Rhode Island, for example, the endorsed candidate's name appears first and is designated by an asterisk.

An analysis by Jewell and Olson shows that although endorsements tend to be decisive in those states where the convention has some control over access to the ballot, the potency of preprimary endorsements varies. Informal endorsements also tend to be decisive among Massachusetts and Wisconsin Republicans. New York's Democrats, however, usually find their endorsements challenged and sometimes upset, despite the strong formal role of the convention. Little is known about lower-level endorsements, but in Minnesota, Connecticut, and Pennsylvania, party endorsement is quite common for seats in the state legislature.[24]

The usual assumption is that endorsement capability is symptomatic of party strength, and laws that make explicit allowance for it represent a party victory of sorts. However, Indiana has no widespread endorsement procedures, even though the parties are quite strong. At the local level especially, political leaders probably can operate very effectively without having their candidate preferences formally ratified or even widely disseminated. Still another possibility is that party organizations and leaders deliberately *avoid* making primary endorsements. We can be certain that this occurs with some frequency, but evidence is scarce.

POLITICAL CAREER PATTERNS

How do politically ambitious people begin their careers? Are there patterns or similarities in the experiences of those who have sought major political offices? Answers to such questions can reveal a good deal about the nature of the political system. Although the experiences of individual office seekers may be distinctive, the fact that these persons share the same political system, society, and culture introduces elements of order into political ambition.

On the surface, the many elective positions in the United States provide political opportunities to people in all parts of the country and at all economic levels. Yet, the system has many restrictive features. Each state has

[23]Ibid., p. 96.
[24]Ibid., pp. 97–106.

unique political outlooks, rules, and practices. Good information about politics in individual states and localities is hard to come by, and it does not travel well. If outsiders experience difficulty finding points of entry, many of the lower offices will be reserved for locals. In a typical year about 18 percent of the American population changes residence. Almost two-thirds of these people will stay within the same county, but even some of these will find themselves in places where they are political strangers.[25]

Experience in one office may help in seeking a better one, but minor offices can also be dead ends. Career movement may be circular or lateral as well as vertical. Politicians may move from one elective position to another because of term limitations, patronage advantages, timing of the election, desire to exclude someone from office, or whatever. They may even contest minor offices to build up name recognition.

Other politicians may gravitate toward the power of local executive leadership—usually the office of mayor. However, the actual powers of mayors are often largely symbolic, and incumbents rarely find themselves in a good position for higher office. Still other local politicians have no particular desire to move up; they may calculate that their chances are too slim, or they may be satisfied with the benefits of local office.

Status Advantages

Elected officials at all levels tend to come from higher occupational, educational, and income levels than the mass electorate. In a sense, this is merely another example of the status bias in participation discussed previously. Office seeking usually reflects two different sets of motives: those of the office seekers themselves and those of the persons who "recruit" others to run for office. Status advantages make it more likely that a person will *want* to run for public office; they also increase the likelihood that "recruiters" will consider that individual. The skills, experiences, and outlooks that are politically advantageous reflect social advantages, at least to some degree.

Bear in mind, of course, that status bias is relative. Thousands of America's elected officials are of modest origins, even though very few come from the society's lowest rungs. Nor is status always an unmixed political blessing. Public perception that a candidate has too much money, formal education, or identification with privileged groups can be politically disastrous. A Nelson Rockefeller fails to obtain a major party presidential nomination; persons like Harry Truman and Richard Nixon reach the top from humble beginnings. Moreover, there is ample room for other influences. A study of city council members in the San Francisco Bay area indicated that most came from the upper two-fifths of their communities in terms of education and income. However, within this pool of "social eligibles," status

[25]In 1975, 8.4 percent of the population eighteen years old or older had lived in a different *state* five years previously. Among those with four years of college education, the figure was 15.1 percent. U.S. Census, *Statistical Abstract of the United States 1972*, p. 36; and "Mobility of the Population of the United States, March 1970 to March 1975," Series P–20, No. 285, October 1975, pp. 24–25.

distinctions did not account for the much smaller number who became politically active.[26] Status differences, important as they are, carry us only a small way toward an understanding of political careers in America.

Then too, persons of the highest status may be the least likely to view politics as a desirable occupation. Entering politics at a very high level of office may appeal to such persons, but this is not easy to do. Activists expect higher officeholders to have some prior governmental experience. Today's individualistic politics is probably more open to socially prominent newcomers than was formerly the case, but at the same time success may now require even greater personal effort over a longer period of time.

Political Careers for Personal Gain

Political careers can be a means to acquire power for the sake of money or other material benefits. Banfield and Wilson emphasize this motivation in their explanation of the political machine, which they regard as basically apolitical: "interested only in making and distributing income—mainly money—to those who run it and work for it."[27]

A fair proportion of people in major elective office are wealthy, and almost two-thirds of the American public claims to believe that "most elective officials are in office for all they personally can get out of it for themselves."[28] One must be willing to consider the possibility that a portion of today's mainstream politicians are more sophisticated than the machine politicians of yore—less blatant and better able to achieve personal advantages by means that are not obviously illegal. Financial disclosure reports filed in the spring of 1978 revealed that at least twenty-four members of Congress were millionaires. The Congressional Quarterly noted that at least thirty senators and sixty representatives had financial interests that could be affected by work of the committees they served on.[29]

This is a large topic and we return to it in Chapter 12 for a closer look. One must interpret with some caution because an element of material gain is present in virtually all successful careers. Also, most people in politics need to maintain a nonpolitical source of livelihood. Some analysts believe that politics for gain is more extensive in states and localities than in the U.S. Congress because of greater public toleration, less press exposure, and (perhaps) less competitive electoral contests. The politician who is in politics for personal gain may not wish to advance to higher office, either because he does not need to or because those in higher office undergo more serious scrutiny by a larger array of interested observers.

Not all politicians get rich. According to Congressional Quarterly, the vast majority who serve in Congress depend primarily on their salaries. The

[26]Moshe M. Czudnowski, "Political Recruitment," in *Handbook of Political Science*, Vol. 2, ed. Fred I. Greenstein and Nelson Polsby (Reading, Mass.: Addison-Wesley Publishing Company, 1975), pp. 2, 94; Kenneth Prewitt, *The Recruitment of Political Leaders* (Indianapolis: The Bobbs-Merrill Co., Inc., 1970).

[27]Edward C. Banfield and James Q. Wilson, *City Politics* (New York: Vintage Books, Random House, Inc., 1963), p. 116.

[28]Sixty percent in the Harris Survey of September 13–22, 1973.

[29]Congressional Quarterly, *Weekly Report*, September 2, 1978, p. 2311.

report goes on to say that "most could count on earnings from stocks, legal fees, partnerships, or businesses back home if their Washington careers were ended by the voters." Many wealthy politicians were affluent before they entered politics. John Danforth and John Heinz (the richest men in the Senate according to Congressional Quarterly) are heirs to important family fortunes. Claiborne Pell, Harry F. Byrd, and Edward Kennedy belong to prestigious families where wealth and political activity have accompanied each other for at least two generations. One can suppose that most individuals who are talented enough to be elected to Congress or a governorship have much more promising ways to become wealthy if that is their major aim. Certainly one would doubt that senators Barry Goldwater, Howard Metzenbaum, or John Glenn became wealthy because of political activity.[30]

Origins of Careers

It is not easy to pinpoint the beginning of a political career, and American politics permits many gradations of involvement in office seeking. With congressional representatives it is easy to think of local offices as political apprenticeships. But in considering seats on a city council, one may find that these politicians served *their* apprenticeships in governmental auxiliaries (such as city planning commissions) or as leaders of civic organizations. Motivations are somewhat obscure, but one should consider office seekers' collective goals as well as their personal ones. Individuals reach important thresholds when their political participation passes from occasional to continuous and when politics becomes their main focus of activity (regardless of source of income) rather than a part-time pursuit.[31]

The odds against political success are rather long, but those who remain in politics for any time tend to develop a high psychic involvement in it. These are the kinds of people who tend to occupy major political offices —not the apolitical types who run reluctantly. Some career origins are a matter of family and in a sense precede any conscious intentions. For example, one investigation found that seven hundred families account for 17 percent of all U.S. senators and representatives who served between 1774 and 1965.[32]

Patterns of Office Holding

One useful concept, developed by Joseph Schlesinger, is the notion of "base" offices. A base office is not necessarily a politician's first elective or appointive position; rather, it is one that provides a common set of experiences for top political leaders. The office of state legislator seems to be especially significant. State legislatures bring together politically minded

---

[30]Ibid. The eight names mentioned in this paragraph account for 40 percent of the senators mentioned by Congressional Quarterly as the Senate's wealthiest members.

[31]Czudnowski, "Political Recruitment," pp. 157–168, 199.

[32]Stephen Hess, *America's Political Dynasties* (Garden City, N.Y.: Doubleday & Co., Inc., 1966), pp. 1, 673. Another study showed that the percentage of congressmen who were close kin of other congressmen steadily declined between the beginning of the Republic and 1958. Czudnowski, "Political Recruitment," p. 188, citing Alfred B. Clubok, Norman M. Wilensky, and Forrest J. Berghorn, "Family Relationships," *Journal of Politics*, 31 (1969), 1035–1062.

persons from all parts of their states and are, therefore, a natural breeding ground for political ambition. Schlesinger's examination of prior offices held by major party nominees for governor and senator showed that in thirty-nine states, 30 percent or more of the candidates had been state legislators at some time. In sixteen states the comparable figure was 50 percent or better.[33]

The broad category "local elective office" is another important base. However, even though these positions are much more numerous (including as they do the city council, county supervisor, mayor, and so forth) a much smaller proportion of leaders had held such a position. A much more significant base is the "law enforcement office," including posts associated with the court system, such as public attorney, sheriff, and judge.

Schlesinger has analyzed these data in terms of a number of office categories and career steps. In his classification, there are thirty-seven possible routes to becoming senator or governor, but a dozen or so account for more than two-thirds of all the cases. In considering governor and senator separately, we find that successful candidates do not differ very much with respect to the last office held prior to the campaign for the top office. (See Table 8–1.) Unsuccessful candidates for either office are slightly more likely to have had either no prior political or governmental office or to have most recently been the occupant of a local office. Possession of a statewide elective office seems to be distinctly advantageous for gubernatorial or senatorial contestants.

The most recent offices held by contestants for top state offices tend to be fairly similar. Generally speaking, the senatorial office outranks the governorship, and the flow of career traffic between them is almost entirely one way. In other words, very few senators even consider running for governor, but a governorship is an excellent springboard to a senate seat. The office of U.S. representative is distinctly less prestigious than either of the other two; it lacks visibility and usually has a local constituency. Nevertheless, this office provides excellent prospects of entry to the other two major offices. Perhaps the most noteworthy thing about Table 8–1 is the high proportion of senators whose most recent office was a seat in the House.

There are many nuances. Higher offices draw personnel from fewer and more conspicuous offices than do lesser offices. This suggests that people in the higher offices have their career lines in "better focus" and that they are therefore more likely to consider or respond to constituencies beyond their own.[34] Some states have more sharply defined patterns of advancement than others.

Unlike most private organizations, elective politics has neither a mandatory retirement age nor a method of keeping younger people out of top offices. The typical age for achieving an office reflects its status, and ambition for higher office is most likely to be successful when the preceding office and the age of the incumbent are appropriately matched. Thus, politicians

[33]Joseph A. Schlesinger, *Ambition and Politics* (Chicago: Rand McNally & Company, 1966), pp. 72–73. The percentages refer to all states in the period 1900–1958 for governor and 1914–1958 for U.S. senator.
[34]Ibid., pp. 116, 196.

Table 8-1
Most Recently Held Office of Major Party Candidates for Governor and Senator,
1900–1958

Most Recent Preceding Office	Candidates for Governor		Candidates for Senator[d]	
	Winners	Losers	Winners	Losers
Statewide Elective[a]	20%	15%	22%	14%
State Law Enforcement	19	21	13	18
State Legislature	19	20	9	14
Administrative[b]	13	14	14	22
U.S. Representative	10	6	27	14
No Prior Office	8	9	8	11
Local Elective Office	7	13	5	6
Other Political Office[c]	4	2	2	1
Total:	100%	100%	100%	100%
	(N = 641)	(N = 440)	(N = 450)	(N = 343)

[a]"Statewide elective" includes all offices voted on by the entire state electorate other than governor or senator. However, the office of Attorney General is classified under "state law enforcement." When used for governor's previous office experience, statewide elective office refers to minor offices such as lieutenant governor and secretary of state. With reference to senatorial careers, the category includes the office of governor as well, and, in fact consists almost exclusively of governors.

[b]"Administrative" is a heterogeneous category that includes any appointive governmental post (other than purely advisory or honorary) at the state or local level.

[c]"Other political office" includes positions such as member of a state constitutional convention and presidential elector.

[d]The time period for senators is 1914–1958.

Source: Adapted from Joseph A. Schlesinger, *Ambition and Politics* (Chicago, Ill.: Rand McNally & Company, 1966), pp. 93, 96. The data base excludes occasional Republican nominees in southern states.

who win House seats tend to do so at an earlier age than those who become governor. Likewise, those who become governor tend to do so at a somewhat younger age than those who first enter the U.S. Senate. When age is appropriate to the pertinent office, people may begin to treat the officeholder as if he were a potential governor, senator, or president.[35]

Occupation is much more than an indicator of status. Skills that go with particular callings may or may not be helpful in politics. Occupations vary in their sociability and in the degree to which they allow part-time performance or temporary absence for the performance of political tasks. The amount of independence is also a factor: Professionals have more of it than nonprofessionals, and some self-employed people have a great deal of it. Political and nonpolitical careers may enhance each other in either direction, and especially at lower levels of office either one may be the individu-

[35]Ibid., pp. 66, 193, 197. Schlesinger does not say so, but high status can probably be very helpful in positioning the ambitious politician in a pertinent office at a relatively early age.

al's primary concern. Some lawyers enter politics, for example, as a way to establish reputations and enhance their practice. Others may choose law for Woodrow Wilson's reason—as a means of entering politics.

There are many possible explanations for the conspicuous presence of lawyers in American politics. Perhaps the United States is more legalistic than most societies in its approach to political issues. This country reveres its constitutional machinery and is happy with the most powerful judiciary in the world. Perhaps lawyers are often available for political office because skills necessary to practice of the law change slowly and thus permit long periods of absence. Schlesinger's research suggests that lawyers' monopoly over law enforcement posts gives them significant advantages in the quest for gubernatorial and (to a lesser degree) senatorial office.

Another scholar reminds us that lawyers have important nonpolitical career alternatives and suggests that there is a broader political role profile centering on *generalist* orientations, ability to perform *complex* operations, and placement in a critical *linkage position* in communication networks. According to him, fifty-two occupational titles share these characteristics. He also believes that the loose structure of American parties has been favorable to "the individual entrepreneur" and that lawyers have been well equipped to play this role.[36]

PRESIDENTIAL NOMINATIONS

The presidency dramatizes more than any other office the enormous importance of political contests that precede the election. Millions of people are constitutionally eligible to serve, but in a realistic sense the electorate is restricted to only two: the Republican and Democratic nominees. Even when significant independent or minor-party candidates have run nobody has expected them to win, and such persons have only affected the outcome by strengthening or weakening the prospects of the major party nominees. So it has been since the third party system took shape in the years following the Civil War. The idea that voters choose between two partisan nominees is deeply engrained in all of the practices and outlooks that determine presidential selection. If this constraint were to lose force, one could be certain that many other features of American politics would also change.

Since national nominating conventions provide the site of selection for major party nominees, actions of these bodies are extraordinarily important. Even so, one must be alert to antecedent events that can influence convention decisions. Conventions limit consideration to only a few persons, and their decisions are often predictable. Thus, with very few exceptions, presidential nominees in the period from 1936 to 1980 led in the final preconvention poll of the party's rank and file.[37]

---

[36]Czudnowski, "Political Recruitment," p. 207. The author cites impressive evidence that lawyers are more numerous in the less rigidly organized of the European political parties.

[37]Nelson A. Polsby and Aaron Wildavsky, *Presidential Elections,* 5th ed. (New York: Charles Scribner's Sons, 1980), p. 87.

National conventions are quite complex in their operations, yet certain key features stand out:

1. *Nomination by absolute majority.* To be chosen by the convention, a candidate must amass more than 50 percent of the delegate votes. This encourages conciliatory tendencies among groups present. After all, failure to agree will ordinarily guarantee victory to the nominee of the other party. By the same token, attempts to boss the convention can be risky. Potential candidates do what they can to attract support from delegates who are not implacably opposed. Delegates have often tried to avoid being isolated, and they have been willing to support choices that were broadly acceptable. The stress toward agreement can make convention balloting unstable, and in the past it often placed a premium on discovering the likely winner and jumping aboard the bandwagon. In recent years, delegate ties to favored candidates have in many cases become stronger. Media emphasis on calling a winner may generate strong bandwagon pressure well before the party convenes.

2. *Public voting.* This feature permits complex negotiations to take place, including the offering of rewards and punishments for decisions about candidate support. It should be noted, however, that large numbers of delegates, high turnover, and short and infrequent sessions make it difficult for conventions to be deliberative bodies.

3. *Varying delegate-selecting and delegate-committing practices.* Despite reform actions that have led to the emergence of some national standards, state and local actions determine the composition of delegations to the nominating conventions. The choice of delegates in each party in each state tends to vary widely. Some states permit voters to choose delegates partly or entirely in primaries. Other states choose delegates in varying combinations of state or district conventions. Presidential primaries may or may not commit delegates to particular candidates, and, if committed at all, the duration and reliability of the commitment may vary.

A number of consequences follow from this diversity. The harvesting of delegates by candidate organizations becomes a very difficult task, demanding expert staff work on a continental scale many months before the convention is held. Diversity also complicates the actual workings of the convention, adding an element of intricacy and even mystery. The wide variety of practices probably favors continuing autonomy of state and local organizations, although the impact of candidate organizations is increasingly important.

4. *Openness to the unexpected.* National party conventions are well-established institutions with the feel of ad hoc assemblages. Each convention differs from the others in its mood and circumstances. If the results are often broadly predictable, few of the participants may feel certain about how things will work out in particular cases. An aura of improvisation surrounds many conventions. Nothing guarantees that a candidate will be selected and effectively supported. Sometimes there is a distinct element of uncertainty, risk, and surprise.

The force of previous commitments, regardless of their origins, may be uncertain if put to a serious test. A candidate going into a convention with a majority of pledged delegates might in some circumstances have difficulty holding them if the convention feared that he could not win the election and a better electoral prospect were available. The convention has an inherent power to be a law unto itself in the matter of nominating a presidential candidate.

5. *Integral relation to the electoral vote system.* Almost all basic characteristics of the national conventions derive from the electoral vote system: treating of states as constituent units, apportionment of delegates, the indivisible linkage between presidential and vice presidential nominees, and the absolute majority requirement. Historically, conventions emerged as vehicles of partisan deliberation after the parties had turned the electoral vote system into a machine for recording partisan preferences. If the Republic were to abolish the electoral vote system in favor of a direct election of the president, it might leave the convention dangling, its basic practices without a clear rationale. Similarly, adoption of a national nominating primary might make the electoral vote system more vulnerable to change or abolition. Each of these possible changes has wide support in opinion polls, but the two are rarely considered together. (For additional discussion, see appendix.)

Who Can Become President?

Most citizens have no conceivable chance of becoming president. Even among political activists, only a small number are real possibilities in any given election year. However, it is very difficult to specify just who is a presidential possibility and how many such persons there are. If we knew their names and thought of them as a group, we could refer to that group as "the availability pool."

Keech and Matthews suggest that we consider 1 percent standing in the polls (among fellow partisans) as a crude measure of presidential availability. Since no one has won presidential office since 1936 who did not meet this criterion, it may define a group that closely approximates the availability pool. For convenience sake we can refer to it as the "one-percent club." Most people belong to the club before the primaries have begun, but not all do; therefore, "membership" is not a necessary condition of nomination. Between 1936 and 1972, 6.6 percent of the group achieved 1 percent support during the primary season. In 1980 George Bush won the Iowa caucuses in January, even though he had not achieved 1 percent poll support even by July 1979. One might think that it would be easy to join the one-percent club. However, between 1936 and 1972 only sixty-two Democrats and only forty-seven Republicans got even this far, and many of these individuals undoubtedly had little real chance of winning a presidential nomination.[38]

A number of factors help us to understand why the number with tangible prospects has been so small. Publicity on a national scale is obviously essential. Not even 1 percent of a party's following will support a candidate if they have not heard of him or if they do not believe that others

---

[38]Harold Stassen, for example, was a member in seven different election years, but he had no chance of getting the nomination more than once or twice. William R. Keech and Donald R. Matthews, *The Party's Choice* (Washington, D.C.: The Brookings Institution, 1976), p. 16. The discussion of the next several pages relies heavily on Keech and Matthews's excellent work at various points.

will attach some credibility to his prospects. Publicity considerations make it difficult for new faces to get the necessary sustained exposure. The publicity must be national, if only because the samples of the major polling organizations are too small to detect important state and local figures. Pressures of news gathering incline attention towards persons perceived as already having substantial prospects of winning.

Interestingly enough, mass publicity has not led to a large influx of theatrical figures, entertainment personalities, and athletes. Some political figures have fit this description, but Keech and Matthews note that none have moved into presidential consideration without first serving in a conspicuous public office.[39] In fact, only one-tenth of those in the one-percent club did not so serve, and almost four-fifths held the office of vice president, senator, governor, or cabinet member.

This does not mean that anyone in a major office automatically receives presidential consideration. Many senators are too old or too involved in the internal operations of the Senate to be available. Almost two-thirds of the governors who polled 1 percent were from eight large nonsouthern states. Cabinet posts are, of course, nonelective, and the capacity of many of their occupants to win elections is doubtful.

Other public offices, of course, also contribute some presidential prospects. Supreme Court justices Fred Vinson and William O. Douglas were prominently mentioned presidential possibilities at one time or another. However, judges are expected to resign from the Court if they wish to pursue the presidency, and this means giving up a prestigious position with an unlimited term. Members of the House serve for such short terms that the would-be candidate must either choose between presidential campaigning and reelection to the House, or coordinate the two simultaneously. Most people who want a presidential nomination must actively seek it. Yet, becoming president is such a long shot that the number who will take necessary steps that would jeopardize other prospects may be extremely limited. A few persons, Eisenhower in 1952 and Ted Kennedy in 1972, could probably have received a nomination with little effort on their part, but such instances are unusual. David Broder suggests that it may be to an aspirant's advantage to "get out of public office so he has nothing to do for two, three, four, or in some cases, six years, except run for president of the United States."[40]

A critic might argue that the system treats the issue of presidential qualifications in a highly stereotyped manner, without giving the slightest consideration to scores of talented people. On the other hand, none of the office expectations operates rigidly. Defenders of prevailing practices could argue that it is not unreasonable to expect presidential aspirants to develop a record in a major elective office. Persons in contention have not been numerous, but an increase in the number could be a mixed blessing. After all, the nominating process is not successful unless each party eliminates all but one contender.[41]

[39]Ibid., p. 10.
[40]John V. Daly et al., *Choosing Presidential Candidates* (Washington, D.C.: American Enterprise Institute for Public Policy Research, 1980), p. 3.
[41]Keech and Matthews, *The Party's Choice*, pp. 242–243.

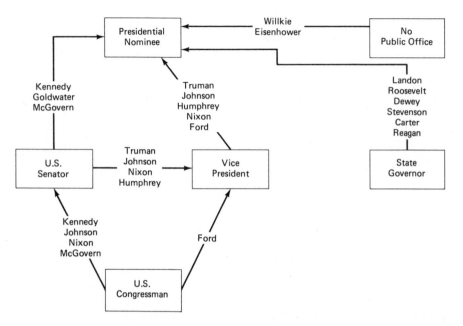

FIGURE 8–1 Major Public Offices Held by Major Party Presidential Nominees, 1936–1980

Source: Adapted from William Keech and Donald R. Matthews, *The Party's Choice* (Washington, D.C.: The Brookings Institution, 1976), p. 20.

U.S. senators have been a markedly favored source of presidential nominees in recent years. This is true regardless of whether we consider the one-percent club, or, as in Figure 8–1, persons who actually succeeded in obtaining nominations. Some senators became their party's choice directly from the Senate, a larger group moved into contention indirectly through the vice presidency. All but two of the governors in Figure 8–1 rose to presidential prominence in the *earlier* half of the period, and none of them took the vice presidential route.

Senators have better prospects than governors because the Senate is at the center of modern politics. Also, Senate norms are permissive, and senators can easily obtain national publicity. Governors serve shorter terms than senators and often find it harder to get reelected. Senators can more easily wait for the propitious election year to try their luck, and they are less frequently faced with either/or choices regarding their current office.

Please keep in mind that the transition from one office to another is not necessarily continuous. Carter left the Georgia governorship in January 1975 to campaign for the presidency. Ronald Reagan finished his second term as governor of California at the same time and maintained credible presidential prospects thereafter without being in any public office. An independent source of income was obviously essential in these cases, and the advantages of one type of office over another seem to have mattered little.

It is not clear why senators have virtually monopolized the track to presidential nomination through the vice presidency. Perhaps the results are one-sided simply because of the small number of cases.

THE CHANGING ROAD TO NOMINATION

Tendencies of the sort we have been describing indicate a good deal of political continuity. Yet many changes are taking place in presidential nominating politics. These are occurring on many fronts in what is probably the most complex nominating system in the world. Let us conclude this chapter by examining a few topics that highlight changes at work in presidential nominating politics.

National party conventions have lacked undivided control over nominations for many years. One recalls William Carleton's brilliant analysis, published more than twenty years ago, which dramatized this idea to the point of overstatement. Carleton said that since 1924 the nominating conventions had been going through a process of "revolutionary transformation" as a response to world crisis and modern mass society.[42] In earlier eras, parties commonly nominated politicians who lacked celebrity status but who were prominent in their own states. National favorites had tended to be one among many, except when there were popular sitting presidents. Now, however, the conventions were increasingly being forced to choose the nominee who was *the* national favorite, and as this took place, delegates to the conventions, "even the biggest of the 'big shots,' " were becoming popular rubber stamps. Presidential primaries were coming to have new significance as a way for politicians to obtain national publicity, and polls were making it possible to determine the identity of *the* national favorite. Carleton thought it likely that "by 1976 or 1980" conventions would simply be ratifying nominations already effectively determined by the various agencies of mass democracy.

Carleton's argument that conventions are now forced to choose national favorites may be impossible to prove or disprove. Perhaps the convention delegates *want* to pick the most viable candidate without being forced to do so. Perhaps, too, anticipation of the convention's procedures has important effects at earlier stages of the process. We have noted that the absolute majority requirement, for example, sets up receptivity to bargaining and compromise.

One should avoid a simple quantum theory of publicity that dictates the existence of a single national favorite. Leaders in the *final* preconvention polls have nearly always won their party's nomination, but earlier poll standings have had less predictive value. In at least four instances since 1936 (the Democrats in 1952 and 1980 and the Republicans in 1940 and 1964), no single leader was an overwhelming party favorite at convention time. Pre-

---

[42]William G. Carleton, "The Revolution in the Presidential Nominating Convention," *Political Science Quarterly*, 72 (June 1957), 224–240.

convention contests are pàrt of a political game in which contestants seek to devise winning strategies against each other. Changes in a candidate's prospects can occur very rapidly in ways that Carleton's analysis does not explain. As the Goldwater and McGovern nominations indicate, the enthusiasms of delegates and other activists can be at least as important in selecting nominees as the acclaim of the mass public.

Recent Changes

The increasing number of states holding presidential primaries is the most widely discussed change in American nominating practices. Yet, political scientists show surprisingly little agreement about its overall significance. The tendency to separate presidential selection from other party operations clearly seems to be at work. And with the current weakness of party organization, delegate selection has been more susceptible to pressures from candidate organizations. However, George Bush's showing in the Iowa caucuses of 1980 suggests that primaries may not be any more vulnerable in this respect than caucuses. Keech and Matthews argue that primaries usually have little independent effect on nomination outcomes. Jeane Kirkpatrick claims their importance can hardly be exaggerated; however, she is primarily concerned with the effects of the primaries on party organizations.[43]

The situation is uncertain, but the following thoughts might be considered.

1. A larger number of primaries permits larger numbers of people to contest actively for a party's nomination, simply because there are more opportunities for candidates to demonstrate voter support. When such demonstrations are successful, the candidates are likely to find financial contributions flowing their way. This does not necessarily mean, however, that the *kinds* of people seeking nomination are changing. A larger number of primaries is symptomatic of a more complex nominating system in which astute planning is apt to be rewarded.

This suggests that the heightened advantage of an early start may offset enlarged opportunities to participate. Small states tend to hold their primaries before the larger states. This exaggerates the impact of atypical states, but it also keeps initial campaign costs low and thus improves the prospects of those with long-shot chances. However, since established candidates can make up their losses in later big state primaries, the net advantage is with those who enter the primary season in a strong position.[44]

2. Primaries tend to magnify the influence of the media. They offer all the elements of news interest: conflict, drama, and suspense. Furthermore, the results of primaries tend to be ambiguous. To make them meaningful to the mass audience, the results must be anticipated and interpreted. This

[43]Keech and Matthews, *The Party's Choice,* p. 229; Jeane Kirkpatrick, *Dismantling the Parties* (Washington, D.C.: American Enterprise Institute for Public Policy Research, 1978).
[44]Keech and Matthews, *The Party's Choice,* p. 112. Another way to state the point is that long-shot candidates cannot afford to do poorly in the early primaries.

often puts the media in the position of deciding how well a candidate must do to "win" a given primary.

The nominating season offers a continuous flow of newsworthy political events with the attendant risk of voter fatigue. However, if it is desirable to have a larger number of contestants, the public may require more time to sort them all out. Therefore, long campaigns are not necessarily bad.

3. The increase in primaries may be lessening the autonomy of the convention. Many of the pre-1968 primaries were merely advisory, with the presidential preference poll completely separate from delegate selection. Outpacing even the increase in the number of primaries has been the tendency to link primary voting more closely to delegate selection. By 1976 and 1980, this had resulted in many fewer genuinely uncommitted delegates.[45] If it is true that these commitments might not be strong enough to survive certain contingencies, it is also true that they make the convention's first ballot (when all major party nominees since 1956 have been selected) highly predictable. One must be cautious, however, about anticipating further decline in the impact of the convention. Proportional and districting rules in delegate selection and incentives from campaign subsidies may decrease the likelihood of one candidate's having a preconvention majority.[46]

Growing importance of the media. Matthews suggests that the impact of media on the presidential nominating process is probably greatest in its earliest phases, when the media and audience are *least* attentive. In a sense, the campaign for nomination begins as soon as a presidential election is over. Early press speculation about the next election tends to structure the initial situation at a time when editors and news budgets subject individual reporters to little restraint. Later, as various politicians put out feelers for the nomination, political reporters in Washington submit them to an informal screening.[47]

As events move forward, the press tends to agree on which persons are worthy of attention and thus begins to define public perceptions of their chances of winning. Frequently the press will ignore all other contenders. As primary season approaches, participants outside the press become more influential. Campaign organizations and the special constituency of campaign contributors begin to be more salient. With the primaries, active elements in the electorate begin to weigh in. As all of this unfolds, the press may increasingly find itself in the position of reacting to the political scene rather than shaping or defining it.[48]

Two themes are especially noteworthy in speculation about media

[45]Polsby and Wildavsky, *Presidential Elections*, p. 84, citing James Lengle and Byron Shafer, "Primary Rules, Political Power, and Social Change," *American Political Science Review*, 70 (March 1976), 84.

[46]Polsby and Wildavsky, *Presidential Elections*, p. 150.

[47]Donald R. Matthews, "Winnowing," in *Race for the Presidency*, ed. James D. Barber (Englewood Cliffs, N.J.: Prentice-Hall, Inc., 1978), pp. 56–57. The classic description of the screening process is by David Broder. See "Political Reporters in Washington," in *Inside the System*, ed. Charles Peters and James Fallows (New York: Holt, Rinehart & Winston, 1976), pp. 211–222.

[48]Matthews, "Winnowing."

influence: the media's emphasis on predicting outcomes and its concern with personalities rather than substantive issues.

Especially in the earliest phases, when indicators are least reliable, the journalistic community is under great pressure to predict nomination outcomes. Among other reasons, this occurs because journalists try to build reputations for sagacity among their colleagues and because of competition among news organizations for rapid yet accurate reporting.[49] Needless to say, readers and viewers often find the horse-race aspects of politics the most interesting.

Although press predictions may create bandwagon tendencies, the impact of the press on campaigns is limited. In 1972 widespread expectations of a Muskie nomination failed to materialize, and in 1976 predictions about the Republican nomination were persistently wrong. The press underestimated Ford's prowess as a campaigner, and with it his early primary strength. Press expectations of an irresistible momentum for Ford, once he started winning, also failed to pan out.[50] However, the prediction fetish may work arbitrarily to eliminate potential candidates in the preliminary stages. It is easier perhaps to dismiss little known figures because they lack prospects of success than to face the question of whether they have qualifications worth considering. Also, the compulsion to examine the contest as a horse race may reduce media attention to electoral issues and characteristics.

There is a widespread view that television avoids exposition, discussion, and analysis of issue positions because of time limitations and the fear of a screen image of "talking heads." In one view, the media tend to focus on factors that might affect electoral outcomes, such as position changes or inconsistencies in positions. Matthews believes that the press largely ignores the merits or demerits of a candidate's policy proposals, except perhaps when they smack of the impractical.[51] Someone has even said that television loves new faces but hates new ideas.

Constraints on working journalists may produce similar results for the print media. For example, reporters from different news organizations find that it reassures their editors if they can agree on the same story leads about a particular candidate's policy statement. In the process, the press may reduce complex issues to labels or symbols. Thus, in 1968, George Romney's position on Vietnam disappeared into the "brainwashing" story. In 1976 the press did not really examine Carter's position on discrimination in housing because of an obsession with some phrases he had used in stating his ideas—including "ethnic purity," "alien groups," and "artificial intrusion."

To the extent that such tendencies occur, the media may unwittingly imply that the issues are not really very important. Such a stance is hard to defend when it is stated explicitly, but one might agree with James Barber that a candidate's positions on issues are not very good predictors of presi-

---

[49]F. Christopher Arterton, "Campaign Organizations Confront the Media Environment," in *Race for the Presidency,* ed. Barber, p. 20.
[50]Matthews, "Winnowing," pp. 62–63.
[51]Ibid., p. 67.

dential action and that what the public most needs is information about the candidates' personal and leadership qualifications. In Barber's words, "Who are these guys, where are they coming from, what are they likely to do to us?" Unfortunately, television news may allot even less time to these matters than to issues.[52]

Such tendencies may combine with other facets of media coverage to produce alienated attitudes toward the political world. The journalistic community tends towards intense skepticism of all politicians. It may also have an implicit tendency to accept solutions presented by "experts." This can work towards a kind of coverage that neglects legitimate political needs (such as the need to compromise) and that understates the value of arrangements that are less than perfect. Barber puts the matter somewhat differently:

> . . . a supposition underlying the skeptical mode is that performance could be
> —and even usually is—much better than the individual lapse being reported.
> A myth of general competence is conveyed, reinforced by the apparently
> exceptional character of the immediate error.[53]

Change in media practices. The media are probably becoming more aware of the fact that their practices influence presidential nominating politics. Although official media spokesmen still insist that the media merely reflect reality rather than shape it, conscious efforts have been made to avoid what are perceived as mistakes in covering the preceding election. Self-examination within the media is likely to increase in the future. In the process, we can hope for even more self-awareness, increasingly relevant political programming, and decreasing intrusiveness. Let us hope also that there will, in Barber's words, be more "newspeople who are themselves genuinely interested in politics and who know instinctively or can learn how to get that caring curiosity through the tube."[54]

COMING TO TERMS WITH POLITICAL AMBITION

Present arrangements may be less of a "system" of nominating politics than a confused groping toward something different. Each recent preconvention season seems to be markedly different from the last, and mistakes are inevitable in a changing political game with emerging characteristics that are as yet poorly defined. Yet the period of maximum confusion may be behind us. Perhaps there is an outside chance that the next two or three presidential elections will bring a simpler, better balanced, and better understood process that will enlist greater sympathy and support from the electorate.

One can easily lose sight of some basic issues amidst the anxieties of political change. For example, we seem to be increasingly reliant on the willingness and ability of individual contestants to beat their own drum.

[52]James D. Barber, "Characters in the Campaign," in *Race for the Presidency,* ed. Barber, pp. 182–183.

[53]Ibid., p. 185.

[54]Matthews, "Winnowing," pp. 58–59; Barber, "Characters in the Campaign," p. 197.

Admittedly, blatant self-promotion may be less hypocritical than practices in earlier periods when presidential hopefuls were supposed to feign disinterest while waiting for the lightning to strike. But it is questionable whether single-minded pursuit of office (especially presidential office) should be so important a requirement. Since we tend to have an innate distrust of politically ambitious people, such a criterion can operate to make our support of political leaders less responsible than it would otherwise be. By making public officials conform to our worst fears—"all they care about is power" —we dissociate ourselves from them and encourage the belief that since it is "they" after all who seek office, "we" are in no way at fault when things go wrong.

We noted at an early point in this chapter that no important candidate is ever simply self-selected. One of the advantages of a strong party system is that the most important support a candidate can get is offered by other politicians in a deliberate and purposeful way. Party politicians, in evaluating the self-serving claims of individual politicians, can in effect say to the wider public: "We have examined the qualifications of all these persons. This is the one that we wish to follow, and the one we think you will be most satisfied with in the office of president. We will not only do what we can to help him get elected, we also accept the responsibility of supporting him in his major policy endeavors."

One may hope that the role of the parties in presidential nominating politics will not be further weakened. For some time now, polls have shown strong support for abolishing presidential primaries and the nominating powers of the national conventions and substituting a nationwide primary in which voters would choose presidential candidates. The national primary idea tends to be indifferent to the role of parties in presidential politics and, like nonpartisan nomination, tends to avoid the key issues.

Many observers believe that a national primary would benefit those with heavy financial support and media attention. Formal or informal preliminaries would still be essential, and one wonders what they would be like. Runoffs might be a frequent occurrence and politics could well become even more personalistic than it is now. If the same reformist spirit should lead us to not only abolish the electoral vote system, but also to adopt a *nonpartisan* national primary, we will have carried antipartyism to a logical but witless extreme.

9

Campaigns

After office seekers obtain a party nomination, politics enters a recognized phase of some weeks or months in which all sorts of activities are undertaken with a view to winning elections. Most Americans think of this as a season when people may be more attentive to political rhetoric—and more tolerant of the silly or spurious.

Activists put together the most elaborate campaigns when major offices are at stake and neither side is certain of victory. Since many contests are neither very competitive nor very major, the scope of campaigning is often quite limited. Hopeless underdogs in minor contests may run as a favor to political organizations or leaders; other candidates experience difficulty obtaining resources and easily become discouraged. Contestants who feel they are sure to win may not believe that an energetic campaign is either necessary or prudent and, like Thomas E. Dewey in 1948, may even try to put the campaign to sleep. All candidates are expected to go through the ritual of campaigning, but only a minority have strong incentives to wage intensive electioneering efforts.

Many people are needed to wage an active campaign for major office, and a measure of organization is therefore necessary to produce significant results. As with other organizations, functional assignments tend to reflect a division of labor. On paper at least, supervision may achieve some coordination. However, there are important differences between formal organization and the informal relationships that lie at the heart of campaign activity. Like all organizations, campaigns emerge from a wider social and political environment.

Perhaps the most distinctive characteristic of the campaign is its short life span. Even if the battle plan extends over many years, the relatively brief campaign season gives campaigning its special flavor. By the time things get into high gear, election day is close at hand. A sense may have developed that everything possible must be done within the limited time available. In such a setting, the adrenalin flow is high, and participants may form a temporary community. Many of the campaign activists are on leave from the regular workaday world. Personalities, surrounding events, and itineraries are new; one can never generate as much action as one would wish, and operating procedures must often start from scratch.

Some inefficiency is inherent in all campaigns. Relations between campaign workers and regular party organizations are often touchy, and authority of the candidate and campaign manager may be largely formal. Those in charge of what are essentially makeshift arrangements cannot afford to subject their campaign staff to controls typical of the workplace. It may be necessary to deal even with paid personnel as though they were volunteers. The campaign may spawn various untidy auxiliaries, with numerous personal contacts reflecting the need to build support in diverse groups. In fact, even the big-league campaign runs the constant risk of becoming a jumble of activities that have little impact on voters. In some cases, the campaign will approach organized chaos.

SIGNIFICANCE OF ELECTIONEERING EFFORTS

Citizens who are unfamiliar with politics sometimes imagine that politicians have access to superpotent methods of persuasion. The prominence of such mysteries as polling, computers, and television production lends plausibility to the notion. Thus, a fictional campaign of some years ago employed simulation techniques for sinister political purposes. In the real world, we have Joe McGinnis's version of how Nixon allowed himself to be merchandized in a series of contrived television presentations in 1968. In Robert Silverberg's *The Stochastic Man,* the central character is adept in the art of statistical projection. He meets aspiring politician Paul Quinn at a New York cocktail party, realizes that Quinn will be president, and abets his rise to power in the election of 2004. The narrative ends in the year 2000, with Quinn's presidency an unpleasant certainty of the future.[1] As Americans continue to feel vulnerable to larger forces, it remains easy to suppose that highly sophisticated techniques win elections.

Actually, there are distinct limits to the contribution any campaign technique can make to the election outcome. Simulation is an interesting technique of political analysis, but it is hardly the political equivalent of the

[1]Robert Silverberg, *The Stochastic Man* (New York: Harper & Row, Publishers, Inc., 1975). Campaign professionals may wish to note that the protagonist develops clairvoyant capacities that take him well beyond simple methodology. "I wallowed in harmonic means, positive skews, modal values, and parameters of dispersion. My office was a maze of display screens and graphs . . . But the heavy math and the high-powered Hollywood technology were simply aspects of the preliminary phases of my work, the intake stage. When actual projections had to be made, IBM couldn't help me." Ibid., p. 9. The earlier works referred to in this paragraph were Eugene Burdick, *The 480* (New York: McGraw-Hill Book Company, 1964), and Joe McGinnis, *The Selling of the President 1968* (New York: Pocket Books, Inc., 1968).

hydrogen bomb. Richard Nixon's 1968 campaign was *not* especially effective. In fact, he almost lost the election, despite an enormous initial advantage.

Political ambition is not confined to a clearly defined season, and most successful politicians are active over a period of years. In the final weeks or months, candidates can react to issue preferences of voters, and they can dramatize certain concerns, but they have little hope of *determining* what those preferences or concerns will be. Party and incumbency connections are in place before the campaign begins, and unforseen events can upset the best-laid plans. Group loyalties change slowly, even if the electorate is more fickle than it used to be. One should certainly be skeptical of all claims that campaigners possess some magic weapon.

Nevertheless, campaigning *is* an important part of the political process. Although it cannot affect everyone's vote, it may produce the critical margin needed for victory. Also, campaign performance may decide more votes today than in earlier years. Technical skills have improved, fewer people cast a straight party vote, and campaigners can try to sway larger segments of the electorate.

Campaigning is a crucial experience that sets political activists apart. Most people do not know what running for office is like; they have never even approached a stranger and asked him or her to vote for someone. Activists, on the other hand, frequently experience campaigns as something more vivid than ordinary life; campaigns tend to "hook" some people on politics.

How to wage an effective campaign therefore becomes a natural preoccupation of all politicians, and the wider implications of electioneering should concern all of us. The way office seekers try to win votes may determine whether many people will be aware of them and, if they are, how they perceive them. "Promises" may turn out to have been misleading or ill-advised; candidates may incur unacceptable obligations or may pander to the whims of the multitude. If one campaign organization is more competent than its rival, voters may be handicapped in deciding who should rule.

Discussion of modern campaigning can extend to topics as varied as the following (doubtless incomplete) listing:

1. Impact of the environment
   Constraints
   Supports
   Events
2. Organization and management of campaigns
   Role of candidate   Units in the campaign
   Role of manager   organization
   Management techniques   Roles of volunteers
3. Strategy and tactics
   Getting out the vote   Getting name recognition
   Persuading the undecided   Reinforcement
   Issues and ideology   Candidate presentation
   Partisanship   Timing

4. Campaign operations
   Research   Scheduling
   Media advertising   Advance[a]
   Media servicing   Direct mail
   Organizational work   Telephone
5. Levels of campaigning
   President   Senate
   Mayoral   Gubernatorial
   Minor offices
6. Campaign effects
   Contest outcomes   Effects on participants
   Political order   Larger society

[a]Note: People doing advance work attend to details of a candidate's appearances some hours, days, or weeks ahead of arrival. They check out speaking arrangements, invitation lists, travel plans, and a host of other practical details. See Jerry Bruno and Jeff Greenfield, *The Advance Man* (New York: William Morris & Company, Inc., 1971).

Each of the main headings in this list can apply to any campaign, regardless of its size or complexity. Small efforts may pose few explicit problems of organization and management, but even a one-man campaign will incorporate some notions of how to win and will generate some activities that are supposed to either implement these notions or meet the expectations of other people. Rather than attempt to deal with all aspects of campaigning, this chapter will focus on selected topics. The reader who wants to acquire campaign skills should get involved in some campaigns. A number of recently published works also offer useful advice.[2]

Major Aspects of Campaigning

A notable development in American campaigns has been the emergence of a corps of professional campaigners who offer services to candidates on a profit-making basis. Such persons often possess skills derived from the world of advertising and public relations and have extensive campaign experience. We noted in Chapter 1 that this trend was natural in a business-oriented society with a mobile and highly dispersed population. In the standard account of this development, demand for propaganda specialists increased markedly in the early years of the twentieth century, a time when big business came under open criticism on many fronts, abandoned its older policy of secrecy, and took on press representatives like Ivy Lee, a former reporter who had served in the press bureau of the Democratic National Committee. By 1924 Lee was no longer a press agent. He regarded himself as a "publicity man," concerned with all aspects of the expression of ideas, who "advises his client what policy to pursue, which, if pursued, would create favorable publicity."[3]

[2]Arnold Steinberg, *Political Campaign Management*, and *The Political Campaign Handbook*, both published in 1976 by Lexington Books, D.C. Heath & Co. See also Robert Agranoff, *The Management of Election Campaigns* (Boston: Holbrook Press, Inc., 1976).
[3]Stanley Kelley, Jr., *Professional Public Relations and Political Power* (Baltimore: The Johns Hopkins Press, 1956), p. 18.

Publicity specialists came to be in great demand not only by business but also by government agencies, professional and religious groups, schools, and colleges. Their services were visible during World War I, in the gas and utilities campaigns of the 1920s, and in a number of New Deal programs. By 1952 professional associations had formed, and many universities were offering public relations courses. Although public relations began in the political world, it reached its full development in the business sphere. It was here that publicity techniques seemed to be more sharply honed, more inventive, and more systematic than the cruder operations of traditional politicians. It was therefore natural that "industrial public relations and commercial advertising came to furnish standards by which to judge the efficiency of party propaganda efforts."

The number of professional campaign management firms expanded rapidly in the 1960s. By 1972, one hundred firms offered complete campaign management services, and another 200 provided their clients with some political services as a part of their business. Sixty of the complete-service firms did the bulk of their work in politics. Professional management services had become a regular feature in elections at all levels in more than thirty states.[4]

In part the blossoming of campaigning as a profit-making enterprise is a response to the needs of candidate-centered rather than party-centered electoral activity. As the burden of getting elected comes to depend on their own efforts, office seekers need to acquire publicity services on short notice. Campaigning in the new form approaches voters as consumers rather than citizens. This may produce a skeptical disposition in which the voter examines the merchandise and chooses accordingly. In such a situation, intermediaries and endorsements that party organizations can provide have less value, and dependence on the purveyors of publicity may be greater. Voters as consumers seek direct access to candidates with minimum inconvenience to themselves. The technical skills needed to accomplish this sense of direct contact center on the media.

As campaign skills available for hire have increased, they have become more specialized. In recent years the older emphasis on "campaign management" seems to have shifted to "consulting services," which do not necessarily emphasize managerial control by persons outside the candidate's inner circle. Different styles have emerged. Some consultants accept clients from one party only; others do not. Matthew Reese specializes in "instant organization" and tries to keep a staff of ten on year-round salary. Joe Napolitan consults on a worldwide scale, spreading the gospel of polling and election communications.

At this stage we should probably look upon campaign consultants as politicians of a special sort rather than as interlopers from Madison Avenue. One of the major studies notes that as recently as 1973 most professional campaign managers had backgrounds in public relations, journalism, advertising, and radio or television rather than in traditional politics. Neverthe-

[4]David L. Rosenbloom, *The Election Men* (New York: Quadrangle/The New York Times Book Co., Inc., 1973), pp. 50–51.

less, the author feels that a vast majority have the overwhelming concern with winning (as opposed to political ideas and principles) and the desire to be "in on the action" that are hallmarks of the professional politician. Indeed he claims that "people who own campaign management companies are professional politicians in the most precise meaning of that term."[5]

When specialists in commercial techniques make the journey from market place to political arena, they must adjust to new stresses. A political advertising campaign is usually more hectic than its commercial counterpart. Deadlines are final, and there is no market share for the losing candidate. Plans and production schedules often must be revamped on short notice. Professionals are apt to experience tension between the need to have a good win–loss record and the satisfaction of supporting personal favorites. Working for a client with a clear termination date can give managers a feeling of independence, but when elections are over there may be no other business waiting. According to Rosenbloom, few political management firms last, and none has survived the departure of its founders. Even some of the most successful ones have difficulty meeting expenses between campaign seasons.

The limited number of major political offices and new limits on campaign finance may put limits on how far such businesses can expand. Ever more frequently, both sides in a campaign have consultants, yet one side must lose, which may make it more difficult for firms to maintain good win-loss records. Thus, Spencer-Roberts lost most of their races in 1970, after riding a tide of successful Republican efforts. The California State Republican Committee did not renew its continuing contract, and the firm soon lost its reputation as "the people to see in California about Republican campaigns."[6] Nevertheless, Stuart Spencer was a key figure in Ronald Reagan's 1980 campaign.

CAMPAIGNS AND THE MEDIA

To the new campaign professionals, media have two components: news and advertising. Of the two, the news component is usually the more challenging because it is not subject to internal control by their campaign organization. In many campaigns, news is also more important in establishing the credibility of the candidate. An efficient campaign will consider all types of media: billboards, weekly and daily newspapers, radio and television stations, magazines, and such special media as trade journals, union newspapers, and ethnic radio and television. Practitioners consider coverage in many media desirable; appearing in a broad range of media increases the chances of getting attention, reaches people within different psychological contexts, and permits highly specific appeals.[7] Campaigners are often advised to coordinate media advertising with such campaign materials as leaflets, bro-

[5]Ibid., pp. 67, 75, 94.
[6]Ibid., pp. 83–84, 96–98, 134.
[7]Agranoff, *Management of Campaigns*, p. 337.

chures, and bumper stickers, so that themes and graphics are consistent and immediately recognizable. A variety of persons can distribute such materials (party workers, volunteers, candidate) in a variety of settings (headquarters, shopping centers, door-to-door, and so forth).

In developing campaign materials, the professional tries to avoid various weaknesses or pitfalls. For example, printed leaflets, useful for presenting issues and positions, can easily contain too much copy and too few photographs. Moreover, lack of a careful distribution plan may nullify the effect of excellently designed materials. Direct mail can target special groups in an effective manner, but direct mail pieces should be designed to exploit this medium's potential. Folklore has it that billboards promote name recognition, but locations must usually be rented by the month and the sheets printed well in advance, which makes them somewhat inflexible. Radio can reach a captive commuter audience, is relatively inexpensive, and requires little lead time. And since particular stations in a district usually appeal to different audiences, radio can target specific groups. Television is probably the most effective avenue to the large, relatively uninterested audience, but it is extremely expensive and requires considerable lead time.[8]

One of the most important tasks of a major campaign is getting effective news coverage—a task that, in the view of campaign professionals, cannot be left to chance. Says Steinberg:

> The political campaign that cannot make news does not deserve coverage. Contrary to civics textbooks, the news media does not exist to help the democratic process. News is a business that succeeds or fails depending on whether it fulfills the public's desire for information. If the campaign does not generate news, the media looks to the opposition, or looks outside politics altogether.[9]

Steinberg emphasizes the importance of "orchestration" in "servicing the news media." Orchestration flows from deliberate choices made at the beginning of the campaign about themes, issues, and the candidate's image. Plans should specify how many times issue positions will be emphasized in order to generate pacing and momentum. Repetition can help establish an association between the candidate and the selected issues. Ideally, the campaign planner finds different and newsworthy ways to dramatize issue positions.[10]

Television news requires visual stories, often achieved by choosing an appropriate environment to film a position statement. Visits to factories, schools, rehabilitation clinics, slums, and shopping centers to illustrate an appropriate issue have achieved television coverage for candidates. Sometimes a single event in the campaign, such as a party rally, can be milked for several press releases extending over a period of time. Effective campaigners become acquainted with journalistic concepts such as "story lead," "reaction statement," and "deadline." The lead is the part of the story which

[8]Steinberg, *Campaign Handbook,* pp. 32–35, 336–337.
[9]Ibid., p. 47.
[10]Ibid., pp. 39–40.

introduces the rest and gets the most emphasis. It conforms to journalists' notions (sometimes not shared by the candidate) of what parts of his statements or activities are most newsworthy. Constraints imposed by deadlines become an integral part of effective campaign discipline. Steinberg emphasizes that the candidate's reaction to a major news event should be succinct and that it should be taped, filmed, or issued as quickly as possible.

The press spokesman plays a vital role in any major campaign because he or she can raise the campaign's prestige in the eyes of the press and bring important skills to the task of getting desired news coverage. The individual in this position should become thoroughly familiar with policies and practices of all media operations relevant to the campaign and should develop personal contacts with the key media personnel. A detailed schedule of the candidate's activities is a basic coordinating device and can be extremely helpful in promoting good press if it is distributed regularly to the media.[11]

Reflections. Mass media have a pervasive impact on campaigns, yet the precise effects are not easy to pinpoint. Print and electronic media can obviously bring candidates to the voters, but political communication through the mass media is susceptible to distortion and mismatching. Stimson Bullitt notes that although mass publics need thoughtful political messages, these must often compete with material designed for moment-to-moment appeal. He says that the sending capability of mass media is in short supply and that we have failed to develop standards of fair access. Rights of receivers are poorly recognized and defined. Media often cater to the young, believing that young people set taste trends and spend the most money. Since younger groups tend to be less interested in elections than older groups, this probably heightens the competitive disadvantages of campaign messages. Television provides the broadest general access to the mass public, but unit costs are relatively high for politicians since they must pay for an audience that includes persons who are not registered or who reside outside of the district.[12]

Media markets do not coincide with political jurisdictions; to cover an entire state a candidate may often use several outlets and still fall short of comprehensive geographic coverage. Print media may also be awkwardly positioned for statewide contests. The *New York Times,* the *Washington Post,* the major weekly news magazines, and the wire services provide important access to voters in a presidential contest and a few noteworthy statewide races. However, the vast majority of candidates must rely on local papers that in combination may reach only a moderate proportion of the eligible electorate.

Bullitt believes that in the present relationship between political life and the media, legitimacy is poorly meshed with the processes of control and communication. He says that satisfaction with traditional political activity has declined as nonresponsible media have risen to power. The resulting

[11]Ibid., pp. 61, 82.
[12]Stimson Bullitt, *To Be a Politician,* rev. ed. (New Haven, Conn.: Yale University Press, 1977), p. 88.

defects in political communication include high expense to candidates; tendencies toward deception, failure to join issues, and failure to present the nature and capacity of candidates. The big need, he argues, is for "media to acknowledge their function as in part a coordinate branch of government, legitimate and responsible, an independent branch, not an arm of another branch, and intended to help the society govern the rest of the government."[13]

   Another scholar who has probed deeply into these matters is Daniel Boorstin. He believes that most of our media problems derive from extravagant expectations that cannot possibly be satisfied in the world of real experience. This results in a continuing demand for "a flood of illusions," which are dished up not only by the media but by many other social institutions as well.[14]

   One of Boorstin's main concepts has to do with the artificial happenings he calls pseudo-events. He says that these help make up for the fact that in any given day there are fewer newsworthy occurrences than we wish to read about in our newspapers. Among the identifying features of a pseudo-event are its lack of spontaneity, the fact that it is arranged for the convenience of the media, and its ambiguous relation to "the underlying reality of the situation." Like the "precooked" news release written in the past tense with a future release date, pseudo-events do not exactly inform us and do not exactly deceive us. Unlike propaganda, which "oversimplifies," the pseudo-event "overcomplicates."

   Boorstin believes that the media's heightened ability to transmit print descriptions, as well as sight and sound images, have made pseudo-events more interesting than spontaneous events to many people. The result is an inherently bewildering state of affairs in which dreams yield to illusions and a "thicket of unreality . . . stands between us and the facts of life." Although the process is not congenial to politics in the heroic mold, television can quickly make a man famous and thus invite confusion between the "big name" and the "big man." "As other pseudo-events in our day tend to overshadow spontaneous events, so celebrities (who are human pseudo-events) tend to overshadow heroes."[15]

   Boorstin's ideas, first penned in the early 1960s, may be pertinent to the pervasive sense of disillusionment that has more recently infected American society. A mood of small-minded selfishness temporarily eclipses traditional American ideals centered on freedom, amity, service, and the dignity of the individual. In terms of Boorstin's discourse, this may result in part from confusion about the difference between dreams and illusions. As Boorstin puts it:

   A dream is a vision or an aspiration to which we can compare reality. It may be very vivid, but its vividness reminds us how different is the real world. An illusion, on the other hand, is an image we have mistaken for reality. We cannot

[13]Ibid., pp. 100–101.
[14]Daniel J. Boorstin, *The Image: or What Happened to the American Dream* (New York: Atheneum Publishers, 1962), p. 5.
[15]Ibid., pp. 3, 13, 19, 35, 36, 37, 54, 66.

reach for it, aspire to it, or be exhilarated by it; for we live in it. It is prosaic because we cannot see it is not fact.[16]

Were we literally *dis*illusioned—freed of our illusions—general rejoicing would be in order. However, the "illusions" that Americans take no satisfaction from rejecting are in many cases not illusions at all, but rather dreams that may be necessary to our well-being. Ideals stand in a healthy relationship to reality; illusions deceive us about reality. Included among our illusions is the notion that selfish individualism is a "realistic" stance towards American society.

The thoughts of both Bullitt and Boorstin suggest that in catering to the mass media, modern campaigning encourages most citizens to be indulged spectators rather than active participants. Crucial campaign activities center on public relations techniques designed to enhance the candidate's prestige and attract attention. In the process, campaigning becomes a type of theater rather than a means of civic communication or political affirmation. Like the convention delegate who needs a portable television set to know what is going on, the reflective campaign activist may well wonder about the underlying reality.

CAMPAIGN FINANCE

Money affects many aspects of campaigning and a flow of financial support is crucial to a campaign's success. Availability of money shapes planning decisions, affects the quality and morale of campaign staff, and sets limits on the scope of campaign activities. Money also tends to index group and individual power.

Nevertheless, one can discern outer limits to the impact of campaign money. A study of Democratic senatorial primaries in Tennessee (for the period 1948 to 1964) found that candidates needed $150,000 to wage a serious campaign. However, the authors ranked money as less important than other political resources. Campaigns could usually convert other resources to campaign funds; money alone could rarely purchase such essential assets as personal capacity, campaign organization, and institutional alliances.[17]

Studies of campaign finances support the popular impression that the amount spent on electoral campaigns has risen dramatically in the past generation, even after appropriate allowance is made for rising prices. Total expenditures by national committees on presidential elections is a fairly good indicator of historical trends. From 1920 to 1956 the dollar figures ranged between $5 million and $14 million; spending tended to be high in years of unusual political intensity, such as 1928 and 1936, and considerably

[16]Ibid., p. 239.
[17]William Buchanan and Alice Bird, *Money as a Campaign Resource* (Princeton, N.J.: Citizens' Research Foundation, 1966). For comments on a variety of studies, see David Adamany, "Money, Politics, and Democracy: A Review Essay," *American Political Science Review*, 71 (March 1977), 289–304.

lower in most other years. Beginning in 1960 presidential campaign spending increased dramatically. Not only did absolute amounts escalate rapidly (increases in spending far outpaced increases in price levels), but cost per vote also soared: starting with 29 cents in 1960 and 35 cents in 1964, and pushing upwards to 60 cents in 1968 and over a dollar in 1972.[18]

According to a study of major contests in seven states, costs in the late 1960s increased at an average *annual* rate of 33 percent. In particular races, the increases could be breathtaking. For example, Democrat Walter Huddleston spent six times as much to win a Senate victory in Kentucky in 1972 as a previous winner in that state four years earlier. If one compares Huddleston with the 1968 *loser* (also a Democrat), his expenditures were *ten* times as great. Scholars know much less about costs of contests below the senatorial level, but it seems clear that campaigns for the House of Representatives paralleled the general trend.[19]

Recent legislation does not seem to have slowed the spiraling costs of campaigns. The 1974 and 1976 amendments to the Federal Election Campaign Act of 1971 instituted serious contribution limits and enforcement provisions. However, in *Buckley* v. *Valeo* (1976), the Supreme Court held that spending limits for nonsubsidized campaigns (originally provided in the 1974 amendments) were unconstitutional. Congress subsequently repealed them in 1976. The ruling also prevented these statutes from limiting spending on behalf of a candidate by persons totally independent of that candidate's campaign.

Election subsidies have apparently eliminated large pressure-group contributions in the presidential contests, but much of this money has surged toward other contests. Corporations and labor unions are both prohibited by law from making direct campaign contributions, but each can set up separate political action committees (PACs) to solicit voluntary contributions, as can other special interest organizations. The Federal Election Campaign Act of 1971 as amended in 1974 and 1976 set up disclosure and reporting requirements for PACs and limited the amounts a committee could contribute to any one contest. The 1976 amendments also required that all PACs established by a company or international union be treated as a single committee for contribution purposes. However, the lack of limits on the total amounts that a PAC may contribute to all campaigns coupled with favorable rulings by the Federal Elections Commission led to an expansion of both the numbers of PACs and their total contributions. In 1978 PACs contributed three times as much to federal candidates as they had in 1974.[20] Despite the huge sums spent in these contests, many contestants undoubtedly lacked the money necessary to wage an effective campaign. Further changes in the legislation are likely, and some observers feel that presidential spending limits in the 1976 legislation are too low to enable candidates to communicate effectively with the voters.

[18]Herbert E. Alexander, *Financing Politics* (Washington, D.C.: Congressional Quarterly Press, 1976), p. 19.

[19]David Adamany, "Financing National Politics," in *The New Style in Election Campaigns,* 2nd ed., ed. Robert Agranoff (Boston, Mass.: Holbrook Press, Inc., 1976), pp. 382–383.

[20]Rhodes Cook, "Political Action Committee Spending Soared in 1978," *Congressional Quarterly Weekly Report,* June 2, 1979, p. 1043.

Soaring money needs, growing weakness in the parties, and the emergence of the new politics campaign professionals have developed hand in hand, with each tending to reinforce the other. Thus, declining party strength probably reduced overall campaign capabilities, opening up opportunites for the new professionals. As the latter became more numerous, they tended to further enfeeble the parties while pushing total cash outlays in political campaigns upwards. Fees charged by today's professionals, and their research and television-centered strategies, may not be much more expensive in net social terms than the large-scale "volunteer" services the parties once provided, but the price tags are more explicit. Larger sums flowing into the electoral arena must finance the efforts of thousands of candidates who can no longer rely on party organizations for the campaign support needed to get elected. Expansion of the money flow probably tends to reinforce personalistic styles in campaigning, but many politicians still cannot obtain enough money to make effective electoral challenges.

Some spending increases seem tied to the rising use of television. Broadcast expenditures in presidential elections held fairly steady in the 1950s, then spurted dramatically upward between 1960 and 1968.[21] Until the Federal Election Campaign Act of 1971, rates for political ads were much higher than for other kinds of advertising. Belief in the potency of television ads began to wane somewhat after 1968, and television spending at the presidential level actually peaked in that year. Nevertheless, television is still the hallmark of modern, big-league campaigning. Ability to "service the media" and generate media events continues to require skills that are in great demand, and participants naturally turn to the specialists in marketing and public relations to obtain them. The idea of free television time for political candidates has made little headway, although it remains an important possibility for the future. Except for presidential debates and national conventions, candidates obtain free television coverage only as items in the news, and this means in a manner consistent with commercial format and product criteria. Candidates for minor offices get free and meaningful exposure from local television stations only with the greatest difficulty.

Getting money. The role of fat cats in national elections seems to have declined somewhat with provisions of the 1974 and 1976 amendments to the Federal Election Campaign Act, which limit the total contributions a person can make and encourage small contributions. No person's combined contributions to federal elections can exceed $25,000 in any given year. This limit does not apply to personal spending by a candidate on his own behalf, nor does it affect personal expenditures that are fully independent of campaigns. However, contributions in other years but for the same election count within the $25,000. Moreover, the law prohibits anyone from contributing in the name of another person.

Among provisions that encourage small contributions are the tax credit for campaign contributions and some of the requirements that must be met to obtain matching funds for presidential primaries. Currently, a

[21]Herbert E. Alexander, *Financing Politics* (Washington, D.C.: Congressional Quarterly Press, 1976), p. 28.

taxpayer may credit 50 percent of all campaign contributions up to a tax credit of $100 on a single return and $200 on a joint return. These tax incentives apply to money contributed at any level: national, state, or local. Subsidies for presidential primaries come in the form of matching funds, and candidates must obtain the first $100,000 from individual private contributions no greater than $250.[22]

Although a few wealthy persons can no longer bankroll a presidential or senatorial campaign, key fund raisers are probably as important as ever. One study suggests that such money people are often prominent in nonpolitical fund raising and that they possess clout based in part on social standing and business positions. The more effective among them are said to maintain up-to-date "tickle lists," which they employ in ways that fit the current fashion in solicitation techniques.[23] Even if effective federal spending limits are imposed in the future, it will probably not diminish the role of fund raisers, since the limits will probably be joined to subsidies in the form of matching funds.

The need to obtain money subjects many contestants to continuous pressure and anxiety. Yet, except for presidential contenders, legislation so far enacted has not really made money raising any easier for most candidates. The contribution limits tend to make fund raising competitive with other contests and (at least for those contributions applied to a tax credit) with electoral politics at other levels of the political system. Legal requirements for detailed financial accountability, accounting requirements, and financial reports place further burdens on campaigns.

Campaigning practices must adapt to the facts just described, and they can do so in different ways. One way to avoid financial pressures is to rely on personal resources of very wealthy candidates. The Rockefeller family, for example, funds most of its own electoral ventures. In the view of one scholar, many of these wealthy candidates, rather than being conservatives representing vested interests, are surrogates for those who otherwise might lack a voice in government. But another scholar bewails popular approval of wealthy candidates on the ground that they "are too rich to be bought" and concludes that such outlooks have "subtly reimposed the means test for office discredited more than a century ago by the Jacksonian movement."[24]

Barring further legislative changes, the candidate for major office who is of modest means had better be popular, an incumbent, or have a good method of raising campaign funds. A candidate's spending does not always need to be on a par with the opponent's. Indeed, available evidence refutes the common belief that the candidate who spends the most wins the election. Although studies by Common Cause of congressional elections in the 1970s indicate that winners did tend to spend more than losers, this could well have been a reflection of incumbency or partisan advantage in particular districts. Throughout the twentieth century, Republicans at the national

[22]Alexander, *Financing Politics*, pp. 272, 275.
[23]George Thayer, *Who Shakes the Money Tree?* (New York: Simon & Schuster, Inc., 1973), as cited by Adamany, "Money, Politics, and Democracy," p. 293.
[24]Adamany, "Financing National Politics," p. 393; Alexander, *Financing Politics*, p. 51.

level have had greater financial resources, and Democrats have had more natural voter support. Nevertheless, from the 1930s on, Democrats won more often.[25]

Most observers feel that, up to a certain point, money is absolutely critical to a campaign. Nobody is certain where this point is, and the uncertainty is increased by the tendency of money to reflect a candidate's popularity. Thus, a popular candidate may receive funds either because contributors are also enthusiastic about such a person or because contributors find it prudent to offer support. The candidate's popularity precedes the influx of money and, in a sense, causes both it and victory at the polls to occur. On balance, however, this only accentuates the importance of raising money. Like Calvinist predestination, money becomes an omen of grace as well as a means of supporting worldly endeavors. "Seed" or "start-up" money is especially important in the early phases of a candidacy.

A recent manual on campaign management emphasizes the technical expertise needed to assure enough revenue. Projections must be based on careful analysis of types of contributors and alternative methods of solicitation. The campaign may approach potential prospects through its top people, peers, telephone solicitation, campaign literature, door to door appeals, newspaper advertising, and special projects. The cost of raising funds is a campaign expense, and managers must be able to subject proposals of professional fund raisers to a fishy-eyed appraisal.[26]

Campaigns have recently turned to direct mail as a way to raise large sums from many relatively small contributions. To date, direct-mail solicitations seem to favor candidates of a pronounced ideological cast. The most widely known direct-mail consultant, Richard Viguerie, has tended to help clients on behalf of rightist causes such as anti-abortion and right-to-work groups. Small donations also provided the main source of revenue for the McGovern, McCarthy, Wallace, and Goldwater campaigns. David Adamany believes that candidates stirring strong sentiments among small but intense parts of the population can obtain a rich harvest, but that moderates fare poorly because they cannot sufficiently arouse their constituencies. As a result, moderates must raise funds, if at all, from traditional partisan and interest group sources. Despite the great potential for direct mail, there are risks for the unwary. Costs can eat up a high proportion of contributions, and managers should carefully examine contracts with direct-mail consultants.[27]

The emergence of large numbers of PACs commented on earlier has also changed fund raising. The 1976 amendments to the Federal Election Campaign Act of 1971 stipulated that no person could contribute more than $5,000 to a given PAC, and no PAC could contribute more than $10,000

[25]Adamany, "Money, Politics, and Democracy," p. 294; Alexander, *Financing Politics,* p. 40.

[26]Steinberg, *Campaign Management,* pp. 140–143.

[27]Adamany, "Financing National Politics," p. 394; Steinberg, *Campaign Management,* pp. 140–141, 165–168. Campaign use of direct mail is by no means limited to fund raising. It can be a very useful approach (especially in small constituencies) to voters with particular social or political characteristics.

to any given candidate ($5,000 in the primary and $5,000 in the general election). However, nothing in the law prevented PACs from supporting as many candidates as they wished (including candidates running against each other) and from contributing up to $15,000 to a national party committee. According to the Federal Elections Committee, almost fifteen hundred PACs contributed $35.1 million to congressional candidates in the 1978 elections.

The sums seemed so large in particular cases and the allocations so blatant that election finance that year received unusually high criticism in the press. PACs provided 56 percent of the money that twenty-two House committee chairmen spent on their reelection campaigns. The average amount of PAC money each received was $45,000—more than twice the 1976 amount. A Congressional Quarterly report noted that incumbents received 2.6 times as much from PACs as their challengers.[28]

The surge of money appeared inordinate in a few conspicuous cases. Thus, Senator Jesse Helms of North Carolina reported expenditures of $7 million, which worked out, according to the *New York Times*, to $13.65 for each vote he received. Eight congressional leaders accepted nearly $1 million in campaign contributions, although none of them faced a serious challenge. As a result support for spending limits and public financing for congressional campaigns grew. A less ambitious approach was to advocate a lowering of the maximum amount a PAC could contribute to any candidate while limiting the funds any candidate could receive from all PACs. In 1979 representatives Obey and Railsback introduced legislation that would also prevent PACs and direct-mail operations from extending credit to candidates who were temporarily short of funds.[29]

Investigations by Gary Jacobson, however, seem to suggest that underfinancing of campaigns is a more serious problem than overfinancing. He notes that PACs provided only about 25 percent of all congressional campaign funds and that individual donations continue to supply most congressional campaign money. He suspects that the PACs drew so much attention because of the diminishing relative importance of labor money as PACs of health organizations, professional associations, and ideological membership groups became more notable. In 1978 Democratic incumbents received a larger share of their funds from corporate, trade, and professional PACs than from organized labor.

Jacobson believes that a solid case can be made for some kind of public subsidy but that its effect would depend on the limits likely to accompany it: "Campaign subsidies will help challengers; restrictions in spending will help incumbents." He believes Congress has shown little interest in changes that would make fund raising easier.[30]

No-contest elections rarely get press attention, but there are many of

---

[28] *New York Times*, July 25, 1979, p. A22; Cook, "PAC Spending," p. 1044.

[29] *New York Times*, July 25, 1979, p. A22. The numbers reported in this paragraph all come from various issues of the *New York Times*: Dec. 25(!), 1978, p. 1; Nov. 26, 1978, Sec. IV, p. 20; Jan. 9, 1979, Sec. III, p. 15; Jan. 4, 1979, p. 16.

[30] Gary C. Jacobson, *Money in Congressional Elections* (New Haven, Conn.: Yale University Press, 1980), pp. xviii, 206, 231, 243. The quotation is at p. xviii.

them. For example, in 1978 the winners in fifty-three House districts had *no* opposition. In twenty-six of a total of ninety-eight districts in Illinois, Massachusetts, New York, and Ohio, winners obtained 80 percent or more of the total congressional vote.[31] Money had to be spent in most of these districts in order to satisfy public expectations. (The $35,000 to $50,000 reported by the *New York Times* is not, in my view, excessive for a ritual campaign. Even a sure winner has campaign costs, and if he or she did not pay, campaign constituents would be resentful.) In most of these cases, the more important fact is that the losing candidates had too little money to wage a campaign that would have given them even a chance at the polls.

Spending money. Spending money effectively in a campaign is almost as difficult as raising it. Whoever manages the campaign should formulate strategy in a way that is concrete enough to be budgeted, maintain the necessary flexibility to meet changing situations, and plan expenditures based on imperfect estimates of the money that will eventually be available. The campaign best designed to produce electoral victory (though not necessarily best from a civic standpoint) will always focus on end results: somehow getting supporters to the polls, somehow persuading doubtful voters, and somehow retaining the support of the faithful. (Converting the opposition is difficult and very seldom enters into most campaign plans.) Basic spending decisions can make the difference between a campaign of maximum impact (though even this will be limited in its effects) and one with negligible results.

Campaign organizations are not always adept at assessing the candidate's real electoral needs. Marjorie Randon Hershey suggests that campaigning may be directed toward satisfying internal wants rather than checking on voter responses or seeking voter support. She observed one campaign in which the campaign staff usually provided the "public" reaction to a new leaflet or press release. Some activities served simply "to impress the candidate or to perk up other staff members."[32]

A difficult problem of big campaigns is judging the proper relationship between campaign spending and campaign revenue or, to put it another way, deciding how much debt to incur. A prudent estimation of the candidate's winning chances may necessarily enter into the determination—making it something like seven-card stud. In an effective campaign both incoming contributions and expenditures often peak late in the game, with fund raising lagging behind spending. According to Steinberg, certain kinds of errors in financial forecasting are common: expecting too much help from party committees, underestimating the value of professional campaign assistance, indulging in wishful thinking, and failing to appreciate the importance of "momentum." He advises managers to budget more money for each successive week on effective television and other advertising and for

[31]Based on data in Richard M. Scammon and Alice McGillivray, eds., *America Votes 13* (Washington, D.C.: Congressional Quarterly Inc., 1979). "No opposition" is defined here as winning by at least 95 percent of the vote.
[32]Marjorie Randon Hershey, *The Making of Campaign Strategy* (Lexington, Mass.: Lexington Books, D.C. Heath & Co., 1974), p. xvii.

distribution of campaign literature. This means keeping early expenditures low enough to assure several upward increments in spending—never spending *less* money later in the campaign.[33]

A broader look. To gain a proper perspective on political money, one should look at it from different angles—a task which is made easier by excellent recent studies of the subject. Keep in mind also a point made earlier—that the costs of campaigns reflect features of the particular governmental and political system. For example, the British election of May 3, 1979, differed from American presidential elections in crucial respects.

The Labour party government lost a vote of confidence in the House of Commons on March 28, and Prime Minister Callaghan's call for new elections precipitated a rapid sequence of events. April 23 was the last day to file, and the balloting occurred only a week and a half later. English voters simply chose members of parliament in particular districts and had no other offices to consider. The electorate could support James Callaghan or Margaret Thatcher only by voting for their followers in parliament, and this meant that votes were heavily oriented to party. Campaign spending limits were severe by American standards. Although major parties obtained modest amounts of free radio and television time under strict groundrules, no candidate was permitted to purchase any broadcast time.

It is true that restrictions on campaign spending in Britain operated only during the election period, but there can be little doubt that campaign costs were dramatically lower than in any recent federal election in the United States. Spending limits and modest campaign subsidies of the British type easily fit a system where party appeals are what count. In the British election, the parties had to be in a state of constant readiness for an election called on short notice, and in a sense the election was simply an extension of proceedings that had been going on in the House of Commons many months prior to the vote of confidence. The focus on structured conflict between sets of party leaders in one legislative chamber meant that there could be a direct carry-over from parliamentary debate to electoral campaigning. Since the results of the election could be decisive (no staggered terms, no independent government authorities, no deadlock between executive and legislature), it was not particularly difficult for campaign appeals to reach a large portion of the British electorate. The spending of large sums on political advertising was not necessary to meet the requirements of electoral democracy.

In comparison, the American presidential election of 1980 differed in many ways that added to its cost. American parties and candidates had to pay the cost of registration drives, which were a government responsibility in Britain. The preceding configuration in Congress did not transpose naturally into the election campaigns, so voters (ideally) had to become familiar with the relevant issues in particular contests. There was little in the way of unified party appeals, and every candidate had to compete for attention against the distractions of many other contests. Instead of merely electing

[33]Steinberg, *Campaign Management*, pp. 146–147.

a few hundred national representatives, American voters had to choose among untold thousands of office seekers. Since many Americans preferred "voting for the man, not the party," the *necessary* costs of attempting to properly inform the electorate were much higher. Nearly all candidates also had to wage costly primary battles earlier in the year. The complex, loose, and multifaceted American election contrasted sharply with its simpler and more closed English counterpart.

Students of campaign finance appear to be in virtually unanimous agreement that the *total* costs of American elections are not particularly high when one considers relevant values and practices. American elections would be less expensive if parties were stronger. But as long as Americans continue to prefer weak parties (however mistaken this preference may be), higher costs commensurate with that preference can be justified. The same logic applies to other aspects of American politics (such as federalism, separation of powers, and the long ballot) which no important segment of the American public usually questions. Even in 1972 (a record year) total nomination and election expenses of all candidates were only $3.04 for each eligible voter.

Adamany and Agree emphasize that if costs were equally distributed, the ordinary citizen would hardly feel the burden. Personal income rose more rapidly between 1952 and 1972 than campaign spending. Total government expenditures have also increased at a greater rate. They argue that private financing does not contribute enough money to support vigorous campaigning for all offices. The money is also poorly distributed: higher for executive offices than for legislative offices, more adequate in competitive than in noncompetitive districts, and more generous to incumbents than to challengers.[34]

Public financing of congressional elections may be the next crucial step in the evolution of public policy toward these concerns. However, it will not necessarily be an easy step to take. Requirements for *X* dollars of matching funds if a candidate accepts a limit of *Y* dollars on his total spending can easily misfire if either *X* or *Y* is too low. Ceilings on spending that are too low encourage financially advantaged candidates to turn down matching funds. When limits are accepted, they may protect the built-in advantages of incumbency. Some observers believe that challengers should receive higher subsidies or limits than incumbents. As one might expect, congressional reaction to this notion has been unenthusiastic.

If Congress does succeed in imposing workable subsidies and limits, it will be even more important to monitor money flows into state level contests. As of 1976, eight states had income-tax checkoff provisions similar to the federal measure. In four of these (Idaho, Iowa, Rhode Island, and Utah), money so raised was distributed directly to state party organizations. Eleven states had some form of public subsidy. Alexander believes that as states establish systems of public financing, there may be increased interest in cutting costs by shortening the ballot.[35]

[34]David W. Adamany and George E. Agree, *Political Money* (Baltimore: The Johns Hopkins University Press, 1975), pp. 26–27.
[35]Alexander, *Financing Politics*, p. 186.

Keep in mind that there are approaches to regulating election finance other than those discussed. Making free time available on radio and television is a possibility, since channnels and frequencies are clearly in the public domain. Automatic voter registration could shift some costs, even if it did not reduce them. Some analysts recommend voucher systems that would enable voters to determine which candidates receive subsidies. Alexander emphasizes the need to think in terms of floors rather than ceilings, and he believes that an element of private financing should be retained. He cautions us not to imagine that campaigns can be kept uncontaminated by the play of political forces and urges a reorientation of civic values so that political giving is upgraded and dignified as an aspect of good citizenship. The overriding need (as yet poorly reflected in federal and state laws) is for funding mechanisms "designed to keep the election process open and flexible rather than rigid, exclusionary and fragmented."[36]

PRESIDENTIAL CAMPAIGNS

Generalizing about presidential campaigns can be difficult. Virtually every presidential campaign has its unusual features: Kennedy's Catholicism and Nixon's performance in the televised debates in 1960; the distinctive mood produced by the assassination of a president and the rise of a new kind of Republican activism in 1964; unprecedented disorder in 1968; party rules changes and the Eagleton fiasco in 1972; and in 1980, the Iranian hostage crisis and Anderson candidacy. All efforts to comprehend the 1976 campaigns confront the fact that one of the candidates was an incumbent who had not been elected either president or vice president by the American people. The decision by one of the country's most popular politicians (Ted Kennedy) not to seek the presidency in two successive elections appears to have been unprecedented.

Efforts of American presidential candidates to claim national support occur in an ambiguous setting. On the one hand, there is receptivity—interest in the contest as a horse race, eager media coverage, attention of political organizations and activists. Yet the size of the nation can overawe even the boldest adventurer, and victory is never complete. Reliable support for the campaign is in short supply. The party apparatus is poorly equipped to assume the burdens of planning and execution, and makeshift arrangements devised in the previous election are irrelevant. Although interested in the presidential contest, the community of partisans is frequently preoccupied with lesser races. At least three-fifths of the electorate has usually decided which candidate to support by the end of the conventions and will not change its mind.[37] Three-fifths is also about the largest share of the popular vote the winner can expect to obtain.

---

[36]Ibid., p. 267.

[37]Herbert B. Asher, *Presidential Elections and American Politics* (Homewood, Ill.: The Dorsey Press, 1976), p. 270.

Presidential campaigning is very demanding. It follows extensive jockeying for the nomination and places heavy burdens on the stamina and physical well-being of candidates. Most campaign activities expose candidates to possible political misadventure for the sake of only the most trifling improvement in their prospects.

Reforms have eliminated some of the pitfalls of presidential campaigning in recent years—most notably the dangerous shortage of campaign money the Humphrey campaign struggled with in 1968. However, assassinations have underscored the difficulty of assuring even the physical safety of our candidates. Organizational weaknesses are more pronounced than ever, and lesser office seekers are not as dependent on presidential outcomes. As "generals" seeking political conquest, presidential aspirants have aides and camp followers, but they can no longer turn to lesser commanders who in turn direct their own foot soldiers.

Office and Party Aspects

Presidency and party are separate entities, but in our most important campaigns, they are subtly intertwined. If an incumbent president is seeking a second term, this will have pervasive effects on the electioneering. Presidents are generally perceived to be a known quantity. They have instant access to publicity, a mixed record in office, opportunity to play the role of international leader, and ability to profit from official actions during the campaign.

Incumbents have taken advantage of the presidency to further their reelection cause in important ways. Thus, Harry Truman called a special session of a Congress dominated by the opposition party to dramatize disagreements with it. Passage of important legislative measures helped Lyndon Johnson in 1964. Both Eisenhower and Nixon were able to detach themselves somewhat from the political battle—the former by a posture of aloofness in 1956, the latter by largely ignoring his opponent and campaigning from the White House in 1972.

Superficially, incumbency appears to be almost irresistible in presidential elections. Incumbents sought the office ten times between 1932 and 1980 and were unsuccessful in only three instances (Hoover, Ford, and Carter). Keep in mind, however, that this tally includes three efforts by Roosevelt prior to the constitutional limit on more than two terms. In two cases (Truman in 1952 and Johnson in 1968) incumbents did not seek reelection—perhaps because they thought their prospects were poor.

The president may even be more *vulnerable* than most other incumbents seeking reelection. His standing in the polls usually declines over time as he remains in office—perhaps because his role requires him to take responsibility for some actions that are both unpopular and well publicized. Presidents are also peculiarly vulnerable to events they may not be able to control. Severe economic crisis, for example, almost guarantees that the incumbent will have trouble getting reelected. According to Arthur Holcombe, in a work published in 1950, each major economic crisis (1837, 1857, 1873, 1893, 1929) was followed by the opposition party gaining control of the presidency at the next election. Wars were almost as hard on the fortunes of the party in power.[38]

One has the impression that Holcombe's ideas continue to have some validity. The Korean War was followed by the election of Eisenhower and a Republican Congress in 1952, and the Democrats clearly lost the presidency in 1968 for reasons that had much to do with the war in Vietnam. None of the post–World War II economic crises have been as severe as those cited by Holcombe, but the ones of 1974–1975 and 1979–1980 had the predicted sequel.

The "successor"—a nonincumbent candidate of the incumbent's party —often seems to be in a difficult position. If there is a natural limit on how long either party can retain control of the presidency, it may work against the fortunes of would-be successors. Between 1932 and 1976 every successor candidate lost. Stevenson in 1952 suffered the handicaps of the Truman administration, although he had no position in it. Nixon in 1960 was closely identified with the outgoing administration, and this seems to have placed heavy constraints upon him. Humphrey's connection with the Johnson administration was probably fatal, and Ford (an incumbent and successor rolled into one) could not shake the effects of his tie to Nixon in the form of the pardon.

Weak as party ties are, they can prevent successors from fully separating themselves from incumbents. In three of four cases, the successor had official position as vice president in the incumbent administration, and everybody expects this role to be played in complete compatibility with the president's wishes.

Candidates can either emphasize their relation to their party or downplay it, and the approach taken usually depends on which candidate represents the stronger party. As long as Republicans are less numerous than Democrats, we can expect Republicans to minimize party appeals. No candidate, however, can entirely escape the partisan context of the campaign. Eisenhower, for example, until 1950 or so was probably one of the least partisan figures in American public life, and he could have been elected as either a Democrat or Republican. Nevertheless, he had to choose, and after he did, one wondered how Democrats could have considered him anything but a Republican. Except for Wendell Willkie, no major party candidate of the twentieth century developed highly visible connections with a different party after his career had begun.

Party does not dictate a candidate's political positions, but it does provide calibration and context for them. The candidate is expected to behave in ways that are at least minimally consistent with his position as party leader. John Connolly's conservatism and personal style required a shift of party if his presidential ambitions were to be credible. The Goldwa-

[38]Arthur N. Holcombe, *Our More Perfect Union* (Cambridge, Mass.: Harvard University Press, 1950), Chap. 4. The opposition party also gained control of Congress each time. However, as our discussion elsewhere shows, incumbency has an impact in Congress that is quite different from its impact on the presidency.

ter candidacy, an anomaly even for Republicans, would have been unthinkable as a Democratic effort. Party traditions set up expectations about future behavior, particularly appointments. The party label links presidential campaigns to images held by the mass electorate, and it subjects candidates to marked differences in outlook that distinguish activists in the Democratic and Republican camps.

Issues in the Campaign

Choosing issue stands poses difficulties for office seekers at all levels of government. The increasing number of policy questions and the apparent capacity of some of them to produce single-issue constituencies have increased the hazards of electoral combat. Although aspiring presidents may enjoy more leeway than other politicians, their positions lead to high expectations and intensive scrutiny. The visible connection between getting nominated and getting elected also places strain on issue positions. Nomination requires candidates to satisfy a somewhat atypical segment of the electorate —the activists in their own party. Positions taken in the spring may have to be moderated after Labor Day, and the risk of well-publicized inconsistency incurred.

Eventually, a great deal of issue material becomes available for electoral consumption in a presidential campaign. A volume put together by the Nixon campaign committee in 1968 listed his views on 227 subjects. After the 1976 election, Carter's White House staff compiled 111 pages of promises, goals, and general principles. Stephen Hess suggests that a sort of Gresham's law may operate, with the peripheral displacing the central, and nothing getting very much attention despite the mass of issue information.[39] However, amidst all the confusion, three recurring features of presidential campaigns have at least the potential of bringing issues to a focus. These are the platforms, the "set speech," and the televised debates.

Party platforms are unfairly maligned rituals that can aid many of the participants in the fall campaign. They are products of the conventions, and they usually reflect the preferences of the chosen candidate. Although convention delegates usually accommodate the nominee's wishes about platform, contentious issues may provoke floor debate or even defection by elements of the party. If participants leave the convention more or less united, the party platform specifies some terms of agreement in ways that are designed to appeal to a majority of voters.

Platforms may be too long to provide a good focus on issues. They may also be silent on difficult matters and expedient in form and intention. They certainly do not achieve enough logical development to destroy the coalitions sponsoring them. However, contrary to general belief, there are usually substantial differences between Republican and Democratic platforms, and anyone bothering to read them can corroborate this for the most recent

[39]Stephen Hess, *The Presidential Campaign*, rev. ed. (Washington, D.C.: The Brookings Institution, 1978), pp. 59–60.

elections. A leading study, moreover, indicates that winners tend to enact much of their party's platform.[40]

The "set speech" is the stump presentation a candidate delivers (with minor variations) at numerous occasions during the campaign. Although it affects the contest in pervasive ways, the media try to avoid reporting it as such, because it quickly ceases to be "new" and therefore a proper element of "the news." Of course, the essence of what a candidate wants to communicate may not consist of logically defended issue positions that one expects to affect government policy in precisely specifiable ways. The candidate may wish to speak in a kind of shorthand ("Don't Let Them Take It Away," "Clean Up the Mess in Washington," "Send Them a Message," "A Government as Good as the People").[41] The set speech may also attempt to set general moods and present the candidate as a certain kind of personality: attractive, accommodating, tough, or whatever.

Televised debates not only dramatize issue positions but can also be a test of intellectual and political skills. The 1976 debates gave both Ford and Carter opportunities to avoid the specific thrust of journalists' questions and present important elements of their set speeches. Since candidates appear jointly, viewers cannot easily avoid exposure to offside propaganda. A ruling of the Federal Communications Commission (FCC) seems to have eliminated most of the legal difficulties that prevented such debates in the past.[42] However, nothing guarantees that such debates will take place, and incumbent candidates are often in a position to decline them. A debate puts candidates at least temporarily on a similar footing, and it is usually to the advantage of the one who is ahead to refuse to debate.

Morton Kondracke argues that the skills required to win television debates are not essential in governing. He believes that the value of debates is exaggerated and endorses John Sears's proposal that each major candidate be given one half hour of prime time per week to speak on subjects of his choice. To have broad appeal, presentations over an eight-week period would have to be interesting and informative; they would also be available for thorough analysis by different kinds of participants and observers.[43]

Strategies

Because of the electoral vote system, presidential candidates naturally try to win particular states that will give them a total of at least 270 electoral votes. Usually this is not too different from getting a strong plurality of the

[40]Gerald Pomper, *Elections in America* (New York: Dodd, Mead & Company, 1975). See also V. O. Key, Jr., *Politics, Parties, and Pressure Groups*, 5th ed. (New York: Thomas Y. Crowell Company, Inc., 1964), pp. 418–422.
[41]Hess, *The Presidential Campaign*, pp. 60–61.
[42]The Commission stated that debates could be exempted from the "equal time" requirements of the U.S. Code (Title 47, Section 315) provided broadcasters determined them to be bona fide news events, provided that there was no evidence of favoritism, and provided that they were covered live (U.S. Code Annotated, Cumulative Annual Pocket Part for Use in 1979, p. 113). Prior to this ruling, the law had been generally understood to require that minor candidates might claim participation rights with major party candidates. The 1960 debates took place because of a special act of Congress for that election only.
[43]Morton Kondracke, "Carter's Debate," *The New Republic*, November 8, 1980, p. 8.

total national vote. However, candidates must pay careful attention to large states where the race is close and where a small shift in support can lose or gain a block of electoral votes. Candidates can shape their itineraries in ways that favor particular states or geographic areas. In the process of doing so, they may display a sensitivity to special groups in pivotal states (grape pickers in California, blacks and Jews in California and New York, auto workers in Michigan, and so forth). Or they may focus on particular local areas: Orange County, Philadelphia, Cook County, or wherever. The home states of the presidential and vice presidential candidates help to focus the ticket's appeal in particular geographic areas.

Elections can be won wherever voters are to be found. In a much discussed work written in 1969, Kevin Phillips saw power shifting from the decaying Northeast to suburbia, the South, and the West. He hoped that the Nixon victory of 1968 represented a new tide in American politics in which plains and mountain states would be joined by the South to become Republican bastions. In his conception, New York, Michigan, and New England would be conceded to the Democrats. Pennsylvania, Maryland, New Jersey, and Delaware together with Kentucky, West Virginia, the Midwest, and the Pacific states would become the critical battlegrounds that could be won by either party. Phillips was, of course, thinking in terms of a viable *party*, not just winning the next presidential election or two. Terrain chosen represented a desire to shift the ideological questions at the pivot points of American politics. An even more influential work by Scammon and Wattenberg spoke of "Quadcali" and argued that the position of maximum campaign advantage is squarely in the middle of the prevailing issue and ideological configuration.[44]

Adding particular groups of voters together to produce victory is usually facilitated by the presence of only two significant candidates. No groups vote solidly for one candidate or the other, and appeals to any group are hazardous if they produce a strong negative reaction from other groups. A coalition of sorts, which can be described as a set of social tendencies, tends to emerge. Ethnicity, religion, economic interest, historical experience, residence, and distinctive local cultures can all figure into the calculations. For example, Phillips based his conclusion about New York and New England on many factors. The region had always been pro-establishment, he noted. In 1968 it was liberal and Democratic; in earlier eras it had been Federalist, anti-Jacksonian, and anti-New Deal. The area was decreasing its share of the total population in each decennial census. In perusing Phillips's analysis of the region we read of all sorts of things: pre–Revolutionary War settlement patterns, the new megalopolis, social cleavages dating from the Civil War, the non-Yankee Northeast, a reinterpretation of the third party system, Catholics, blacks, silk-stocking districts, and much else.[45]

---

[44]Kevin P. Phillips, *The Emerging Republican Majority* (Garden City, N.Y.: Anchor Books, Doubleday & Co., Inc., 1970); Richard M. Scammon and Ben J. Wattenberg, *The Real Majority* (New York: Coward-McCann, Inc., 1970). *Quadcali* is based on a line drawn from Massachusetts to Washington, D.C. to Illinois to Wisconsin with *Cali*fornia added in. Pp. 68–69.

[45]Phillips, *Emerging Majority*, pp. 43–187, 461–474.

Another analyst notes that campaigns rarely articulate their strategies in official form and that they often change as the campaign progresses. To find out about them, one must usually depend on third- or fourth-hand reports.[46] Improvisation probably looms a good deal larger than strategic plans meticulously executed. Candidates react to concurrent events, exploit opportunities, and try for any gains they can realize. Miscalculations play a role: Carter's reference to "lust in my heart" in a 1976 *Playboy* interview, Ford's remarks about Eastern Europe in the second televised debate of that year, and McGovern's seemingly desperate search for an Eagleton replacement in 1972 come to mind. Poll results and crowd counts may be as significant as the moves of the candidates.

Length of the Campaign

The publicized parts of presidential campaigning now begin with the earliest caucuses and primaries. As the preliminary skirmishes have become more visible, participants and public alike have come to feel that the presidential campaign is almost interminable. It is tempting to agree with those who argue that the campaigns should be shortened, either because they exhaust the candidates to no good purpose or because they bore the electorate. However, on this matter there is definitely more than meets the eye.

In the past century and a half, ambitious men have usually begun their search for this office well ahead of the election year for reasons quite natural to the political situation. The preceding midterm election usually marked the time when the search became especially serious, and presidential ambitions often had to progress amidst delicate negotiations among powerful state and local party leaders. The Republic could conceivably revert to semiclosed nominating politics, and this would undoubtedly make the campaigns *seem* shorter. However, such a development appears to be neither likely nor desirable.

In fact, it might be difficult to shorten campaigns without producing undesirable side effects. A national presidential primary would not eliminate the need for preliminaries of some sort, although these might not be as newsworthy as the present state primaries. Reduction of matching funds by the amount a candidate chose to spend before a certain date might give undue advantage to better known candidates or simply lower the visibility of early political moves. Presidential campaigns are long in part because of the fixed term of office, the office's enormous importance, and the relative openness of the contests to persons beyond a small circle of insiders. Almost anyone who seeks the office must work long and hard to succeed.

Stephen Hess suggests that long campaigns are less open to manipulation than short ones and that they help to give underdog candidates time to catch up. If voters rely less on party cues than formerly, events occurring during the campaign may be necessary to help them decide. Beyond this, Hess takes the position that the grueling nature of the campaign is beneficial, even though it is hard on the candidates.

[46]Herbert Asher, *Presidential Elections*, p. 269.

It is exactly because the campaign is both long and arduous that it eventually penetrates into the field of vision of many Americans; the longer a candidate participates in the ordeal, the greater is the likelihood that his character and instincts will be perceived by the electorate.

What Americans have constructed, mostly by accident, is a partial simulation of the presidency.[47]

CAMPAIGNS AND THE POLITICAL ORDER

Electioneering is a necessary part of politics in a democratic society. It not only has symbolic significance, but also inculcates appropriate attitudes on the part of politicians and gives citizens a practical basis on which to decide who should rule. Increasing expenditure of material and psychic resources on the great American bullshine machine may therefore be a sign of health. Taken as a whole, the nation cares about political campaigns, even if it is no longer very much entertained by them and even if it has not succeeded in working out inequities and distortions in a coherent way.

The most serious continuing problems have to do with democratic citizenship, systems of mass communications, lack of competition in many races, and the failure to give nonpresidential races the attention they deserve. None of these matters enters the field of public policy at all easily, although evolving legislation on campaign finance provides some leverage. Most of them reflect partially submerged contradictions between the nation's business and political cultures. The proper role and significance of campaigns for hire, for example, poses a nice question. Do the new politics professionals undermine the democratic civic arena, or will they be coopted by it so as to provide a new and unexpected source of support? Indeed, have they not already rescued it from the incompetent manipulations of the bosses and thus vastly improved it?

Regardless of the answers to these questions, one may well be concerned about how appropriate marketing operations are to democratic political campaigns—even if they do help elect candidates. A wide range of consumer choices is desirable and may be analogous to free political choices in important respects. The democratic process, however, seems to require a sense of obligation, as well as a willingness to assert oneself, to be involved, and to be inconvenienced. These values have little relevance in the marketplace, and we may be losing ground on them in this society. You might want to reflect a bit on Steinberg's statement quoted earlier that campaigns that do not generate news do not deserve coverage.

A clash of values is inherent in the question of whether news dissemination should be regarded as a business, a branch of government, or a part of the educational system. So far, the tilt has been heavily towards news for profit. In addition, questions centering on mass media are complicated by the relative novelty of broadcast technology. Contradictions between capitalism and democracy are at least a hundred years old in this country, but

---

[47]Hess, *The Presidential Campaign,* pp. 47–49; quotation on p. 49.

television as a political force has been with us only thirty years or so. The new communications technology seems to have destabilized American campaign practices and shifted or distorted most of its basic relationships.

Perhaps a new pattern of political campaigning will emerge after the novelties of recent years have had time to be assimilated. If the Republic could somehow evolve strong political parties, it might obtain significant improvements over the present situation. Issues could be simplified and more sharply focused, and campaign financing could be more easily managed. Strong parties could also help contestants in the important but little-publicized races and give citizens enhanced opportunities for meaningful participation. The present situation seems both ambiguous and unstable. There is still great openness to change in our institutional life, and few of the possibilities for the future have been foreclosed. In part, the challenge is one of political imagination: thinking clearly about what kind of political system we want and then going about the business of achieving it.

10

Elections

No other nation holds as many elections as the United States. Indeed, Americans quite possibly do more electing than all the rest of the world put together. According to the most recent tally in 1977, we elect about 490,000 officeholders at all levels of government.[1] (The figure was down by about 20,000 from 1967, but special district offices had increased 27 percent.) Even the scheduling of so many contests is a formidable task, and many states hold elections at least three years out of every four. Furthermore, since it is necessary to select most candidates in primaries, this usually doubles the number of times voters may go to the polls.

POTENTIALS AND LIMITS

Elections require the counting of individual choices in a decisive way, and they make it necessary for office seekers to court popular approval. People who vote are likely to feel that they have been consulted, hence voting tends to promote allegiance to the political system. Yet, somewhat paradoxically, competitive elections encourage criticism of the regime, and perhaps even disaffection from it if favored candidates and programs always lose.

Elections do not perform any of the functions identified in Table 10–1 in an all-encompassing or exclusive way. Even with many elective offices, elections restrict choices to a few contestants for any position and to a few designated times in an ongoing process. Exchange of influence does not control or even reveal all actions of public officials, and there may be some two-way relationships between mass and elite elements even in societies without democratic elections.

[1]U.S. Bureau of the Census, *1977 Census of Governments,* Vol. 1, Number 2, "Popularly Elected Officials," issued October 1979.

247

Table 10–1
Functions of Elections

	For Individual Voters:	For Political Systems:
1. *Choice*	Count individual choices in selecting rulers	Provide succession in leadership
2. *Power*	Provide continuing exchange of influence between voters and office holders	Influence governmental policy decisions[a]
3. *Support*	Promote allegiance to regime	Help secure legitimacy of regime
4. *Opposition*	Encourage criticism of government[b]	Promote limited (constitutional) government[b]
	Encourage disaffection from regime	Permit mass repudiation of regime

[a]Voters sometimes *control* policy decisions through initiative, referendum, recall, and the like. However, these effects are rather limited in scope.
[b]These entries differ from Rose and Mossawir's treatment.
Source: Adapted from Richard Rose and Harve Mossawir, "Voting and Elections: A Functional Analysis," *Political Studies*, 15 (June 1967), 173–179.

The special contribution of democratic elections is that they regularize, protect, and dignify the making of individual political choices. In so doing, they depend upon a fair approximation to a free election ideal in which

1. Votes are equally weighted
2. Voters register their choices secretly, without fear of coercion or reprisal
3. There is accurate registration, counting, and reporting
4. Suffrage is universal
5. Voters are free to know and to discuss, and activists are free to organize and contest
6. Choices are meaningful, and information about them is widely disseminated
7. Losers accept defeat, and winners take temporary control of government
8. Future elections are guaranteed—there are no elections to end elections.[2]

Individual choice is paramount, and other functions listed in Table 10–1 tend to depend on it.

Please note that the exchange of influence between voters and office seekers can be continuous, even though elections only occur at certain times. Officeholders who want to be reelected often make their performance

[2]Adapted with some changes from Austin Ranney, *The Governing of Men,* 4th ed. (Hinsdale, Ill.: The Dryden Press, 1975), pp. 144–147.

in office part of an ongoing campaign in which they try to anticipate future voter reactions. National elections bear upon more than the selection of personnel and policies. Basic political practices and the structure of the regime itself may also be at stake. At an even deeper level there is the political community—that is, the identification of a people who expect to be governed by common institutions.

As noted above, the tendency of elections to both support and oppose political regimes is something of a paradox. But this is essentially a matter of balance. When resistance to government becomes too widespread and too intense, it can tear the political community apart. Yet, a certain amount of opposition is essential to a democratic order. It ensures that support is neither total nor unconditional. Free elections legitimize criticism of government and thus encourage government to be limited while it is obeyed. Opinion polls are an important adjunct to competitive elections and can often transmit more timely and precise information than an election. However, a regime that does not permit electoral contests is rarely interested in polling.

Important as elections can be, there are limits to what we should expect of them. Voters often possess important resources of skill and information, but elections do not call on these in a very efficient manner. A group of a thousand persons selected at random is likely to contain different individuals who can do a number of difficult things well. If it had to, the group could depend on different members who had particular knowledge and skills. Although the group as a whole is anything but "dumb," there are very few things that most or all of the persons in it can do well.

A potentially serious problem with elections is that in any group of one thousand voters, there may be twenty or thirty with outstanding political insight and perhaps a hundred or so who are politically well informed. The remaining individuals are apt to be short on political information and poorly positioned to draw on the resources of the group as a whole when they vote. Democracy ultimately rests on a faith in ordinary people, but it is not necessary to assume that human nature is ideal or that the electorate is omniscient. Successful democracy depends to a significant degree on having satisfactory alternatives on the ballot.

Although elections influence governmental policies, they rarely provide a "mandate" to pursue specific courses of action, and claims to the contrary usually lack substance. American policy in Vietnam between 1964 and 1966 is one of the more arguable instances. Persons opposed to the military escalation in Vietnam often interpreted Lyndon Johnson's landslide victory in 1964 as a mandate for limited involvement. In some cases, the perceived violation of this "mandate" produced bitter disillusionment with electoral politics.

Johnson said little about Vietnam in the 1964 campaign, but despite some ambiguities, the remarks he did make suggested that he intended to stay out of the shooting war. Nevertheless, the 1964 Michigan data indicate that he won the vote of 52 percent of the "hawks" as well as 63 percent of the "doves." Furthermore, the hawks were much more numerous. Even more important, Johnson received most of his support from neither hawks nor doves, but rather from those who chose the option: "Keep our soldiers in Vietnam but try to end the fighting."[3] In 1966 Senator Wayne Morse and others stated that Johnson's expansion of the conflict had been contrary to promises made in the 1964 campaign. However, most of the people who had voted for Johnson did not feel they had been betrayed. In 1966 better than two out of every three who said they had voted for Johnson also said that they approved of his Vietnam policies.[4]

Voting choices reflect party loyalty and personal evaluations of candidates as well as issue concerns. Even if issues were the only criterion for voting, the number of potentially important issue judgments would obscure the meaning of most elections. In the usual case, most voters are not aroused by a single overriding issue. A variety of concerns may mean that the final choice is an overall judgment in which neither candidate obtains 100 percent approval.

However, elections do provide elected officials with a provisional license to govern. As one scholar puts it: "An electoral victory does not commit the politician to the voters' program, but rather serves as a popular endorsement of his policies; the politician offers a proposal, and the electorate approves, condemns, or fails to respond."[5] In this view, initiative remains with those citizens who are politicians. In their control over politicians' jobs, voters possess a final sanction, but they can more easily use it to punish politicians for past actions than to direct their future behavior. The electorate's most effective judgments are retrospective rather than prospective.

That such limits seem to be inescapable is not necessarily bad. Citizens can affect public policy other than by voting. Moreover, important theorists in the liberal tradition have seen dangers in *direct* voter control and found benefits in *indirect* influence. Among those fearing too much direct voter influence were John Stuart Mill, John Locke, and James Madison. Locke thought that the major purpose of elections was to prevent government oppression. Mill voiced a similar thought when he stated that "Men, as well as women, do not need political rights in order that they may govern, but in order that they not be misgoverned."[6]

HOW VOTERS DECIDE

Efforts to understand the decisions of voters begin with an examination of the election returns themselves, especially those that can be broken down by state, county, or even smaller units. People in different social groups tend

---

[3]Eric Goldman, *The Tragedy of Lyndon Johnson* (New York: Alfred A. Knopf, 1969), pp. 234–237; John H. Kessel, *The Goldwater Coalition* (Indianapolis: The Bobbs-Merrill Co., Inc., 1968), p. 290.

[4]Gerald M. Pomper, *Elections in America* (New York: Dodd, Mead & Company, 1975), p. 251. The 1966 evidence is reported in Sidney Verba et al., "Public Opinion and the War in Vietnam," *American Political Science Review*, 61 (June 1967), 319, 325.

[5]Pomper, *Elections in America*, p. 253.

[6]Ibid., Chaps. 2, 10. Pomper adduces Locke's views from passages in *Of Civil Government* (New York: E. P. Dutton, 1943), pp. 187–193. The Mill quotation is from *Considerations on Representative Government* (New York: Liberal Arts Press, 1958), pp. 53–54. Pomper's book is now available in an updated 1980 edition.

to support different candidates, and matching election returns with known characteristics of particular areas can tell one a good deal. In 1978, for example, Chicago's Eleventh Ward returned the city's heaviest Democratic pluralities for the Democratic candidates for senator and governor, Alex Seith and Michael Bakalis. The Eleventh Ward runs north and west from the intersection of Wentworth and West Forty-seventh Street on Chicago's South Side. Its Polish, Irish, Hispanic, and German elements contrast markedly with the Forty-eighth Ward on the northern lakefront where Charles Percy and Frank Thompson obtained pluralities. To take another example, Gerald Ford's vote in 1976 in some of Indiana's rural counties showed the persistence of political traditions that go back to the Civil War. In Dubois and Sullivan counties (which went Democratic in 1860) Ford averaged 44.2 percent of the vote. In Monroe, Lawrence, and Green counties (which supported Lincoln in 1860) Ford averaged 54.8 percent. All of these counties are clustered in the southwestern part of the state, and they strongly resemble each other in their economic and social makeup.[7]

In a presidential election especially, it is helpful to supplement this kind of analysis with data on a representative sample of American voters. Comparing election returns by county, ward, or precinct cannot tell us directly what individual voters were thinking. Another problem known as "the ecological fallacy" can occur when we try to infer the characteristics of individuals from characteristics of an area or group.

Findings from polls and surveys will be subject to error, but the ability to match attitudes and behavior at the personal level will often more than compensate. The potential sources of error in polls and surveys include confidence limits, sampling, response rate, quality of questionnaires and interviews, and the validity of answers given by respondents. Declining response rates have posed serious problems in recent years.

Questionnaires administered to representative samples permit investigators to acquire information about many characteristics of individual voters. These include:

Personal attributes, such as the voter's educational level, age, sex, income, ethnic identity, residence, and occupation

Psychic states, such as degree of trust in government, sense of political efficacy, expectations of the future, and level of happiness

Political perceptions, such as information level, matters seen as major national problems, evaluation of the president's performance, and images of the parties

Preferences, such as positions on issues, ideological labels, and the names of leaders that the voter likes

Loyalties to party, leader, community, family, church, or region

Behavior, such as group membership and participation, campaign activity, political communication within small groups, and media usage

There are few limits on what might be relevant to a person's voting decision, and well-designed questionnaires provide hundreds of items of

[7]John H. Fenton, *Midwest Politics* (New York: Holt, Rinehart & Winston, 1966), pp. 158–159; Richard M. Scammon and Alice V. McGillivray, eds., *America Votes 13* (Washington, D.C.: Congressional Quarterly, 1978), pp. 113, 118–119.

information. Researchers can explore factors distant in time by asking about recollections from childhood. They may explore more immediate influences by obtaining reactions to recent campaign incidents or finding out about earlier voting decisions. Sometimes respondents are reinterviewed one or more times to pinpoint short-run sources of change. Within an acceptable likelihood of error, it is possible to compare the results of large numbers of comparably conducted surveys and in the process to check up on previous findings or get a picture of change in the electorate.

You will recall from Chapter 7 that survey data have yet to yield a satisfactory explanation of why some people vote and others do not. Social scientists have a somewhat better understanding of choices made by those who do vote. The University of Michigan's Survey Research Center has developed the most commonly used approach, and it focuses on three aspects of voter choice: party identification, orientation to issues, and orientation to candidates. Other factors are assumed to affect a voter's decision only if they impinge on his awareness within one or more of these three spheres. The individual voter is making choices, is aware that he is doing so, and can state "reasons." Thus a fifty-eight-year-old widow in Grosse Point, Michigan, would not be likely to say that she voted for Ford in 1976 because she was a northern Protestant who lived in a high-income suburb. However, she might tell the interviewer that she was a Republican and that she thought it was important to keep government spending down. If her age, religion, or residence affected her vote, relationships to her party, issue positions, or candidate preference would have to be present.

Party identification, you will recall, is a person's sense of attachment to a political party. We have seen that it applies to a large proportion of the population, and that it tends to remain stable over long periods. Let me remind you again that party identification is *not* a matter of simply putting a partisan label on the voter's choice. A person who identifies with one party may well vote for the other's party's nominee because of issue or candidate considerations. A fair number of voters do so in every presidential election. Important examples would be Democrats voting for Nixon in 1972 and Republicans voting for Johnson in 1964.

Some political literature may convey an unwarranted sense that party is a disembodied force that operates on people from the outside. The reality is that party attachment lies within individual persons. People develop these and other attachments in the process of becoming human in modern society. Party identifications are seldom the result of purely rational calculation, but neither are many other attachments. To give qualified support to a party out of loyalty to it may in principle be no more irrational than to give similar support to one's church, country, or children.

The importance of party identification in voting is quite easy to understand. Graham Wallas suggested many years ago that people need something that can be loved and trusted and that can be recognized at successive elections as being the same thing that was loved and trusted before. That "something" is party. People pick up their partisan attachments at an early age, find them easy to maintain, and can apply them in many different elections. When many offices are contested, the difficulty of evaluating candidates or issues increases. Party label becomes a "cue" that simplifies the voter's task. In fact, party label is ordinarily the *only* cue available when the act of voting takes place. In the privacy of an American polling booth, voters have only a set of positions, candidates' names, and party labels. The ballot format (or array of offices on machines or other devices) may even present party as the main choice. In recent years party identification explains presidential voting less well than congressional voting—perhaps because the availability of much more information about presidential politics lessens people's need for the party as a cue.

Candidate appraisals can turn on different things. At the most primitive level is simple name recognition. A pleasant manner, an ethnic name, or a conventionally attractive family may attract some voters but not others. Perceptions about the candidate's trustworthiness, intelligence, qualities of judgment, personal magnetism, or leadership ability may be decisive in some instances. In principle it is possible for people to be swayed more by negative than by positive evaluations of a candidate.

There is no set manner in which to ask the questions that determine a respondent's orientation toward the candidates. One very straightforward method is to request that the respondent state in his own words what he likes and dislikes about each of the candidates. Researchers can then code and classify the answers.

Orientation toward candidates provides a natural and plausible basis for explaining vote decisions. For presidential elections at least, voters have enough information to form distinct images of the candidates. It is often tempting to personalize complex problems of modern society, and for many people "voting the man, not the party" is a badge of honor. Here again, it is essential to distinguish voter attitudes from voter choices. The ballot offers choices between parties as well as between candidates. The alternative selected may also reflect the voter's stake in particular issue controversies.

The third domain, issue orientation, can in principle be as important to voters as either of the others. A major contest is apt to have more issues than candidates. The analyst may examine a respondent's orientation to many single issues or to combinations of issues as an ideological patterning. Open-ended questions may reveal concerns that the investigator had not anticipated. Polls and surveys taken over many years show that the issues people think are important can change a good deal. This may be especially true of foreign policy issues since they may touch on matters that are remote from the personal experience of most Americans.

Despite its high prestige, issue voting has its limitations. Some issues are both complex and technical. If voters wish to choose candidates whose issue stands will benefit them personally, they may find it difficult to make the correct determinations. Effective issue voting is more difficult than implementing a party or candidate preference. Candidates may not differ on the issues of immediate concern, or a voter may prefer candidate A's stand on one issue and candidate B's on another. Some office seekers try to be "all things to all men," in effect disguising or ignoring the issue alternatives. Public and media alike tend to perceive many local contests as basically issueless.

The authors of the Survey Research Center's landmark study of the 1956 election suggested that the American voting public did not grasp the logical connections among various issues. They found that less than a fifth used ideological terms such as *liberal* and *conservative,* similar ideas in different words, or other broad organizing concepts. Another 45 percent (in what the authors termed "ideology by proxy") articulated concerns linked to particular groups, such as "big business," "the little man," and "the farmers." Another 23 percent linked evaluations of the parties and candidates to "the nature of the times." For more than 17 percent the authors could find no issue content whatever in the recorded comments.[8]

These findings were consistent with indications from the polls that levels of political information in the mass public tend to be quite modest. The current situation may be somewhat different, but even today as many as half of those polled are not likely to know the name of their congressional representative, know how many senators there are from each state, know the approximate percentage of oil the nation imports from abroad, or know whether the United States is a member of NATO. In 1960 Gallup polls indicated that a majority of the American people did not realize that Kennedy was a Catholic until after he had received the Democratic nomination.[9]

For the person who wants to use his or her vote intelligently, no one of the three domains is necessarily superior to the others. Each can be the basis of a perfunctory or even stupid action at the polls. If one pays little attention to political matters, straight party voting may be the most sensible course. People who cannot think in terms of more than a single issue, or who know little about the candidates, or who evaluate them in ways that have little to do with their character, aims, or qualifications might be well advised to support candidates of the same party for most offices.

Impact of Party Identification

For many years the best election analysis emphasized the impact of party identification on voter choice. In *The American Voter* (1960) this was the variable which gave greatest coherence to the political attitudes of the electorate. Not only did party attachments correlate very strongly with the vote; the authors also found that party attachments had a pronounced, consistent, and systematic impact on assessments of Eisenhower, Stevenson, foreign policy issues, and domestic issues. Citizens who were attentive to, interested in, and informed about politics tended to be party identifiers rather than independents.

The findings suggested that candidate and issue orientations were less important in understanding electoral behavior. For example, the authors of

[8]Angus Campbell, Philip E. Converse, Warren E. Miller, and Donald E. Stokes, *The American Voter* (Chicago: University of Chicago Press, 1976), Chap. 10. This study was originally published in 1960 by John Wiley and Sons. See esp. pp. 234–236, 249. For a different, highly interesting approach to political thinking at the mass level, see Robert E. Lane, *Political Ideology* (New York: The Free Press, Macmillan, Inc., 1962).

[9]James D. Barber, ed., *Race For the Presidency* (Englewood Cliffs, N.J.: Prentice-Hall, Inc., 1978), p. 182.

The American Voter analyzed sixteen different domestic and foreign policy issues. Taken one by one, proportions of people holding an opinion, knowing what the government was doing about the matter, and correctly perceiving the nature of party differences represented by the candidates ranged between 18 percent ("give aid to neutral countries") and 36 percent ("act tough toward Russia and China"). Even these people did not necessarily vote in terms of their issue concerns. They merely constituted the segment in which issue voting *might* have occurred. Many of these persons could well have based their choices on other attitudes. Taken as a whole, the findings did not indicate any coherent patterns of belief. The authors stated that the electorate appeared unable to appraise either the goals of government or the appropriateness of means chosen to serve those goals.

Evaluations of candidates figured much more prominently in the election results in 1956 than in 1952. However, even though the balance of feelings heavily favored Eisenhower in 1956, only a small segment of the electorate had especially strong feelings toward him. Most people acted in ways that were consistent with their party identification, and there were more voters with strong party identifications than with strong candidate preferences. Although it was apparent that candidate appraisal influenced the 1956 outcome, the Michigan researchers thought this was a deviation from the more usual case in which partisan proportions of the vote would reflect levels of party identification in the electorate.[10]

Changing Interpretations

A Michigan survey has been conducted on each successive presidential election since 1956, and resulting data are available to interested scholars for independent analysis. Three major studies based on these materials through 1972 (undertaken prior to 1976) agreed in a general way that party identification had become a less significant determinant of the vote and that ideological or issue voting had become more significant.[11] One or two of these studies pointed to a number of other changes in electoral politics without contradiction from the others. Thus, by 1972 independents were about as well informed as identifiers. Although independents were still less involved in electoral political activity, they were more likely to have opinions and to know candidates' stands on new issues such as legalization of marijuana, law and order, and Vietnam. The studies also found that blacks had become more involved in politics, and a broad racial division had developed in regard to most political attitudes. The influx of new young voters through

[10]This and the preceding two paragraphs draw on Campbell et al., *The American Voter*, pp. 69, 128–132, 139, 182–183, 529–531, 543. For a more detailed summary of *The American Voter* and a useful discussion of its relation to other significant research of the 1950s, see Norman H. Nie, Sidney Verba, and John R. Petrocik, *The Changing American Voter* (Cambridge, Mass.: Harvard University Press, 1976), Chap. 2.

[11]In order of publication, the three studies were Gerald Pomper, *Voters' Choice* (New York: Harper & Row, Publishers, Inc., 1975); Warren E. Miller and Teresa E. Levitin, *Leadership and Change* (Cambridge, Mass.: Winthrop Publishers, Inc., 1976); and Nie, Verba, and Petrocik, *The Changing American Voter.*

"replacement" and through lowering of the voting age had left its mark. Thus 7 percent of the electorate had been 24 or under in 1952; the proportion rose to 15 percent by 1974. New voters contributed significantly to increases in the number of independents, and they accounted for much of the change in positions of key population segments. Thus, northern WASPS had become less Republican and more independent, lower status native white southerners had become less Democratic and more independent. With the exception of blacks, most segments had become less clearly aligned with either party.[12] The studies tended to agree that issues had become more important in voting.

There was no arguing with the fact that larger proportions of the electorate now said they were independent and that fewer were strong party identifiers. However, these studies differed markedly in their appraisal of partisanship in the electorate. In the most emphatic picture of growing party weakness, the study authored by Norman Nie, Sidney Verba, and John Petrocik pointed to a declining correlation between party and vote choice, increases in split-ticket voting, and a growing tendency of partisans to be dissatisfied with their own party. The authors claimed that partisanship was not transferring across generations from parents to children as much as previously, and they cited evidence that party had become less important as a basis for evaluating candidates. Even among people who did identify with a party, relatively fewer mentioned the candidate's party as a reason for liking or disliking him.[13]

The authors drew pessimistic conclusions. They felt that growing party weakness had brought a loss of continuity and predictability to elections, with individual voters evaluating candidates on the basis of short-term forces conveyed by the media. Candidates could no longer be held responsible for what fellow partisans had done in office, and unless an incumbent was running, party weakness meant that people could no longer be retrospective in their voting. The shift towards voting on the basis of issues also suggested a shift towards a prospective rather than retrospective basis for voting. The difficulties of having voters control government through prospective voting were left unstated but clearly implied.

In sharp contrast to this, Gerald Pomper's study claimed that in the previous twenty years or so the Republic had achieved greater political development. Traditional attachments were less likely to determine voters' choices, and the electorate seemed to be capable of changing with times and events. Voters of the 1950s had been largely dependent; now a new "responsive voter" was emerging who no longer gave blind loyalty to the parties. Party ties were becoming significantly related to views on policy issues, and people were more aware of policy differences between the parties. Pomper thought that institutional party weakness was a serious problem, but he viewed the larger scene with considerable optimism. He thought

[12]Pomper, *Voters' Choice,* pp. 28–29, 33–34, 40, 140; Miller and Levitin, *Leadership and Change,* pp. 193–194, 198; Nie, Verba, and Petrocik, *Changing American Voter,* pp. 233, 237, 238.
[13]Nie, Verba, and Petrocik, *Changing American Voter,* pp. 48, 56, 70–71. Information on transmission of party identification across generations was based on questions about the party identification of parents during the years when the respondent was growing up.

that it would be difficult but not impossible to revive the parties as responsive and capable organizations.[14]

The study authored by Warren Miller and Teresa Levitin contended
that the party system was still largely intact, despite unmistakable increases
in issue and candidate voting. In their view, a surprisingly strong tendency
of independents to lean towards one party or the other obscured the impact
of party. Also, ticket splitting was not as persuasive evidence of party weakness as many believed. They pointed out that from the 1950s to the 1970s
the congressional vote had remained close to "normal vote" expectations
—that is, the way people would have voted if party identification was the sole
consideration. They thought it improbable that voters would support their
party's candidate for Congress, then turn to the opposition party's candidate for president in order to split their tickets. In their words: "Much of
the recent increase in ticket splitting reflects choices of specific presidential
candidates that many party members could not support; as such it does not
indicate the weakening of general ties to the political parties."[15]

Despite the obvious importance of candidate evaluations in almost all
elections since 1956, it was difficult to integrate this fact into a satisfactory
theory of voting behavior. After all, partisanship and issue positions could
lend coherence to a voter's choices across many elections. However, researchers had not been able to specify candidate characteristics of enduring
importance to the voters. Miller and Levitin noted that this was the most
variable of the three determinants of voting choice. Although it had often
had much to do with election outcomes, there was a tendency towards
"chaos . . . at the theoretical or conceptual level." Candidate attributes still
tended to be "a catchall category containing whatever seems unrelated to
issues or to party."[16]

The increased importance of issues seemed to be clear. According to
Miller and Levitin, 1972 was the first election in twenty years "in which
survey data showed issues to be the most important determinant of the vote
for a substantial portion of the electorate." They felt that issue polarization
was one of the crucial political facts of the 1970s, and they depicted it in
terms of a clash between "new liberals" and the "silent minority." The latter
term labeled those people (16.7 percent in 1970) in the interviews who were
opposed to protest, who were unequivocally hostile to the counterculture,
whose first priority was to maintain law and order, and who gave more than
average support to the military and the police. (President Nixon had
thought of such views as belonging to the "silent majority," so the term
carried an ironic twist.) "New liberals" (14.3 percent in 1970) was the term
applied to people who took the exact opposite positions on these issues. In
1972 the two groups combined made up about 29 percent of the electorate,
with all other respondents giving mixed answers. New liberals and silent
minority differed hardly at all in party terms, and each included all shades
of the party spectrum. In their vote for president, however, only 57 percent

[14]Pomper, *Voters' Choice*, pp. 215, 223–226.
[15]*Leadership and Change*, p. 226.
[16]Ibid., pp. 44–45.

of the new liberals voted for McGovern, whereas the silent minority over-whelmingly supported Nixon.[17]

1976 and Beyond

The studies just reviewed analyzed American electoral politics from 1964 to 1972. Since equally exhaustive analyses have not appeared for the years since, we must be careful not to let the quality of these analyses obscure the possibility that further important change has taken place. Evidence so far available suggests that party identification continues to play an important role in presidential elections. In 1976 party identification was an especially strong determinant of the vote. If it was not behaving precisely as it ought to have in a technical sense (see footnote 35, page 125), a preliminary report on the 1976 Michigan data nonetheless indicated that party identification was more important than any other factor that impinged on the voters' choices that year. This included evaluation of candidates, the Nixon pardon, political ideology, and reactions to the improved state of the economy.

In 1976, relationships between the vote and most demographic categories (except race) were not very strong. People who did not vote in terms of party seemed to be using ideological labels: 79 percent of self-identified liberals voted for Carter; 80 percent of their conservative counterparts voted for Ford.[18]

In sum, regardless of the state of the parties as organized institutions (and survey data tell us little about that), party is still lending coherence to American voting. At this time, divisive issue positions so evident in 1972 have faded somewhat and change in the direction of factional fluidity (hypothesized in *The Changing American Voter*) are not so readily apparent. Continuity of choices between 1972 and 1976 seems to have been present despite the unprecedented upheavals of the 1968–1974 period, and it also appears in the transition from 1976 to 1980.

As of this writing, reports on the relationship of party to issues or ideology are not available for 1976 or 1980. However, Pomper's notion of the responsive voter remains plausible. Although partisanship was strong in 1976, it does not appear to have been mindless. The choice between Carter and Ford turned on eminently reasonable criteria such as party loyalty, perceived competence of the incumbent, and ideological position. In the early weeks following the 1980 election, political observers tended to perceive the result as a partisan victory for the Republican party, not simply a Reagan triumph. As in 1976, the competence of the incumbent was an issue. Most observers sensed a close connection between Republican victory and a resurgence of political conservatism.

[17]Ibid., pp. 69–70, 82, 86, 90, 127, 230.
[18]Arthur H. Miller, "The Majority Party Reunited?" in *Parties and Elections in an Anti-Party Age,* ed. Jeff Fischel (Bloomington: Indiana University Press, 1978), pp. 133, 137–138. Additional support for the continued importance of party came from a report of a study in which investigators interviewed the same respondents in 1972, 1974, and 1976. See Philip E. Converse and Gregory B. Marks, "Plus ça change . . .: The New CPS Election Study Panel," *American Political Science Review,* 73 (March 1979), 32, 34.

Realignment Possibilities

Realignment is a topic with perennial appeal. Those who are frustrated with the ambiguities of American politics may long for the more clear-cut alternatives they think a realignment would provide. Others see fresh possibilities for displacing the tired controversies of the older politics. One can seldom rule out the possibility of realignment, and this makes the subject a natural one for political columnists and inside dopesters.

When the party system has changed, as in the elections of 1896 and 1932, it has happened in an atmosphere of high risk, intense feeling, and even a sniff of real danger. There may well have been tendencies of this sort in the 1964–1974 period. One scholar, for example, believes that if the Wallace movement had penetrated lower and lower-middle strata to the point where it constituted a quarter or more of the electorate, there would have been a threat of civil war.[19] You will recall from Chapter 5 that basic political changes occur in crisis periods, when a major new issue or issues cut athwart the existing party system.

It is conceivable that political restructuring could now take place in response to new issues. Many activists are dissatisfied with the state of contemporary politics, levels of trust in government are still very low, and the country is having obvious difficulty with problems of global interdependence, energy shortages, unemployment, and inflation. The present scene does not exclude the possibility of a soft shuffle of political forces, or even a sea change.

Popular interest in a new kind of party system may also be greater than usual. According to a Gallup poll conducted sometime between late 1978 and February 1979, more than 40 percent of Americans believe there is a place for a new center party with Republicans representing the conservative right and Democrats the liberal left.[20] The public seems open to change, and in the world we now inhabit, new problems affecting large segments of the population could blow up almost over night. The Wallace campaigns demonstrated that it is by no means impossible for a major leader to get a third party on the ballot in many states, even if minor-party voting and identification has usually been miniscule.

Analysts sometimes base their theories of realignment on a notion of party as a combination of groups in uneasy alliance. If a major group defects from one party to the other, the system is transformed. Recent survey data do not encourage this approach because partisan differences in major population segments have been so small. Class voting has not been very significant in recent years, and political differences between regions have declined. In 1976 Catholic and Protestant voting choices were only 11 percentage points apart.

If electoral politics has become more individualized and if voters are more responsive to issues and events, activists may determine whether

---

[19] Walter Dean Burnham, *Critical Elections and the Mainsprings of American Politics* (New York: W. W. Norton & Co., Inc., 1970), p. 170.
[20] *Family Weekly*, January 28, 1979. Gallup noted that in recent decades the polls have usually indicated that only a small minority is attracted to the prospect of third parties.

realignment will occur. Thus, Tom Hayden has attempted to forge a coalition on the left consisting of people who either encompass the usual group differences or who are a minority in all groups, such as racial minorities, young people, workers, consumers, environmentalists, and the handicapped. Don Rose, an operative who helped put together Mayor Jane Byrne's 1978 victory in Chicago, began working with the Citizens' party in 1979. The group's heroes were Ralph Nader and Barry Commoner, and it attempted to coalesce public interest lobbyists, environmentalists, and disarmament activists for an effort in 1980. This and another new party, the Libertarians, appear to be relaxed and unaccountably cheerful about their prospects.[21]

In the political mainstream a two-party format contains more numerous factions. In addition to five major factions identified by Nelson Polsby (Main Street Republicans, Wall Street Republicans, New Left Democrats, Welfare State Democrats, and Quasi-Populist Democrats), there are undoubtedly many smaller ones (such as traditional Southern Democrats) as well as cross-cutting movements such as feminism, environmentalism, and so forth. He observed that such factions tend to stay within the Democratic and Republican parties because of coalition-forcing aspects of American political institutions.[22] If his view was correct that Jimmy Carter neither belonged to nor was aligned with *any* of these factions, the status quo of the late 1970s may have been somewhat unstable. Different factional combinations could perhaps crystallize at any time. Moreover, large numbers of independents and nonvoters now on the sidelines could be drawn into a realigned system in new and unexpected ways.

One scenario, sketched out in 1973, contemplates an updated and clarified version of the New Deal party system. Issues that cut across party lines (Communism, Vietnam, the social issue, and race) were (except for race) already losing their potency, according to this analyst. Perhaps the next set of dominant issues would center on class conflict and government activism, much as they had in the 1930s. The Democrats could then reassert their claim on those who were relatively deprived and who favored an active government; the GOP could represent those of the opposite persuasion.[23]

The underlying logic for this line of speculation was quite interesting. Much of what had been going on could be interpreted as a delayed reaction to the New Deal. Surveys in 1960 and 1970 indicated that party independence was only on the increase among *white* Americans. Blacks were already largely Democratic by 1960, but in the next ten years they became overwhelmingly so while the proportion of independents dropped. It was possible that many white independents were moving toward the other party. Conservative Southern Democrats, for example, an anomaly in the

[21]Tom Hayden, "The Left-Progressive Coalition," in *Emerging Coalitions in American Politics,* ed. Seymour M. Lipset (San Francisco: Institute for Contemporary Studies, 1978), p. 365; *Newsweek,* September 17, 1979, p. 44.

[22]Nelson W. Polsby, "Coalition and Faction in American Politics: An Institutional View," in Lipset, *Emerging Coalitions,* pp. 110–115.

[23]James L. Sundquist, "Whither the American Party System?" *Political Science Quarterly,* 88 (December 1973), 559–581.

New Deal coalition of the 1930s, began voting for Republican presidential candidates in the 1950s, and by the early 1970s were much more inclined to say they were independent than to say they were Republican. Much of the split-ticket voting and political independence represented the persistence of discordant loyalties at lower levels of the system. However, these were becoming increasingly harmonized as more and more of the states became competitive in presidential politics. Perhaps these thoughts still retain some plausibility. Socioeconomic status was again consistently related to the vote in 1976. If the differences were not nearly as great as in 1960 and earlier, at least the inversion effects of 1972 were absent.[24]

Everett Ladd disagreed. He felt that the country was in a new postindustrial era with correspondingly new social classes and centers of power. New Deal liberalism was no longer contested, but a newer liberalism that supports nontraditional personal values, quality of life concerns, and related issues, had become highly controversial. The forces that produced Carter's victory in 1976 bore only a superficial resemblance to the New Deal coalition. Groups that were repelled by the party's espousal of the new liberalism (such as manual workers, big city dwellers, Catholics) and that had been the bedrock of the New Deal coalition, voted in a manner very similar to the general electorate.[25]

Another view, penned on the eve of the 1980 election, saw portents of change on all sides. Public and experts alike were changing their minds about government activism. Hawkish internationalism was on the rise among the general public, and highly visible liberals were experiencing electoral difficulty. The GOP was coming to be the party of ideas, and its main adherents could even fashion a credible claim that it was becoming the party of the people. Not just Reagan but much of the Republican establishment had moved toward the center. The era of American liberalism was over, and a new parade was marching down Main Street. However, these authors cautioned us not to underestimate the ability of the Democratic party to "steal, swipe, pilfer, and appropriate the ideas of the other party."[26]

NONPRESIDENTIAL RACES

One might suppose that voters would use party cues more extensively in nonpresidential contests, since media provide relatively less information about candidates and issues and since mass interest in other offices is usually not as great. Thus, as we have already noted, the net results of presidential voting deviate from party affiliation more than comparable results of congressional contests. The point is an important one, and it bears repetition.

[24]In 1972, high and middle SES groups voted 32 percent Democratic; middle SES groups voted only 26 percent Democratic. Everett C. Ladd, Jr., "The Shifting Party Coalitions 1932–1976," in Lipset, *Emerging Coalitions*, p. 98.

[25]Ibid., p. 94.

[26]"When you hear Democrats, in private, practicing to say the words 'capital formation,' you know the process is well under way." Richard M. Scammon and Ben J. Wattenberg, "Is It the End of an Era?" *Public Opinion*, October/November 1980, p. 10.

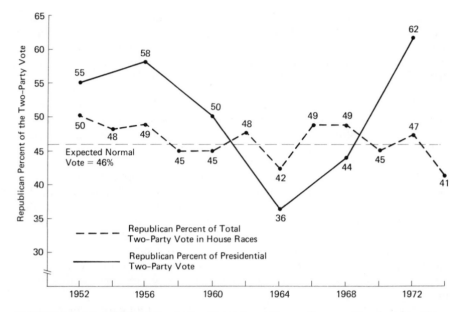

FIGURE 10–1 Republican Vote in Presidential and House Contests Compared to "Normal Vote" Expectations

Source: Warren E. Miller and Teresa E. Levitin, *Leadership and Change* (Cambridge, Mass.: Winthrop Publishers, Inc.), p. 41. Reprinted by permission of Winthrop Publishers, Inc.

Note: The normal vote is simply the vote that would have been cast if party identification were the only political factor relevant to partisan vote choice. Notice that the normal vote is understood to reflect the long-term force of party identification, and that it remains the same from 1952 to 1974. For a further discussion of the concept, see source pp. 37–41.

A careful examination of Figure 10–1 may help to solidify your understanding of the matter.

Survey-based reports on state and local contests are surprisingly scanty, but some informed speculation supports the notion that party identification is especially important at that level. We know, of course, that there is considerable ticket splitting, but we do not know how extensive it is across the entire range of relevant offices. Ticket splitting may well be concentrated among the highly visible contests. One study showed that there was a consistently strong association between party identification and vote for governor and U.S. senator in the Michigan surveys from 1964 to 1970. Another study suggests that party loyalty has a very important impact on state legislative contests. The candidates to these offices are often obscure, and they usually lack the campaign resources needed to make themselves familiar to the voters.[27]

[27]Andrew T. Cowart, "Electoral Choice in the American States," *American Political Science Review,* 67 (September 1973), 843; Malcolm E. Jewell and David M. Olson, *American State Political Parties and Elections* (Homewood, Ill: The Dorsey Press, 1978), p. 252.

262

Nevertheless, there are contrary considerations. Many local elections are nonpartisan. At the very least this means that ballot choices offer no party cue, and it often means a good deal more. The value of incumbency in most lower offices ranges from important to overwhelming. Many Americans move into new communities where partisan affiliations may have unfamiliar connotations. Where constituencies are very small, as they are in more than half of the counties of the United States, it may be easy for contests to be approached in a "friends and neighbors" spirit. Partisanship is weaker in some states (California, for example) than it is in others (such as Massachusetts or Indiana).

A survey taken in 1968 based on a very large sample discovered that, contrary to expectation, the association between party identification and electoral choice was *weaker* for gubernatorial and senate contests than it was for presidential voting in that year. This clashed with the notion that people vote in terms of party affiliation when they are less concerned, or when they lack better information: In 1968 both of these things were more evident at the presidential level. In order to make sense of the findings, the author speculated that "individuals experience a strain toward consistency among attitude elements, and this strain increases with the salience or value placed upon the elements." If this is true, it may be psychologically easier for people to defect from their party at lower levels. He also suggested that many voters may consider party to be a less relevant criterion in state and local politics.[28] Note, however, that 1968 seems to have been a special instance. As you can see from Figure 10–1, 1968 is the only year between 1952 and 1972 in which the presidential vote was very close to normal vote expectations.

Governors

Although party identification plays a substantial role in voters' choices of governors, other factors condition these elections in ways that make them somewhat distinctive. Also, the evident party connection is somewhat puzzling since there are indications of rather drastic declines in the consistency of partisan voting for governor and other major offices. In other words, gubernatorial contests, like their presidential counterparts, are becoming somewhat "office-specific." One can illustrate the point by comparing partisan vote spreads in senatorial and gubernatorial races in recent elections. In 1978, 24 states elected both a senator and a governor. In six states the vote spread was greater than 15 percent, and in five others the spread was from 9 to 14 percent. Ten of the states exhibited split-party victories, with a Democrat winning one office and a Republican the other.[29]

---

[28]The associations referred to were substantial in each case (with correlation coefficients varying between .53 and .73) but slightly and consistently lower in both the Michigan data and the much larger sample on which the major findings of the study were based. Gerald C. Wright, Jr., *Electoral Choice in America* (University of North Carolina at Chapel Hill: Institute for Research in Social Science, 1974), pp. 39, 145–148. The quotation is on page 146.

[29]Jewell and Olson, *American State Political Parties and Elections*, pp. 243–244; *Newsweek*, November 20, 1978, p. 52.

On balance, incumbency seems to help governors who seek reelection, even though it helps them less than congressional candidates. Over time, about two-thirds of the governors who seek reelection win. For a variety of reasons, politicians tend not to make a career of being governor. Twenty-nine or so states either prohibit consecutive reelection or restrict governors to no more than two terms. For politicians in many states, the U.S. Senate offers greater security and national visibility. Positions in the national administration and national judiciary also seem to attract governors.

Incumbency is not an unmixed blessing for those governors who seek to exploit it. As highly visible partisan leaders, they cannot easily avoid controversial policy issues, and, like presidents, they can become scapegoats for general frustrations in the society. Those who are reelected frequently win with smaller margins.[30] In 1978, however, twenty-one incumbent governors tried for reelection and sixteen of them won. None of the five incumbents who lost (Bennett of Kansas, Perpich of Minnesota, Thompson of New Hampshire, Straub of Oregon, and Schreiber of Wisconsin) received less than 45 percent of the vote.

The notion has been widespread that incumbent governors (or their parties) suffer at the polls when they raise taxes. However, evidence presented by Gerald Pomper provides very convincing refutation for the period from 1948 to 1964. He found low and inconsistent relationships in this period between either incumbent party victory or incumbent party vote change and several plausible measures of state tax increase.[31] His analysis emphasizes that, for many reasons, state tax and spending policies are not controlled through state elections, and he cautions against interpreting gubernatorial elections in any single-minded way. Governors must function in a complex federal system, and nationwide trends can affect their electoral prospects.

Congress

Although Congress and presidency are coordinate branches, differences between presidential and congressional elections are so great that they almost belong in separate political universes. Aside from the electoral vote system and the complex nominating procedures, a presidential election is a very simple event. It is a contest between (usually) two major party candidates, which turns on sentiments in the entire nation. The presidency is, of course, different from the person who happens to be president, but everyone understands that the winning candidate will be "in charge" of the presidential institution.

Congressional elections differ in almost every respect. Nomination and election to Congress are quite simple. Except for the few states that have runoff primaries, the candidate simply runs in a single primary; if he gets more votes than anyone else, he receives the nomination. The general election is even simpler and has none of the complications analogous to

[30]James E. Piereson, "Source of Candidate Success in Gubernatorial Elections, 1910–1970," *Journal of Politics*, 39 (November 1977), 943.
[31]*Elections in America* (New York: Dodd, Mead & Company, 1968), pp. 130–133, 146–148.

those produced by the electoral vote system. The task of understanding congressional elections only becomes complex when we try to find out what they mean in terms of institutional power. The effect of an election on the institutional power of the presidency is quite straightforward. However, the impact of elections on Congress is neither obvious nor simple, and patience is necessary to an understanding of it.

The mass public seems to hold contradictory views about Congress. The idea of a coequal legislative branch that ought to "check" presidential power appears to be widely approved. Yet most Americans seem to focus their limited knowledge and concern almost exclusively on their own state or district or on a particular area of public policy. Voters appear uninterested in gaining control over congressional positions with the greatest influence on Congress's institutional power.

A December 1979 mailing to liberals from the Democratic National Committee illustrates the point:

Dear Friend
Does this sound like a bad dream to you?
   Chairman Strom Thurmond of the Senate Judiciary Committee
   Chairman Jesse Helms of the Senate Agriculture Committee
   Chairman Jake Garn of the Senate Banking Committee
   Chairman John Tower of the Senate Armed Services Committee
This bad dream could become a reality in America starting in 1980 and for years to come.
How?
If the Republicans capture control of the United States Senate in next year's election, these men will become Chairmen of their committees.

The letter did not mention that if Democrats maintained control of the Senate, such conservatives as John Stennis, Russell Long, and Lloyd Bentsen would also continue to chair important committees. One could sense, however, that aside from voters in the states these men represented, few voters in the 1980 elections would know or care about these vital aspects of Senate elections.

Elementary knowledge of how power is organized and exercised in Congress appears to be practically nonexistent at the mass level, and the question of how voters might get control of Congress (rather than mere piecemeal representation in it) is hardly ever posed, let alone debated. The public holds Congress in low esteem, yet 90 percent or more of incumbents running for reelection win.

Relating results of congressional elections to realities of congressional power is difficult even for professional observers. There are, after all, 535 elected officials to be considered, and not all of them are elected at the same time. The two chambers operate under different procedures and spawn a large number of powerful but specialized committees. These in turn generate a staggering volume of legislative activity, more or less simultaneously, with effects that may be trivial, obscure, specific to a few interests only, or broadly important to the entire nation.

As you try to understand the realities of congressional elections, keep the political differences between Senate and House in mind. U.S. senators are very important figures. They represent entire states and can be influential at both the national and state level. The Senate must approve all major executive appointments and ratify all treaties. Six-year terms allow senators to pursue individual political interests, and for some this means presidential ambitions. In contrast, most members of the House have little visibility. They serve districts created by state legislators, and these districts are often either removed from or swallowed up by the major metropolitan centers, leaving the representative in something of a political no man's land.

Incumbency advantage. Special features of congressional elections begin with the campaigns. A study made by the division heads of the Democratic and Republican national committees some years ago gives an interesting perspective. The authors were fully aware of incumbency advantages in House elections, and this led them to investigate the motives and operations of those who challenged incumbents.

Using questionnaires mailed under national party committee auspices, they found a number of things. State legislatures constructed districts in a way almost guaranteed to make them safe for many incumbents. National party organizations wrote off most of the challengers as sure losers, and the local parties concerned themselves with other races. As a result nearly three-fourths of the seats went virtually unchallenged. Challengers had to work without a meaningful record of their own and without effective party support against opponents who had better sources of funding and better control over issue agendas. The authors contended that such feeble competition reflected weaknesses of party organization. They urged that state party chairmen or executive directors serve on a full-time basis and that regional party units be formed to service clusters of forty or more districts. They hoped that contests would become more competitive as parties became more evenly balanced in the states and as districts came to be apportioned more equitably.[32]

These hopes have not been realized. In 1978, 95 percent of House incumbents seeking reelection won; in 1962, when Huckshorn and Spencer gathered their data, 93.6 percent won. Furthermore, the proportion of incumbents who won by at least 60 percent was higher in 1978 than at any time since 1956.[33] Despite some evidence of stronger state party organization, incumbent members of Congress maintain more of a lock on their districts than before, and this situation may well persist. Incumbents now have large staffs whose duties, we may properly assume, are in no way permitted to interfere with their employer's re-

[32]Robert J. Huckshorn and Robert C. Spencer, *The Politics of Defeat* (Amherst: University of Massachusetts Press, 1971). The study dealt with the congressional elections of 1962. See especially Chap. 8.

[33]Albert D. Cover and David R. Mayhew, draft of chapter for Lawrence C. Dodd and Bruce I. Oppenheimer, eds. *Congress Reconsidered* (Washington, D.C.: Congressional Quarterly Press, 1981).

election. Furthermore, the separation between presidential and congressional contest results depicted in Figure 10–1 may make it more difficult for lopsided presidential results to disturb incumbency advantages in the future.

Redistricting. Court-mandated redistricting has largely eliminated the marked disparities in population or numbers of voters that once characterized some congressional districts. Nevertheless, some scholars believe that incumbents still gain significant advantages from districting arrangements. Judicial guidelines have permitted states to ignore county lines to meet precise standards of numerical equality among districts. According to one analysis, this has given states greater freedom in their redistricting arrangements, and it has enabled members of Congress and their allies back home to use redistricting for political gain.[34]

Such tendencies are difficult for courts to eliminate, and it is likely that however political boundaries are drawn, they will provide advantages to some groups at the expense of others. Even so, the courts should be able to determine whether districting plans are reasonably fair in *partisan* terms. One scholar urges courts to consider all of a state's districts simultaneously and to specify minimum standards of "responsiveness" and "bias" for the entire set. A "responsive" set of districts is one that enables a party to increase its share of the seats if it obtains a substantial increase in its statewide congressional vote total. An "unbiased" set of districts is one which treats Democrats and Republicans alike. He has developed both of these concepts to the point where he believes they can be reliably measured. His indicators show that there had been a noteworthy decline in responsiveness between 1952 and 1970, and an increase in bias between 1958 and 1970 in House elections.[35]

Other aspects of incumbency advantage. Districting considerations are almost certainly not the only reason for recent increases in incumbency advantage. Cover and Mayhew suggest that declining partisanship has also benefited incumbents. Voters dissatisfied with party cues may be ready to use other kinds of cues. Using survey data from the period of 1958 to 1974 they demonstrate that people who defected from their partisan identification in casting their congressional vote tended to favor the incumbent and that the trend in this direction was increasing. Thus, by 1974, 74 percent of those who identified with one party but voted for the House candidate of the other party had voted for the incumbent, and only 26 percent had voted for the challenger. Comparable figures for 1958 were 57 and 43 percent respectively.[36]

[34]Ibid.

[35]Edward R. Tufte, "The Relationship Between Seats and Votes in Two-Party Systems," *American Political Science Review,* 67 (June 1973), 550, 553–554. Among the more notable treatments of Congress and electoral politics are David R. Mayhew, *Congress: The Electoral Connection* (New Haven, Conn.: Yale University Press, 1975); and Morris P. Fiorina, *Congress: Keystone of the Washington Establishment* (New Haven, Conn.: Yale University Press, 1977).

[36]The comparison only refers to contested elections in which one of the candidates was an incumbent. Chapter by Cover and Mayhew in Dodd and Oppenheimer, *Congress Reconsidered.*

Another possibility is that increasingly complex bureaucratic arrangements encourage representatives to emphasize constituency service rather than policy making. From the constituent's point of view, it is sensible to prefer the incumbent if this is the preferred congressional role, since experience presumably enables a representative to intercede more effectively with the bureaucracy and thus benefit constituents. From the representative's point of view, "The nice thing about casework is that it is mostly profit; one makes many more friends than enemies."[37]

The political consequences of incumbency advantage are most easily understood if one thinks in partisan terms. As incumbency advantage increases, electoral mechanics become less sensitive to changes in partisan vote shares. For example, if in 1978 Republicans had increased their share of the vote by 5 percent in each district, they would have increased their share of the seats by considerably less than 5 percent. The reason is that the *size* of the incumbency advantage is now large enough in most cases to cushion substantial losses of support. Most incumbents have been Democrats in recent years, and the insensitivity of House elections to partisan vote shifts has been a major obstacle to a resurgence of Republican strength. The principle which this illustrates is sometimes referred to as the "Matthew Effect."[38] In the final analysis, incumbency advantage accrues to particular legislators rather than to political parties, and this makes for a more individualistic legislative style.

High rates of reelection mean that membership of the House changes rather slowly, thus fortifying traditions of continuity in House operations. However, incumbents do not always win. From 1956 to 1976, between 86 and 95 percent of House members sought reelection. In each election year, 1 to 3 percent or so of these members did not survive the primary; some of the remainder (3 to 13 percent) lost the general election. Cumulative effects over two or three elections could be substantial. For example, 49 percent of the House membership was different in 1979 from what it had been in 1973.[39]

Senate

Senate elections substantially differ from House elections. Incumbent senators have been somewhat less successful in their bids for reelection: Only 64 to 72 percent of those who survive the primary are reelected. Even so, a senator has only to be elected twice to become a veteran legislator as he approaches a third term. Total turnover between 1973 and 1979 was about the same as in the House.

U.S. senators have been likened to the barons at Runnymede; their electoral contests, accordingly, are often believed to turn on the rather visible personalism of Senate politics. Personalistic or not, however, votes for U.S. senator are closely associated with party identification:

[37]Morris P. Fiorina, "The Case of the Vanishing Marginals: The Bureaucracy Did It," *American Political Science Review*, 71 (March 1977), 177–181.
[38]From the proverb in Matthew 13:12: "For whosoever hath, to him shall be given . . . but whosoever hath not, from him shall be taken away. . . ."
[39]William J. Keefe, *Parties, Politics and Public Policy in America*, 2nd ed. (New York: Holt, Rinehart & Winston, 1976), p. 39. *Newsweek*, November 20, 1978, p. 56.

	Percentage Voting Democratic for U.S. Senator			
	1964	1966	1968	1970
Strong Democrat	90%	92%	90%	98%
Weak Democrat	83	68	75	85
Independent	59	43	44	62
Weak Republican	27	9	21	23
Strong Republican	7	7	9	8

Interpret the upper left entry in this array as follows: Among respondents classified as strong Democrats, who lived in a state in which there was a Senate contest, and who reported their vote for senator in 1964, 90 percent said that they voted for the Democratic candidate. University of Michigan data.

Source: Andrew T. Cowart, "Electoral Choice in the American States," *American Political Science Review*, 67 (September 1973), 843.

Long terms and staggered elections tend to insulate the Senate somewhat from partisan tides. Even if the weaker party enjoys a strong temporary surge of support, it cannot easily obtain control. Thus Republicans in the period 1959 to 1979 only held 32 to 44 seats. Since only a third of the seats come up in any given year, it has been difficult for Republicans to win enough seats to obtain control.

The 1980 election offers an interesting illustration. As the GOP approached 1980, its Senate prospects were better than usual. In late 1979 it appeared that the Carter administration was vulnerable, and conservative groups were targeting a number of liberal Democratic senators for defeat. Democrats held twenty-four of the thirty-four seats to be contested. To get control of the Senate, Republicans would need to accomplish a prodigious political feat, but perhaps they could bring it off. If they could beat off all challengers to the ten seats they had to defend, they would need to win only nine or ten of the twenty-four Democratic seats to control the Senate. Fourteen of these Democratic senators appeared somewhat vulnerable: Mike Gravel of Alaska; Alan Cranston of California; Gary Hart of Colorado; a successor to Senator Abraham Ribicoff of Connecticut; Richard Stone of Florida; Herman Talmadge (or his successor) in Georgia; Frank Church of Idaho; the nominee who would defend retiring Senator Adlai Stevenson's seat in Illinois; Birch Bayh of Indiana; John Culver of Iowa; Russell Long of Louisiana; John Durkin (or his successor) in New Hampshire; George McGovern of South Dakota; and Patrick Leahy of Vermont.

The peculiar rhythms of Senate elections had an important bearing on the situation. Incumbents in the 1980 races had fought their previous battles in 1974—one of the best Democratic years in the entire postwar period. Presumably, some of those 1974 Democratic victors would not have won in a more normal year. Presumably too, Republican senators who survived such a sweep would have good reelection prospects. The rhythm of Senate politics explained why such a large number of the 1980 seats were held by Democrats and why Republicans were more optimistic than usual. It would still be an uphill fight, however. Democratic contestants were already raising a good deal of campaign money in 1979, and it was even possible that the

Democrats would only lose two or three seats.[40] As it turned out, the Republicans achieved a remarkable six seat margin of control in the Senate. A few unexpected victories enabled the GOP to accomplish this feat by taking only eight of the seats listed above. Democrats such as Gary Hart and Alan Cranston, who survived the onslaught, appeared to be well positioned for the future.

The Midterm Battle

There are essentially two types of House elections: those that occur in presidential election years and those held in the "off-year," or "midterm." As you can see from the figure that follows, voter turnout in presidential years is always much higher: The same number of seats is at stake, and the presidential race makes voting somewhat more dramatic and consequential.

With only one exception, in every midterm election since the Civil War the party opposed to the incumbent president has gained seats in the House. The reason for this pattern is not very clear. If voters were basing their choices on qualifications of individuals, the results would hardly have been so consistent in party terms. Perhaps voters consider each party's legislative record and react against the party in power because it has promised too much and delivered too little. However, this explanation seems to exaggerate the degree to which party organizes the perceptions most people hold of the legislative process. For example, a study of the 1958 midterm found that a majority could not even recall which party controlled Congress, let alone specify its major legislative accomplishments.[41]

In the 1950s and 1960s political scientists believed that in the larger presidential-year turnout, partisan political forces would carry some congressional seats that would later be vulnerable. Two years later, the absence

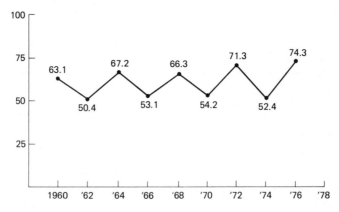

Votes Cast for U.S. Representatives in Millions

[40]Michael Barone, "A Republican Senate?" *The New Republic,* October 13, 1979, pp. 8–12.
[41]Donald E. Stokes and Warren E. Miller, "Party Government and the Saliency of Congress," *Public Opinion Quarterly,* 26 (Winter 1962), 531–546.

of some voters who had helped put the president in office would weaken the presidential party's prospects in these marginal districts. In other words, midterm election results reflected forces at work in the previous election and the decline in turnout two years later.[42]

The tendency today is to see midterm elections as negative referenda on the *president's* performance. Analysts theorize that voters who are dissatisfied with the president tend to express this sentiment by voting against the congressional candidate of the president's party. Even though some voters approve of the president and vote accordingly, the dynamic balance tilts towards negative evaluations rather than positive ones. In other words, the tendency to punish the president for perceived misfortunes seems to outweigh the tendency to reward him for perceived benefits.

Thus, a study using poll data for six midterm elections from 1946 to 1966 found that persons who disapproved of the president's performance were more likely to get to the polls than those who approved. Furthermore, among those who voted, disapprovers were more likely to vote *against* the House candidate of the president's party than approvers were to vote *for* that candidate. A complementary study by Edward Tufte found that the presidential party's total congressional vote share is greater when the economy is doing well or when the president enjoys high popular approval. The number of seats lost depends on the responsiveness of the districting system as well as total vote share. Tufte believes that voters do their best to send a message, but that the message is often poorly reflected in the new distribution of seats.[43] Unfortunately, there seems to have been little research on midterm Senate elections. Since 1932, however, there have been two instances, 1934 and 1962, in which the president's party did not suffer net Senate losses.

It is important not to exaggerate the scope or importance of the newer interpretation of midterm elections. Incumbents still enjoy enormous advantages, and many other factors doubtless contribute to midterm outcomes in particular years or districts. Yet, negative voting at midterm, even if it operates only at the margin, appears to have considerable policy significance. It encourages new thoughts about presidential politics, congressional politics, and the crucial but almost hidden way in which party links the two together.

ELECTIONS AND PUBLIC POLICY

Survey data show that there are a very large number of policy concerns in the electorate. Even when single concerns are combined into categories, the list remains long. In the 1972 Michigan data for example, many of the

[42]V. O. Key, Jr., *Politics, Parties, and Pressure Groups*, 5th ed. (New York: Thomas Y. Crowell Company, 1964), pp. 568–569. See also Angus Campbell, "Voters and Elections," *Journal of Politics*, 26 (November 1964), 745–757.

[43]Samuel Kernell, "Presidential Popularity and Negative Voting," *American Political Science Review*, 71 (March 1977), 44–66. Edward R. Tufte, "Determinants of the Outcomes of Midterm Congressional Elections," *American Political Science Review*, 69 (September 1975), 812–826.

answers could be combined under "law and order" and "Vietnam." However, one tabulation included fifty-six additional response categories, and an office seeker would have been ill-advised to discount their importance. They included school prayer, medical care in general, black civil rights, gun control, taxes, and power of government.[44] Voters could not easily communicate these concerns from the polling booths, and, except in a few states where propositions were on the ballot, electoral choices were limited to selecting *people* for public office. Elections can best communicate policy preferences when strongly held opinions of large numbers of people become focused on one or a few particular concerns.

Policy made in response to elections (or in anticipation of them) is not necessarily elaborate or highly sophisticated. One study notes evidence that government outlays for various services correspond to the election calendar. Thus, monthly totals of government transfer payments including social security, disability insurance, and the like tend to peak in December because of growing population and a larger pool of eligible beneficiaries. However,

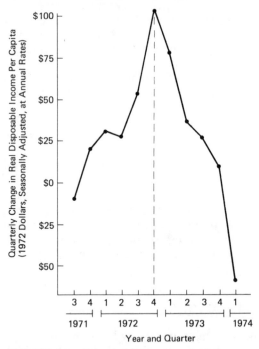

FIGURE 10–2 Quarterly Changes in Real Disposable Income surrounding the 1972 Election

Source: From Edward R. Tufte, *Political Control of the Economy* (© 1978 by Princeton University Press): Figure 2–7, p. 46. Reprinted by permission of Princeton University Press.

---

[44]Robert Weissberg, *Public Opinion and Popular Government* (Englewood Cliffs, N.J.: Prentice-Hall, Inc., 1976), pp. 174–175.

in four of seven even-numbered years between 1962 and 1974, transfer payments peaked in October or November.

Election-year expansion of the American economy even spills over to other nations:

> The growth rates in real GNP in *other* countries are nearly double in the years of U.S. presidential elections compared to years without elections in the U.S. or the country itself. . . . A presidential election in the United States is nearly as effective in producing accelerated economic growth in Canada, France, Germany, Japan, and the United Kingdom as an election in the country itself.[45]

The author of this study presents convincing evidence that electoral calendars in the large capitalist democracies are becoming more synchronized to the political advantage of incumbents in these nations. He speculates that internationalization of the U.S. "electoral economic cycle" may partly explain the appearance of economic interdependence and urges that calendars be desynchronized.

The impact of an election on government policy depends in part on the year and office being contested. Midterm congressional elections, as we have seen, may convey a special message of their own. The extreme situations are represented on the one hand by many minor office contests and on the other by presidential elections in "critical" years. Races for minor office may be devoid of policy significance regardless of when they take place, because official responsibilities are too routine, because the public pays them little heed, or for other reasons. At the other extreme the presidential elections of 1896 and 1932 established new directions in public policy that lasted for decades. The earlier contest settled questions concerning tariffs, the gold standard, and extension of territory in ways that assured an industrial future for the United States. The latter event, as we have seen, brought a new scale of government activity, transformed nation/state relationships, and initiated a new emphasis on social welfare in government policy.[46]

It is too simple to say that in such elections voters communicated specific policy directives to the government. It would be more accurate to regard critical elections as political earthquakes whose shockwaves rearrange the materials of the political universe. Turnout in such elections is unusually high and people develop the feeling that something different needs to be done. A larger than usual number of new faces turn up in positions of congressional leadership, facilitating new courses of governmental action. Social structures and social roles outside of the political arena also change, and the country may enter a new historical era.

It is not necessary to have a realignment in order to get important new legislation, but elections with a major policy impact come somewhat infrequently. The elections of 1912 and 1964 stand in a category by themselves,

---

[45]Edward R. Tufte, *Political Control of the Economy* (Princeton, N.J.: Princeton University Press, 1978), p. 66. The discussion of transfer payments is at p. 39.
[46]David M. Brady, "Critical Elections, Congressional Parties and Clusters of Policy Changes," *British Journal of Political Science*, 8 (January 1978), 79–80.

and neither was a product of a major social crisis. In each case, a temporary change in the partisan balance permitted the advantaged party to enact important new legislation. In a very broad sense, these were electoral accidents caused by problems in the Republican party. In 1912 the party split, and this virtually guaranteed Woodrow Wilson's election. Important legislation that followed included the Federal Reserve Act, the Smith-Lever Act, the Federal Trade Commission Act, and the Clayton Antitrust Act. In 1964 the GOP nominated a candidate with unusually narrow electoral appeal. The result was a large enough influx of Democrats into Congress to permit enactment of many liberal measures.

If we combine these two categories and add the election of 1876, it becomes possible to say that over the past hundred years a national election with especially important policy consequences occurs at intervals varying between sixteen and thirty-two years. Underlying controversies tend to be durable, and contestants fight important skirmishes in intervening years. Thus, a midterm surge in 1946 enabled Republicans to pass the Taft-Hartley Act over President Truman's veto. In 1934, a unique reversal of the midterm election pattern led to the "second new deal." At other times, such as many of the Eisenhower years, an absence of new policy initiatives may have reflected the prevailing public mood.

You should be aware that legislative enactments are not necessarily translated into precisely corresponding results. Policy decisions often fail to achieve the results that supporters desire, and they may even be forgotten entirely. Other policies may be sabotaged in their administrative arrangements or come to grief in their encounters with organized interests. Stated differently, policy "implementation" is not synonymous with policy "determination," and the one does not flow automatically from the other. You should be prepared to discover in particular cases that the political process has produced "policies" that amount to little more than symbolic reassurance that Something Has Been Done. If Murray Edelman is right, this has typically happened with regulatory policy.[47] Other examples are all about us. Every policeman knows the community neither wants nor will permit enforcement of the letter of all laws. Commercial considerations dictate the piecemeal physical development of most communities, even though there is usually something called a "Comprehensive Plan." Political accommodations and special favors soften the contours of many official policies, and not always with ill effect.

In other instances, "policy" flows inexorably into "action." If the Federal Reserve Board raises reserve requirements, banks will sell some assets from their portfolios. If policy makers lower personal income taxes, taxpayers will spend more on cars, cameras, and vacations. If the president orders a military action against some opposing military force, guns will fire real bullets and real people will be killed. Many policies produce tangible (if not precisely measurable) benefits and costs and the relation of such policies to electoral politics is often close. Other examples would be import

[47]Murray Edelman, *The Symbolic Uses of Politics* (Urbana, Ill.: University of Illinois Press, 1967), p. 60.

quotas, agricultural price supports, veterans' bonuses, highway construction grants, gasoline rationing, and rivers and harbors projects.

Electoral Ideals

The policy concerns we have been discussing provide a natural bridge from this chapter to the next. Before moving on, however, let me caution you against judging elections against some inappropriate standard. In its concern with "congruence," some of the recent public opinion literature comes close to doing this. The emphasis is placed on making public policy resemble popular preferences, and the effectiveness of elections tends to be judged in terms of how well elections can communicate public opinion.[48]

Such a conception of the role of elections can easily degenerate into an overly simple theory of issue voting with little place in it for organization, leadership, changing circumstances, pursuit of long-range objectives, persuasion, compromise, or expertness. The question of congruence between mass opinion and public policy is interesting and important, but there are limits on its usefulness as a criterion of public policy.

The proper standard for judging elections should center on getting a government that can deal capably with complex problems in ways that are acceptable to the people and preserve their freedom. Beyond this and just as important, our political ideals should be concerned with healthy relationships among the people themselves. This includes developing political awareness on a broad scale and reinforcing democratic practices of compromise, taking responsibility for one's actions, and respecting other people's rights. Efforts to achieve such ideals are bound to be imperfect in their results. The contribution of elections is identified in the early pages of this chapter; if these ends are achieved, this is quite enough to expect of them.

---

[48]Weissberg, *Public Opinion and Popular Government,* Chap. 8; Norman Luttbeg, *Public Opinion and Public Policy,* rev. ed. (Homewood, Ill.: The Dorsey Press, 1974), pp. 1–10.

11

Partisanship
in Government

The nation's top governmental decision makers operate within the three coordinate "branches" that are supposed to "check" and "balance" each other. The branches can align in various ways. Rivalry, for example, could pit two branches against a third. One branch could well have a greater impact on society than either of the others at any given time. Conflict between two major parties could reinforce these institutional rivalries or, by cutting across branches, defuse or suppress them.

The Constitution does not mention parties, and the tripartite structure partly reflected antiparty intentions. As E. E. Schattschneider put it:

> The authors of the Constitution set up an elaborate division and balance of powers within an intricate governmental structure designed to make parties ineffective. It was hoped that the parties would lose and exhaust themselves in futile attempts to fight their way through the labyrinthine framework of the government, much as an attacking army is expected to spend itself against the defensive works of a fortress.[1]

Describing how the complex of party and government works in practice—or how it ought to work so as to realize specified values—is something like an exercise in geometry, only more tricky. The three branches constitute a policy-making system, with activities of one branch affecting each of the others. Yet attempts to follow main lines of activity often lead into other arenas, such as the bureaucracy or the various units of state and local government.

Many observers have detected tendencies toward deadlock in our con-

[1]E. E. Schattschneider, *Party Government* (New York: Holt, Rinehart & Winston, 1942), p. 7.

276

stitutional setup—with proposed actions stalling out or being postponed or booby trapped in conflicts between branches of government or houses of Congress, or in failing to run the gauntlet that is required for passage. All of this seems as logical as a geometric theorem. Yet, if Martin Shapiro is correct, there is an important countertendency that few have noticed. He argues that the system of checks and balances implies redundancy, because one unit cannot check another unless it can perform some vital functions of the other. He says that this permits each participating agency to meet veto threats from another by moving to perform tasks of the threatener. In the process, politicians may successfully explore alternative avenues or detours, and the scope of government activity can increase.[2]

In recent years people have begun to question earlier notions of how the branches should be related, and many important constitutional issues are open to reexamination. Some of these have an important bearing on the proper role of the parties and the closely associated issues of leadership and popular choice. Partisanship in government is so pervasive that it will undoubtedly continue to affect what our institutions can do and how well they do it.

JUDICIAL PARTISANSHIP

At the state and local level, the judicial function is, more often than not, closely intertwined with partisan politics. Most of these judges are elected in some manner and, like other elected officials, must concern themselves with practical requirements that elections entail. Judges of major state trial courts are frequently among the notables of state politics, even though their participation is usually somewhat circumspect. State judgeships are often an attractive form of patronage to political parties, and judges may themselves dispense extensive patronage in the legal system. Auctioneers, clerks, guardians, receivers, referees, trusteeships, and probate appointments in addition to a wide variety of nonjudicial posts may all be filled by judges. The latter may include boards of education, park commissioners, welfare boards, hospital building authorities, and so forth. Judicial rulings often come into play on such potentially partisan matters as election disputes, zoning challenges, and jurisdictional conflicts between government agencies.[3]

Federal judges, of course, are appointed, not elected, and unless impeached they remain on the bench until they choose to resign. Supreme Court justices produce reasoned positions on issues raised in particular cases. Impartiality is the ideal, and justices are not supposed to represent

[2]Martin Shapiro, "Courts," in *Handbook of Political Science,* ed. Fred I. Greenstein and Nelson W. Polsby (Reading, Mass.: Addison-Wesley Publishing Co., Inc., 1975), V, 345.
[3]Kenneth N. Vines and Herbert Jacob, "State Courts and Public Policy," in *Politics in the American States,* ed. Herbert Jacob and Kenneth N. Vines (Boston: Little, Brown & Company, 1976), p. 250; Hugh A. Bone, *American Politics and the Party System,* 3rd ed. (New York: McGraw-Hill Book Company, 1965), p. 262.

anybody. Necessarily political aspects of their decisions (such as striking compromises with colleagues or rallying support among them for a particular interpretation of law) take place mostly in private sessions. Yet, differences between federal and lower courts should not be overstated. Norms of impartiality are also strong at lower levels, and judicial systems of the nation and the states are interdependent. Governors often appoint lower-level judges when vacancies occur. The style of judicial decision making, with its appearance of passivity and objectivity, its special requirements for access, its specialized procedures, and its focus on particular cases is basically similar at all levels. The national judiciary has always been an important source of patronage, and party leaders have always perceived the federal courts to be a major instrument for exercising control over the substantive content of public policy.[4]

Federal judges cannot escape being political in a broad sense, and the essential work of judging fits all of the usual definitions of politics—"Who gets what, when, how" (Lasswell); "the authoritative allocation of values" (Easton); and "a struggle among actors pursuing conflicting desires on public issues" (Van Dyke). This is true despite all claims and appearances to the contrary and despite the very real presence of other values. As a coordinate branch of government with discretionary powers, a political role for the Supreme Court is inevitable. Yet to say that judging is political is not necessarily to say that it is partisan in the usual sense.

Backgrounds of judges and circumstances that bring particular individuals to the bench are, of course, unmistakably partisan. Candidates for district judgeships receive state and local political clearance, and individual senators often use the privilege of senatorial courtesy to push candidates of their own. Appointments to the Supreme Court rarely cross political lines, and when they do, appointments usually reflect an unmistakable conservative or liberal preference.[5]

Everybody understands and expects that presidents will select persons for the Supreme Court who they hope will be sympathetic to their policy views. Other important criteria are perceived merit and personal friendship, and presidents also take into account traditional political considerations such as race and religion. Although candidates must by common consent be lawyers, no particular kind of prior experience is necessary or desirable, making many kinds of persons available. Justice Felix Frankfurter believed that the essential qualities needed are those of the philosopher, historian, and prophet. He once told an audience that "the correlation between prior judicial experience and fitness for the Supreme Court is zero."[6]

John Schmidhauser's research of some years ago clearly delineated

[4]Glendon Schubert, *Judicial Policy Making* (Glenview, Ill.: Scott, Foresman & Company, 1974), p. 13.

[5]As when President Nixon appointed Lewis Powell and President Wilson appointed Louis Brandeis. According to Glendon Schubert, the only example of a president crossing party *and* ideological lines was President Hoover's appointment of Benjamin Cardozo. *Judicial Policy Making* (Glenview, Ill.: Scott, Foresman & Company, 1974), pp. 13–14.

[6]Henry J. Abraham, *Justices and Presidents* (New York: Oxford University Press, 1974), p. 44.

the political background of all justices up to 1957. One of his findings was that "political participation of a very advanced kind appears as a crucial ingredient in the life careers of all but one of the members of the Supreme Court. . . ." Another was that nearly two-thirds of the justices had been raised in families with consistent and frequently successful records of political involvement. Although presidents had possibly used appointments in a few instances to pay off political debts or to kick bothersome people "upstairs," Schmidhauser believed that "the so-called crasser political motives" had not usually been uppermost. Perceived commitment to the values of the president had been the dominant consideration throughout American history.[7]

One might deduce from these facts that partisanship tends to link the Supreme Court to the Democratic and Republican coalitions in the rest of the society. The idea is not entirely fanciful. The legal profession is a major force in this nation's electoral politics. As persons who have usually held political posts before coming to the Court, it would be strange if Supreme Court justices were not sensitive to the issues of the day and even passionately concerned about some of them. We know that for many people political outlooks and identifications often develop at an early age and resist change later on. We know too that partisan pressures on and in the Court existed in the earliest days of the Republic (witness *Marbury* v. *Madison*!). If you told a person who was unfamiliar with the Court that justices disagree about "political questions," "judicial activism," the commerce power, and the equal protection clause, you could forgive him for supposing that they were embroiled in partisan controversies.

Perhaps there are tendencies towards inclusion of the Supreme Court within the wider associations of national partisanship. However, if this is true, it is not easy to bring the Court into full partisan alignment with the other branches. For one thing, justices sometimes behave in ways quite contrary to the hopes of the president who appointed them. Justice Story's behavior on the Court distressed James Madison, and Oliver Wendell Holmes infuriated Theodore Roosevelt by deciding against the government in the Northern Securities case. Eisenhower was almost as irked with William Brennan's opinions as he was with Earl Warren's.[8] Another consideration is that vacancies on the Court occur infrequently, and at any given time the "partisan" lineup on the Court is likely to be out of phase with the rest of the political system. For example, consider the Supreme Court of January 1981.

The dates of appointment span nineteen years and four presidents. Although the Democrats were the majority party in the country throughout the period, justices appointed by Republicans outnumbered those appointed by Democrats by better than four to one. Today's Court is probably not as liberal as it was under Chief Justice Earl Warren, but the seven justices appointed by Republican presidents cover a wide spectrum. In one version,

[7]John R. Schmidhauser, "The Justices of the Supreme Court: A Collective Portrait," *Midwest Journal of Political Science*, 3 (February 1959), 13, 35–36.
[8]Abraham, *Justices and Presidents*, pp. 62–63; 245–246.

Table 11-1
Supreme Court Justices as of January 1981

	Circumstances of Appointment		
	Year	President	Inferred Political Intention
John Paul Stevens	1975	Ford	Conservative
Wm. H. Rehnquist	1971	Nixon	Conservative
Lewis Powell	1971	Nixon	Conservative
Warren Burger	1970	Nixon	Conservative
Harry Blackmun	1970	Nixon	Conservative
Thurgood Marshall	1967	Johnson	Liberal
Byron White	1962	Kennedy	Liberal
Potter Stewart	1958	Eisenhower	Conservative
William Brennan	1956	Eisenhower	Conservative

Note: "Inferred political intention" merely registers the assumption that Democratic presidents want liberal justices, while Republican presidents want conservative ones. The categories are crude, and in two or three cases, the term "moderate" might be more appropriate. Other justices appointed after 1955 were Charles Whittaker (1957–1962), Arthur Goldberg (1962–1965), and Abe Fortas (1965–1969).

Brennan occupies the liberal end (along with Marshall) while Burger and Rehnquist defend the Court's conservative extreme. The other justices tend to provide swing votes that vary between the two. "Party cohesion" appears to be low; for example, in the 1977–1978 term, the four Nixon appointees voted together only 36 percent of the time.[9]

It would be unrealistic to expect the Supreme Court to clash with dominant political outlooks in the nation for very long. In an influential analysis published some years ago, Robert Dahl put the matter more sharply. He argued that the Court was usually an element in the leadership of the "dominant alliance" and that it supported the major policies of that alliance. Exceptions were the short-lived transitional periods between old and new alliance systems.[10] One indication of this was that the Court had not often overturned federal legislation in order to help minorities against overbearing majorities. A more recent analysis seems to confirm the main thrust of his analysis and to press it somewhat closer to the ebb and flow of the electoral cycle. Its author believes that the Court's most notable collisions with elected branches have occurred during periods of partisan realignment. Realignment periods bring in new legislative majorities. The Court comes to reflect the new majority after presidential appointments change its composition. In this sense the Supreme Court can be regarded as following the election returns.[11]

[9]Sandra Stencel, "Burger Court's Tenth Year," *Editorial Research Reports*, September 22, 1978, p. 685.
[10]Robert Dahl, "Decision-Making in a Democracy: The Supreme Court as a National Policy Maker," *Journal of Public Law*, 6 (1957), 279–295.
[11]Richard Funston, "The Supreme Court and Critical Elections," *American Political Science Review*, 69 (September 1975), 796, 803.

Although the present Supreme Court has a rather different partisan cast than the other branches, it does not appear to be markedly out of step with the rest of the political system. Even so, it would take heroic efforts to locate the 1980 Court in the New Deal coalition. Not only is its partisan makeup discordant with such a notion, but the Court has also departed from the rather passive role envisioned for it in New Deal thinking. In its stands on some controversial issues (desegregation, pornography, abortion, and so forth), the Court might be considered a bastion of establishment liberalism, but if this is so, the intentions of appointing presidents have in most cases come to naught. Shapiro believes that such decisions represent a response to changing standards of enlightened opinion in the society and that the Court is not acting directly in an election-oriented way, even if its actions are consistent with electoral trends.[12]

THE EXECUTIVE BRANCH

The executive branch of the United States government extends from the one individual who is vested with all of "the executive power" in Article II, Section 1, of the Constitution, to the 2.9 million civilians in departments, agencies, boards, committees and commissions who constitute more than 99.8 percent of the federal government. Executive branch outlays in 1977 constituted all but 0.003 percent of total federal outlays and all but 0.018 percent of total federal civilian employment. In addition there were two million or so other persons in the armed services.[13] The executive branch is diverse in its aims, activities, and talents; untidy in its organizational contours; variously peculiar in its constitutional position; and not easily comprehended by looking at successive slices from the top down—or indeed in any other way. It is wise to examine it from different perspectives. Ideals of legal accountability, group and national interest, administrative policy making, the art of getting things done, and notions of political responsibility are some of the more important ones.

The executive branch reflects the impact of persistent antiparty outlooks in American society as well as the growing weakness of party organizations.[14] Even so, the partisan political perspective is still a useful approach to the executive branch as a whole. Even in the many areas where partisanship does not extend, like the dog in the night-time, its absence is an important clue to what is happening.[15]

[12]Martin Shapiro, "The Supreme Court: From Warren to Burger," in *The New American Political System,* ed. Anthony King (Washington, D.C.: American Enterprise Institute for Public Policy Research, 1978), pp. 179–211.

[13]Employee counts do not include consultants, contractors, universities, local units, and other middlemen involved in delivery of federal programs. U.S. Bureau of the Census, *Statistical Abstract of the United States,* 1978, pp. 263, 278.

[14]Joyce Gelb and Marian Lief Palley, *Tradition and Change in American Party Politics* (New York: Thomas Y. Crowell Company, Inc., 1975), p. 263. See also their excellent discussion of antipartyism in the American political culture, pp. 7–19.

[15]"Is there any point to which you would wish to draw my attention?" [asked Inspector Gregory] "To the curious incident of the dog in the night-time." "The dog did nothing in the night-time." "That was the curious incident," remarked Sherlock Holmes (Arthur Conan Doyle, "Silver Blaze").

The president is, of course, the central protagonist in the executive branch. In a widely respected book first published in 1956, Clinton Rossiter confidently proclaimed that the presidency was "one of the few truly successful institutions created by men in their endless quest for the blessings of free government." Twenty years later, when the ravages of Vietnam and Watergate were still fresh in everybody's mind, Richard Neustadt maintained that the Johnson and Nixon years had only dented the office and that the presidency had even gained some net advantages of influence over time.[16] It is perhaps too early to say whether Neustadt was right. What is striking, however, is how great is the presidency's loss of the aura of assured success. Today, Rossiter's praises seem extravagant. Textbooks still say that the president is chief of state, chief legislator, chief administrator, and chief of a lot of other things, but we seem to have our fingers crossed.

That it should be so is perhaps inevitable after the tribulations of the 1960s and early 1970s. However, the situation reflects deeper factors. Rossiter's formidable mentor, Edward S. Corwin, was much less enthusiastic about the presidency. For him, the president as "boss of the works" had no convincing connection with reality; the presidency was a potent manifestation of majority-rule democracy, but it was "dangerously *personalized*" in two respects:

> . . . first, that the leadership that it affords was dependent altogether on the accident of personality, against which our haphazard method of selecting Presidents offers no guarantee; and secondly, that there is no governmental body that could be relied on to give the President independent advice and that he was nevertheless bound to consult.[17]

Each of these dangers seems more serious today. Everett Ladd is not exaggerating by much when he describes presidential nominee selection as "flea-market politics" or a system of "chaotic individualism."[18] The number of persons who can conceivably enter what we have termed the "availability pool" for the presidential nomination is probably larger than when Corwin wrote, and success in getting a nomination probably depends to a greater degree on luck and self-promotion.

Vice presidents have risen to the office of president with disturbing frequency, even though their initial selection has usually been cursory and lacking in systematic input from many sectors of the party. The problem is not merely that vice presidents accede to the office when presidents suffer mishap (Harry Truman, Lyndon Johnson, Gerald Ford). Vice presidents also can press strong claims to a party nomination when the incumbent

---

[16]Clinton Rossiter, *The American Presidency,* rev. ed. (New York: Harcourt Brace Jovanovich, Inc., 1960), p. 15; Richard Neustadt, *Presidential Power* (New York: John Wiley & Sons, Inc., 1976), pp. 22, 61.

[17]Edward S. Corwin, *The President: Office and Powers 1787–1957* (New York: New York University Press, 1957), p. 312. Emphasis in original. The identical words appeared in the work's first (1940) edition.

[18]Everett Carll Ladd, Jr., *Where Have All the Voters Gone?* (New York: W. W. Norton & Co., Inc., 1978), p. 69.

finishes a second term (Nixon). Since the president is paired with the vice president on the ballot, the electorate cannot register separate verdicts for each. None of the four individuals named in this paragraph (except possibly Nixon) could have received a presidential nomination if he had not been vice president, and all became vice president for reasons that had little to do with their qualifications to serve in the nation's highest office. In thinking about the dangers of the vice presidency, the reader should also reflect on the Eagleton and Agnew sagas. Agnew was well on his way to an eventual Republican nomination when scandal destroyed his career.

With respect to Corwin's second aspect of presidential personalism, Neustadt tells us that in Truman's time, members of Congress and other high officials could expect to see the president for fifteen minutes or so on one or two days' notice. Eisenhower broke this tradition, and the breach continued under Kennedy and Johnson. Neustadt believes that their freedom to choose whom they would see paved the way for the reclusiveness of the Nixon administration, and he comments, "A generation ago, Nixon's practice would have seemed almost an abdication, and Ford's a grudging restoration. Now they are considered matters of style, and the next man can do as he likes."[19]

Neustadt believes that White House staffers have tended to be courtiers ever since Herbert Hoover. However, the "White House" as a pseudosovereign entity did not materialize until the 1960s when the inclinations of its occupants were given an important assist from the media. The monarchical atmosphere that some discerned during the Johnson and Nixon years seems to have dissipated with Ford and Carter, but there is still no reliably independent and reliably obligatory advice available to presidents. The smoothness of White House machinery may produce more serious temptations than staff flattery. Neustadt says it encourages self-indulgence and allows our chief executives to rise above "the courtesies and duties of American public life as practiced by most politicians including previous presidents."[20]

The cabinet as a consultative organ is probably no more clumsy or inconvenient than it always has been. However, the lessened ability of most agency heads to get access to the president, at its most conspicuous during the Nixon and Johnson years, seems to have persisted under Ford and Carter, with little public comment by participants or media.

Partisanship strongly affects the provision of "independent advice" that the president is "bound to consult." In a healthy two-party system, the president would be expected to consult regularly with congressional leaders and major notables of his party. These persons would not have unlimited access to the president, and he would not have to follow their advice;

---

[19]Neustadt, *Presidential Power*, p. 13.

[20]White House food was notoriously bad in the Roosevelt years, but by the time of Johnson and Nixon everything from air conditioning to helicopters was "at hand and in order." Ibid., p. 28. For broadly corroborative thoughts on monarchical tendencies in the presidency, see Philip B. Kurland, *Watergate and the Constitution* (Chicago: University of Chicago Press, 1978); and George E. Reedy, *The Twilight of the Presidency* (New York: William Collins, World Publishing Co., Inc., 1970).

however, they would not tolerate the imposition of people who could deny access, and they would have to be consulted on important policy matters as well as on personnel. In a weak two-party system such as we have today, the president sees only those he wishes to see. Party weakness lessens the political value of partisan consultation because party leaders cannot deliver support in exchange for having their advice carefully considered; that is, they are much less able to help the president get reelected, get his choice of a successor nominee named by the convention, or get his program through Congress.

Many thoughtful persons have wrestled with the problem. Corwin proposed that the president "constitute his Cabinet from a joint Legislative Council to be created by the two houses of Congress and to contain its leading members."[21] A basic difficulty with providing any kind of reliable advice is that it carries a potential danger of intruding on the president's proper discretion. For example, Stephen Hess has pressed for a markedly different cabinet under the slogan of "a more collegial presidency." He believes that modern presidents have been mistaken in their attempts to make themselves chief manager of the federal government and wants to see reversed what he concedes is a forty-year trend. His goal is a setup in which presidents would have to rely on department and agency heads for management and major advice. Such ideas conflict with optimistic assessments of the presidency in the conventional wisdom of yesteryear. If Hess is right, we will need to rethink the nature of the president's prerogative in a fundamental way. We will also have to discover some way to get presidential assent to the kind of cabinet that Hess proposes. Hess's modified cabinet would be strictly limited in size, would accurately reflect the power base in the executive branch, would meet frequently on a regular schedule, and would be the focal point of the White House machinery. Cabinet members, not White House aides, would speak for the administration.[22]

Elements of Presidential Partisanship

The president is the only public official other than the vice president with a national constituency. Since the office enjoys greater power and prestige than any other, and since partisan arrangements largely control which office seekers will have a chance to be elected president, it is natural for political activists and general public alike to think of the president as chief of the party. Arthur Holcombe said many years ago that presidents who tried to govern without benefit of any organized partisan support never succeeded well enough to inspire imitation.[23]

In the sweep of American history, the presidency and the two-party system have complemented each other. If the parties had not transformed

[21]Corwin, *The President*, p. 297. Since the cabinet is an extraconstitutional body, a constitutional amendment would not be required.

[22]Hess is not arguing that his proposals be somehow imposed on unwilling presidents. He merely wishes to support presidents who are sympathetic with his aims. Stephen Hess, *Organizing the Presidency* (Washington, D.C.: The Brookings Institution, 1976), p. 10, Chap. 11, and p. 218.

[23]Arthur N. Holcombe, "Presidential Leadership and the Party System," *Yale Review*, 43 (1954), 321–335; Rossiter, *The American Presidency*, p. 31.

the electoral vote system, it is possible that the office would not have emerged in its present form. Similarly, without the presidential office, it would have been difficult for parties to become national in scope. The only national party organs of note have been the conventions and the national committees. Our parties created these devices in order to nominate presidents and to coordinate presidential campaigns, and they have never gone very much beyond that.

The president's standing as party leader is especially clear in relationship to the national committee chair. The president selects this individual, who serves at the president's pleasure, despite formal appointment by the national committee. The situation in the other party is comparable. A nominee who loses the race for the presidency may remain as titular party leader, but with poor chances of being renominated. As election year approaches, claims of competing leaders become more insistent until the convention again decides. At this point defeated rivals are expected to rally around the nominee before the television cameras. One or more individuals will have chaired the national party throughout this sequence, but nobody will have mistaken this person for leader of the party.

A practical aspect of presidential leadership is the president's apparent ability to affect other election outcomes. Although direct intervention is notoriously unsuccessful, the electoral fortunes of a presidential candidate often correlate with those of other office seekers in the party. Most people think of this as "coattails effect"—one of those notions that seems perfectly clear until one reads some of the crucial literature.[24] The subject is in fact rather quirky—loaded with pitfalls for the unwary. Warren Miller points out, for example, that to measure presidential coattail influence by excess of a presidential candidate's vote over the congressional votes for his party is to make it paradoxically dependent on his failure to exert that influence. In other words, the usual *indicator* of coattail influence may actually measure the candidate's *lack* of influence. Coattails influence, of course, implies substantial partisan consistency in voting, as well as movement toward or away from a party's candidates. However, these things do not depend on coattails. That people think they do reflects the general American tendency to underestimate and devalue political parties.

Partisan sweeps do sometimes occur, but the precise nature of these events remains unclear. One may feel confident about coattails in a particular election (such as Lyndon Johnson's apparent pulling power in 1964), yet wonder why it is lacking in another year (such as Nixon's inability to help other Republicans in 1972). In both cases, the opposing presidential candidate was especially vulnerable. However, an alternative view would be that coattails influence is not nearly as pronounced in the *weaker* party.[25] It is hard to imagine a more irresistible candidate than Eisenhower, but he did not bring conspicuous electoral success to office seekers of the weaker party.

[24]A good introduction is Warren Miller's, "Presidential Coattails: A Study in Political Myth and Methodology," *Public Opinion Quarterly*, 19 (1955–1956), 26–39.
[25]Frank J. Sorauf, *Party Politics in America*, 3rd ed. (Boston: Little, Brown & Company, 1976), p. 369.

When truly important party shifts occur, as during critical elections, explanations in terms of coattails are particularly unsatisfactory. (Consider, for example, the flow of power toward the Democrats from 1928 to 1936, described in Chapter 3. For yet another angle of vision, look again at Figure 10–1.)

If coattail effect is mostly a myth, it is an important one for presidential leadership. If office seekers of his party perceive that their electoral fortunes are linked to the president's, they will presumably be more likely to support him. Persistent split-ticket voting could conceivably shatter the myth and turn the president's role as party leader into an empty formality.

Legislative Leadership

The president's role as party leader is entirely extraconstitutional. However, the requirement that he be "chief legislator" is firmly grounded in the letter of the Constitution, in practical realities of modern government, and in the way Congress has chosen to organize its activities. Even so, Congress is rarely eager to submit to presidential leadership. Antipresidential instincts are part of the congressional ethos, and they run strong even in the president's own party. That Congress is the most powerful legislative body in the world results partly from its considerable success in resisting even strong presidents.

V. O. Key noted many years ago that Congress tends to be the bulwark of particular interests. He believed that it tended to resist actions in the general interest and agreed with Henry Jones Ford that American democracy instinctively resorts to executive power as the historic agency for removing public authority from the control of particular interests.[26] Congressional arrangements normally make it difficult to pass controversial legislation or legislation with no persistent group support. Party support for a president's program can override such obstacles if the president's party controls Congress.

Some of President Carter's first term difficulties resulted from low levels of support for his programs by congressional Democrats. *Congressional Quarterly*'s analyses indicated that Carter's success rate in his first two years was only comparable to Nixon's despite the fact that Democrats controlled Congress in each case. The Senate backed Carter on 84.8 percent of selected measures; the House on 69.4 percent. It is not clear how many of his proposals required action by both houses, but presumably his overall success rate was lower than either of these figures. As usual, support of the president was strongly related to party.[27]

Presidential "batting averages" should be accepted with skepticism because they require difficult judgments about what votes to include and because presidents can improve their scores by not pressing for difficult measures. Carter's legislative initiatives in energy, strategic arms limitation,

[26]V. O. Key, Jr., *Politics, Parties, and Pressure Groups*, 5th ed. (New York: Thomas Y. Crowell Company, Inc., 1964), p. 661.
[27]*Congressional Quarterly Weekly Report*, December 9, 1978, pp. 3407–3408.

hospital cost containment, tax reform, and other areas met considerable resistance in Congress. Although this may have reflected weakened party ties, other factors should also be considered. Carter's legislative liaison operation seems to have been ineffective until at least mid-1978. Two of Carter's most important items were treaties requiring the support of two-thirds of the Senate for ratification. The greater staff resources available to individual legislators enabled them to compete with the executive branch on more even terms in matters requiring technically proficient policy analysis. The increasing safety of incumbents, dissensus in American society, and a drift towards unusually decentralized legislative practices could also have been factors.

Party and Administration

In the final edition of his text on political parties, V. O. Key was able to argue that a victorious party was responsible for controlling and directing the federal bureaucracy. He did not have a rigid kind of party control in mind. Rather, he saw a place for administrative initiatives if they did not "run counter to the dominant inclinations of the party in power." He did not see partisan control as a simple matter of commands issuing from political superiors to bureaucratic subordinates. Good results would require a collaboration between permanent staff and skillful administrative politicians. The interests of particular agencies usually catered to particular clienteles. Although it would be difficult to bring these into accord with a "party program dedicated to the general welfare," a small number of presidential appointees presumably had a realistic chance to guide the machinery of government in a way that fulfilled the party's responsibility to the electorate.[28] Today, partisan control of administration is a less tangible prospect. "The party" is more of a symbol, complexities have escalated, and the president is more distant from domestic program administration.

The president's increased isolation from the rest of government is apparent from the institutional development of White House staff and the related inability of agency heads to obtain reliable access. Foreign policy crises also help explain presidential isolation. Military and foreign policy agencies are in a clearer line of presidential control than many of the agencies that deal with domestic programs. Since the position of the United States in world affairs is both dangerous and declining (not necessarily in relation to the Soviets or any other particular nation), foreign crises naturally rank high on any president's list of priorities.[29]

Nor should one forget the president's uncomfortable personal responsibility (greater than anyone else's) to decide about the launching of nuclear

[28]Key, *Politics, Parties, and Pressure Groups,* Chap. 25, "Administration and Politics." The notion of partisan responsibility for administration is a major theme of this chapter. See pp. 690, 691, 696, 699, 711, 717.

[29]The appearance of statesmanlike actions also tends to boost the president's popular standing. Witness Nixon's reluctance to terminate the Brezhnev visit in 1973 and Carter's exuberance after the Camp David agreements between Egypt and Israel.

missiles. The unmistakable capacity of the Soviets and this country to inflict *mutually* unacceptable damage on each other ("irreversability become irreparable" in Neustadt's words) only dates from the late 1960s. Its ability to isolate presidents "in heart and mind" may have taken some years to sink in.[30]

One aspect of declining partisanship is the increasing proportion of federal administrative positions that are under general or special merit systems—by 1950 the proportion was better than 85 percent of all civilian employment, and by 1975 it stood at about 90 percent. Abraham Lincoln had much more patronage at his disposal in 1861 than Ford or Carter in the 1970s, even though the federal establishment was seventy-seven times larger by 1975.

At present, the largest proportion of persons exempted from any merit system (about 281,000 in 1975) are foreign nationals and American teachers working at bases and embassies abroad. Attorneys in all departments and a variety of other miscellaneous positions are also exempt. Although one cannot rule out patronage and favoritism, it is safe to assume that most of these positions are not available to presidents as patronage. Positions of greatest concern to the president in 1975–1976 were the 3,773 noncareer positions that the personnel agencies classified as political, excepted, or noncareer. Of this number, 2,453 were in the supergrades (GS–16 to GS–18) or higher.[31]

As government has become more complex, objectives emphasized in presidential appointments have also changed. The post office closed up shop as an engine of patronage in the late 1960s, and the postmaster general's cabinet-level patronage role disappeared. Federal appointments offered as reward for party and electoral support have declined in importance, amidst rising concern for program support, managerial skill, and personal compatibility with the president. Processes at work here have, of course, been going on for a long time. Expansion and modernization of government means that sophisticated talents in sciences, health, finance, legal affairs, engineering, contract work, intergovernmental relations, and other specialized fields are needed. The gap between modern personnel requirements and resources available to party organizations has grown. The parties have lagged in developing new skills—even those necessary to the winning of modern elections. In the public image (and to some extent in reality), party organizations have increasingly stood for bossism, amateurism, and parochialism.

Given the persistent underestimation of party in American outlooks, one must be careful not to overstate these points. Some of the nation's

---

[30]In explaining "irreversibility become irreparable," Neustadt says: "By this I meant not only that some choices were beyond recall once made—an old dimension—but worse, that nothing later could ward off, reduce, repair, or compensate for costs to one's society." *Presidential Power*, p. 26.

[31]Hugh Heclo, *A Government of Strangers* (Washington, D.C.: The Brookings Institution, 1977), p. 38. Other numbers in this paragraph are from O. Glenn Stahl, *Public Personnel Administration*, 7th ed. (New York: Harper & Row, Publishers, Inc., 1976), p. 48. Data on federal employment in 1861 are from U.S. Census, *Historical Statistics of the United States* (Washington, D.C.: 1975), Part 2, p. 1103.

technological capacities and needs appear to be matters of inflated labeling. Traditional political practices may have continued to a greater degree than commonly recognized. Old ethnic concerns may have been decked out in new political attire, and modern presidents may apply partisan criteria with more finesse. John F. Kennedy, for example, told the people responsible for seeking top-level talent that he wanted the best people they could find.[32] However, Arthur Schlesinger's account attests to the importance of partisan or pseudopartisan considerations of deciding who the "best fellow" was. These included conservative versus liberal outlooks, capacity to deal with a Congress narrowly controlled by Democrats, geographic balance, past record of partisan activity, and current position in the Democratic party.

A comparable account of staffing the Carter presidency is not yet available, but the intentions and results may not have been too different. Although Kennedy had deliberately gone outside normal political channels in his recruiting, Carter went even further in this direction, setting up panels of mostly nonpartisan evaluators. According to Heclo, "these supposedly objective efforts produced a few obvious choices and a host of chancy compromises as their goals became blurred under personal, political, and interest group pressures."[33]

By the late 1970s the ideal of coherent management of the federal bureaucracy in accord with general rather than particular interests seemed more distant than ever. In its concern with obtaining tight White House control, the Nixon administration seemed to have discredited major executive branch studies going back to the Brownlow Commission of 1937. In Neustadt's account, the Nixon men did this in part out of political ignorance and a failure to understand basic elements of Rooseveltian practice (as opposed to Rooseveltian rhetoric), including the distinctions between White House and Executive Office of the President, and between president and executive branch.

> They thought the Constitution's "take care" clause made him a general manager as though ours were a unitary government with powers hierarchical, not shared. . . . Nixon's men thought they were carrying on and tidying up what Democrats did badly but had always meant to do.[34]

If we are to give up on having the president manage the executive branch, one may wonder whether some other instrumentality will accomplish this.[35] The luxuriant complexity of today's bureaucracy makes this problematic. One possibility might be the strengthened cabinet discussed earlier. Even though this runs deeply against the grain of American practice,

[32]"Now on these key jobs, I don't care whether a man is a Democrat or an Igorot. I want the best fellow I can get for a particular job." Arthur M. Schlesinger, Jr., *A Thousand Days* (Boston: Houghton Mifflin Company, 1965), p. 129.
[33]Heclo, *A Government of Strangers*, p. 94.
[34]Neustadt, *Presidential Power*, pp. 55, 56.
[35]For a more optimistic assessment of the president's managerial opportunities, see Dwight Ink, "The President as Manager," *Public Administration Review*, 36 (September/October 1976), 508–515.

something of the sort could conceivably come to pass, with several hundred noncareer appointees carrying much of the load. The task appears difficult now, but it may be possible to develop rational political oversight if the United States can return to a greater degree of consensus.

At present the critical relationship between political overseers and top-level careerists appears at best undeveloped and at worst chaotic. On this critical front, much may depend on the new Senior Executive Service created in July 1979. In working out a new kind of political oversight, the role of partisanship may turn out to be empty formality, major criterion, or anything in between. If partisanship is not to be a major factor, it is not at all clear what political vehicle would be used to impose general interest policies.

Perhaps we should note that some scholars question the desirability or the possibility of comprehensive control of government. A leading textbook in public administration, published in 1978, advised us that pyramidal concepts in administration are passing. Hierarchy is giving way to "the all-connected network" or the "matrix organization." The author stated that in advanced organizations of the future, we will see an increasing similarity between public and private organizations; boundaries between the two will "tend to be loose and low, easy to bend and easy to break." He seemed to believe that elected officials should influence but not control administration. A major implicit value (if I judge the work correctly) was the desirability of administrative autonomy. When the author referred to politicians, it was usually in a negative or trivial context. He liked the idea of democratic administration but tended to equate it with employee freedom, participation of diverse interests in administration, and consensus in the work group. He did not address the question of how the electorate is to obtain explicit control of the administrative process. The discussion of administrative responsibility stressed professionalism, publicity, and participation. "Participation . . . means that administrators must consult more and more interests and listen to more and more points of view."[36]

A somewhat related line of thinking stresses the limitations of comprehensive policy making. Charles Lindblom, for example, has argued that complex decision making is necessarily "fragmented, disjointed, and incremental," rather than "synoptic." He believes that coordination by mutual adjustment, as in market situations, is often superior to coordination by central direction, common purpose, or command. A multiplicity of decision makers having varied attitudes and interests is apt to be best at solving complex problems. Furthermore, he says, in a democratic society, no set of politicians has unilateral authority of the sort that would eliminate interdependence among agencies, legislators, and executives. Such an assessment raises normative as well as empirical questions. The author presented it in the early 1960s when the American political system seemed to be working

[36]George E. Berkley, *The Craft of Public Administration* (Boston: Allyn & Bacon, Inc., 1978), pp. 492–495, 502–515, 525–534. Quotations on pp. 493 and 504. The 1981 edition of this book (same publisher) may incorporate some changed views on these matters.

well. Today, when many of our delivery systems seem to be working badly, the desirability of highly complex decision-making arrangements may be more doubtful.[37]

THE PARTISAN CONGRESS

Partisanship is more conspicuous in Congress than in either of the other branches. Members serve as Democrats or Republicans and organize their activities on partisan lines. Although communication is open, personal contacts and friendships tend to be greater among legislators of the same party. Moreover, it is the *two*-party system that is entrenched in all congressional arrangements. This is especially obvious with the many committees and subcommittees that constitute the heart of congressional operations. All are composed of majority party and minority party contingents. The majority party is in nominal control of *each* committee and designates *all* committee chairmen. Congressional leadership is also explicitly partisan. For example, Congress's most important leadership role, Speaker of the House, has the usual prerogatives of a presiding officer combined with status as leader of the majority party. He is expected to be "fair," but he is is *not* expected to be impartial.

Party arrangements are loose, but they undoubtedly help Congress do its work. Despite numerous obstacles to legislation, the amount that must be passed is substantial. Passing laws is not Congress's only function, of course, but it is the one that most depends on strong coalitions. Legislative coalitions could conceivably be put together one measure at a time (and to some extent they are), but this would make it difficult to pass the more than two hundred public bills and resolutions a year that is now Congress's minimum work pace.

Congressional parties stand at a point of critical balance in American politics: On the one hand, they are durable coalitions that cut across many issues. On the other, one can easily see tendencies that subject such coalitions to stress or even threaten to destroy them. Winner-take-all election rules in the states and districts force coalitions at the local level within the particular constituencies and thus account for the very small number of legislators who are not Democrats or Republicans. Perhaps law making itself to some degree also forces coalitions. Once details of legislative proposals have been worked out (a vital activity!), members must at some point vote yea or nay. Drastic limitation on voting alternatives at the final stage guarantees that one side or the other will have at least a majority. And, there is obviously pressure in the system to pass legislation.

What about opposing forces that tend to break coalitions apart? There are many of these. Party labels in congressional elections mask local or

[37]Charles E. Lindblom, *The Intelligence of Democracy* (New York: The Free Press, 1965), pp. 3–9, 99, 151, 331–333. Another important study in this line is Aaron Wildavsky, *The Politics of the Budgetary Process* (Boston: Little, Brown & Company, 1964).

regional variations in political outlooks. Personality appeals in congressional campaigns may mean that self-conscious coalitions of like-minded groups rarely emerge to put elected representatives in office. Expectations that members of Congress should get specific benefits for their own districts or that they should express their own individual views in congressional votes often work against durable cross-issue coalitions.

Of special importance on the disintegrative side of the ledger are (1) bicameralism, (2) weak leadership, and (3) special vote requirements. A legislature composed of two roughly equal houses obviously places added burdens on coalitions wishing to pass legislation, since it is harder to get majorities in each of two houses than in only one. Bicameralism also contributes to weak congressional leadership. Congress has House leaders and Senate leaders but does not (and probably cannot) have any members who could be made responsible as leaders to *both* chambers.[38] Lacking powerful leadership, authority may flow downwards—enhancing the discretion of individual legislators and the power of various committees charged with particular pieces of legislation. An opposite tendency is for leadership to flow towards the president. However, cross-issue coalitions that support the president tend to be somewhat partisan.

Special vote requirements include the two-thirds vote necessary to ratify treaties, the 60 percent needed to shut off a senate filibuster, and the separate procedures for authorization and appropriation of money, which may be needed for a measure to have any real effect. The legislative obstacle course usually requires concurrence from many separate groups. These may include two kinds of committees (authorizing and appropriating) at two levels (subcommittee and parent committee) in two houses. If measures pass the two houses in different form, still another committee (the conference) will be necessary to resolve the differences. If the president vetoes a bill, a two-thirds vote in each house will be needed to override.

Democrats versus Republicans

The most visible aspect of legislative partisanship is the extent to which parties consistently differ in legislative voting. From 1955 to 1977, the proportion of all roll calls that were party votes (defined as a majority of one party opposing a majority of the other) has varied between about 29 and 54 percent. Data assembled by Jewell and Patterson show that throughout this period the House and Senate were never more than about twelve or so percentage points apart in degree of party voting, and that party voting in both chambers tended to change in a somewhat parallel fashion. Thus, party voting was lowest from 1967 to 1970 in both houses, and it rose rather steadily thereafter. (The trends are not easy to evaluate because of unanimous roll calls, and because roll-call patterns vary among different kinds of measures.) If a stricter standard is applied—90 percent opposing 90 percent —party voting is much lower: around 6 or 7 percent of house votes since

[38]This is true despite the fact that the same party is usually in control of both chambers. In this century, 1911–1983, and 1981–1983 have been the only years of divided partisan control of House and Senate.

1950. This figure compares with the 17 percent or so that generally obtained from 1921 to 1948.[39] Perhaps a few examples from the 1978 session of the U.S. Senate will illustrate the variety of oppositional patterns. Congressional Quarterly has identified fifteen votes that it considered to be particularly important. One of these, ratification of two Panama Canal treaties by an identical vote, showed considerable partisan difference, with Democrats supporting the treaties five to one and Republicans opposing them almost one and a half to one:

	Vote on Panama Canal Treaties	
	Democrats	Republicans
Yea	52	16
Nay	10	22
	Index of partisan difference[40] = 41.8	

Notice, however, that at least a few Republican votes would have been necessary to pass the treaties, even if every Democrat had supported them. Interestingly enough, no significant split showed up between Southern Democrats and Democrats outside the South on these votes, and even the Southern Democrats supported the treaties by better than two to one.

In another action, the Senate approved a resolution allowing states an additional thirty-nine months to ratify the Equal Rights Amendment (ERA). According to Congressional Quarterly, the key division was on a proposal offered by Senator Garn of Utah, which would have allowed states that had already ratified ERA to rescind their action during the extension period:

	Vote on Garn's Motion to Allow *States to Rescind Approval of ERA* *during Extension Period*	
	Democrats	Republicans
Yea	20	24
Nay	41	13
	Index of partisan difference = 32.1	

Even though the index of partisan difference is rather low, partisan differences are quite noticeable. Unlike the previous vote, a considerable split

[39]Samuel C. Patterson, "The Semi-Sovereign Congress," in *The New American Political System,* ed. King, pp. 169–170; William J. Keefe, *Parties, Politics, and Public Policy in America,* 2nd ed. (Hinsdale, Ill.: The Dryden Press, 1976), pp. 139–140.

[40]The index of partisan difference is the positive difference between the percentage of Democrats voting yea and the percentage of Republicans voting yea. If the total yeas and nays are not taken as fixed, the index can vary between zero (indicating no difference between the parties) and 100 (indicating complete difference). However, the index cannot reach 100 on lopsided votes. In the vote at hand 83.9 percent of the Democrats voted yea, and 42.1 percent of the Republicans voted yea. The difference between these two figures is 41.8.

developed between Southern and non-Southern Democrats (index of difference = 67.0), which did not, however, affect the partisan complexion of the
outcome.

Several of the votes cited by Congressional Quarterly produced splits
between yeas and nays of better than three to one, and with this degree of
consensus, there is a limit to how different the parties can be. However, one
such vote was rather partisan despite the lopsided outcome: The Senate
rejected an amendment to the defense spending authorization bill proposed
by Senator Tower, which would have increased the total by $1.6 billion. His
measure lost, twenty-one to seventy-four. This would not count as a party
vote even under the simple majority criterion discussed earlier, because the
Republicans divided seventeen to seventeen. However, Senate Democrats
voted overwhelmingly to reject, and the index of partisan difference was
43.4.

The net impact of party in Congress resists precise description. Many
important actions (especially by leaders) do not involve voting, and members' positions on some votes are not recorded. As one examines Congress
over time, changes in the kinds of recorded decisions may affect the comparisons. For example, a recent updating of an older study documents a considerable decline in the number of roll calls dealing with patronage when the
1921–1944 period is compared to the 1948–1964 period. Conversely, the
number of foreign aid measures increased considerably in the latter period.
Both of these shifts in the composition of recorded actions would tend to
depress party differences in the more recent period. Another view is that the
increase in partisanship since 1970 reflects an unusual degree of Democratic
opposition to Republican presidents.[41]

The updated study suggests a possible trend toward more consistent
partisanship in congressional roll calls. Even though overall partisan differences were less pronounced in the 1948–1964 period, votes tended to even
out over the various categories. Matters that had been sharply partisan in
the earlier period become less so; issues on which party stands had been
similar became more partisan. In foreign affairs especially, the decline of
party voting did not signify a return to bipartisanship. The author believes
that the factor of party continues to be more influential than any other
political pressure in producing distinctive voting behavior among members
of Congress. This includes metropolitan versus rural, foreign-born versus
native, black versus white, and South versus non-South pressures.[42]

Differing Party Outlooks

Since partisan cleavages persist in Congress, we would expect them to
have some basis in distinctive attitudes or policy preferences. Lacking these,
and making full allowance for expediency and divisions within the parties,
one would wonder what the point of the partisan differences could possibly

[41]Julius Turner, *Party and Constituency*, rev. ed. by Edward V. Schneier, Jr. (Baltimore:
The Johns Hopkins Press, 1970), p. 45; Patterson, "Semi-Sovereign Congress," p. 171.
[42]Turner, *Party and Constituency*, pp. 1, 39, 67, 131, 164, 168.

be. On the other hand, distinctive partisan outlooks are obviously not so pronounced, even among these most active people, that they constitute unified groupings.

To shed further light on this subject, it is useful to examine ratings of individual members of Congress that Americans for Democratic Action (ADA) and Americans for Constitutional Action (ACA) publish each year. This approach is not faultless. Since members are aware that they are being rated, an interactive, even incestuous, relationship between raters and ratees could develop over time. The advantage of the ratings is that they are based on explicit procedures and reflect judgments by knowledgeable observers concerned about legislative outcomes. The two groups regard each other as ideological opponents, and they rate legislators on different sets of

Table 11-2
Ratings of U.S. Senators, 1978

	ADA Ratings		ACA Ratings	
Highest Scorers	KENNEDY	METZENBAUM	H. BYRD	Scott
	SARBANES	RIEGLE	Goldwater	McClure
	CLARK	CRANSTON	Lugar	Bartlett
	BAYH	CULVER	Garn	Hatch
	WILLIAMS	GRAVEL	Curtis	Helms
	MUSKIE	MATSUNAGA	Hansen	Thurmond
	CHURCH	Javits	Tower	
	PELL	Brooke		
	NELSON	MCGOVERN		
Lowest Scorers	McClure	ALLEN	HATHAWAY	RIEGLE
	Laxalt	Helms	BAYH	CRANSTON
	Young	Garn	MATSUNAGA	MUSKIE
	Hatch	Wallop	Case	MOYNIHAN
	Scott	H. BYRD	Javits	PELL
	Tower	Thurmond	JACKSON	SARBANES
	Bartlett	Curtis	GRAVEL	ANDERSON
	EASTLAND	STENNIS	EAGLETON	WILLIAMS
	Griffin	Lugar	ABOUREZK	
	Goldwater	Stevens		
Average Rating All other Democrats	45.4		35.0	
All other Republicans	35.8		49.3	

Ratings of both the ADA and ACA consist of the percentage of times senators voted in accord with the particular group. ADA used 20 selected votes, ACA 24. Only four roll calls were used by both groups. Failure to vote lowers ADA ratings but not ACA. Highest scorers: ADA 70 or higher; ACA 86 or higher. Lowest scorers: ADA 10 or lower; ACA 12 or lower. "All other" ratings were calculated independently of each other, so that the ADA figures average senators not listed among highest and lowest ADA scorers only. Democrats in capitals, Republicans in lower case.

Source: Congressional Quarterly Weekly Report, June 2, 1979, p. 1067.

votes. When the ratings are in general agreement, one may sense that something meaningful is being measured.[43] Bear in mind, however, that two legislators with the same scores can have very different voting records. William Keefe's portrayal of the 1974 ratings revealed marked partisan differences. Many Democratic senators had ADA ratings higher than 70 and ACA ratings lower than 30. Southern Democrats and Republicans were usually at the other extreme.[44] In 1978, the patterns of party difference depicted in Table 11–2 seemed to be very similar, and senators who were in office in both years tended to receive similar ratings. Most senators with particularly high ADA ratings and particularly low ACA ratings were Democrats. The fact that eight senators are common to both groups confirms our assumption that the differences are reliable. Note that party makes a difference even after highest and lowest scorers are eliminated. Whether one thinks the differences matter will depend on how one regards the substantive questions at issue in the particular votes.[45]

The most obvious exceptions to consistent partisanship are regional. Conspicuously conservative Democrats tend to come from the South; unusually liberal Republicans tend to come from the Northeast. If one examines ratings within regions, important party differences still persist. Southern Democrats are conservative, but Republicans from the South tend to be *more* conservative. Northeastern Republicans are liberal, but northeastern Democrats are *more* liberal. Even so, if we restrict attention to eleven former Confederate states, and to nine northeastern states, regional differences dominate. More precisely, the differences between regions within each party are greater than differences between the parties within each region.

The finding is an impressive testimonial to a conflict that originated at least a century and a half ago. However, you should keep in mind that these findings reflect only nineteen states. The scope of contemporary partisan conflict is much broader than the scope of these ancient regional differences. Democrats and Republicans organize congressional proceedings, not southerners and northeasterners. The proportion of southerners among Democratic legislators has declined dramatically in the last thirty years, and the proportion of Democratic seniority leadership positions controlled by southerners is now less than 25 percent.[46]

[43]Liberal Democrats, including Hubert Humphrey and Eleanor Roosevelt, founded the ADA in 1947. The ACA emerged eleven years later, and Ben Moreell, Chairman of the Board, Jones and Laughlin Steel Corporation, was its first chairman.

[44]Keefe, *Parties, Politics, and Public Policy*, p. 144.

[45]Protecting the redwood trees; cutting individual income taxes; prosecution for obscenity; the B–1 bomber; the Panama Canal treaties; budget ceiling for Department of Health, Education and Welfare; emergency farm bill; mideast fighter plane sales; overall budget targets; labor law revision; foreign aid; airline deregulation; government corporation for oil shale research; loan guarantees for New York City; sanctions against Rhodesia; full voting representation in Congress for District of Columbia; exemptions of small businesses from requirements of OSHA; spending for HUD, Interior, and Agriculture; court-ordered busing; natural gas pricing; use of Labor-HEW funds for abortions; ERA deadline extension; and taxation of corporate income earned abroad. *Congressional Quarterly Weekly Report*, June 2, 1979, pp. 1062–1075.

[46]Patterson, "Semi-Sovereign Congress," p. 157.

Table 11-3
Ratings of Southern and Northeastern Senators in 1978

	Average ADA Rating	Average ACA Rating
A. Southern Democrats (N = 17)	28.2	54.0
B. Southern Republicans (N = 5)	12.0	89.6
C. Northeastern Democrats (N = 10)	66.5	10.8
D. Northeastern Republicans (N = 8)	57.5	22.4
Party differences among southern senators (A − B)	16.2	35.0
Party differences among northeastern senators (C − D)	9.0	11.6
Regional differences among Democratic senators (A − C)	38.3	43.2
Regional differences among Republican senators (B − D)	45.0	67.2

"South" consists of Va., Ala., Tenn., Fla., Ga., S.C., La., Ark., N.C., Miss., Tex. "Northeast" consists of Me., N.H., Vt., Mass., R.I., Conn., N.Y., N.J., Pa. Signs are ignored in calculating differences.

Source: Congressional Quarterly Weekly Report, June 2, 1979, p. 1067.

Party and Congressional Performance

Congress has changed in many ways in the last fifteen years or so, and persons of many different viewpoints can sympathize with much that has happened.[47] Our national legislators have curtailed the arbitrary powers of committee chairmen, and they no longer apply seniority as an automatic rule in selecting these leaders. They have also opened the process of decision making through recording of teller votes and campaign disclosure and open meeting requirements. With very few exceptions our legislators have always worked hard at their jobs, and this is even more true today. Congress has increased its staff, and greatly improved the quality of policy analysis available to it through units like the Congressional Research Service, the Office of Technology Assessment, the General Accounting Office, and the Congressional Budget Office.

There is, of course, the matter of increased incumbency advantage. Our evaluation in Chapter 10 tended to be negative. What is chiefly disturbing, however, is the increasing *margin* by which successful incumbents were being returned to Congress. Less disturbing is the large *number* (or proportion) of incumbents who are reelected. A system in which a large proportion of incumbents are returned to office gives legislative operations continuity and helps members develop needed expertise. Patterson suggests that the high rate of return may not be too different from other democratic legislatures. Moreover, it is difficult to quarrel with an incentive system that

[47]Two of the most useful descriptions of these changes appear in Patterson, "Semi-Sovereign Congress," and Leroy N. Rieselbach, *Congressional Reform in the Seventies* (Morristown, N.J.: General Learning Press, 1977).

emphasizes reelection as the reward for hard work and attending to constituents' needs. At root, some of the problems of incumbency advantage may be problems of Republican weakness in the two-party system. Throughout the 1970s, Democratic incumbents fared better than Republican incumbents, and much of the turnover of membership in both houses was at the expense of Republicans.[48]

Judgments about Congress's partisan arrangements should depend in part on performance criteria, but these are difficult to establish. At present, members of Congress must attend to local as well as national concerns. As an institution Congress is expected to orient itself in some manner to the president and his program while identifying its own particular objectives. In addition, it must decide how much authority it will delegate to administrative agencies and how much it will reserve to itself.

In a book published in 1977, Leroy Rieselbach suggested that we use three standards of evaluation in thinking about what Congress should do: responsibility, responsiveness, and accountability. *Accountability* exists when the electorate can evaluate congressional decisions regularly: "If the decision makers are found wanting, the 'rascals' can be 'turned out' of office." *Responsiveness* concerns legislators' openness and their listening to and taking account of those many persons who are affected by congressional decisions. *Responsibility* involves successful problem solving by an assertive Congress.[49]

Although Rieselbach found congressional performance to be considerably short of ideal in each respect, he believed it achieves a higher degree of responsiveness than of responsibility or accountability. Responsibility is lost because, while Congress lets others set the national agenda, it reacts to these initiatives in a ponderous and somewhat willful manner. Accountability exists in theory but is dissipated in practice because citizens are uninformed and because they often lack a clear and substantial choice in primaries or general elections. Rieselbach's book states that widespread agreement on a fundamental congressional reform package is not likely, and it proposes incremental changes that take off from what he believed to be the best of the 1971–1975 reforms. He seeks to improve responsibility and responsiveness by strengthening Congress in its relation to the executive and by attending to both the deliberative and decisional phases of policy making.

To achieve responsive deliberation, Rieselbach's 1977 analysis would accept individualized campaigns attuned to local issues in the hope that legislators would be a highly diverse group. He is willing to accept the very considerable diffusion of power in Congress and would welcome additional diminution of the power of committee chairmen. He would encourage more committee hearings and more persistent efforts to obtain testimony from underorganized interests. The deliberative stage would take time, but it would not be allowed to drag on unduly. Responsible decision making would stress letting the majority act once deliberation is concluded. Obsta-

---

[48]Patterson, "Semi-Sovereign Congress," pp. 143, 155.
[49]*Congressional Reform*, pp. 8–9, 51–56. The quotation appears on p. 9.

cles such as House Rules Committee procedures, delaying tactics, the filibuster, and difficult discharge requirements would be modified or eliminated. Accountability was important, but Rieselbach seemed to feel that less could be done about it directly. He advocated minimal secrecy in congressional proceedings and expanded media coverage. He hoped that candidates would present specific views on issues so that watchful citizens could vote intelligently. He also hoped that an enhanced congressional image would induce more citizens to be attentive to congressional politics.[50]

Throughout Rieselbach's treatment the parties play a distinctly minor role. One reason for this may be fear that stronger congressional partisanship would either enhance the power of the president or centralize congressional policy making to an undesirable degree. Another reason is that he (correctly) regards parties as weak at the constituency level and senses that little can be done to reverse the trend towards more personalistic and less partisan congressional races. Third, Rieselbach appears to be rather sanguine about interest group lobbying, even though he concedes that access to Congress is highly unequal and that it depends a great deal on experience, money, and know-how.

Certainly factors other than partisanship need to be considered in efforts to improve our legislative process. Yet, party continues to have an important bearing. Take responsiveness, for example. We know that only tiny fragments of the mass public will regularly communicate with members of Congress, and we have no reason to suppose that such persons are representative of the larger society. These people are not evil, they may be making an important contribution to good government, and they certainly are exercising basic constitutional rights. But to what extent should Congress do what they want? Ideally, it would seem that mass-based political parties should be able to override such pressures because they represent more inclusive interests. As things stand now, congressional Democrats and Republicans may not be cohesive enough to do this. In congressional politics, weak parties can often mean that organized special interests have disproportionate influence.

Rieselbach apparently believed that relations between Congress and the presidency should approach parity.[51] One wonders if this goal is consistent with increasing the prerogatives of individual members of Congress. Up to a point, extensive sharing of power within Congress helps Congress offset executive power and protect its own autonomy. However, fragmentation may also result, making it difficult for legislators to enact controversial legislation. Presidential power has compensated for decentralized congressional power in the past. For Congress to be more than a junior partner of the president, an enhanced capacity for collective action by Congress may

[50]Ibid., Chap. 5.
[51]He did not use the word *parity*, but he said that Congress must be able to "produce decisions that have a reasonable chance of prevailing against presidential power," p. 110. For a more recent statement of Rieselbach's views, see his "Assessing Congressional Change, or What Hath Reform Wrought (or Wreaked)?" Boston College Symposium, January 31, 1981.

be required. Or, perhaps more likely, the system will work best, as it has in the past, when a strong president dominates the policy-making process.

The recent tendency (quite widespread in the entire society) towards flight from leadership and an embrace of consensus can be dangerous. Americans have often been skeptical of political leadership claims, and the excesses of Vietnam and Watergate have undoubtedly reinforced this skepticism. However, to reject authority and to make legitimate action depend entirely on consensus is to invite drift and mediocrity.

In the 1970s, Congress seemed to have gone very far in the direction of minimized leadership responsibility. The authority of party leaders in Congress became weaker than ever, despite some formal appearances to the contrary.[52] Committee chairmen remain important, but one wonders how much influence they really will have—especially in a Senate now controlled by the GOP. In most cases, seniority is still the most important factor in their selection, and the element of deliberate choice may be largely lacking. If chairmen displease any important segment of their party, on the committee or in the caucus, perhaps their colleagues can reject them on the next round of organizational decisions. In the 1970s, individual members of Congress often refused to assume responsibility for the actions of Congress as a whole (even when they were Democrats), and in seeking reelection they often scored points by running against Congress. House Democrats opened up many of their caucus meetings to the public, but their election of committee leaders and party leaders remained closed and off the record.[53]

The pre-1971 arrangements were faulty in many respects, but they at least made some provision for leadership. People who chaired committees achieved their position entirely on the basis of continuous party seniority in their committee, and they often exercised their powers arbitrarily. However, they could and did exercise independent authority that left a mark on the legislative product, and they usually gave conspicuous support to Congress as an institution. And, of course, as we have noted above, the president was expected to exercise leadership.

Rieselbach's analysis seems to reflect the persisting distrust of leadership. It opposes centralization in either branch and, by omission, deemphasizes the president's constitutional responsibilities as legislative leader. He wanted those who chair committees to become even less powerful than they were, and, if successful in this, appeared largely indifferent to how they might be selected. On the whole, he was content with the proliferation of subcommittees and tended to see this as enhancing congressional responsiveness.

Changes in the opposite direction should also be considered: strengthen congressional leadership; simplify the committee structure; make committee chairmen powerful, but be very concerned with how they are selected; remove leadership selection from the veil of secrecy and make

---

[52]These include the resurgence of the party caucuses, the new policy and steering committee arrangements among House Democrats, and the new relationship between the Speaker and the Rules Committee. On these matters see ibid., pp. 46, 57–58.

[53]Ibid., p. 63.

it the most visibly controversial and well publicized of congressional decisions; develop more coherent and reliable party programs so that voters who are not experts in congressional politics will have some chance to understand the alternatives before them. If Congress is unwilling to implement such changes, or to improve its leadership capabilities in other ways, Americans may have to rely on the president (and the Supreme Court) rather than the Congress in the future as in the past as the place where the buck finally stops.

Finally, we must not forget the administrative agencies as we think about partisanship in Congress. The congressional relationship to the executive branch affects bureaucratic as well as presidential power. Although this has always been true, it appears to be especially relevant now that the capacity of the president to be an administrative manager is waning. Delegation of rule-making authority to administrative agencies has proceeded very far. The melange of issue networks and middlemen in the delivery of federal services also threatens to deprive agencies of the control they have a constitutional duty to exercise. If rigid centralization in Congress, whether through party or other means, will not solve these problems, neither will the addition of more congressional staff personnel. In this context, fragmentation of congressional authority is definitely part of the problem.

THE RESPONSIBLE-PARTIES DEBATE

The discussion to this point has suggested that partisanship is an important element in each of the elected branches of our government and, to some extent, in the judicial branch as well. We have seen that it is impossible to discuss partisanship in one branch without considering the others. Partisanship tends to link the branches, and if parties were stronger, those linkages would be tighter. This concluding section will consider partisanship more explicitly by examining some doctrines or theories about the proper role of parties in government.

One view, of course, is that parties have no constructive place in public life. This opinion was widespread among the framers, received formidable support from John C. Calhoun, and was well articulated in a later era by Herbert Croly and M. I. Ostrogorski. For the person with a serious interest in constitutional democracy or public affairs, however, the antiparty view offers little comfort. It ignores the role of parties in making mass political participation a practical reality. Its serious adherents are, with few exceptions, antipolitical or apolitical.

Another segment of informed opinion believes that the parties are satisfactory as they are (or rather as they were as recently as 1965). Its most vigorous and interesting expression is Pendleton Herring's *Politics of Democracy*, written in 1940. Herring believed that the esence of democratic politics is patience, flexibility, and a willingness to accommodate differences through practical arrangements. The United States had been individualistic from the outset and had achieved unity only through struggle. The basic role of the parties was not to frame issues or draw up programs but "to discover some way of bringing together into a reasonably harmonious relationship as large a proportion of the voters as possible." Party politicians had to maintain ties to people of differing classes, group interests, and political outlooks. It was quite acceptable for each member of Congress to deal with the play of interests in his or her own way and not be bound by party stands. "Little would be gained," Herring said, "by shifting the struggle to a party conclave and compromising differences in private caucuses in order that the party might offer the appearance of solidarity." Disciplined parties representing more clear-cut differences might easily result in a hardening of the political arteries. He conceded the difficulty of executing coherent national programs and was willing to rely in part on presidential leadership to provide it. He also hoped that the democratic milieu would enable a science of society to emerge that could apply intelligence to our common problems.[54]

In his preface to the 1965 edition, Herring noted the considerable gap that separated his views from those who favored a more responsible party system. This other approach went back to the writing of Henry Jones Ford, A. Lawrence Lowell, Frank Goodnow, and Woodrow Wilson—early and major figures in the emergence of political science in the United States. By 1956 "responsible party government" was probably the most widely held approach to the problems of the parties among American political scientists. It received its definitive modern exposition in the writings of E. E. Schattschneider and in the 1950 report of the Committee on Political Parties of the American Political Science Association (which Schattschneider chaired).[55]

Those who espouse responsible parties generally support the following notions:

1. Modern democracy requires that the people be able to maintain control *over* government rather than participate *in* government on a regular basis. The emphasis should be on popular choice of decision makers rather than having the people make governmental decisions themselves.

2. To achieve this kind of popular control, it is necessary to have competitive

---

[54]Herring's book was reissued in 1965 by W. W. Norton & Co., Inc. See pp. xiv, 102, 107.

[55]Austin Ranney and Willmoore Kendall, *Democracy and the American Party System* (Westport, Conn.: Greenwood Press, Publishers, 1974), p. 151. (This book was originally published in 1956 by Harcourt Brace Jovanovich.) Some key works of the early writers were: Henry Jones Ford, *The Rise and Growth of American Politics* (New York: Macmillan, Inc., 1898); A. Lawrence Lowell, *Public Opinion and Popular Government* (New York: Longmans, Green and Company, 1913); Frank J. Goodnow, *Politics and Administration* (New York: Macmillan, Inc., 1900); Woodrow Wilson, *Congressional Government* (Boston: Houghton Mifflin Company, 1885); *Consitutional Government in the United States* (New York: Columbia University Press, 1908). More recent works include E. E. Schattschneider, *Party Government* (New York: Holt, Rinehart & Winston, 1942) and *The Semisovereign People* (Hinsdale, Ill.: The Dryden Press, 1975). This latter work was originally published in 1960. The report referred to was entitled "Toward a More Responsible Two-Party System," and it was published both as a supplement to *The American Political Science Review,* 54 (September 1950), and as a separate publication (Rinehart & Company, Inc.), also in 1950.

parties that offer alternative sets of rulers. The rulers must be identifiable, answerable, and strong enough to run the government. The parties must be unified and disciplined, and the majority party must be responsible for the conduct of government.

3. American parties as we have known them are unsatisfactory for the roles envisaged. They are too decentralized, too loosely organized, and too undisciplined. Policy differences between the parties lack clear definition, and national party leaders lack reliable partisan support.

4. In a period of continuing crisis, the United States needs coherent, expertly designed programs of action, democratically arrived at. Such policies are conspicuously lacking, and cohesive national parties are the only vehicles that can possibly provide them in the American system. Our governmental system is too complex to permit our many leaders to serve up such programs on the basis of each one's personal preferences. We cannot rely on the pressure groups to provide them because these groups represent special rather than general interests and are not accountable to the general public.

5. Specific changes will enable us to achieve the kind of party system needed. (The details have been numerous and varied. They typically include transferral of power in the parties from the state to the national level, stronger party leadership in Congress, wider margins of party control on congressional committees, four-year terms for representatives and eight-year staggered terms for senators, with elections timed to coincide with presidential elections, strong party caucuses in each house, clear caucus responsibility for congressional leadership, and so forth.)[56]

A number of political scientists subjected the doctrine of responsible party government to searching criticism in the early 1950s. The major issues in contention seemed to concern the nature of American society versus English society, the costs or undesirable consequences of changing to the more cohesive parties that the doctrine's proponents advocated, and the nature of American parties as then constituted. There were, of course, differences among particular critics, but we shall ignore these in the following brief summary.

Advocates of responsible parties often admired English parliamentary arrangements and to some extent took these as a model for the United States to follow. However, critics believed that British society was very different from ours: English society was smaller in scale and more homogeneous; its leaders came from a narrower segment of the society. Some argued that the British party system did not operate as its idealizers thought it did. British parties were cohesive, but their differences were not particularly clear-cut. Between 1911 and 1950 a single majority party had controlled British cabinets only about a third of the time. The rest of the time that country had experienced coalition governments or control by a single party having less than majority support.[57]

Critics argued that advocates of unified parties had understated the costs and overlooked some consequences. Some believed that American

[56]This summary is adapted from Ranney and Kendall, *Democracy and the American Party System*, pp. 151–152, 525–527.
[57]Ibid., pp. 529–530.

parties were loosely organized because of the nature of our governmental structure. If so, making our parties resemble the English would require drastic changes in the Constitution. Moreover, many Americans would find it difficult to relate to programmatic parties. Americans were accustomed to using parties for patronage, social activity, or business advantage. They were also accustomed to entering the political arena via the personal attractions of particular leaders. If successful, the responsible-parties doctrine might produce centralized bossism that would be worse than anything previously experienced at the local level. Others thought that the effort to achieve such parties might set up self-destructive tendencies. For example, the lesser party might narrow its appeal to satisfy only those adherents left in its ranks; this, however, would reduce its appeal at the next elections. If it again closed ranks, its appeal to the mass electorate would dwindle still further. Another possible consequence of insisting on party cohesion might well be a multiparty system.

Critics also stated that contributions of the existing party and group system were more significant than implied by the responsible-party advocates. Party platforms did differ in important ways, and most of the platform of the winning party was usually enacted. Considerable party cohesion was evident on important congressional votes. Some believed that the bias against pressure groups was unduly strong and that the public interest conception underlying the proparty–antigroup philosophy was faulty. Society held too many interests and too many groups for all of them to be effectively subordinated to the parties or absorbed by them.[58]

In the past quarter century, advocacy of responsible parties has probably lost ground. Political science is larger, more diverse, and less centrally concerned with American political parties. Changes in the parties themselves have been ambiguous. Some trends appear to make responsible parties a more likely prospect than before: the declining position of southerners in the Democratic party and with it the decline of the conservative coalition in Congress; the increasing nationalization of public life; the apparent growth of issue concerns in the mass electorate; and the structural changes in Congress that make it possible for caucuses to exercise meaningful choice in selecting congressional leaders. Weighed against these currents, however, are all the accumulated indications of weakness in the parties: weaker voter loyalties, weaker organizations, and weaker claims of parties on people in public life. English practices are less inspiring, and American society now seems too fractious to accommodate itself to the collaborative effort that would be required. An important segment of the citizenry seeks direct, not mediated, participation.

It is sometimes said that the dominant view among parties specialists in political science is now that of Pendleton Herring.[59] If so, some important

[58]Ibid., pp. 527–533; Ivan Hinderaker, *Party Politics* (New York: Holt, Rinehart & Winston, 1956), pp. 659–675.

[59]E. M. Kirkpatrick, "Toward a More Responsible Two-Party System: Political Science, Policy Science, or Pseudo-Science?" *American Political Science Review*, 65 (December 1971), 984–985. Kirkpatrick was a member of the Committee on Political Parties, and his article is a useful point of departure for readers interested in the methodological issues involved in the debate.

qualifications should be noted. Herring's thoughts on the subject were developed at a time when parties were strong—"in power" in his words. He was also accepting of a strong presidential role, confident of the nation's emerging administrative capabilities, and hopeful about a science of society. One can be certain that many specialists now view these conditions and assumptions in a new light.

If one had to choose the view of a single individual, it would be more correct to say that V. O. Key's ideas now predominate. Key did not enter the responsible-parties debate, but he had some affinities with the responsible-parties view. His many writings suggested that parties were vital institutions that could link the various parts of government together. They tended to perform best under conditions of factional simplicity in a hospitable political environment. For him, the critical issues of democratic politics centered on the factors that either facilitated or impeded widespread party competition. Unlike Herring, he was distinctly (though moderately) pro-party and antigroup, and he did not endorse the present condition of the parties. He said that the American constitutional system is not designed to be a party government, but that its operation requires at times that it approximate party government.[60]

Responsible-party government has its greatest appeal in a less than total or extreme form. Thus, Judson James makes a distinction between "party government" (which requires absolute majority rule and great capacity of parties to coordinate government), and "responsible parties" (requiring qualified majority rule and some capacity for coordination). The latter approach is the one he favors, and he believes that it is also superior to either the status quo or to other possible approaches to the coordinative capacities of parties and views on majority rule.[61]

Everett Ladd argues that the basic concept of responsible-party government is sound, but that the "full 'party government' position" convinces many of its impracticality by asking too much. Says Ladd:

> Only parties can so organize the issues that mass publics are enabled to speak effectively upon them. . . . If they [the parties] make elected officials in some sense collectively—rather than individually—responsible to the electorate, parties enormously expand the level of meaningful public control over government.[62]

CONCLUSION

The responsible-parties debate raises fundamental issues that can engross anyone wishing to understand the political workings of our national government. Even though the central issue may now be of less concern to special-

---

[60]Key, *Politics, Parties, and Pressure Groups*, p. 665.

[61]For him, the status quo is a situation in which parties have no capacity for coordination. Adherents of the status quo are in effect opposed to majority rule. A "progressive" approach implies that there should be absolute majority rule, but that parties should play no role in coordinating government. Judson James, *American Political Parties in Transition* (New York: Harper & Row, Publishers, 1974), pp. 12, 258–260.

[62]Ladd, *Where Have All the Voters Gone?*, p. xxi.

ists, citizens interested in political reform should consider the ideas carefully. Many educated Americans are now concerned with the "imperial" presidency, the changing Congress, the runaway bureaucracy, and what many see as an arbitrary Supreme Court. The parties provide a thread of continuity to organize one's thoughts about these matters. If Americans arrive at a new consensus on how our institutions ought to work, and if they succeed in making the national government more pleasing to them, it is quite possible that a more responsible party system will also have emerged. Achieving the kind of government we want by means of calculated change in the party system is technically possible today. However, those who prefer responsible parties are less certain than before about how to obtain them.

Rieselbach's analysis of Congress is useful because it attempts to specify some of the trade-offs. He is undoubtedly right that we shall not enjoy the luxury of finding a program of reform that satisfies all goals equally well or that does not have important costs associated with it.

A person attracted to the cause of congressional resurgence ought not to reject responsible parties on that account. Rieselbach's opinion that responsible parties would strengthen the president is debatable. Many responsible-parties adherents did favor a strong presidency, but this was a general view with few dissenters in the political science of the 1950s. One of the issues in the debate was whether a *lack* of such parties in time of crisis might encourage "presidential dictatorship."[63] Indeed, the experience of recent years suggests that the ability of the president to isolate himself at will from the advice of other partisan figures may in the long run be an extremely dangerous tendency in American politics.

[63]See Ranney and Kendall, *Democracy and the American Party System*, pp. 526, 530.

12

Political
Corruption

To some extent, the ethical difficulties of politics resemble those in other areas of life. Few if any of us can cope without some resort to selfishness and expediency. It does not matter whether we are speaking of people in businesses, universities, religious orders, or most other human settings, and we should expect the same to be true in politics. However, ethical difficulties in politics extend to government, and this takes us beyond these common dimensions for at least two reasons.

First, government is a mechanism of unusual power, and we "know" that power corrupts. There is no legitimate wordly authority above the modern state that is capable of punishing its transgressions. If an evil group succeeds in tapping the resources of government for personal benefit, its members may feel that their new-found largess is inexhaustible. Furthermore, since the power of government includes its ability to persuade and to induce compliance, successful malefactors may even earn the applause of their victims.

The second reason is that government is an instrument of collective or national purpose. This means, for example, that it can become the weapon of a fanatical ideology. Well short of this but far more usual are practices justified by the doctrine that personal morality is not precisely applicable to the actions of the state. Thus Hans Morgenthau was a leading exponent of "realism" as opposed to "moralism" in international affairs. His view was that "Ethics in the abstract judges action by its conformity with the moral law; political ethics judges action by its political consequences." The counterpart of this idea in domestic policy is what Robert Dahl calls "the ethics of responsibility," referring to a domain of action that lies "between the simple extremes of unprincipled politics and rigid morality."[1]

If we wish to make ethical judgments about politics, the most difficult cases concern rulers who must employ morally questionable means if they are to achieve legitimate ends. Leaders such as Abraham Lincoln and Winston Churchill were not saints, but historians have admired them because they judge their basic choices to have been sound. Moreover, the courses of action implied by those choices were not easy to carry out. In both cases, success required acumen, courage, flexibility, and persistence.

It is not easy to say when rulers should take actions that would be immoral by purely personal standards. Choosing the lesser of two or more necessary evils is one approach. Max Weber argued that politicians should have a deep devotion to a cause, accept responsibility for the things they do in advancing that cause, and maintain a sense of proportion regarding both.[2]

Governments can commit especially serious breaches of ethical principles, and some of these violations cannot be properly justified by any reasonable principle of political prudence. Rulers have used the state to torture, kill, and enslave innocent people. One study estimates that in the twentieth century one out of every thirty inhabitants of the globe died as the result of deliberate crimes against humanity by governments. The authors note that scapegoating, diabolization, and propaganda inciting to violence against the victims almost always accompanied these crimes.[3] Admittedly, one cannot blame all such excesses on the state. Man's inhumanity to man may be innate in the sense that many ordinary people acquiesce in the depravity of a few. Except in the very worst cases, the state undoubtedly prevents many injustices that would occur in its absence.

It is even less helpful to blame such excesses on politicians as such. Politicians, of course, are intricately involved with the operations of the state, but so are administrators, police officers, soldiers, news reporters, foreign powers, and other groups. Communal hatreds and frustrated aspirations at the mass level almost always figure in the most serious human rights violations.

Political corruption is usually understood as the abuse of public authority for private advantage. One may fairly consider it to be a much less serious problem of political ethics than forced migrations, slavery and forced labor, torture, and extermination of primitive communities.[4] But

[1]Hans Morgenthau, *Politics Among Nations*, 4th ed. (New York: Alfred A. Knopf, Inc., 1967), p. 10; Robert A. Dahl, *Democracy in the United States*, 3rd ed. (Chicago: Rand McNally College Publishing Company, 1976), p. 78.

[2]Max Weber, "Politics as a Vocation," in *Essays in Sociology*, trans. H. H. Gerth and C. W. Mills (New York: Oxford University Press, 1946).

[3]Kurt Glaser and Stefan T. Posony, *Victims of Politics* (New York: Columbia University Press, 1979), pp. 44–45.

[4]According to Sean MacBride of Amnesty International, the practice of torture has become especially serious in recent years—more widespread in its use and in many cases practiced with the direct or implied consent of a large number of governments. James A. Joyce, *The New Politics of Human Rights* (New York: St. Martin's Press, Inc., 1978), p. 83.

although we reach this conclusion with something of a sigh of relief, we should not be tempted to further conclude that political corruption can be equated with petty corruption. Large-scale corruption for high stakes is serious enough to be a top-priority concern.

Even petty corruption can be a serious problem. The existence of petty corruption certainly does not preclude the existence of the most depraved conduct imaginable, as the regime of Idi Amin in Uganda demonstrated. Petty political corruption at lower levels of the political system can encourage corrupt practices outside the political arena and thus promote a sense that fraud and exploitation are pervasive.

HISTORICAL BACKGROUND

People who engage in corrupt acts usually seek tangible material benefits such as jobs or money. The pursuit of material gain is quite general, however, and cultural attitudes toward it therefore come into play. Americans are probably no more materialistic than other peoples, but in this country the stress on material gain did acquire distinctive features worth noting. Nineteenth-century American democracy had both "realistic" and "romantic" aspects, and each tended to fortify materialism. Realistic democracy, says Ralph Gabriel, involved "caucuses and logrolling, the struggle for office among individuals, and the sparring for advantage among sections or pressure groups."[5] Americans have always expected this side of democratic politics to be seamy, and they have tended to tolerate some corrupt practices within it.

Romantic democracy, on the other hand, was a national religion that enshrined the ideals of the Declaration of Independence: belief in the fundamental equality of all persons, the possession of inalienable rights by all (including the right to pursue happiness), and the conviction that government is an instrument of the people. These ideals implied that all individuals, not just a few, had the right to strive towards material improvement.

In the agrarian society of nineteenth-century America, idealism tended to fortify the acquisitive impulse. Freedom was supposed to be "holy" in its purposes, and progress was supposed to represent an advance in virtue, but Americans often regarded material betterment as the outward proof of this advance. In the experience of most Americans, closeness to the land had a moral value that was consistent with the desire to make a profit from its use.[6] Religious faith in a moral order combined with a pervasive belief in progress to dignify the material strivings of free individuals. The belief took hold (and still persists) that good people get ahead. Even today, American children are urged to "make good," and cutting corners to achieve that end is not strongly disapproved.

[5]Ralph Gabriel, *The Course of American Democratic Thought* (New York: The Ronald Press Company, 1940), p. 13.
[6]Daniel J. Elazar, *American Federalism: A View From the States*, 2nd ed. (New York: Thomas Y. Crowell Company, Inc., 1972), pp. 92–93.

The scope of political corruption could be great in a large, rough, and expanding American society. In 1795 four land development corporations persuaded the Georgia legislature to sell them land in the Yazoo tract at one and one half cents per acre; the total area was larger than the present state of Alabama. When it became known that interested persons had bribed many of the legislators, the next legislature cancelled the grants. However, by this time the original grantees had unloaded most of their grants on third parties of varying degrees of innocence. Spain had claims in the Yazoo area, as did the federal government and a confederation of Indian tribes who occupied it at the time of the sale. Before the affair was concluded, years later, Georgia ceded her claim to the United States, Congress passed a measure that awarded the claimants over $4 million, and the Supreme Court held Georgia's recision of the grant to be an unconstitutional breach of contract. A recent account lists twelve or more prominent politicians who were directly involved in the affair, including five notables in Massachusetts and Connecticut who were members of the New England Mississippi Land Company.[7]

The rise of a corporate industrial order in the latter nineteenth century was a pertinent development. One must suppose that by concentrating wealth, the new corporate structures increased the capacity of money to corrupt the political system. Large corporate enterprise also confused American thinking about differences between the public and private spheres. By perceiving these collective entities as private rather than public, Americans may have given greater scope to the more permissive norms of private enterprise where, Paul Douglas noted, expense accounts are padded, and managers "think nothing of awarding contracts, insurance, and underwriting privileges on the basis of friendship and relationship rather than the quality and price of the goods and services supplied."[8]

Twentieth-Century Experience

America's traditional values are, of course, a special instance of Western civilization, and these have suffered unusual strain in the twentieth century. Some of this can be attributed to a general decline of morale in Western nations that has been occurring at the same time that Western technology and culture have diffused over much of the globe. Western political power has ebbed despite Western superiority in science and technology, and European colonial enterprises have disappeared, in many cases with surprisingly little apparent residue. The decline has been going on for a long time, but World War I seems to have been a critical event.

The war's essential stupidity, with its frightful slaughter, had catastrophic effects and put an end to the earlier faith in progress. The cream of Western youth had gone off to fight, the poet Ezra Pound was later to say,

[7]Larry L. Berg, Harlan Hahan, and John R. Schmidhauser, *Corruption in the American Political System* (Morristown, N.J.: General Learning Press, 1976), pp. 14–16.
[8]Paul Douglas, *Ethics in Government* (Cambridge, Mass.: Harvard University Press, 1952), p. 25.

"for an old bitch gone in the teeth, for a botched civilization." The war discredited all aspects of the older European society. After 1918 the dominant stance of Western intellectuals, artists, and composers was usually opposed to conventional norms in esthetics and politics. Under mediocre leaders, Western governments lurched towards totalitarianism—and another total war.

Today, things have proceeded to the point where the United States is the only surviving example of a major Western power. This seems to have implicated the Republic one way or another in the dubious moral practices of a large number of unadmirable regimes. To deal effectively with these sorts of ethical problems, the country must not only look deeply into its own practices but must become much more sensitive to the consequences of its actions abroad on other peoples. The United States may even have to lead in the creation of a new world order, not because it is suited for the task but because no other nation can possibly do it.

In recent years, there has been much pessimism and confusion. John Lukacs claims that we are experiencing the passing of the modern age and that it is a time of a strange and unprecedented mixture of darkness and light. The rule of democracy, he says, has made people feel powerless and weak; the spread of civilization has led people to discover the emptiness of their aspirations; universal education has led to the discovery that the schools are teaching little or nothing.[9]

In the 1970s columnists in one of the country's major new magazines frequently commented on the darker aspects of the period. About a month after Carter's election in 1976, Meg Greenfield claimed that what the American electorate wanted above all else in its foreign relations was a restoration of a sense of national honor. Two years later she was appalled by the sense of "absolute bafflement" in Washington about events in the outside world (particularly in China, Iran, and Guyana) and asked: "How is it that we have all this information, but we never seem to know anything?" In commenting on her own question, she wondered if we had not developed a bias against knowing things, "as distinct from perpetually looking into them." "We need," she said, "historians and deciders and people who are not afraid of facing the implications of what they know . . . and people with guts to turn around this really weird and dangerous condition of government."[10]

Two other columnists were concerned about America's youth. One cited a survey of twelve hundred junior-high-school children that found that the most popular response to the question: "Who is your hero?" was "None." He suggested that we offer our students some true stories about people of quality along with the usual examples of corruption, degradation, and so forth. The other columnist argued that society's interest in youth was

[9]John Lukacs, *The Passing of the Modern Age* (New York: Harper Torchbooks, Harper & Row, Publishers, Inc., 1970), pp. vii–ix, 9–10.
[10]*Newsweek*, December 18, 1978, p. 112. The earlier column appeared in *Newsweek*, December 6, 1976, p. 104. Copyright 1978 by Newsweek Inc. All Rights Reserved. Reprinted by permission.

waning and that America had lost its ability to see youth as a dream fulfillment.[11]

In the 1970s, it often seemed that corrupt practices touched every
aspect of American life. Jack Valenti defended the movie industry with the
televised assertion that it should not be singled out for blame since the
entire nation was awash in an ocean of corruption. The popular television
program "60 Minutes" often described some outrageous ripoff, and frequently the perpetrators were lawyers, doctors, other professionals, and
businessmen.

A number of observers noted the increasing sophistication of white-
collar crime, and the extraordinary investigative resources needed to bring
effective prosecutions. The *New York Times* reported the belief of law enforcement officials that white-collar swindlers based in Arizona were bilking
Americans out of at least $100 million per year. Broad-based investigations
growing out of the murder of reporter Don Bolles were said to have uncovered a vast array of sophisticated fraud. An article in *U.S. News and World
Report* told of massive abuses in chain-owned nursing homes, linked to
medical clinics and pharmacies that were highly susceptible to kickbacks,
extortion, bribery, and padded claims. The corruption included use of elaborate computer programs by medicaid billing agents for fraudulent purposes.[12]

There were also indications that the society had become more sensitive
to its crime and corruption problems. Commissioner Patrick Murphy took
important steps in the early 1970s to reduce New York City police corruption. The Organized Crime Act of 1970 makes it a federal crime for state
and local law enforcement officials to protect gambling operations, and
federal strike forces have moved against organized crime with considerable
vigor since the mid-1960s. In one instance a two-year investigation led to
the 1975 conviction of fifty persons for defrauding the FHA and Veterans
Administration in Los Angeles.[13]   By 1977 some twenty-four states had
ethics laws with boards or commissions to administer them. California's
Political Reform Act of 1974 (passed through the initiative process as Proposition 9) contained sweeping provisions on campaign disclosure, campaign
expenditure limits, lobbying, conflicts of interest, and other matters.

THE CONCEPT OF POLITICAL CORRUPTION

Unethical political behavior in the United States has not received as much
attention from political scientists as other aspects of the American political
process. Representative data are difficult to obtain either from records or

---

[11]William J. Bennett, "Let's Bring Back Heroes," *Newsweek*, August 15, 1977, p. 3; and
Peter N. Stearns, "The Fading of Youth," *Newsweek*, July 23, 1979, p. 15.

[12]*New York Times*, May 21, 1979, p. 1; "Medicaid Abuse: Even Worse Than Feared," *U.S.
News and World Report*, June 4, 1979, pp. 43–45.

[13]George C. S. Benson, Steven A. Maarinen, and Alan Heslop, *Political Corruption in
America* (Lexington, Mass.: Lexington Books, D. C. Heath & Co., 1978), pp. 247–250; Lester
A. Sobel, ed., *Post-Watergate Morality* (New York: Facts on File, 1978), p. 160.

interviews, and definitions are apt to be slippery. Joseph LaPalombara believes that many leading American social scientists have been upwardly mobile persons who, as increasingly staunch defenders of the existing system, have been likely to ignore or play down political corruption.[14] Since the study of corruption requires fortitude, it may be easier on the psyche to investigate other countries or earlier eras. Then too, high voltage moralizing can easily degenerate into simplemindedness and self-righteousness. In many cases it is wise to suspend ethical judgments temporarily in the interest of getting a better understanding of social phenomena.

There has, of course, been a critical awareness of corruption in the popular culture, in political movements such as populism and progressivism, in investigative journalism, and in the works of such "hardboiled" mystery writers as Dashiell Hammett and Raymond Chandler. All nations develop a colorful vocabulary to refer to corrupt practices. Unethical fees to public officials are referred to as *la mordida* in Spanish-speaking countries, *la bustarella, baksheesh, speed money,* or *dash* in other settings.[15]

Most of the English words used to describe corruption are American in origin, and many of them are richly expressive. *Graft, kickback, fix, rake-off, payola, grease,* and *spoils* resist precise definition, yet each conveys a somewhat different shade of meaning. Most of these words apply only to the political arena, but *payola, kickback,* and *rake-off* can also pertain to commercial transactions. (None is as broad as *baksheesh,* which in India shades into legitimate tipping practices.) The words convey a mixture of distaste, amusement, and awe for practices that the speaker expects to occur in shabby or otherwise dubious social settings. In recent years, these older terms have been joined by *hustle, rip-off,* and *scam.*

Abuse of public authority can be defined as a deviation from the formal duties of a public role as measured against a legal standard, public opinion, or some conception of the public interest. The legal criterion is useful for purposes of comparative analysis, but because legal norms change, such a criterion raises difficulties where the concern is with corruption over long periods of time. Moreover, corruption is not primarily a legal problem. At their best, the laws of the state are products of political compromise achieved through relatively impersonal processes. Aleksandr Solzhenitsyn has correctly decried the "atmosphere of moral mediocrity" that results from an excessive reliance on legalism in the West:

> If one is right from a legal point of view, nothing more is required, nobody may mention that one could still not be entirely right, and urge self-restraint or a renunciation of these rights, call for sacrifice and selfless risk: this would simply sound absurd. Voluntary self-restraint is almost unheard of; everybody strives toward further expansion to the extreme limit of the legal frames.[16]

[14]Joseph LaPalombara, *Politics within Nations* (Englewood Cliffs, N.J.: Prentice-Hall, Inc., 1974), pp. 373–374.
[15]Ibid., p. 403.
[16]Aleksandr Solzhenitsyn, *A World Split Apart* (New York: Harper & Row, Inc., 1978), p. 17.

One recent study is particularly helpful in thinking about the "grey areas" associated with corruption. This approach focuses on the circumstances under which corruption *may* occur and explores how different groups perceive the same behavior and how the same people attach varying blame to different kinds of actions. The key formulation can be most simply presented in the form of a statement in which the key terms are italicized, as follows:

> Corruption *may* occur when *officials* extend *favors* that benefit *recipients* in *exchange* for *payoffs* received from *donors.*[17]

Note that one can describe ordinary democratic politics in these terms without regarding it as corrupt. All legislation favors some groups more than others, and favoritism must be marked for any taint of corruption to be properly inferred. The payoff may be reelection or greater popularity.

In speculating about the variations, the authors make some interesting points. Canons of correct behavior often vary in stringency with the nature of the official role. For example, people usually hold judges to higher conflict of interest standards than legislators; among legislators, favors for constituents are less likely to be perceived as corrupt than favors to nonconstituents. People may single out donations by a single individual for greater blame than donations by a large group of individuals or firms. Consider some of the responses in questionnaires filled out by state senators: Nearly all agreed that it would be a corrupt act for a city crew to pave the driveway of the mayor's home; however, only 24 percent thought it was corrupt for a public official to use his influence to get a friend or relative admitted to law school. More than half thought most public officials would not consider it corrupt for a presidential candidate to promise an ambassadorship in exchange for campaign contributions, but 81 percent believed that most of the *public* would condemn it![18]

Larger Considerations

There is a tendency to visualize corruption only in its petty forms. A veneer of legality may disguise larger-scale corruption and make it appear respectable. Although corrupt acts probably occur with greater frequency at lower levels of government, they are likely to have more serious consequences when they occur at higher levels. As previously noted, a single campaign donor is more easily castigated than a large group of donors. The same study notes that people tend to think that private favors are more corrupt than those providing large public benefits. Major corruption, such as the systematic looting of the public domain that has occurred in most countries at some time, or the Teapot Dome scandal, or the abuses associated with Watergate may be so extensive and so brazen that we cannot

[17]John G. Peters and Susan Welch, "Political Corruption in America: A Search for Definitions and a Theory, or If Political Corruption Is in the Mainstream of American Politics Why Is It Not in the Mainstream of American Politics Research?" *The American Political Science Review,* 72 (September 1978), 976.
[18]Ibid., 976–981.

easily adjust our thinking to them. People feel that bribes, which occur rarely, are outrageous, but campaign contributions given in hope of preferred treatment are probably the rule rather than the exception, and the public has tended to view them with tolerant suspicion.

Not all corruption is necessarily bad, but most of the claimed justifications apply to less developed societies and have little applicability in the United States today. In a poor country, opportunities for nepotism may attract qualified persons to poorly paid positions. By making structures and practices more flexible, corruption may also be a means of avoiding violence in some countries. LaPalombara, who cites these points, deplores premature attacks against corruption in underdeveloped nations and feels that they can retard the emergence of needed bureaucratic and party structures. He also notes that these points are widely debated among scholars. Another student of the subject urges us to look at the groups that are excluded from power in estimating the probable strains caused by corruption. If the wealthy are systematically excluded from power, large-scale corruption is likely to occur. He feels that corruption often cements a conservative coalition that is likely to hold back on collective demands.[19]

Some analysts of American politics speak of "systemic corruption." The term draws attention to the fact that the trading of payoffs and favors is not merely an isolated phenomenon. Different students of American politics use the expression in different ways. For Berg, Hahn, and Schmidhauser, political authority tends to be pervasively corrupted by the holders of the major economic resources in the society.

> Through subtle and covert process, as well as from direct bribery and favoritism, powerful economic interests in America have reaped political subsidies and rewards that shift the burden of the cost of government to the rank-and-file citizen who must pay for these through taxes.[20]

These authors do not suggest that this kind of corruption cannot be corrected in a capitalist society. They urge instead that more attention be focused on the role of money in political campaigns and hope that certain reforms will enable citizens to surmount political corruption. In their discussion of Watergate, they identify institutional shortcomings as the focus of systemic corruption. They argue, for example, that the House Judiciary Committee should have held Nixon in contempt for his refusal to provide the committee with pertinent evidence, that Congress avoided doing its duty by not passing judgment in an impeachment proceeding, and that only small portions of the news media were able to play an effective role as the "loyal opposition."[21]

Philip Kurland also tends to believe that abuses of power have been pervasive, although he does not use the term "systemic corruption." He

---

[19]LaPalombara, *Politics within Nations*, pp. 414–417; James Scott, *Comparative Political Corruption* (Englewood Cliffs, N.J.: Prentice-Hall, Inc., 1972), pp. ix, 33.
[20]Berg, Hahan, and Schmidhauser, *Corruption in the American Political System*, p. 13.
[21]Ibid., pp. 27, 72–75, 80–82.

rejects theories that make money the root of all evil, and argues that love of power is more dangerous than love of money. Watergate, he says, was a constitutional crisis that involved cumulated political power, and the primary malignancy was the "growing cancer of the dictatorial presidency." He asserts that the focus on campaign finance in the wake of Watergate gets at palliatives rather than cures, symptoms rather than causes.[22]

Contemporary American Corruption

Looking back in time an observer can easily get the impression that political improprieties were more serious and more frequent in earlier eras. If early America was underdeveloped, and if corruption plays a constructive role in underdeveloped societies, one might be tempted to infer that rampant corruption of the post–Civil War era somehow assisted in the development of a new political and industrial system in the United States.

Does it follow that corruption is less of a problem in the United States now that the country is relatively developed? Tempting as such a conclusion is, we should view it with deep suspicion. It is true that growing affluence, the rise in educational levels, and professionalism in administration have lessened the availability and appeal of certain kinds of political favors. The era of the machines seems to be over, and modern legislative bodies are regarded by those that know them best as much improved at all levels of government. It also seems to be true that the society has become more sensitive to such injustices as traditional treatment of aged, handicapped, and homosexual persons, as well as women.

However, we have no good evidence that formal education, technology, or wealth have purifying effects on individuals. If in some cases they lessen the incentive to engage in corrupt behavior, in others they increase a person's capacities for corruption. The transition from a predominantly working-class to a predominantly middle-class society may have increased the proportion of white-collar crimes, which are difficult to prosecute. The decline of political machines, rather than reducing corruption, may have only dispersed the exchange of payoffs more widely. Government has greatly expanded its scope of operations, and other things being equal, this increases the potential for political corruption.

Variations

The idealistic impulse in a society vacillates, and even at its strongest it does not always lower the society's level of corruption. Excessive idealism can even produce a reaction in the opposite direction—as when Americans fought the Civil War and World War I in the spirit of moral crusades, then lapsed into periods of low ethical practices afterwards. When idealism is translated into legislation to control gambling, prostitution, alcohol, and drugs, the results are often undesirable. When laws set standards that im-

---

[22]Philip B. Kurland, *Watergate and the Constitution* (Chicago: University of Chicago Press, 1978), pp. 4–5, 180–183. For other important reflections on corruption—especially its relation to violence, betrayal, secrecy, and propaganda—see Carl J. Friedrich, *The Pathology of Politics* (New York: Harper & Row, Publishers, 1972).

portant segments of the society will not accept, they not only encourage illicit businesses but also give lawbreakers an inducement to corrupt law enforcement personnel. For example, the effort to eliminate alcoholic beverages by constitutional amendment in 1920 was motivated by idealism, and Prohibition achieved some good results. However, Prohibition also led to major smuggling operations, secret bars operated under police protection, and criminal control of liquor traffic. The most notorious instance was "Scarface Al" Capone of Chicago, who presided over a small army of hoodlums and accumulated a gross income of $60 million before being jailed for income tax evasion in 1931.[23]

Differences in the American political culture stemming from early settlement patterns also color attitudes toward political corruption. One such cluster of values and practices, according to Daniel Elazar, is the "individualistic political culture." It began, he says, with the distinctive emphasis on individual freedom to pursue private goals held by most of the persons who originally settled in New York, New Jersey, Pennsylvania, Delaware, and Maryland. These groups were ethnically and religiously diverse. They differed markedly from the more homogeneous Puritans and Yankees in New England with their predominantly religious motivations. The thinking of those in the middle Atlantic states also differed from that of the plantation-centered society of the South. As the nation expanded, the descendants of these middle states moved westward and left their imprint on many parts of Ohio, Indiana, Illinois, Missouri, and points further west.

In Elazar's view, the individualistic culture looks upon the political order as a marketplace. Politics becomes a "business" and political parties become "business corporations" that provide the necessary organization to maintain the political marketplace. People in such cultures think that government exists to satisfy individual needs, not to improve the community or harness itself to some cause. The general view is that politics is best left to professionals. The public does not become agitated about political corruption unless it becomes extraordinary in scope or degree.[24]

A major problem in studies and analyses of corruption is the degree to which it is exposed. Unless it has already been at least partly exposed, the researcher has nothing to investigate. Yet the corruption that has been uncovered (and that we therefore know something about) may be only a small and unrepresentative part of the total. For example, the morning after a court convicted Maryland Governor Marvin Mandel on charges of profiteering, an English newspaper stated that Maryland was the most politically corrupt American state. However, scholars know of no reliable way to rank states in the degree of corruption. Corruption has been conspicuous in Maryland, but perhaps that state has greater capabilities of exposure and prosecution. One might say the same of New Jersey, where prosecutors have obtained numerous convictions of political figures in recent years. Nobody knows whether these states are more or less corrupt than many others.

[23]John A. Garraty, *A Short History of the American Nation* (New York: Harper & Row, Publishers, Inc., 1974), p. 402.

[24]Elazar, *American Federalism*, pp. 92–114. The other two cultures depicted by Elazar (the "moralistic" and the "traditionalistic") are less tolerant of political corruption.

Perhaps corruption in top echelons of the three branches of national government is the most serious as well as the most likely to be exposed. Media attention and public concern is greatest at this level. Also, if past corruption is easier to study than present corruption, we might expect that historians would by now have exposed much of the high-level corruption of earlier eras.

Common Features of Political Corruption

One recent analysis focuses on three major scandals involving presidents: the Grant scandals, the Harding scandals (Teapot Dome, abuses in the Veterans' Bureau, the alien property scandal and other incidents), and Watergate.[25] The author detects a number of interesting parallels, including the following:

1. In each instance "the seemingly reflexive response of the president was to deny scandal and/or to cover it up and protect his associates." Each president regarded efforts to clear the government of corrupt friends as a personal attack.
2. In each instance those interested in exposing and prosecuting had good reason to distrust the Department of Justice. A combination of congressional hearings and a legal process outside regular Department of Justice channels brought many of the cases to the fore. Interestingly enough, the role of the press became increasingly important over time, and during Watergate it was virtually "a full partner in the investigative process."
3. Each episode came in the aftermath of a relatively unpopular war and an expansion of presidential powers.
4. Each episode resulted in a breakdown of public trust in government and perhaps even in the moral fortitude of the general population.[26]

Nobody seems to have attempted a careful investigation aimed at discovering whether offenders in major observed incidents of political corruption received suitable punishment. As Berg, Hahn, and Schmidhauser point out, there may be a greater need for swift and certain punishment than for severe sentences. They argue that serious violations of campaign laws should carry mandatory jail sentences of from six months to two years. Evidence from the sources already cited suggests that extreme leniency is the usual rule. The principal participants in the Yazoo land frauds, say Berg and his associates, "ultimately enjoyed greater economic and political success than the opponents who condemned their actions." Nobody went to jail, and many of the original speculators continued to be accepted in the most distinguished circles. All of the main participants in the Credit Mobilier operation escaped any punishment, and some of those who moved against the Grant scandals suffered for it. Thus, after General George A.

---

[25]Jarol B. Manheim, *Dejavu* (New York: St. Martin's Press, Inc., 1976), Chap. 4. The Grant scandals included Credit Mobilier, the gold conspiracy, the whiskey ring, the treasury scandal of 1873, Belknap's sale of appointments and abuse of contracts, and many other incidents. This source gives a good summary account of each of these episodes.

[26]Ibid., pp. 127–132.

Custer testified about abuses in the Indian Bureau, Grant removed him from command and placed him in charge of a six hundred-man regiment. Manheim notes that it was "an angry, disgraced and humiliated Custer who led his troops rather incautiously into the valley of the Little Big Horn." Grant also forced Secretary of the Treasury Benjamin Bristow to resign because of his role in ordering an investigation of Orville Babcock. The Treasury agent who had headed the successful investigation of the whiskey ring was framed for extortion and dismissed.[27]

In the Harding scandals, two officials committed suicide and two others, Charles Forbes and Albert Fall, received jail terms of two years and one year respectively. Forbes was head of the Veterans Bureau. Among other things, he is said to have purchased a hundred-year supply of floor cleaner and wax at more than thirty times its actual value. Secretary of Interior Albert Fall was the first cabinet member in American history to receive a jail sentence. He had received $168,000 from oilmen Harry Sinclair and E. L. Doheny and had secured the transfer of naval oil reserves in California and Wyoming from the Department of the Navy to the Department of the Interior. Thereafter, he had privately arranged the leasing of the reserves to Doheny and Sinclair. Paul Douglas noted that Doheny was acquitted of offering the same bribe that Fall was convicted for accepting. (Sinclair received a nine-month sentence.) In his view, this illustrates a tendency to attach greater blame to guilty public officials than to equally guilty people in private life who usually initiate the corruption.[28]

Watergate, of course, resulted in an unprecedented number of jail sentences. Although Ford pardoned Nixon after becoming president, the Appellate Division of the New York State Supreme Court subsequently disbarred Nixon from the practice of law. It is not easy to say whether all of the various malefactors received appropriate punishment because Watergate had so many different facets: unethical sabotage of the opposition party, burglary, questionable campaign finance practices, perjury, coverups, surveillance, taping of private telephone conversations, enemies lists, personal enrichment, and presidential relations with the Internal Revenue Service, FBI, and CIA.

Unlike other major scandals in American history, much of the initiative for this one seemed to come from the public officials themselves, and corruption as we have defined it was a relatively minor element. Persons who played major roles in resisting or exposing the various abuses do not seem to have suffered particularly, but not many of them have been conspicuously rewarded by the society they served. However, investigative journalists Robert Woodward and Carl Bernstein received accolades for their role in exposing the scandals, thereby gladdening the hearts of the few hardy souls in the United States who are secure enough, concerned enough, or imprudent

---

[27]Manheim, *Dejavu*, pp. 105, 107; Berg, Hahan, and Schmidhauser, *Corruption in American Politics*, pp. 15, 16.

[28]Douglas, *Ethics in Government*, pp. 24–25; Manheim, *Dejavu*, pp. 116–117. Sinclair's punishment stemmed from contempt of Congress and contempt of court. He had refused to testify before a congressional committee, and he had hired private detectives to spy on his jury. Ibid., p. 118.

enough to actively oppose corrupt political practices. Although Archibald Cox missed out on an appointment to the Supreme Court, he became Chairman of Common Cause in February 1980.

CORRUPTION IN CONGRESS

Problems of political corruption in Congress are among the most significant we could discuss. Maintaining a satisfactory climate of political morality is difficult if the nation's elected leaders do not maintain the highest possible ethical standards. Yet the power of Congress and its remarkably individualistic values make it difficult to attain such standards. The U.S. Congress is the strongest legislative body in the world and, as such, becomes a natural magnet to those who seek economic benefits through political channels. Strongly established prerogatives of individual members make it possible for any representative or senator to become a target of pressure. These same prerogatives create the need for complex procedures that lower the visibility of congressional decision making.

Americans have always expected members to represent local constituency interests. The pertinence of this for possible corruption was well stated by Alistair Cooke in 1951. He noted that in the House of Commons, every member of a standing committee must swear that his constituents have no local interest in the bill under discussion.

> This is quite different from watching the Congress bring up a bill and expecting your man to amend it in your interest. This difference may not be so good for the folks back home . . . but it does make possible a national legislature and encourages the honesty of its members.[29]

Ethical shortcomings of Congress are an old story. Modern standards of conduct in the courts crystallized early in the nineteenth century, but comparable canons for legislative bodies appear to be, even now, only in the formative or exploratory stage. H. Hubert Wilson, writing in 1951, detected a nationwide contempt for Congress that had begun many years earlier and persisted up to that time. He thought that this attitude was lamentably indiscriminate but not without foundation since Congress had ignored countless accusations against its members and tacitly acknowledged their truth. Things had been even worse, of course, in the nineteenth century. Henry Adams, says Wilson, recollected a cabinet officer telling him in the Andrew Johnson era: "You can't use tact with a Congressman! A congressman is a hog! You must take a stick and hit him on the snout!"[30]

[29] *Balancing Moral Responsibility and Scientific Progress,* report of the 20th annual New York Herald-Tribune Forum, October 22–24, 1951, p. 44. The quotation appears in George B. Galloway, *The Legislative Process in Congress* (New York: Thomas Y. Crowell Company, Inc., 1953), p. 385.
[30] "As for members of the Upper House," notes Wilson, "even Adams admitted that the senators passed belief." H. Hubert Wilson, *Congress: Corruption and Compromise* (New York: Holt, Rinehart & Winston, 1951), p. 6.

There is little doubt that greater corruption occurs in Congress than in legislatures of other modern democracies such as Britain, France, Japan, Sweden, Switzerland, and Holland. How long this has been so is not clear. One study claims that many of these countries were worse than the United States in 1800. It is possible that the comparison among legislatures reflects generally higher levels of corruption in American society as a whole, although there are those who believe otherwise. William James, for example, in a letter from Europe at the time of the Dreyfus affair, spoke of the "solidly entrenched and permanently organized corruptive geniuses of monarchy, nobility, church and army." To him, these had far more sinister effects than America's "improvised and shifting agencies of crude pecuniary bribery."[31] Even if corruption is not more entrenched in Europe, legislatures there are generally less powerful than the American Congress and thus provide a less inviting target.

General sensitivity to congressional ethics seems to have increased substantially in the past twenty years. The escapades of Bobby Baker and cases involving Adam Clayton Powell and Thomas Dodd came to light almost simultaneously in the 1960s and seem to have triggered a search for new institutional responses.

Baker had come to Washington in 1943, at age fourteen, from Pickens, South Carolina, to be a Senate page. When Lyndon Johnson became majority leader in 1955 he made Baker secretary to the majority. Baker worked closely with Senate leaders, helped them keep track of votes, and assisted in political fund raising. The press began to investigate Baker closely after a $30,000 out-of-court settlement on a civil claim that Baker had used his influence to obtain contracts for a vending machine firm in defense plants. Probes revealed that Baker had become a millionaire on a salary of $19,000 a year. Baker resigned in October 1963, and a two-year spate of Senate investigative activity followed. A federal district court convicted him of income tax evasion, theft, and conspiracy to defraud the government in January 1967.[32]

The House expelled Powell in 1967 after numerous irregularities, including charges of misuse of public funds. The Supreme Court ordered that he be readmitted, but when he returned to Congress in 1969, the House fined him and stripped him of seniority. The Senate censured Dodd in June 1967 for using campaign funds for personal purposes.

Each of the three episodes tended to be a drawn-out affair, and their impact was probably cumulative. Thus, there was a gap of eight years between Baker's resignation and the beginning of his prison sentence. One could only speculate or how many people knew what he had been doing for how long. Powell was a talented individual whose flamboyance, self-aggrandizement, and racial assertiveness had been intermittent items in the news

---

[31]Benson et al., *Political Corruption*, p. 4; the James quotation is to be found in Kurland, *Watergate and the Constitution*, p. 180.

[32]Baker began a four-year jail sentence in 1971 and was paroled in June of 1972. *Congress and the Nation* (Washington: Congressional Quarterly, Inc.), *Congressional Quarterly*, 1 (1945–1964), 1773–1778; 20 (1965–1968), 644–645; 37 (1969–1972), 417; Edmund Beard and Stephen Horn, *Congressional Ethics* (Washington: The Brookings Institution, 1975), pp. 1–2.

for years. In his own summation of his congressional career, he once said: "As a member of Congress, I have done nothing more than any other member and, by the grace of God, I intend to do not one bit less."[33] In 1958, for example, there had been a grand jury probe of his tax returns, and Tammany leaders in New York voted to drop him as a candidate. The charges against Dodd came initially from the Drew Pearson/Jack Anderson column in 1966, but an initial Senate inquiry cleared him of any wrongdoing. As the press raised new charges, the Senate mounted a second investigation, and this ultimately produced effective action.[34]

Following these and other episodes, each house established an ethics committee, and the legal profession moved to discourage the practice of law by members of Congress. The early 1970s brought a case of influence-peddling in Speaker John W. McCormack's offices, and a federal court convicted one of McCormack's top aides, Martin Swieg, of perjury and of misusing the Speaker's office to influence government decisions. Nathanial Voloshen also pleaded guilty to conspiring to use the Speaker's office for illegal purposes and lying to a grand jury about the charges. According to a book published in 1972, Voloshen had paid McCormack a $2,500 monthly fee for working out of the Speaker's office so that he could obtain favorable agency rulings for business clients. The author claimed that companies paid substantial fees to Voloshen, which he would split with McCormack and perhaps one or two others.[35]

The Voloshen/Sweig episode did not have the impact of the earlier instances cited, but Watergate, of course, placed enormous pressure on Congress. The feeling grew that Congress should be more independent of the president and more assertive in policy making. But for Congress to do this effectively, it would have to demonstrate sensitivity to issues of congressional corruption. A study of earlier attitudes, published in 1975, suggested that pressures generated by publicized scandals were forcing changes in the House, but mainly on the basis of self-interest and political realism. The authors stated that the House had strongly resisted the creation of an independent federal elections commission in 1974.[36]

The later 1970s seemed to witness a continuing stream of incidents and a raising of critical standards. In 1976 the House disciplined Wayne Hays and Robert Sikes but failed to investigate or take action against possible misdeeds of numerous other members. The most pervasive scandal that year, according to Congressional Quarterly, centered on illegal campaign contributions from Gulf Oil to dozens of legislators. Also, eighteen members admitted to receiving unreported free hunting trips from various defense contractors. The *Wall Street Journal* reported charges that ten House members had filed false travel expense claims, and these never got beyond the preliminary stages of investigation. The House shouted down a move to strip Andrew Hinshaw of his office because of his conviction on bribery

[33]*New York Times Biographical Edition,* April 1972, p. 846.
[34]Beard and Horn, *Congressional Ethics,* pp. 1–5.
[35]Robert N. Winter-Berger, *The Washington Payoff* (New York: Dell Publishing Co., Inc., 1972), as cited in Benson et al., *Political Corruption,* p. 141.
[36]Beard and Horn, *Congressional Ethics,* p. 83.

charges.[37] According to Congressional Quarterly: "Unlike the Watergate scandal, which prompted both houses to launch highly publicized, lengthy investigations, most members tried to ignore the allegations of impropriety on Capitol Hill."[38]

Between 1976 and 1978 attention turned to probes begun by the Securities and Exchange Commission and Justice Department into a South Korean influence ring in Washington ("Koreagate") that centered on businessman Tongsun Park. This was a multifaceted episode, and at the end of 1976 five different investigations were under way, including those of three different House committees. Various strands of the affair involved the former Korean ambassador, the Korean Central Intelligence Agency, Suzi Park Thomson (an employee in Speaker Carl Albert's office), and Reverend Sun Myung Moon. Investigations headed by Representative Donald Fraser found that the Korean lobbying effort had begun in 1970 and suggested the possibility that executive branch agencies had covered it up beginning in 1971. House and Senate ethics committees completed their work in October 1978 without recommending severe disciplinary actions against any members, even though early reports had indicated that as many as 115 had taken illegal gifts from Korean agents. According to Congressional Quarterly, the House ethics investigation had ended "in a bang of hyperbole, a whimper of opprobrium, and a mass of uncertainties about the future of the ethics process."[39]

Scandals continued to unfold after the Korean influence episode, but the general reaction suggested that outside pressure would force Congress to upgrade its ethical standards and its methods of securing compliance. In 1979 a court sentenced former representative Joshua Eilberg on criminal conflict of interest charges, the House censured Charles Diggs, the Justice Department began a jury-tampering inquiry on a mistrial involving Daniel Flood, and the Senate voted to "denounce" Herman Talmadge for financial misconduct. In 1980 the FBI's "Abscam" operations provided new evidence of wrongdoing while raising questions about procedures and actions of investigative agencies. By April 1981, six members of the House had been convicted in connection with the Abscam investigation. Five of the six individuals convicted had failed in their attempts to seek reelection: John W. Murphy of New York, Frank Thompson, Jr., of New Jersey, John W. Jenrette, Jr., of South Carolina, Michael Myers of Pennsylvania, and Richard Kelly of Florida. Jenrette resigned from the House on December 12 under threat of an expulsion proceeding.

[37]Congressional Quarterly, *Congressional Ethics,* p. 3.
[38]Ibid. The House forced Wayne Hays to resign as chairman of the House Administration Committee because of allegations by Elizabeth Ray that he had given her a job in exchange for sexual favors. The House reprimanded Sikes for financial misconduct in 1976 and the Democratic caucus ousted him as chairman of the Military Construction Appropriations Committee the following year.
[39]*Congressional Quarterly Almanac 1978,* pp. 803–811. Although the House did not censure any of its members, it did reprimand several.

Congressional Perquisites

Traditionally congressional service was assumed to be part-time work and members were expected to have other sources of income. Even the Legislative Reorganization Act of 1946 assumed that Congress could adjourn before August, and in 1950 the congressional salary was still only $12,500. Even if one included the $2,500 tax-free expense allowance, congressional remuneration was far below the $22,500 that cabinet members received or the $25,000 earned by Supreme Court justices. By the mid 1950s virtually continuous congressional sessions had become the rule, and informed observers were calling for pay increases. Congressional salaries in selected years reveal the rate of increase since then:

	Congressional Salaries	Consumer Price Index (1967 = 100)
1950	$12,500	72.1
1960	22,500	88.7
1970	42,500	116.3
1977	57,500	181.5
1980	60,662	233.2

The 1980 price index figure is for January. U.S. Dept. of Labor, Bureau of Labor Statistics, *Monthly Labor Review*, Ap. 1980. p. 89.

Sources: Congressional Quarterly, *Congressional Ethics*, p. 30; U.S. Census, *Statistical Abstract of the United States 1978*, p. 490.

Considering the shift to full-time service, the desirability of making members less dependent on outside income, the desirability of attracting qualified people, and the rise in price levels, the salary increases have not been excessive.

However, congressional fringe benefits and perquisites, taken in their totality, raise more difficult questions. One problem with them is that there are so many that it is hard to state an overall value. They begin with perquisites that are normal for most professional or mid-level executives in the regular society: free parking, office space, telephone service, office supplies, and travel allowances as well as health insurance, life insurance, and retirement benefits. Members enjoy informal perquisites that stem from being a VIP: probability of press coverage when desired, special treatment by government agencies, ability to delay departures of planes, and so forth. These, too, are not unknown in the regular society, although few entertainers, professionals, or executives attain VIP status. Washington social life is unusually intensive and becomes a fringe benefit in a sense, but most legislators must restrict their participation in it and do a good deal of entertaining at their own expense. Members get free preparation of packages for mailing (by "Jack the Wrapper" on the Senate side); extensive computer assistance; free wall calendars and government publications; unrestricted parking (any car with Congressional plates) anywhere in Washington while on official business; gymnasium, swimming pool, paddleball court, and sauna; and individual photographic service.

A staff of doctors and nurses gives members free medical care while at work. There are tax deductions for Washington living expenses and special allowances for traveling abroad. Additional money that can be earned through speaking, writing, and publishing. There are also franking privileges, generous allowances for long-distance phone calls, WATS lines, sophisticated radio and television recording facilities, special discount merchandise in office building shops, low-cost food services from cafeteria to catering, low-cost or free beauty and barber service, IRS office on Capitol Hill to help members prepare income tax returns, and so on.[40]

How does one decide what an appropriate array of perquisites should be? Probably, most of us want the members of our highest legislative body to have emblems suitable to their status and power. If national legislators did not receive VIP treatment, we might wonder what to do about it. Some perquisites help Congress do its work in a distinguished manner. In this respect, personal and committee staff resources (the most important perquisites of all) loom very large, as do specialized congressional agencies such as the General Accounting Office, Congressional Budget Office, and Congressional Research Service.

Having said all this, Americans might well be concerned if enjoyment of the perquisites was to become a major reason for people to seek congressional office. The fringe benefits have expanded somewhat in the last twenty years, and they may isolate legislators too much from life as ordinary Americans experience it. A degree of isolation is inherent in VIP treatment, of course, but the emblems of prestige need not be elaborate in a properly functioning republic. Dignity and style should have greater weight than unusual privileges.

Another question is whether perquisites give unwarranted advantage to members seeking reelection. Incumbency advantage may not be any greater in the United States than in legislatures of other democratic nations, but most of us would not want this advantage to result from the tangible rewards of office holding. We could better assess this matter if we knew how much incumbency advantage was "too much." Many political scientists believe that a high probability of reelection gives legislators a chance to become experienced and that it therefore adds to the capacity of Congress to assert itself in national policy.

We have a fair idea of the factors that make the probability of reelection to a House seat better than 90 percent, but we do not know how they rank in importance. Perquisites are undoubtedly among these factors, especially the large numbers of persons legislators can hire at their own discretion. In fact, the size of congressional staff has now expanded to the point

[40]Ibid., pp. 27–55.

where it raises other concerns, among them the potential bureaucratization of Congress, and the possibility of legislators losing influence as the staff imprint on policy becomes greater. A related issue is how legislators should balance their policy-making responsibilities against the need to service state or district interests. Much of the increase in staff has possibly resulted from a simple increase in communication traffic. In this context, moral issues are relatively minor.

Congress Reacts

The most noteworthy congressional response to its ethics problems consists of new codes of ethics adopted in 1977 by special resolutions in each house and a government-wide ethics law that went on the books in 1978.[41] Senate and House versions of the codes differ somewhat. Both place detailed restrictions on gifts, office accounts, use of franked mail, foreign travel, and outside earned income. Excluding the financial disclosure provisions (which were the principal focus of the ethics law), the major provisions of the codes on these matters are summarized in Table 12–1.

Financial disclosure provisions of the ethics law apply to all legislators, all principal assistants, and all legislative branch employees paid at the GS–16 level or higher. Any candidate for congressional office must also file a report. Reports are due by May 15, the public must have access to them within fifteen days, and reports must remain available for five years. Early versions of the bill restricted outside earned income and supplied criminal as well as civil penalties, but these did not survive the legislative mill.

The degree of detail required in the reports is extensive, although dollar amounts are mostly reported by broad categories of value (such as $5,000 to $15,000 and $15,000 to $50,000). Those filing reports must provide information on source and type of any outside income, and information of varying detail on gifts, honoraria, property holdings, debts, trade or business interest, finances of spouses and dependent children, and qualified blind trusts. House and Senate ethics committees have responsibility for reviewing reports to see if they are properly filed, and the General Accounting Office also monitors compliance. Violations are subject to civil penalties up to $5,000.[42]

How Much Progress?

It is difficult to determine how much real progress has been made in decreasing the likelihood of congressional corruption, exposing it when it occurs, and dealing with it in an appropriate manner. However, checking the current situation against responsible complaints of some years ago provides some perspective. Cabell Phillips penned one of the more thought-

[41]H. Res. 287 and S. Res. 110, 95th Cong., 1st Sess., PL 95–521.

[42]*Congressional Quarterly Almanac, 1978,* pp. 835–841. The law imposed similar disclosure requirements on top-level executive and judicial branch personnel. It also established an Office of Government Ethics in the new Office of Personnel Management. Other provisions dealt with the mechanism for appointment of a special prosecutor and restrictions on postgovernment employment.

Table 12-1
Main Provisions of Congressional Codes of Ethics 1977

Gifts

No gifts of $100 or more to be accepted in any year by any member, officer or employee from any lobbyist or foreign national. (Senate ban extends to spouses and dependents.)

Office Accounts

Office costs in Washington and home district to be paid from a single "official expenses" allowance.

No unofficial office accounts.

No conversion of campaign funds to personal use.

Foreign Travel

No per diem for expenses paid by other sources.

No lame duck foreign travel.

Franked Mail

No franked mass-mailing less than 60 days before a primary or general election in which the member is a candidate.

No franked mass-mailings unless preparation and printing costs are paid entirely from public funds.

Outside Income

No outside earned income over 15 percent of official salary. (Does not apply to dividends or other unearned income, or in most cases to income from a family controlled business.)

No honorarium of more than $750 for a representative, or $1000 for a senator.

NOTE: In March 1979, the Senate voted to postpone the beginning of the 15 percent limit for four years.

Special Senate Provisions

No Senate lobbying for one year after leaving the Senate.

No discrimination in Senate employment or promotion because of race, religion, sex, or physical handicap.

No personal services for senators by employees.

Senate ethics committee to enforce the code.

Source: Congressional Quarterly, *Congressional Ethics*, April 1977, pp. 18–24. This summary does not include financial disclosure provisions. In August 1979 and January 1980, the Senate and House respectively substituted provisions of the Ethics in Government Act (PL 95–521) for the disclosure provisions of the Senate and House codes of ethics. See Congressional Quarterly, *Congressional Ethics*, 2nd ed., 1980, p. 77.

ful analyses, and it appeared in George Galloway's text published in 1953.[43] Phillips thought Congress had a smaller proportion of deliberately dishonest persons than the population at large. However, he found congressional corruption to be serious in the following respects:

[43]Galloway, *The Legislative Process in Congress,* pp. 386–391.

1. The use of a double standard of morality that markedly favored the legislators over other public officials. "No one ever investigates Congress," Phillips asserted.
2. Abuse of influence. "A telephone call from a Senator or Congressman can paralyze the will of a government executive and alter the course of national policy. A vengeful member of Congress can shatter a reputation or destroy a program."
3. An "influence racket" that grew out of this. "Influence peddling" was common, and some members may have been taking fees for representing clients before an agency of the government (a statutory felony). Members often could squeeze concessions from regulatory agencies or affect administrative decisions that could "spell fortune or disaster for various interested citizens."[44]
4. A general dulling of ethics at the edges "by the nature of their calling and its rules of survival. . . . Their adult lives have been lived in the atmosphere of the deal, the compromise, the reciprocal personal favor."
5. The avoidance of bribes but the taking of illegitimate rewards "clothed in political raiment" (such as campaign contributions), which enabled recipients to rationalize their acceptance.
6. Lack of any written or unwritten code of conduct. "Each member is his own censor and his morals and his motives are nobody's business but his."
7. Refusal to seek out and punish congressional wrong doers. Use of the "club spirit" to "cover up evil."

If this was an accurate portrayal of the main problems, congressional ethics have probably improved a great deal. Congress still tends toward a double standard, but it is much less able to maintain it these days. Investigations by the Justice Department, Securities and Exchange Commission, and other agencies are now facts of life for individual legislators who may be engaged in wrong doing. Although self-policing and the even-handed punishment of infractions are not yet the rule, it is no longer true that "no one investigates Congress." Press attention to congressional corruption is also more intensive than it once was.[45] Abuse of influence with the executive branch is undoubtedly a continuing problem but possibly less so than formerly. In the complex issue networks of today, the influence racket may now appear more crude and more likely to boomerang.

Cabell Phillips thought that the dulling of ethical sensitivity grew out of the members' background in old-style organization politics. However, most members of Congress today have *not* "fought their way up through precinct, city and state political machines." The politics of recent years—at least for national legislators—has relied more on personal style and publicity than on favor from party leaders. (This may incidentally have impaired the capacity of members to compromise their differences and follow political leadership.) Codes of conduct and comprehensive disclosure requirements are undoubtedly not all they should be, and one might prefer to see stiffer penalties for infractions of the codes, tighter restrictions on post-

[44]Phillips's comments, published in 1953, claimed that in the past twenty years Washington had supplanted Wall Street as the wielder of financial power. Ibid., p. 390.

[45]To get a sense of current press concern, see the heading "U.S. Congress" in the *New York Times Index* for any recent year.

congressional employment, better regulation of lobbying, and so forth. However, if the hesitation and general discontent of the legislators in formulating these measures are any indication, the codes are by no means an empty gesture.

Progress has been most questionable in the area of campaign finance. Even though statutes now limit contributions from particular sources and require extensive reporting and accountability, the amounts of money needed have expanded enormously in the past twenty years. The possibility of abuse is ever present, and the image of key congressional incumbents awash in a sea of campaign money is not reassuring. The study of corruption by Berg, Hahn, and Schmidhauser spotlighted campaign finance as perhaps the most critical issue today. They said: "In fact, it is the central thesis of this book that a major source of systemic corruption in America can be found in the interface between economic resources and political power that occurs primarily in election campaigns and to the inequities it produces." They called for public financing of congressional campaigns and lower spending limitations on incumbents than on challengers.[46] It is conceivable that if public financing with spending limits and advantages to challengers turns out to be unachievable (for constitutional or other reasons), reformers will begin to call for arbitrary limits on the number of terms our national legislators can serve.

Perhaps the worse thing to be said of congressional ethics today is that improvement seems to come only as a result of *outside* pressure. Related to this is the sense that everything achieved is in flux and subject to possible change as public interest waxes or wanes. The attitudes of defensiveness and mutual self-protection are still very strong in Congress. More than any other institution one can think of, Congress needs to become *self-directed* in the pursuit of morally defensible standards of behavior if it is to satisfactorily meet the nation's contemporary expectations.

LIMITING CORRUPTION

In terms of sheer volume, most American political corruption probably occurs at the local level. Even so, improving the commitment to ethical standards at the national level may be the key strategic issue. Local corruption will not decline appreciably as long as local citizens and politicians feel (at best) that no example is being set in Washington. The lack of such an example may also encourage white-collar crime in the society at large.

Corruption at the top is both the least defensible and the most dangerous. It is least defensible because salaries and perquisites do not need to be supplemented and because the granting of illegitimate favors by Congress does not usually benefit disadvantaged individuals or groups. (In both respects congressional corruption today may even compare unfavorably with old-style machine politics.) High-level corruption is the most dangerous

---

[46]Berg, Hahn, and Schmidhauser, *Corruption in the American Political System*, pp. 27, 171, 188–190. Quotation on p. 27.

because it threatens the heart of our constitutional order. It does this by destroying legitimacy, by awarding benefits to interests that are already too powerful, and by impairing the capacity of one political branch to check the other.

The belief most members of Congress apparently held in the 1960s—that their behavior was no worse than that of others in the society—is not adequate as a standard of congressional conduct, even if it significantly understates the level of congressional rectitude (as I think it does). Nor is it adequate after all allowance has been made for the quality of congressional work, which, as such, is generally quite good. The public rightly expects its high-level politicians to set an example of rectitude.

The movement towards open meetings and financial disclosure make it more likely that congressional corruption will be exposed *from the outside*. Although this represents genuine progress from an earlier era, success depends ultimately on Congress's perfecting its own standards of conduct and developing pride in them. Outside checks are necessary, but Congress should not have to depend on the FBI or the *New York Times* to generate the needed pressure for disciplining errant members.

Former Senator J. William Fulbright discerns what he believes to be a new breed of legislator that promotes only what is in current demand—reacting to public opinion rather than working for what is in the public interest. He also says that the new breed has discarded the role of educating the people in favor of performing services for the best organized, best funded, and most politically active groups.[47] A self-directed Congress would admittedly be somewhat less responsive to public and group opinion, but a nation hungry for genuine leadership might not object.

Such a Congress would probably have to give its internal leaders strong authority. It would put much less emphasis on localism and individual member freedom—and probably devote less of its staff and its attention to constituency services. Unless citizens are willing to pay such costs, their hopes for a more ethical and assertive Congress may be much more difficult to achieve. The romantic ideal of individual member freedom is that it enables the members to follow their consciences and in the process permits citizens to "vote the man rather than the party." In practice, individual member freedom often means the spreading of local favors and a loss of institutional responsibility and accountability.

We should note that the public may want an *ethical* Congress more than an *assertive* Congress. Even the concern over congressional ethics may be more verbal than actual. If we could find the bottom line in the swirl of public values and practices, we might discover that the public would prefer to rely on the presidency as the motor of government (despite fear of the imperial presidency), while preserving access to Congress as a way to bend the process of government to local or group advantage.

If citizens do want a more assertive and ethically committed Congress, how can they achieve it? At least four strategic opportunities ought to be explored:

[47]J. William Fulbright, "The Legislator as Educator," *Foreign Affairs*, 57 (Spring 1979), 723.

1. *Public financing of congressional campaigns.* Despite many technical difficulties, including constitutional ones, at least some specialists in political finance believe that a sound system of public financing is both possible and desirable. David Adamany is a strong advocate of public financing, and in a recent work he has proposed a voucher system that deserves continued study. He may well be correct in his belief that public finance for one branch but not the other jeopardizes the esteem and power of the unfunded branch.[48]

2. *Revival of congressional parties and the strengthening of congressional leadership.* The natural way to support political leaders is through the device of the political party. This idea was central to H. Hubert Wilson's study of congressional corruption in 1951 and bears repeating today, even though congressional parties seem even weaker now than when he wrote. Perhaps in these times, the emphasis on party must be more modest. The overriding need is to establish leadership in Congress that a majority of members can respect and follow. If some way can be discovered to do this through nonparty means, the revival of parties beyond their present strength might not be necessary. However, what the alternative technique would be or how it would be superior to stronger parties remains elusive. Without stronger leadership in an institutional sense, and without leadership that is willing to press for higher ethical standards, the instincts for mutual self-protection that have inhibited action in the past may prevail.

3. *Regulation of lobbying.* The 1946 Regulation of Lobbying Act should be replaced by a more comprehensive and enforceable statute. In 1978, the House reported a measure which failed in the Senate, even though it was considerably weaker than a measure that never went to conference in the previous Congress. The 1978 bill would have required annual registration and quarterly reporting by major paid lobbying groups and would have applied to about 100,000 executive branch officials as well as national legislators.[49]

4. *More vigorous discipline of errant members.* Each house has the power to censure a member, and next to expulsion this is considered the most severe action that Congress can properly take against a member. The Senate censured Joseph McCarthy in 1954 and Thomas Dodd in 1967; prior to the censure of Diggs in 1979, the House had not censured a member since 1921. Expelling a member in either house requires a two-thirds vote, but as of April 1981 neither chamber had taken this step against a member since the 1860s. H. Hubert Wilson noted, quite correctly, that "throwing the rascals out" is only the beginning of the good fight, but he also offered the sensible suggestion that the beginning must be made.[50] (In May 1981, Representative Raymond Lederer resigned after the House Ethics Committee recommended expulsion for his involvement in the Abscam investigation.)

Censure and expulsion can be abused, but the larger risk is that Congress invites disrespect when it exercises these powers too timidly. Some argue that it is up to the voters to punish the transgressors and that if they elect persons of dubious character, Congress should not supercede that judgment. There is perhaps a grain of truth in this. Voters do have responsibilities, and we should not minimize them. Whether voters in fact usually

[48]David W. Adamany and George E. Agree, *Political Money* (Baltimore: The Johns Hopkins University Press, 1975), p. 176. See also Gary C. Jacobson, *Money in Congressional Elections* (New Haven, Conn.: Yale University Press, 1980), pp. 12–58.
[49]*Congressional Quarterly Almanac, 1978*, p. 782.
[50]Wilson, *Congress: Corruption and Compromise*, p. 12.

censure errant politicians in such cases or support them out of misguided sympathy for the underdog is a nice question. Even so, the separate constitutional responsibility of Congress is clear enough.

Perhaps it would be best to conclude on a note of sympathy for the Congress. Coming to grips with problems of corruption is distasteful and even agonizing. The folkways of mutual deference are deeply rooted in the past and have in many ways served the society well. Some of the approaches listed above may enable Congress to improve its standards with little damage to the comity that ought to exist among legislators. Perhaps too there should be greater emphasis on punishing those who attempt to corrupt public officials. A sense of perspective, along with patience and persistence, will be necessary as we grope our way towards a more legitimate political order.

13

Conclusion

The novelist Aldous Huxley believed that most ignorance is vincible—that we do not know because we do not want to know. Plausible as this idea sounds, it may be insufficient to explain some widespread deficits in political understanding. Admittedly, many people do resist acquiring political knowledge, but one must also concede that getting to the bottom of almost any basic political question poses impressive difficulties. Anthony Downs has even suggested that it is irrational to be well informed about politics "because the low returns from data simply do not justify their cost in time and other scarce resources."[1]

Many intellectuals suppose themselves to be wise yet disdain to think seriously about the needs of democratic politics. Political activists on the other hand often have inhibitions similar to those of Rogers Hornsby (the great right-handed batter) who, legend tells, never read books because he feared they might hurt his eyes.

Today's voters are probably more sophisticated than those of yesteryear, but their knowledgeability is frequently exaggerated. In 1972, for example, best available data indicate that one-fifth of Vietnam "doves" thought that Nixon was closer to their preferred position than McGovern. Another one in six saw no difference between McGovern and Nixon on this issue. In 1974, shortly after the midterm elections were over, almost two-thirds of those interviewed could not recall the name of either the incum-

[1]Anthony Downs, *An Economic Theory of Democracy* (New York: Harper & Row, Publishers, Inc., 1957), p. 259.

bent U.S. representative or the challenger. In 1958 better than 10 percent more people could recall at least one of the names.[2]

PARTIES AND AMERICAN DEMOCRACY

The setting of American electoral politics permits elite, business, and interest group formations to wield considerable power. However, deteriorating capacity to govern is, in my view, more to be feared than the hidden hand of elite rule. The title and content of *Washington Post* reporter Haynes Johnson's recent book *In the Absence of Power* is illustrative. Johnson had first come to Washington during Eisenhower's second term, a progovernment New Deal liberal. But by the late 1970s, he was deeply disturbed by the staggering complexity and ineffectiveness of American government. He found that dedicated people within the bureaucracy showed serious fatigue and resentment. They spoke to him of reaching and exceeding the saturation point in programs, services, benefits; of programs eventually turning inward and becoming self-destructive; of the uselessness of struggling to simplify legislative dictates affecting those programs. Johnson believed that greater burdens on government might make it collapse of its own weight.[3]

Although such problems undoubtedly relate to many aspects of our society, party arrrangements may be among the more significant ones. When the parties are weak, collaboration among elected officials becomes more difficult, and alternative packages of public policies are less available to the citizenry in a reliable form. Leadership becomes more personalistic. Administration expands in response to organized group pressures and becomes less accountable to the larger society through the electoral process. The morass that Haynes Johnson tells us about often disappears from view in the public administration literature. That literature even tends to endorse administrative complexity and absence of overall direction by its stress on such slogans as "devolution," "leadership by change facilitation," "planning is acting," and "authority in the group."[4]

The United States stands at an unprecedented distance in time (a half century or so) from its most recent party realignment. The political situation is fluid, and the country has yet to put the troubles of the 1960s and early 1970s behind it even as new challenges crowd to the fore. Even so, the election of 1980 could easily be interpreted in partisan terms, and it may have marked something new in the making.

Many kinds of party systems are possible in the United States. About the only arrangement Americans cannot have is the elections-without-par-

[2]The recall figures are from Albert D. Cover and David R. Mayhew, draft of chapter for Lawrence C. Dodd and Bruce I. Oppenheimer, eds., *Congress Reconsidered* (New York: Congressional Quarterly Press, 1981). The perceptions of Nixon and McGovern by "doves" is from Warren E. Miller and Teresa E. Levitin, *Leadership and Change* (Cambridge, Mass.: Winthrop Publishers, Inc., 1976), p. 141.

[3]Haynes Johnson, *In the Absence of Power* (New York: The Viking Press, 1980), p. 71.

[4]H. George Frederickson, "Public Administration in the 1970's: Developments and Direction," *Public Administration Review*, 36 (1976), 564–576.

ties that they sometimes seem to most prefer. We can be sure that parties of some sort will exist as long as elections are held and as long as people are permitted to exercise basic political freedoms. The present party system could become even weaker, but advantages of parties to both voters and office seekers almost certainly guarantee that a party system of some sort will continue.

Those who advocate stronger parties at present hold quite different viewpoints. To use somewhat different labels from those of Chapter 11, we can identify roughly three "proparty" groups: traditionalists, modernizing reformers, and new politics reformers. Traditionalists favor parties in the old mold. They admire the skills of the professional politician and emphasize the need for compromise and coalition building. Modernizing reformers find the old parties unsatisfactory—too parochial and too job oriented. They want responsible parties that support strong leadership and that are capable of supporting coherent courses of public policy. New politics reformers also reject old-style politics, but they stress participatory democracy and openness within the party. They tend to be sympathetic to the McGovern-Fraser party reforms, and they tend to be less concerned with building organizational strength than with eliminating corruption. Some of them are especially interested in nonparty channels of participation. In the late 1970s, none of the three positions was sustained by a broad consensus in political science or in public life.

My own position has elements of those mentioned above but is most sympathetic to modernizing reform. My hope is for a system that accords central importance to elections and that elicits much more popular participation in all phases of electoral politics. I believe that the United States would be best served by parties that are not only strong in the traditional sense but also more cohesive and policy oriented at the national level. Governmentally, stronger parties should serve to help achieve more capability, more democracy, and more legitimacy. Culturally, stronger parties should help us establish a healthier relationship with our own past and future.

If capability, democracy, and legitimacy have top priority, it seems reasonable to reassert the importance of mechanisms that can give majorities a major influence, and that can help leaders take difficult but necessary political actions in a responsible way. Voting for leaders in terms of their personalities does not produce such a mechanism. The government is too complicated for us to control it simply by choosing attractive political figures and letting them exercise their personal charms. Moreover, a political process stressing personalities can be a long-term danger. The most serious excesses in presidential prerogative occurred during Watergate, when antiparty feelings were especially strong and when the president was less subject to partisan restraint than at almost any time since the Civil War.

I do not want to overstate the case, and my own views do not extend to all aspects of these problems. America's parties labor under severe handicaps. They are localistic anachronisms in an age of electronic technology. Direct primaries have gone hand in hand with divided party organizations and weaknesses in the nominating activities that constitute their basic reason for being. American political parties must operate in a governmental system that divides authority into many separate compartments, and they must confront persistent antiparty feeling in the wider society.

To be realistic, one must concede that an important revival of party strength does not appear imminent. As the 1980 election entered its final phases, a leading political journalist expressed a belief that unless the major party conventions stipulate that their nominees must be willing to debate each other, and unless they defend their mutually arranged control of the debate format, there may be nothing left of a two-party system in the 1984 presidential election.[5]

Another observer argues that party revival will only follow, not precede, a new sense of national direction.

> Reformers who urge the revival of parties as abstract good things in themselves or look to the reinvigoration of the jumbo coalitions of years gone by are marching up a blind alley. Purpose comes first, then party. In the rush of campaigning, the urgent work is to discover themes of unity so compelling that they will attract allies whose allegiance might survive the selection.[6]

Obstacles to stronger parties are formidable, but the most important ones concern attitudes rather than rules or structures. Americans tend to admire political independence and to distrust political organizations. If attitudes could be changed, Americans would find ways to strengthen the parties. As Ladd puts it:

> The basic change that is needed . . . is simply a renewed appreciation of what useful things parties—as institutions and not just labels—are to have around. If this should somehow come to pass, it would then be relatively easy to rebuild the parties as instruments for planning and representation.[7]

What specific steps might be taken? The national parties could simplify delegate selecting and committing rules and leave events more open to the free play of partisan politics. Convention rules could require states to reserve delegate places for senior elected officials and party chairmen, and these persons could be urged to arrive at the convention uncommitted. More states could use caucus systems instead of presidential primaries. As one analyst notes: "Caucuses are good party-building devices, requiring intense organization at the precinct level. Once enough energy to organize a precinct is expended, people tend to stay interested in party affairs—that is, in the issues and personalities that comprise politics."[8] States retaining the presidential primary could be permitted and even encouraged to allow

---

[5]David S. Broder, "For Future Debate: Anderson Factor Four Years Hence," *Today,* October 10, 1980.

[6]James D. Barber, *The Pulse of Politics* (New York: W. W. Norton & Co., Inc., 1980), p. 322.

[7]Everett Carll Ladd, Jr., *American Political Parties* (New York: W. W. Norton & Co., Inc., 1970), p. 255.

[8]*The New Republic,* March 22, 1980, pp. 5–8.

voters to elect uncommitted delegates. Beyond this, delegate commitments could be officially declared to be nonbinding political undertakings.

Of course, if the society wants stronger parties, there will be some disagreement about how best to obtain them. One wonders if new politics reformers would be willing to agree that commitment to party is more constructive than momentary commitments to particular presidential candidates. Perhaps they would concede this point if they felt certain that the stronger parties would be open. However, an open party with genuine influence may be especially vulnerable to informal methods of control. If one believes that it is necessary to guard against this, rules and regulations are a natural recourse.

One can make a case that stronger parties would emerge from a policy of deregulation. Taken to the extreme, such a policy would result in parties without labels on the ballot. With statutory regulation removed, parties would be forced to win offices through active organizing and campaigning. Such a policy is most unlikely, however, because it would probably mean the end of the direct primary. Proparty scholars disagree about the merits of primaries in a system of responsible parties, even though most would probably support a drastic simplification of the relevant statutes. The country is accustomed to primaries, and primaries will probably remain an integral feature of our electoral system. If it is our intention to construct a new kind of party built from the top down, we shall be operating in terra incognita.

One of the more important questions facing us today is whether recent declines in voting reflect a feeling that elected officials are losing their dominant position in government. If they are, the expression of national purpose may become ever more difficult, even impossible, unless new institutions are devised. Within existing institutions, we have the alternative of moving again toward a system based on presidential leadership or of trying to develop parity between Congress and the president. However, this predominant influence we are speaking of cannot be total or unilateral. In a properly functioning arrangement of authorities, room must be available for administrative initiative and independence from arbitrary fiat. Ideally, strengthened partisan capability would go hand in hand with improved management by means of such devices as the Senior Executive Service. Taken together, these would help Congress achieve greater coherence and simplify its oversight of administration.

At present, the United States seems reluctant to make basic choices in an explicit way. Perhaps so many adaptations are called for on so many fronts that no one can know what courses of action will most likely produce particular results. If so, much can be said for hedging all bets and "muddling through." However, high levels of cynicism and distrust suggest a condition of immobility rather than (or more important than) one of uncertainty, in which case "muddling through" may only increase the rigidities in a society of formed groups.

There is, of course, some risk of mistaking the truly central issues. Ralf Dahrendorf, for example, suggests that enabling people to operate in a market environment may be more important than issuing directives from government. He reminds us that many important problems can no longer be solved in a national context, and he wonders if giant companies and powerful trade unions do not have a more powerful impact on people than parliamentary institutions.

> The greater demand for participation, the removal of effective political spaces from the national to the international level, and the removal of the power to determine people's life chances from political institutions to other institutions are all signs of what might be called the dissolution, perhaps the dilution of the general political public which we assumed was the real basis of democratic institutions in the past.[9]

If this is the proper way to look at the democratic prospect, representativeness and capable national government may not be the most crucial matters. Dahrendorf emphasizes the need to reestablish an effective general public. Others might argue that protection of human rights has the highest priority, even if this must be tackled in the context of highly imperfect international organizations.

CONTINUING CONCERNS

Aspects of electoral politics most frequently discussed include campaign financing, presidential selection, and the role of television. Although earlier chapters include many comments on these matters, a few final words may be appropriate.

Since 1971, a body of campaign finance legislation has been evolving toward greater complexity and uncertainty. Perhaps it is now necessary to digest what we have already attempted in this field and, where possible, to simplify and even retrench. Attempts to regulate the give and take of electoral politics often have unintended consequences. For example, it seems to have been necessary for John Anderson to continue his campaign after September 1980 because of dependence on future campaign subsidies. Campaign finance regulation also seems to have taken some of the spontaneity out of national politics.

Although public financing of some sort for congressional campaigns would be highly desirable in principle, to work well in practice the sums must be large enough to cover modern campaign costs, and they must be properly allocated. Unless substantial sums are channeled through party organizations (rather than given directly to contestants), public financing could take us further from the collaborative effort and stronger leadership needed in Congress. Much of the increase in campaign costs represents part of the price we pay for preferring personalistic politics to partisan politics. Despite the great increases in campaign outlays, many contestants still receive too little money to have a fair chance against better known opponents.

---

[9]Ralf Dahrendorf in Michel J. Crozier, Samuel P. Huntington, and Joji Watanuki, *The Crisis of Democracy* (New York: New York University Press, 1975), p. 191.

Our present method of nominating presidents, despite conspicuous shortcomings, also has important hidden—perhaps too well hidden—advantages. One may hope that the Republic will hesitate before moving toward a drastic revision of our presidential nominating procedures. The arrangements we now have do require a good deal of campaigning, but such activity is a healthy and necessary part of a democratic process. The sense of political exhaustion felt by so many in the 1980 election derived from a number of factors, including long-term trends toward party weakness and changing custom (in the really old days, ambitious men were not supposed to undertake a visible search for party nomination). In 1980 we were almost thirty years into the television age. An unusually large number of primaries were held, and media were aware of the crucial importance of the Iowa caucuses. Frustrations centered on American hostages in Iran had an unprecedented and negatively tinged impact on campaigning, beginning almost a year ahead of the election.

Institutional changes endorsed in the polls frequently reflect traditional disinterest in political parties and needs of political leadership. Thus, George Gallup identifies nationwide primaries, direct election of the president, limits on congressional terms, and national initiative procedures as being among the six reforms Americans want most.[10] Such changes have "quick fix" appeal, reflecting a widespread tendency to make political choices, like marketplace choices, on the basis of rapid appraisal. Although support for these measures is numerically large among persons polled, no grassroots clamor can be heard for any of them.

The proper role of television is a crucial issue of contemporary politics, but as yet no one knows how to get it on the main agenda for serious consideration. As presently constituted television does serve some governmental and educational functions and occasionally turns in a very fine performance in these areas. However, television spokesmen are reluctant to acknowledge such responsibilities; they prefer to make the invalid claim that television merely mirrors reality. Perhaps television and the other mass media should ultimately become, as Stimson Bullitt suggests, a branch of government or even an educational enterprise.

At present, television is mostly a business, and the top priority of the network operations is to expose viewers to the propagandists who wage unrelenting war on such threats to the nation as acid indigestion, lower back pain, and hemorrhoidal symptoms. All of the changes in modern electoral politics connect in some significant way to television, but these relationships are likely to be transformed as society becomes better adapted to the new medium and more resourceful in using it for diverse and broadly constructive purposes.

---

[10]George Gallup, "Six Political Reforms Most Americans Want," *The Readers Digest*, August 1978, pp. 59–67. The other two reforms are congressional campaigns financed exclusively by public funds and advance of election and inauguration to September and November, respectively.

E. E. Schattschneider pointed out some years ago that the American government had survived and grown strong despite a pervasive distrust of government, a structure that hobbled it, a hostile intellectual environment, and a nostalgia for the society's small government origins. At the time he wrote, it seemed that the society with one of the most antigovernmental civilizations in history had produced the most powerful government ever known.[11]

In more recent years all forms of authority have come under attack, yet American government has expanded even further. It grew in response to rising political demands even while our pessimism and distrust of government mounted and our sense of security eroded. If negative attitudes and escalating demands continue, governmental preformance is likely to deteriorate even further. This declining quality of performance may in turn reinforce the pessimism and distrust. Aspirations are essential in politics, but our appraisals should take into account means as well as ends; politics remains the art of the possible.

People who describe the technological, media, and cultural factors that have produced the politics of today sometimes imply that the new condition is permanent. This is perhaps a possibility; after all, contemporary economies and technologies do differ from anything ever experienced before. However, continuing change is much more likely. Perhaps we can hope for a reaction against the present mood of selfish individualism and fragmented political interests.

Unrelieved pessimism about the American condition is not justified. In most historical periods we find a mixture of good and bad, and this one is no exception. American moods may fluctuate between extremes of optimism and pessimism in ways unwarranted by objective conditions. The sense of unlimited optimism that pervaded the early 1960s was certainly unjustified, but then again, perhaps things have not been as bad as they sometimes seemed in the 1970s.

So many astonishing things have come to pass that people no longer know what *is* possible. Many seem to be credulous, yet simultaneously disinclined to believe anything or anyone in particular. Amidst dramatically expanded expectations of what is our due, we remain anxious about our ability to achieve some fairly simple things. Americans know, for example, though it is seldom discussed, that in an age of "space-age technology" freight train derailments occur at a rate unheard of fifty years ago. This country's remarkable achievements now inspire little satisfaction, and its various vulnerabilities and malfunctionings are pervasively disturbing.

At this stage of the game, it appears quite clear that a political system built *exclusively* on the pursuit of "selfish" interest is a dead end. In a nation of individualists, voting itself may rest on an irreducible element of civic generosity. Admittedly, most of what goes on in politics and in other parts of life is in some sense "selfish" (although the word is too narrow to be

---

[11]E. E. Schattschneider, *Two Hundred Million Americans in Search of a Government* (New York: Holt, Rinehart & Winston, 1969), pp. 29–32.

suitable), and the system must work with that. However, a loss of vision is much more likely to do us in than excessive idealism.

The United States has defined its reason for being in terms of political democracy, and if we devalue the instruments of that purpose, we strike at the heart of our civilization. Elections have been central experiences in which we discovered where we stood and where we were headed. Reaffirmation of our faith in electoral democracy carries with it hopes for rediscovered connections with the past, a sense of larger common purpose, and renewed hope for the future.

In his 1976 Nobel lecture, the novelist Saul Bellow noted that art has not been connected to the main human enterprise for a long time, and he voiced the wish that writers would return from the periphery to the central concerns of mankind.[12] The validity of a call to artists to return from the periphery has its political counterpart in the need for all sorts of people (artists and intellectuals included) to support the democratic enterprise.

The case for investing more of our energies in electoral democracy is not unassailable, but it has more validity than such fashionable approaches as chic Marxism, single-issue politics, expansion of judicial power, or dropping out. Elections have helped to unify us in the past and may do so again, even while we seek a more effective and just world order.

[12]Saul Bellow, "The Nobel Lecture," *American Scholar* (1977), pp. 324–325.

APPENDIX

The Electoral
Vote System

Americans instinctively think of presidential elections as straightforward national contests in which the people, by popular vote, choose the winner. In its larger significance, this perception is substantially correct. Actually, however, voters in each state choose slates of electors who are usually pledged to a candidate. The electoral vote count, on a state by state basis, normally determines who will be president and vice president. Since electors never meet as a national body, and since they rarely deliberate, *electoral vote system* is a more accurate term than *electoral college*.

National statutes set down the timetable for presidential elections. Voters choose electors on the first Tuesday after the first Monday in November; electors meet in the states on the first Monday after the second Wednesday in December; the president of the Senate counts the electoral votes on January 6.

In most states, names of presidential candidates rather than names of electors appear on the ballots. However, this does not significantly alter the electoral vote system. In 1976, for example, voters choosing "Gerald Ford" were in fact voting for electors pledged to Ford in their state. The same was true of "Jimmy Carter" (and of "Eugene McCarthy" in those states where his name was on the ballot). It was generally assumed that electors would be faithful to their party or candidate commitments, and everyone therefore "knew" who won before the electors met.[1]

[1]Let us note in passing that one of Ford's electors from the state of Washington voted for Reagan. Also, we have Senator Robert Dole's testimony that in a few close states, Republicans were "looking around" for electors. "The Electoral College and Direct Election," *Hearings Before the Committee on the Judiciary,* United States Senate, 95th Congress, First Session, 1977, pp. 36–37. Hereafter, this source will be cited as *1977 Senate Hearings,* and supplementary hearings of that year under the same title and auspices as *1977 Supplementary Hearings.* As of October 1980, there had only been eight instances of an elector being faithless to his candidate commitments in all of American political history. Most electors are chosen at state party conventions, but some are chosen by party committees or in party primaries. Electors' names do not appear on the ballot in thirty-nine states. *Congressional Quarterly Weekly Report,* October 25, 1980, pp. 3184–3185. In 1960, all of the electors chosen in Mississippi were "uninstructed," and six of Alabama's eleven electors were "unpledged."

BASIC ELEMENTS

The electoral vote system is a blend of constitutional requirements and long-standing political practice. The essential constitutional elements are as follows:

1. Each state is awarded electors equal to the number of its U.S. representatives and senators. The District of Columbia also receives three electors under the terms of the Twenty-third Amendment.
2. Electors meet in their respective states on the same day throughout the United States for the sole purpose of voting by ballot for president and vice president. Electors tally their votes for president and vice president separately, then transmit the lists of all persons voted for to the president of the U.S. Senate, who counts them in the presence of the senators and representatives.
3. The person with a majority of electoral votes for president becomes president. If no individual receives a majority of electoral votes, the House chooses from among the top three electoral vote winners; each state's House delegation has one vote, and a candidate must win a majority to be elected. The Constitution prescribes a similar contingency for the vice president, with the Senate choosing among the top two. A further contingency makes the new vice president the acting president if the House fails to choose a president by January 20.
4. The Constitution allows each state legislature to determine how that state's electors are to be chosen. With negligible exceptions, popular election has been the method used in every state since the Civil War. No senator, representative, or U.S. officeholder is eligible to be an elector.

HISTORICAL BACKGROUND

The framers of the Constitution had difficulty deciding how the president should be selected, and we are not certain how they expected the electoral vote system to work. They may have rejected direct popular election because communication difficulties and varying suffrage practices among the states made it impractical. They probably assumed that voters would choose the electors and that the electors' deliberations would reflect popular sentiment.[2]

The framers' assumptions (if any) about political parties or about presidential *nominations* are not known. Some believe that they expected many parties to emerge. Others have wondered if they did not expect electors to merely nominate presidents, with the House making the actual selection. Most likely, the framers wanted a mechanism that would reflect popular opinion yet insulate the president from political entanglements.[3]

George Washington was certain to be the first president under any system, but choices of successors were more doubtful. By the end of

---

[2]Lucius Wilmerding, Jr., *The Electoral College* (New Brunswick, N.J.: Rutgers University Press, 1958), pp. 12, 19–22.
[3]William H. Riker, *Democracy in the United States,* 2nd ed. (New York: Macmillan, Inc., 1965), p. 230; American Enterprise Institute for Public Policy Research, "Direct Election of the President," *1977 Supplementary Hearings,* pp. 388–389.

Washington's second term, the electoral vote system was under severe pressure. Instead of being apolitical deliberative bodies, electors usually belonged to slates of partisans allied with like-minded slates in other states. Competition between Federalists and Jeffersonians was producing a national system of party politics that fundamentally altered the original scheme.

Under the original provisions of the Constitution, electors simply wrote two names on a ballet without designating one as president and the other as vice president. Under the emerging impact of partisan organizations, this meant that a majority giving equal support to its two candidates might tempt minority party electors to support the majority's vice presidential nominee and make him president. Majority electors could not completely eliminate this possibility, even if they scattered a few of their second votes. In 1800 a famous tie vote between Jefferson and Burr threw the election into the House. Federalists were in control there, and after toying with the notion of making Burr president, finally chose Jefferson on the thirty-sixth ballot.

To eliminate further difficulties, Republicans secured passage of the Twelfth Amendment in 1804, in time for the fall elections. The amendment required electors to indicate their choice of president and vice president in distinct ballots. It also established the contingency provisions described above and stipulated that at least one of the names listed by any elector could not be an inhabitant of the elector's state.

It was in this context that the parties, operating through state legislatures, moved toward the winner-take-all arrangements that lie at the heart of the electoral vote system. In the early years, legislatures selected electors through a variety of methods that were often subject to frequent sudden changes. The complexity and capriciousness of these devices apparently led to pressures for a stable and uniform practice.[4] Attention focused on essentially four different ways that this could be achieved.

1. Select the president by direct popular election
2. Have state legislatures designate the individuals who would be electors
3. Have the voters choose electors on a general ticket (winner-take-all) basis
4. Have the voters choose electors within districts[5]

Three of these approaches have dominated debate on the electoral vote system since the 1830s. The first was impractical in the early years for reasons cited above, and democratic ideals precluded the second. Until the 1960s, most reformers favored the fourth approach in one form or another. Although recent critics have rallied behind direct election, the idea of selecting electors within districts may again come into favor at some future time.

[4]Wilmerding, *The Electoral College*, p. 53.
[5]Ibid., pp. 55–57. There are, of course, other possibilities. For an especially interesting one, see Twentieth Century Fund Task Force on Reform of the Presidential Election Process, *Winner Take All* (New York: Holmes & Meier Publishers, Inc., 1979).

The general ticket system probably won out because it did not require a constitutional amendment. Dominant parties in at least a few states could make their greatest impact through a general ticket system, and other states would be inclined to go along out of self-interest. Participants could achieve a uniform practice through parallel actions powered by the political interest of state parties. By 1836 all but one of the states had adopted the general ticket system, and few have departed from it in the years since.[6]

Dissatisfaction with the electoral vote system is almost as old as the Republic itself. Today's critics see it as archaic, unfair, arbitrary, and hazardous, a view that dates at least from the Jacksonian era. Senator Thomas Hart Benton, for example, complained in 1824 that the electors had "degenerated into mere agents, in a case which requires no agency, and where the agent must be useless, if he is faithful, and dangerous, if he is not."[7]

The impetus toward direct popular election in the 1960s and 1970s had several causes. George Wallace's winning of forty-five electoral votes in 1968 showed that minor party candidates might manipulate the system, and the elections of 1960 and 1976 were also quite close. If Wallace had prevented either Richard Nixon or Hubert Humphrey from getting a majority of electoral votes, his electors might have determined which candidate would become president before the House could act. It is also worth noting that the doctrine of "one man, one vote" received special emphasis in reapportionment cases in this period.[8]

Advocacy of direct election went hand in hand with declining party influence, a disposition to simplify complex issues, and widespread concern about the performance of American political institutions. However, the Senate decisively rejected direct election in a 1979 roll-call vote, and the proposal will probably be given less emphasis in the 1980s.

Under the plan former Senator Birch Bayh advocated for many years, voters would cast a single vote for two persons who consented to the joining of their names as candidates for president and vice president. No candidate could join his name with more than one person. Persons qualified to vote for members of the most numerous house of the state legislature would be eligible to vote for president, and paired candidates receiving the greatest

---

[6]Ibid., pp. 64–65. Among these is the state of Maine, which selects two of its four electors in its two congressional districts. Wilmerding notes that reformers who favored the district system in principle often found it expedient to work for a general ticket system in practice. Thus Jefferson, in a letter to Monroe of 1800, stated: "All agree that an election by districts would be best, if it could be general; but while 10 states choose either by their legislatures or by general ticket, it is folly and worse than folly for the other 6 not to do it." Ibid., p. 60. Theoretically, the states could abandon the general ticket system at any time, but in practice they are not likely to do so unless there is a constitutional amendment. See Judith Best, *The Case Against the Electoral College* (Ithaca, N.Y.: Cornell University Press, 1971), pp. 22–23. Sometimes the term *unit rule* is used to refer to choice of electors by general ticket.

[7]Wilmerding, *The Electoral College*, p. 171. Another of Benton's complaints was that the general ticket system "is not the case of votes lost, but of votes taken away, added to those of the majority and given to a person to whom the minority is opposed." American Enterprise Institute, "Direct Election," p. 391.

[8]American Enterprise Institute, "Direct Election," p. 384.

number of votes would be elected unless they received less than 40 percent of the total vote. If no candidates received 40 percent, voters would choose between the two highest pairs in a runoff election.[9]

PROS AND CONS

The merits of particular selection methods depend crucially on expectations of how various participants would react. Supporters of direct election, for example, often see runoffs as unlikely under their proposal, since at least one candidate has almost always received more than 40 percent of the popular vote. Critics, however, suspect that new rules would change electoral behavior. More candidates might contest presidential elections since they would not have to carry entire states to accumulate significant numbers of votes. Moreover, minor candidates might discover a shared interest in forcing a runoff if they thought they could bargain for concessions before the next round of voting.

Other possible reactions make direct election a more desirable prospect. Suppose, for example, that we have another election in which a candidate obtains a majority of electoral votes but trails in the popular vote. Such a development is unlikely but certainly not impossible. It happened in 1888, and some would say in 1876 and 1824 as well.[10] Such an election might bring on a major constitutional crisis in the America of today. Moreover, a switch of only ten thousand or so votes in Ohio and Hawaii in 1976 would have given Ford the presidency, even though Carter had 1.7 million more votes. For Birch Bayh, such possibilities make the present system a game of Russian roulette with the pistol pointed at the temple of the Republic.[11]

On the other hand, defenders can argue that Americans would accept an outcome of the sort hypothesized for 1976. It would have resulted from constitutional provisions, and the nation cannot have a constitutional crisis by following the specific instructions of its basic charter. People would have noted that Carter obtained much of his plurality in southern states, and this would have enabled the nation to accept the victory of his opponent as fair. More exotic kinds of malfunctionings of the electoral vote system could be

[9] 96th Congress, 1st Session, S.J. Res. 28.

[10] The election of 1876 was so clouded by frauds and irregularities that, as Judith Best says, "only an eccentric majoritarian would single out the technical runner up Presidency of Hayes as a matter for criticism and concern." *The Case Against the Electoral College*, pp. 52–53. For the election of 1824, see Chapter 2 of text.

[11] More fanciful results cannot be dismissed as absolutely impossible. For example, *Newsweek* described a possible "Mondale scenario" for 1980. This could have unfolded if Anderson had received enough electoral votes to deprive Carter or Reagan of an electoral vote majority, and if no deal were made with faithless electors. If the contest had then gone to a newly elected House in which Democrats and Republicans controlled an equal number of state delegations, a deadlock could well have ensued. If, however, the Democrats still controlled the Senate, they would presumably select Mondale vice president, and if the House had failed to select a president by January 20, Mondale would have taken office as president under the terms of the Twentieth Amendment. *Newsweek*, May 26, 1980. p. 35.

prevented by passing a perfecting amendment of the sort that Lyndon Johnson advocated in the early 1960s.[12]

Debate about the electoral vote system ranges over a broad terrain. Even among thoughtful analysts, virtually every major political value has been invoked by each side. This tends to exaggerate the importance of the issue and distract attention from other important aspects of the presidential selection process.

The fact that so few Americans understand the electoral vote system is perhaps the most telling point against it. Moreover, those who are familiar with the institution cannot claim that its major features are ideal. A technical perfecting amendment would undoubtedly eliminate undesirable elements, but if the nation is to bother with amending the Constitution, the appeal of direct election is very great. One might suppose that the principle of a direct vote would not have to be defended in this day and age.

Even so, persons who carefully study the matter often conclude that the electoral vote system should be retained. Whatever its disadvantages, it has the merit of proven success. It has produced presidents accepted by the American people, and, except in 1800 and 1824, it has accomplished this result in the initial voting. Even though in many cases the winner received less than 50 percent of the popular vote, there has been little resort to contingency arrangements.[13] Continuing disagreements among knowledgeable persons about the actual effects of the system indicate that we do not understand it very well. Since the benefits of changing to direct election are speculative, the changes necessary to achieve them should not be risked. More succinctly, "If it ain't broke, don't fix it."[14]

RELATION TO THE TWO-PARTY SYSTEM

A connection undoubtedly exists between inherited arrangements and the nature of our party system, but its character is hotly disputed. In the debate over direct election, preference for the two-party system is often a compulsory platitude. Yet disputants may feel a dissatisfaction with the two-party framework that they are reluctant to express.

[12]Abolish the electors as physical entities and cast a state's electoral vote automatically for the candidate pair receiving the greatest number of votes in that state. If no pair received a majority of the electoral vote, Congress would choose a president in joint session by a majority of individual votes of members. This is sometimes referred to as "the automatic vote plan." Senator Birch Bayh argued for this proposal in 1965 and 1966. By May 1966, however, he had changed his position and became the leading advocate of direct election. American Enterprise Institute, "Direct Election," p. 385.

[13]In recent years Harry S. Truman won with 49.6 percent of the popular vote, John F. Kennedy with 49.7 percent; and Richard Nixon in 1968 with 43.4 percent.

[14]Words attributed to Bert Lance, President Carter's hapless budget director, by columnist George Will. *Hearings Before the Subcommittee on the Constitution of the Committee on the Judiciary United States Senate,* Ninety-sixth Congress, First Session (hereafter cited as *1979 Hearings*), p. 224. Although direct election has received heavy support in the polls, there is no public outcry against the electoral vote system. According to Will, "Fear of the electoral college ranks just below fear of college presidents." Ibid.

Supporters of direct election can claim that parties would have to work harder in areas where they have a heavy advantage or disadvantage, and that this would tend to make parties more competitive over larger areas. They also argue that minor party candidates who win electoral votes may exploit electoral tallies in a mischievous manner. Winner-take-all features, they believe, encourage power plays by minor candidates with a regional base, and they cite a succession of such candidates, beginning with the 1948 parties of Strom Thurmond and Henry Wallace. In 1976 Eugene McCarthy might have deprived Carter of the presidency and given it to Ford, if McCarthy had received about 24,000 more votes in Ohio and Wisconsin.[15]

Nevertheless, defenders of the electoral vote system seem to have the more cogent arguments on this particular issue. They emphasize that winner-take-all at the state level seriously handicaps independent or minor party efforts by favoring candidates with large, geographically dispersed followings. In fact the winning ticket has received a higher proportion of the electoral vote than of the popular vote without exception in every election since 1832. Defenders tend to believe that overrepresentation of the winner may explain why the House has not chosen a president since 1824. Any system of elections must have contingency provisions, and the more these are invoked, the more likely they are to distort the initial voting results. The electoral vote system penalizes minor parties because votes that do not help carry entire states tend to be wasted. Furthermore, since contingency arrangements are seldom invoked, minor candidates who *do* win electoral votes have little hope of being able to bargain with them.

It is true that some very astute supporters of a strong two-party system (such as David Broder and Judson James) are on record as supporting direct election. However, other important scholars and analysts such as Theodore Bickel, Philip Kurland, Austin Ranney, Martin Diamond, Aaron Wildavsky, Arthur Schlesinger, Jr., and Kevin Phillips have contended that the electoral vote system strengthens the two-party system. Schlesinger emphasizes that it rewards parties with a strong geographic base and thus discourages parties based on such ideological causes as antiabortion, black power, antibusing, antigun control, homosexual rights, communism, or fascism. At least two of these authorities have found themselves in opposition to the two major parties at one time or another. Martin Diamond, for example, in his Senate testimony, recalled his earlier days as a Socialist, and suggested that the Socialist party would have enthusiastically endorsed direct election.[16]

In a January 1977 column, Kevin Phillips argued that direct election was long overdue. The two-party system had become unresponsive, he said, and new parties would be able to press popular demands that the major parties ignore. Four months later, however, a different essay by Phillips argued that direct election would balkanize American politics. Although the

[15]Kenneth Kofmehl, *1977 Hearings*, pp. 353–354.
[16]For Martin Diamond's comments, see *1977 Supplementary Hearings*, pp. 149–158; for Schlesinger's analysis, see ibid., p. 514; see also Judson James, *American Political Parties in Transition* (New York: Harper & Row, Publishers, Inc., 1974), pp. 61–69.

implicit value placed on the two-party system was more favorable in the second article, the empirical assessments were not too different.[17]

Please bear in mind that presidential selection requires nomination as well as election, and the two elements are closely related. Advocates of direct election seldom specify what kind of nominating system would be matched with direct election. Birch Bayh strongly opposes a national presidential primary because he believes that it would interfere with consensus building in the major parties. Yet in the opinion polls support for the national primary has been almost as one-sided and persistent as support for direct election.[18]

Presumably, direct election would eliminate states as significant pieces of turf in presidential politics. If this occurred, the states could easily lose their role and separate identity in platform drafting and in caucus or convention nominating procedures. The natural corollary of direct election, despite Bayh's opposition, could therefore be the national presidential primary. Even if this primary did not evolve toward a nonpartisan format, and even if primary and/or election runoffs did not become the norm, it might be difficult for the two-party system to adapt successfully. We would be moving further from the notion that political parties make presidential nominations and further from acknowledging the role of parties as intermediaries between voters and electoral choices. The alternative to a two-party system might not be a three- or four-party system, but a fragmented political order.

The relation between nomination and election could also be considered from the other direction. For example, if Congress were to pass legislation setting up regional or national primaries, prospects of changing the electoral vote system could be affected. Ideally, one might hope that policy makers would consider these issues in tandem rather than in isolation. However, arriving at an intellectually defensible package of nominating and selecting practices is a formidable task. As prosaic a matter as the election and positioning of the vice president may be in greater need of change than electoral vote mechanics.

Those who favor direct election can make a fair case that the electoral vote system is not one of the important "causes" of the American two-party system. Thus, one study says that the following factors are usually cited by those who try to account for the two-party system:

1. Election of officials from single-member districts by plurality vote
2. Tendency towards consensus on national goals and a tendency towards cultural homogeneity
3. Political maturity
4. Persisting tendency towards dualism.[19]

[17]Kevin P. Phillips, "Abolish the Electoral College," *Viewpoints*, Vol. 2, no. 3 for March 1977, Card No. 72, Accession No. 34. *1977 Supplementary Hearings*, pp. 516–517.
[18]George Gallup, "Six Political Reforms Most Americans Want," *The Readers Digest*, August 1978, pp. 59–62.
[19]Adapted from Lawrence D. Longley and Alan G. Braun, *The Politics of Electoral College Reform* (New Haven, Conn.: Yale University Press, 1972), p. 88.

Even if this line of argument is correct, a direct-election amendment might work against a two-party system if it changed the nature of the political arena. Charles Black, for example, says that it would be the most deeply radical amendment ever to enter the Constitution. Theodore White considers it a revolutionary measure that would change the entire system of elections and upset two hundred years of American history.[20] White is especially concerned about putting all presidential votes into a single pool. He says that vote manipulators would have a field day in a system where votes poured into Washington "undisturbed by state, without color or character or history." He claims that the new bosses would be the media professionals and that state boundaries that give us a sense of place in presidential politics would yield to maps of major media markets.

> This plebiscite proposal will withdraw from us a large and throbbing memory of our history—all those lovely maps of elections which tell schoolchildren as well as grownups how the country has swung section by section from mood to mood. Instead, we will have this boiling pot of 75 million votes stirred by mixmaster, manipulators, and television—understandable only by statisticians and social scientists.[21]

White did not address the two-party issue directly in his 1979 Senate testimony. If presidential selection were to take on these characteristics, however, it could mean a decline in the pragmatism, consensus building, bargaining, and continuity that the two-party system's staunchest supporters see as its major virtues.

---

[20]American Enterprise Institute, "Direct Election," p. 392, citing Black's testimony before the Senate Judiciary Committee in 1970; Theodore White, *1979 Hearings*, p. 342.

[21]*1979 Hearings*, pp. 342, 345, 346. This quotation is on p. 345; the earlier one is on p. 346.

Index

Page numbers in italics indicate data from tables included.

Authoritarian political systems, 4–10
Automobile industry, U.S., 75

Bagehot, Walter, 14
Bain, Richard C., cited, 24, 128n
Baker, Bobby, 321
Baker, Howard, 76
Baker, Ross K., cited 156n
Baltimore Sun, 105
Ballots: absentee, 138; bedsheet, 25; party designation on, 17; in primary elections, 200, 202–203; secret (Australian), 17; shortening of, 188–189
Banfield, Edward C., cited, 35n, 116n, 170n, 205n
Banks, Arthur S., cited, 5n
Barber, James D., cited, 217–218, 336
Barone, Michael, cited, 121n, 270n
Bayh, Birch, 269; on presidential election reform, 345, 346, 347n, 349
Beard, Edmund, cited, 321n, 322
Beauvoir, Simone de, 56
Beer, Thomas, quoted, 40n
Begin, Menahem, 76
Belknap, William, 31
Bell, Daniel, cited, 81n, 84
Bellow, Saul, cited, 341
Bennett, William J., cited, 312n
Benson, George C. S., cited, 312n, 322n
Benton, Thomas Hart, 345
Berelson, Bernard, cited, 107n, 163n
Berg, Larry L., cited, 310n, 315, 318, 329
Berkley, George E., cited, 73n, 290
Bernstein, Carl, 64, 319
Best, Judith, cited, 346n
Bicameralism, 292
Bickel, Theodore, 348
Big business (see also Corporate enterprise): electoral power of, 144–145; government regulation of, 39, 145, 146; in Grant administration, 30–31; interest group influence of, 141–146, 156; party political influence of, 30–31, 35–36, 42, 145–146, 156–157 (see also Republican Party); political corruption and, 310, 317; progressivism vs., 39–40; as systemic institution, 145
Bill, James A., cited, 137n, 138n
Binder, Leonard, quoted, 19
Binkley, Wilfred, E., cited, 21n, 40n, 107n
Bird, Alice, cited, 229n
Black, Charles, cited, 350
Black, Hugo, 44
Black Friday episode, 30
Blackman, Paul H., cited, 173n, 186n
Blackmun, Harry A., 280
Black Panther party, 55, 60
Blacks, American: as Carter supporters, 71, 156; Democratic party identification of, 260; employment gains by, 54; as freed-

Blacks, American (cont.)
men, 1865–1867, 32–33; integration efforts of, 46, 54, 160; political activism by, 156, 158, 178, 255; residential location of, 96; social segregation of, 95–96
Bone, Hugh A., cited, 193, 196n
Boorstin, Daniel J., cited, 228–229
Bossism, 30–31, 35, 117–118, 304
Bower, Robert, cited, 105
Brady, David M., cited, 273n
Brandeis, Louis, 278n
Braun, Alan G., cited, 349n
Brennan, William, 279, 280
Brezhnev, Leonid I., 75
Broadcasting, campaign, 226, 231 (see also Television)
Broder, David, cited, 105, 212, 336n, 348
Brown, Edmund G. (Pat), 51, 70
Brown, Edmund G., Jr., 67, 76, 195
Brown, Richard Maxwell, cited, 27n
Brownlow Commission, 289
Brown v. Board of Education of Topeka, Kansas, 47
Bryan, William Jennings, 37–38, 42
Bryce, James, cited, 117
Buchanan, James, 25
Buchanan, William, cited, 163, 229n
Buckley v. Valeo, 230
Bullitt, Stimson, 227, 339
Burdick, Eugene, cited, 221n
Bureaucracy (see also Administrative agencies): administrative frustration in, 334; elective government vs., 181–182, 191; mass society and, 81, 82; merit system vs. patronage in, 288–289; partisan control of, 287–288
Burger, Warren E., 280
Burnham, Walter Dean, cited, 31n, 38n, 174–175, 259n
Burr, Aaron, 344
Bush, George, 76, 211, 215
Business, see Big business

Cabinet, presidential liaison with, 283–284
Caddell, Pat, cited, 63
Calhoun, John C., 23, 24, 301
California: nonpartisan elections in, 200; partisan affiliation in, 125–126, 200; party disestablishment in, 50, 109; Political Reform Act (1974) in, 312; primaries, 53, 58, 200; Proposition 13, 74; voter registration in, 200
Calley, William, 61
Campaign(s), political: advance work in, 223; advertising media in, 225–226; financing of, see Campaign financing; length and inefficiency of, 220–222; news media in, 18, 105, 216–218, 226–228; nonpresidential, 261–271; presidential, 238–245 (see also Presidential campaigns); professional

Corruption, political (*cont.*)
campaign finances and, 315–316; characteristics of, 308, 312–315, 318; in Congress, 320–329; exposure vs. assessment of, 317–318, 329; legislation against, 316–317; power vs. money in, 315–316; prevalence of, 309–310, 315–316; social scientists on, 312–313; as systemic, 315–317, 329; in underdevelopment, 315, 316
Corwin, Edward S., cited, 282–284
Cotter, Cornelius P., cited, 129*n*
Counterculture of the '60s, 54
Cover, Albert D., cited, 121*n*, 266*n*, 267, 334*n*
Cowart, Andrew J., cited, 262*n*
Cox, Archibald, 65, 320
Cox, James M., 42
Crane, Philip, 76
Cranston, Alan, 269, 270
Crawford, William H., 23
Credit Mobilier, 31, 318
Crime, 54
Croly, Herbert, 40, 301
Crotty, William J., cited 132*n*, 134*n*
Culver, John, 269
Curtin, Philip D., cited 34*n*
Custer, George A., 318–319
Czudnowski, Moshe M., cited, 205*n*, 206*n*, 209*n*

Dahl, Robert A., cited, 5*n*, 83*n*, 280, 307–308
Dahrendorf, Ralf, cited, 337–338
Daley, Richard J., 58
Daly, John V., cited, 212
David, Paul T., cited, 24*n*
Davies, James C., cited, 54*n*, 55*n*
Davis, David Brion, cited, 28*n*, 128*n*
Davis, James, cited, 130*n*
Davis, Jefferson, 28, 29
Davis, John W., 42
Debs, Eugene, 37
Deleware, 202
Democratic government(s): characteristics of, 6, 10, 19, 137; dissolution of, projected, 337–338; elite power and, 137; in Great Britain, 12–13; libertarian rule and, 137; mass opinion and, 83–84; modernization and, 1–2, 12–14; moralistic ideas about, 309; one-party politics and, 10; political parties in, 4–6, 12–15, 301–302; popular majority rule and, 159; ranked by population, *5*; secret ballot in, 16, 17
Democratic National Committee: control of, by Carter, 69, 128; delegate selection reforms by, 61–62, 68, 129–133; southern delegate control and, 129
Democratic National Convention(s) (*see also* National nominating conventions): Chicago protests riots (1968) at, 58–59, 60; delegate vote apportionment at, 127–128;

Democratic National Convention(s) (*cont.*)
nominee selection at, 57–58, 62–63, 127, 133; two-thirds rule at, 128–129; unit rule at, 128
Democratic party: after Civil War, 31, 32; in congressional legislation, 291–305; convention delegate selection reforms by, 62, 68, 130–131, 132; Jacksonian emergence of, 24; labor support of, 156, 234; New Deal and, 43–44 (*see also* New Deal); presidential candidates and campaigns of, 37–38, 41–42, *43*, 48, 51, 53, 57–58, 62; in presidential elections, *see* Presidential elections; primary elections and, 201–202; southern conservative realignment in, 260–261; urban work force and, 62; white supremacy and, 39
Depression(s): of late 1880s, 36; of 1893, 36–37; Great, of 1929, 41–42, 114
Deutsch, Karl W., cited 142
Dewey, Thomas E., 45, 229
Diamond, Edwin, cited, 105*n*
Diamond, Martin, cited, 348
Direct popular presidential election, proposed, 344–350
Direct primaries, by parties, 16–17, 133–134, 198–199, 349 (*see also* Primary elections)
Districts, congressional, 266–267
Dixiecrats, 45, 129
Dodd, Thomas, 321, 322, 331
Dole, Robert, 342*n*
Douglas, Paul, cited, 310, 319
Douglas, Stephen A., 24
Douglas, William O., 45
Downs, Anthony, cited, 333
Doyle, Arthur Conan, cited, 281*n*
Draft, military, 60, 77
Dunn v. *Blumstein*, 177*n*
Durkin, John, 269
Duverger, Maurice, cited, 3*n*
Dye, Thomas R., cited, 116*n*, 138*n*, 141–143, 195*n*

Eagleton, Thomas, 63, 101
Easterlin, Richard A., cited, 99*n*
Ecological fallacy, in election results, 250
Economic crises (*see also* Depression[s]): in presidential elections, 239–240
Economic Opportunity Act (1964), 52
Economic Stabilization Act (1970), 61
Economic status, 89–93 (*see also* Social status)
Edelman, Murray, cited, 274
Education, 47
Eisenhower, Dwight D., 45, 50, 240; administration of, 45–46; Democrats for, 45*n*, 122; official deportment of, 283
Elazar, Daniel J., cited, 309*n*, 317
Election(s): analysis of area characteristics and result of, 250; balloting in, *see* Ballots; big business and, *see* Big business; cam-

National Education Association (NEA), 153
National nominating conventions, 209–211 (*see also* Democratic National Convention; Nominating process; Republican National Convention)
National Opinion Research Center, 90, 93–94 (*see also* Public opinion poll[s])
National presidential polling, *see* Direct popular presidential election; Direct primaries
National Republicans, 24, 25
Nebraska, 58, 194
Nelson, Michael, cited, 189*n*
Neuman, Sigmund, cited, 4, 81
Neustadt, Richard, cited, 282–283, 288
New Deal, 42–44; delayed reaction to, 260; Democratic party and, 42, 43–44; Supreme Court vs., 44, 110; younger generation and, 99
New Hampshire, 53, 57, 69, 76
New Jersey, 317
New Republic, The, cited, 336
News media (*see also* Broadcasting; Television): as campaign expenditure, 231; in corruption exposure, 315, 318; political role and influence of, 18, 105, 225–228; in presidential process, 216–218; pseudo events by, 228; in U.S. vs. western Europe, 17–18; in Watergate affair, 315
Newsweek, cited, 71*n,* 75, 160, 187*n,* 311, 312, 346*n*
Newton, Huey, 55
New York, 118, 157
New York Sun, cited, 31
New York Times, 61, 105; cited 30, 52*n,* 156, 234, 311, 329
New Zealand, 10–11
Nichols, Roy F., cited, 1*n*
Nie, Norman H., cited, 123*n,* 172*n,* 173*n,* 179*n,* 255*n,* 256
Nixon, Richard M., 46, 48, 50, 51, 53, 58, 59, 333, 345; administration of, 60–67; autocratic deportment of, 67, 283; "Checkers" speech by, 50; currency devaluation by, 61; illegal campaign contributions to, 66–67; impeachment proceedings against, 65; impoundment operations by, 67; minority popular vote for, 347*n;* poll standings of, 60, 61; presidential candidacy of, 48, 50, 59–64, 222, 240; press relations of, 51, 66; resignation of, 65; Supreme Court appointment of, 278*n;* tax evasion by, 67; television use by, 50, 101; Vietnam war involvement of, 61, 333; in Watergate affair, 64–66, 315; White House control under, 289
Nominating process, presidential; candidate availability in, 129–130, 211–212, 282; by congressional caucus, 22, 127, 197; development of, 21–28, 196–199; by insider cooptation, 196–197; national party conventions in, 24*n,* 127–133, 209–211 (*see also*

Nominating process, presidential (*cont.*)
Democratic National Convention[s]; Republican National Convention[s]); news media roles in, 130, 216–217; nonpartisan approach in, 194–196; partisan approach in, 196–199, 209; party weakness and, 199; polling procedures in, 210–211; precovention poll ratings and, 209, 211, 214; primary elections in, *see* Primary elections; by Republicans, *see* Republican National Convention; reformation of, 62, 68, 130–132, 334, 336, 339; states' roles in, 197, 198, 201–203, 214–215
Nondemocratic governments, 4, 6, 6*n,* 7–8
Nonpartisan candidates, 195–196
Nonpartisan elections, 193
Nonpartisan League, 112
Nonparty political systems, 9, 19
Nonvoting, 171, 175–177, 182–184, 190 (*see also* Voter participation)

O'Brien, Donal B. Cruise, cited, 7*n*
O'Brien, Lawrence, 63
Officeholders, elected: base positions of, 206–207; party affiliations of, 119–120; political careers of, 203–209; residency rules for, 120
Office of Technology Assessment, 297
Olsen, David M., cited, 119, 156*n,* 198*n,* 200*n,* 201, 262*n,* 237*n*
One-party political system(s): authoritarian, 10; competitive, 7–8, 10; as democratic, 10; military force as, 7–8; in U.S., 38
Organized Crime Act (1970), 312
Organized labor, *see* Labor unions
Ortega y Gasset, Jose, cited, 82
Ostrogorski, M. I., 301

PACs, *see* Political action committees
Padover, Saul K., cited, 83*n*
Palley, Marian Lief, cited, 281*n*
Panama Canal treaties (1978), 73, 293
Panic of 1893, 36–37
Pareto, Vilfredo, cited, 136, 137
Parties, political, *see* Political parties, *and specific parties by name*
Partisanship: in Congress, 291–201; in the judiciary, 277–281; in the presidency, 284–286; regional differences vs., 296; role for responsible, 301–305
Partisan swing, 175
Party identification: candidate evaluation and, 254; changes of, 124; concept of, 122; decreasing strength of, *123,* 123–126, 256; of the independent, 123–124; issue orientation and, 253–254; registration as, 122; in Senate elections, 268–269; in state and local elections, 262–263; support as, 122 (*see also* Voter participation)

Posony, Stefan T., cited, 308n
Postindustrial society, 84–86
Postmaterialism, 85–86
Pound, Ezra, quoted, 310–311
Poverty, 90
Powell, Adam Clayton, Jr., 321, 322
Powell, Bingham, Jr., cited 2n
Powell, Lewis, 278n, 280
Preprimary endorsements, 202
Presidency/President, the: administrative agency management by, 288–289; citizen's potential access to, 211–222; collegial, 284; congressional relationships of, 283–284, 299–300; direct access to, 282–284; executive branch mangement by, 287–289; federal patronage and, 288; foreign policy role of, 287–288; legislative role of, 286; monarchal tendencies of, 67, 100, 282–283; nomination and election to, see Nominating process, Presidential campaign(s), Presidential election(s); Primary election(s); partisanship of, 121, 284–286; as party leader 284–286; White House staff and, 283, 287, 289
Presidential campaign(s) (see also Campaign[s], political): of Carter, 69, 70, 71, 77–78; economic crises and, 239–240; electoral vote strategies in, 242–244; financing of, 66, 68, 229–233, 236–237; by Ford, 70, 71; by incumbents, 239; issue positions in, 241–242; length of, 244; of McGovern, 62, 63; miscalculation in, 244; by Nixon, 59, 61–62; partisan affiliation in, 240; by Reagan, 71; television in, see Television; of Wallace (G. C.), 59–60
Presidential dictatorship, 306
Presidential election(s): automatic vote plan for, 347n; campaigning for, see Presidential campaign(s); coattails effect in, 285–286; Congressional elections and, 121; constitutional provision for, 342–343; direct popular vote in, 16–17, 23, 342, 344–350; electoral college vote in, see Electoral vote system; by minority of votes cast, 346–348; by national direct vote, 344–350; party identification in, 253, 263; policy changes and, 273–274; religion of candidate in, 51; runoffs in, projected, 346; television's role in, see Television; tie-breaking role of House in, 243; timetable for, 342; voter runout in, 174 (see also Voter participation); winner-take-all issue in, 343, 344, 348
Presidential primaries, 16, 17, 62, 76–77, 130, 132, 133–134, 198–199, 215–216, 349 (see also Direct primaries; Primary elections)
Press, in presidential campaigns, 217 (see also News media)
Primary election(s): blanket, 199–200; for Congress, 263–264; Democratic party, 58, 59–60, 62–63, 69, 70, 76; Democratic party

Primary election(s) (cont.)
reforms for, 62; direct, national, 16–17, 133–134, 198–199, 349; media publicity and, 215; nominating conventions and, 216; nonpartisan, 194: one-percent club in, 211; open, 199–200; partisan, types of, 199–201; party organization and, 198–199, 335; party weakness and, 199, 215, 335; presidential, see Presidential primaries; Republican, 53, 59, 70–71, 76, 77; state regulation of, 16–17, 198–199, 200, 202–203; uncontested, 201–202; voter participation in, 201, 202
Progressive movement, 38–40
Progressive party: of T. Roosevelt (Bull Moose), 114; of H. Wallace, 45, 113; in Wisconsin, 112, 114
Prohibition party, 112, 113
Pro-life party (New York), 157
Property: concept of, 89; earned income vs., 89–90
Proportional representation, 12
Protestants, 68–70, 94–95
Protest movements, 54–56, 60–61, 75, 157–158
Public opinion poll findings: on approval of the president, 60, 71, 75; on the Bible as literal truth, 70; on the 'born again' experience, 70; on candidate vs. issues invoting, 255; on Carter-Reagan-Anderson candidacies, 77–78; on a centrist, third party, 259; on confidence in leadership, 72; on corruption in politics, 314; on crime, 54; on Democratic nominee preference, in 1980, 76; on direct presidential balloting, 349; on election day registration, 187; on energy crisis, 73; on ethnic self-identification, 93–94; on issue orientation, 253–254; on labor unions vs. big business, 153; on McGovern's candidacy, in 1972, 63; on national primaries, 349; on party affiliation in state and local elections, 262, 263; on personal participation, 162; on party candidate selection, 129–130; on presidential balloting in union households, 156; in presidential campaigns, 244; on religious affiliation, 124n; on segregation, 114; on social class self-identification, 90; sources of errors in, 250; on television watching and influencing, 102, 105; Harry Truman and, 45; on Vietnam war, 114; on voter affiliation, 163; on voter characteristics, 250, 252–253; on voter participation, 183–184
Public sector employees, 151–153
Putnam, Robert D., cited, 137n, 138n, 140n,

Quadcali, 243n
Quie, Albert, 133

Racial conflict, 57, 95–96
Radicalism, 54–56

Spencer, Robert C., cited, 266n
Spencer, Stuart, 225
Spoils system, 15
Stahl, O. Glenn, cited, 288n
Stassen, Harold, 211n
States: with blanket primaries, 199; congressional campaign financing by, 237; delegate selection patterns in, 197–198; direct primary regulation by, 16–17, 198; election regulation by, 16–17, 186, 343; governors of, 206–207, 263–264; incumbency advantages within, 263–264; machine politics within, 117; nominating caucuses in, 215; nominating conventions in, 197–198, 202; nonpartisan political tendencies within, 109, 126–127, 196; with open primaries, 199, 200; presidential elector selection in, 23, 343; presidential primaries in, 16n, 198–199, 201, 215; primary ballot variations in, 200, 202–203; uncontested primaries in, 201; voter participation variations by, 167–168, 201–202; voter registration requirements of, 186, 198, 200
States' Righters, 25, 45, 112, 113
Steinberg, Arnold, cited, 223, 226, 233n, 235, 245
Steiner, Gary, cited, 107n
Stencel, Sandra, cited, 280n
Stevens, John Paul, 280
Stevenson, Adlai, Jr., 130n, 240
Stewart, Potter, 280
Stokes, Donald E., cited, 164n, 165n, 254n, 270n
Stone, Richard, 269
Strauss, Robert, 69
Strikes, industrial, 37
Student Nonviolent Coordinating Committee (SNCC), 55, 158
Sundquist, James L., cited, 115n, 260n
Supreme Court: civil rights positions of, 47; liberalism of, 281; New Deal vs., 44; partisanship of, 277–281; political pressures against, 159–160; sovereignty of, 181n

Taft, Philip, cited, 152n
Taft, William Howard, 128
Taft-Hartley Act, 274
Talmadge, Herman, 269
Taney, Roger B., 25
Tauber, Karl and Alma, cited, 96n
Tax cutting incentives, 74, 75
Teapot Dome scandal, 318, 319
Television (see also Broadcasting; News media): campaign advertising on, 226, 231; Carter-Reagan debates on, 77–78; free political coverage on, 231; influences on public political behavior of, 100–103; Kennedy-Nixon debates on, 50; local elections and, 102; as news source, 102–104; Nixon-McGovern debates on, 101; presidential campaign role of, 101–104, 130,

Television (cont.)
217–218, 242; proper role of, 339; race riot coverage by, 57; Watergate affair coverage by, 64
Temperance movement, 27
Thayer, George, cited, 232n
Three Mile Island incident, 74, 75
Thurmond, Strom, 45, 348
Ticket splitting, 257, 262
Tilden, Samuel J., 31
Time, cited, 6n, 102, 155n
Tocqueville, Alexis de: cited, 159; quoted, 86–87
Tower, John, 294
Transportation, 47
Truman, David B., cited, 159n
Truman, Harry S., 44, 45, 283, 347n
Tufte, Edward R., cited, 267n, 271, 273n
Turner, Julius, cited, 293n
Two-party political system(s), 10–11; alignment and realignment of, 115, 256–261; development of, in U.S., 20–22, 109–111 (see also Party political developments); direct popular presidential vote vs., 347–350; fading of, in U.S., 335–336; minor political parties and, 10–11, 113–115; multiparty political systems vs., 12; revival of, projected, 336
Two-thirds rule, 128; abolition of, 129

Ujifusa, Grant, cited, 121n
Unemployment, 67
Union party, 113
United Automobile Workers (UAW), 156
United Pacific Railroad, 31
United Press International, cited, 105
U.S. News and World Report, 155n, 312
United States Steel Corporation, 75
Unit rule, in delegate balloting, 128, 345
University of Michigan, Survey Research Center, cited, 163, 249, 252–256, 262
Unruh, Jesse, 58, 71
Upper class status (see also Social status/class; Wealth): identification with, 90, 91; liberal values and, 142; political power and, 136–140; property and, 89–90; special interest groups and, 154

Van Buren, Martin, 24, 25, 26
VanDeusen, Glyndon G, cited, 25n
Van Devanter, Willis, 44
Verba, Sidney, cited, 97n, 123n, 172n, 173n, 179n, 255n, 256
Vergers, 184
Vice presidency: accession to presidency from, 282–283; selection of candidate for, 50, 52
Vietnam war, 53, 73; electoral mandate on, 249; perception of policy on, 57–58, 333; protests against, 55–56, 60–61, 311